Vice President of Editorial	Melissa Wagner
Director of Acquisitions	Mikaela Felty
Director of Book Development	Jocelynn Hessler
Production Manager	Mike Brehm
Cover Design	Jose Rosado

Published in the United States of America by
IGI Global Scientific Publishing
701 East Chocolate Avenue
Hershey, PA, 17033, USA
Tel: 717-533-8845
Fax: 717-533-7115
Website: https://www.igi-global.com E-mail: cust@igi-global.com



Library of Congress Cataloging-in-Publication Data

Names: Kam, Kenn Jhun, 1986- editor | Gunasagaran, Sujatavani A/P, 1976- editor
Title: Fostering resilience and quality of life through sustainable urban evolution / edited by: Kenn Jhun Kam, Sujatavani A/P Gunasagaran.
Description: Hershey, PA : IGI Global Scientific Publishing, [2026] | Includes bibliographical references and index. | Summary: "This book aims to explore how sustainable urban development can boost both resilience and quality of life in cities. It looks at key strategies, design principles, and policies that help create urban spaces that can adapt to environmental, social, and economic challenges"-- Provided by publisher.
Identifiers: LCCN 2025004362 (print) | LCCN 2025004363 (ebook) | ISBN 9798337303901 hardcover | ISBN 9798337303918 paperback | ISBN 9798337303925 ebook
Subjects: LCSH: Sustainable urban development | Resilience (Personality trait) | Quality of life
Classification: LCC HT241 .F68 2026 (print) | LCC HT241 (ebook) | DDC 307.76--dc23/eng/20250618
LC record available at https://lccn.loc.gov/2025004362
LC ebook record available at https://lccn.loc.gov/2025004363
British Cataloguing in Publication Data
A Cataloguing in Publication record for this book is available from the British Library.

# Table of Contents

# Detailed Table of Contents



Urban landscapes are at the forefront of global transformation, driven by rapid urbanization, population growth, and the intensifying impacts of change in climate. It is essential to adopt sustainable development principles that balance environmental stewardship, economic vitality, and social equity in order to guarantee the resilience and well-being of urban populations. This study analyses the evolving dynamics of urban landscapes, emphasizing sustainability's role in fostering resilience and enhancing quality of life. The study explores novel approaches to urban planning and development, including green infrastructure, smart city technologies, and circular economy practices. It highlights the challenges due to urbanization. Fuzzy AHP has been used to analyse these challenges in detail. The result of fuzzy AHP showed that Environmental challenges has the highest impact. Through a multidisciplinary lens, this chapter underscores the interconnectedness of resilience and quality of life, advocating for urban ecosystems that are inclusive, adaptable, and future-ready.



Smart Infrastructure and Sustainable Urban Systems integrate advanced technologies with sustainable practices to tackle urbanization challenges. Focusing on environmental sustainability, social equity, technological integration, and climate resilience, it highlights strategies like IoT, renewable energy, and nature-based solutions to enhance urban quality of life. Emphasizing collaboration and inclusive policies, it offers a roadmap to develop adaptive, resource-efficient, and equitable cities for a sustainable future.



This research focuses on the issues and challenges in relation to passenger dissatisfaction with the accessibility into MRT train stations. Frequent MRT users often face numerous unpleasant experiences but lack a suitable platform to voice their concerns and resolve these issues. The research will employ a quantitative method for data collection, using relevant questionnaires targeted at frequent MRT passengers. The findings show that lack of parking spaces, ticketing issues and proximity to residential areas are the main concern of the passengers. Ultimately, the outcomes of this study may form the basis for considerations and improvement to enhance the accessibility of MRT Line train stations, ensuring a seamless and satisfactory travel experience for all passengers and promoting inclusivity within Malaysia's public transportation system.



Residential satisfaction plays a crucial role in gauging the quality of living in low-cost housing. In order to better understand the elements that affect residential satisfaction, this study examines the social interactions, design features, and planning policies in low-cost housing environments. The study utilizes a quantitative approach to assess the satisfaction levels of residents in low-cost housing, focusing on key variables such as user comfort, building services, and social cohesion. Data was collected from residents related to accessibility and proximity to urban facilities, had the greatest impact on resident satisfaction. The quality of construction materials, the availability of essential building services, the overall design of housing units were found to significantly influence both the comfort and safety of residents. The findings underscore the need for comprehensive planning that addresses both the physical infrastructure and social dynamics of low-cost housing to improve quality of life and resident satisfaction



United Nations predicts that 70% of the world's population will be living in urban areas by 2050. Malaysia is among the developing countries hopping on this bandwagon by realizing the nation's digitalization agenda towards Malaysia's smart city journey. Currently, Malaysia's smart city plans focus on two major areas: transport issues and cashless payments. However, there are more areas to be further developed in the smart city plans. To ensure Malaysia is ready, research into consumer behavior is needed. This is aligned with the 12th Malaysian Plan on digital transformation; Shared Prosperity Vision 2030; and fulfillment of SDG9. Nevertheless, empirical studies on factors influencing Malaysia's intention to purchase homes in smart cities are scarce. The current study conducts qualitative study of 20 in-depth interviews among diverse individuals in Malaysia. Findings from the major themes point to five main factors including security and privacy; environmental initiatives; digital infrastructures and smart mobility; digital literacy and knowledge expectancy; and price value.



This paper explores how lighting permutation methods, inspired by Islamic ornamentation, can improve indoor environmental quality, focusing on lighting design. Islamic ornamentation, with its intricate geometries and symbolic patterns, offers a unique foundation for creating natural lighting strategies that are both functional and aesthetically meaningful. By examining the cultural significance and contemporary uses of Islamic ornamentation, the study identifies design principles to inspire innovative natural lighting solutions. Using computational tools and parametric design methods, the research presents a design analysis for integrating these ornamentation-based lighting techniques into modern architecture. The findings highlight the potential of culturally grounded design traditions to enhance visual comfort, energy efficiency, and spatial harmony, contributing to a more sustainable built environment. This paper offers valuable insights for architects, lighting designers, and engineers on the role of ornamental design in improving indoor spaces.



This chapter focuses on studying urban pollutants in Colombia's most populated cities by developing local instrumentation and implementing chemical transport models (CTMs). The instrumentation includes Scanning Depolarization Lidar System, MAX-DOAS and low-cost in situ devices. Additionally, particulate matter is collected for chemical and morphological analysis using different techniques to identify the main sources of emissions. The chapter aims to provide examples of the findings from a study that is set to establish a foundation for adapting chemical and transport models to complex topography, such as coupling WRF-Chem with LOTOS-EUROS and setting the basis for incorporating data assimilation techniques to enhance the models' predictive capabilities in tropical conditions.

In an increasingly interconnected world, reimagining community resilience demands the integration of digital innovation. Digital platforms facilitate real-time information sharing, enabling members to respond effectively to challenges, whether they stem from natural disasters or social issues. Innovative tools such as mobile apps and social media can gather diverse voices and build inclusive environments, promoting empowerment through participatory decision-making. Virtual town halls, community forums, and online workshops encourage dialogue, bridging gaps between local government and citizens. Digital innovation also enhances access to resources, providing residents with essential information on health services, educational opportunities, and local initiatives. By utilizing data analytics, communities can better understand their needs and priorities, ensuring tailored solutions for improved resilience. As communities continue to evolve, embracing digital innovation will be pivotal in nurturing resilience and active participation.



The long, linear, upward, and single-directional traditional career path in the architectural profession is a rigid and inflexible career model, which is unable to keep pace with the evolving nature of work in the 21st century. This is an interdisciplinary study connecting architecture and career studies to reveal the evolving career path in architecture and identify the push and pull factors leading to a multiple-career pathway in the profession. The participants were a purposive sampling of 20 millennial architects, who had transitioned from a single career to having multiple careers, including architecture, during the interview. The study revealed that the rigidness of the traditional career pathway itself is a push factor that indirectly causes the millennial architects to move towards a career pathway that is more flexible and controllable. The study suggests that an on-going evolution towards embracing

# Preface

In a time when cities across the globe are grappling with the complexities of climate change, rapid urbanization, resource scarcity, and social inequality, the call for resilient, inclusive, and sustainable urban environments has never been more urgent. *Fostering Resilience and Quality of Life Through Sustainable Urban Evolution* brings together diverse voices, disciplines, and perspectives to explore how sustainable principles and innovative technologies can work in harmony to transform urban life.

This volume presents a multidisciplinary dialogue on the evolving dynamics of cities and communities, highlighting the need for integrated strategies that promote environmental stewardship, social equity, and economic adaptability. The chapters delve into critical themes ranging from sustainable infrastructure and smart technologies to low-cost housing satisfaction, urban pollution monitoring, and the cultural integration of traditional design principles in modern architecture. Each chapter offers unique insights grounded in rigorous research and practical analysis, offering frameworks that are both contextually rich and globally relevant.

## CHAPTER OVERVIEW

**Chapter 1** explores the transformation of urban landscapes under the pressure of climate change and urbanization. It emphasizes the importance of sustainable development strategies, such as green infrastructure and smart technologies, to enhance resilience and quality of life. Using the fuzzy AHP method, environmental challenges were found to have the most significant impact on urban sustainability.

Focusing on smart infrastructure, **Chapter 2** outlines the integration of technologies like IoT and renewable energy within urban systems. It emphasizes collaboration, inclusivity, and resource efficiency as key strategies for building climate-resilient and socially equitable cities.

**Chapter 3** investigates accessibility challenges faced by frequent MRT train users. Through quantitative analysis, it identifies core issues such as limited parking, ticketing inefficiencies, and inconvenient station locations. The findings aim to guide improvements in Malaysia's public transportation infrastructure to enhance user satisfaction and inclusivity.

**Chapter 4** examines the factors influencing satisfaction among residents in low-cost housing. Key elements include planning policies, user comfort, building services, and social interaction. Data indicates that proximity to urban facilities and construction quality significantly affect resident comfort, safety, and overall satisfaction.

Exploring Malaysia's digital transformation, **Chapter 5** investigates factors influencing consumer interest in smart city home ownership. Through qualitative interviews, five major themes emerge: privacy and security, environmental initiatives, digital infrastructure, digital literacy, and pricing. The findings align with national development agendas and highlight gaps in current smart city planning.

**Chapter 6** examines how Islamic ornamentation can inform innovative lighting strategies in architecture. Using computational and parametric design methods, it demonstrates how culturally inspired geometries can enhance indoor environmental quality, energy efficiency, and visual comfort in modern buildings.

Focused on Colombia's urban areas, **Chapter 7** details the use of in-situ instruments and remote sensing technologies for air pollution monitoring. It combines chemical analysis and transport modeling to better understand pollution sources and improve predictive modeling in tropical and topographically complex environments.

**Chapter 8** discusses the role of digital innovation in strengthening community resilience and engagement. It showcases how online platforms, mobile apps, and data analytics enhance civic participation, improve access to services, and facilitate inclusive decision-making in response to social and environmental challenges.

**Chapter 9** addresses the shift from traditional career models in architecture, this chapter explores the motivations behind multi-career trajectories among millennial professionals. It identifies the limitations of rigid career structures and highlights the benefits of adopting flexible, interdisciplinary paths to align with evolving personal and professional needs.

We are grateful to the many scholars and practitioners whose contributions shape this volume. Their work illuminates pathways toward a future where cities are not only efficient and technologically advanced but also equitable, livable, and deeply connected to the communities they serve. We hope this collection inspires continued inquiry, cross-disciplinary collaboration, and action toward more resilient and life-affirming urban environments.

**Kenn Jhun Kam**

*Taylor's University, Malaysia*

**Sujatavani Gunasagaran**
*Taylor's University, Malaysia*

# Chapter 1
# Evolving Urban Landscapes:
## Building Resilience and Promoting Quality of Life Through Sustainability

**Shweta Saini**
https://orcid.org/0009-0009-1216-062X
*Graphic Era University, India*

**Ankita Singh**
https://orcid.org/0009-0004-9448-062X
*Graphic Era University, India*

**Manish Bisht**
*Graphic Era Hill University, India*

**Shwetank Avikal**
https://orcid.org/0000-0001-9210-850X
*Graphic Era University, India*

## ABSTRACT

*Urban landscapes are at the forefront of global transformation, driven by rapid urbanization, population growth, and the intensifying impacts of change in climate. It is essential to adopt sustainable development principles that balance environmental stewardship, economic vitality, and social equity in order to guarantee the resilience and well-being of urban populations. This study analyses the evolving dynamics of urban landscapes, emphasizing sustainability's role in fostering resilience and enhancing quality of life. The study explores novel approaches to urban planning and*

DOI: 10.4018/979-8-3373-0390-1.ch001

*development, including green infrastructure, smart city technologies, and circular economy practices. It highlights the challenges due to urbanization. Fuzzy AHP has been used to analyse these challenges in detail. The result of fuzzy AHP showed that Environmental challenges has the highest impact. Through a multidisciplinary lens, this chapter underscores the interconnectedness of resilience and quality of life, advocating for urban ecosystems that are inclusive, adaptable, and future-ready.*

## 1. INTRODUCTION

The 21st century has been defined by rapid urbanization, population expansion & mounting effects of environmental change-forces which are dramatically reshaping the global urban landscape. The United Nations reports that more than 55% of the world population currently lives in urban areas, with projections indicating an increase to 68% by the year 2050 (United Nations, 2018). Urban regions have emerged as centres of revenue generation and creativity but they also confront significant difficulties of our era. Issues include environmental degradation, social inequality, and the need for sustainable resource management (UN-Habitat, 2020). As cities expand and evolve, they must reconcile the demand for growth with the imperative to create environments that support human well-being and ecological health.

Urbanization brings with it a dual-edged reality: while it drives economic progress and technological innovation, it also intensifies tension on infrastructure, resources from the earth & social systems. Such uncontrolled expansion of cities often leads to severe environmental consequences, such as deforestation, loss of biodiversity, and increased carbon emissions (Seto et al., 2012). Furthermore, urban populations are progressively susceptible to the effects of climate change, such as severe weather phenomena, elevated sea levels, and urban heat islands. These difficulties jeopardise the resilience of metropolitan places and diminish the standard of life for its residents, especially marginalised people, who frequently endure the most severe impacts caused by such crises (IPCC, 2021).

To address these challenges, urban areas must embrace sustainable development principles that integrate environmental stewardship, economic vitality, and social equity (Elmqvist et al., 2018). Sustainability in urban planning is no longer a luxury or an abstract ideal; it is a necessity for ensuring the long-term resilience of cities. In this sense, resilience denotes the capacity of city structures to endure and recuperate from shocks while adjusting to evolving conditions (Meerow et al., 2016). Equally important is the enhancement of quality of life, which encompasses not only physical and material well-being but also social cohesion, cultural vibrancy, and access to opportunities (Gehl, 2013).

The subject matter here examines the complex interplay amongst resilience & the quality of life within the framework of sustainable urban development. This delves into transformative potential of innovative urban planning strategies, such as green infrastructure, smart city technologies, and circular economy practices.

A key emphasis is placed on the integration of nature-based solutions, energy-efficient systems, and participatory governance frameworks in urban planning. These approaches represent a shift from traditional, siloed planning methods to holistic, multidisciplinary strategies that address the interconnected challenges faced by urban ecosystems. Solutions derived from nature yield environmental advantages while also enhancing social and economic results through improved urban livability and increased community participation (Frantzeskaki et al., 2019). Participatory governance enables residents to actively influence the development of their metropolitan areas, ensuring that the planning of cities aligns with the requirements and goals of various demographics (Arnstein, 1969). It examines how urban systems function as complex, interdependent networks and argues for the necessity of systems thinking in creating sustainable cities (Satterthwaite, 2011). This chapter offers a thorough guidance for legislators, designers for cities, and academics by integrating concepts from urban planning, environmental science, sociology, and technology to address the concerns of urbanisation and climate change.

In presenting these strategies and insights, this chapter aims to inspire a vision of cities that are not only functional and efficient but also inclusive, adaptable, and future-ready. Urban regions has the capacity to function as catalysts for sustainable growth, wherein financial possibilities, equitable society, and ecological wellness remain fundamentally interconnected (Evans, 2019). By adopting sustainability, cities may evolve into resilient ecosystems that flourish amidst global difficulties, simultaneously improving the standard of life for all residents.

The chapter begins by examining the forces driving urban transformation and the challenges urbanisation poses before moving on to apply fuzzy AHP to find out the challenges of urbanization and which challenge impacts more than the others. This research aims to provide learners with the information and resources necessary to reinvent urban landscapes as dynamic, sustainable, and resilient environments for future generations.

The aim and scope of this chapter is to talk about urbanisation and the challenges of urbanisation, the different categories of challenges of urbanisation and to apply fuzzy AHP to determine which challenge of urbanisation needs to be addressed more than the others.

## 2. LITERATURE REVIEW

The lightening-fast modernisation of the 21st century, together with mounting impacts on climate change, has created a pressing need to rethink urban development practices. A growing body of literature has explored sustainable urban design as a means to address these challenges.

The unprecedented rate of urbanization is reshaping the global demographic landscape. With over 4.4 billion people, fifty five percent of the global population living in metro cities, this number is expected to increase to sixty eight percent by the year 2050 (United Nations, 2018). Urbanisation has propelled economic development and innovation, although it has also exacerbated issues with housing, infrastructure, and resource allocation.

Seto et al. (2012) highlight the environmental repercussions of urban growth, such as biodiversity loss and the deterioration of essential ecosystems. Informal settlements, sometimes situated in hazard-prone regions, shelter nearly one billion individuals worldwide and illustrate the inadequacy of several cities to properly manage increasing populations (UN-Habitat, 2020). These towns are devoid of essential amenities such as potable water, sanitary facilities, and power, rendering inhabitants susceptible to environmental and social hazards.

Studies also highlight the uneven nature of urbanization across regions. For example, developing countries in Sub-Saharan Africa and South Asia face greater challenges in managing urban growth compared to developed regions in Europe and North America. Satterthwaite (2011) notes that unplanned urbanization in these regions exacerbates inequality, underlining the importance of incorporating sustainability into urban planning.

The change in climatic conditions is a significant critical problem to urban areas, amplifying existing vulnerabilities. The Intergovernmental Panel on Climate Change (IPCC, 2021) designates metropolitan regions as hotspots for climate impacts, including rising sea levels, extreme heat, and flooding. Urban heat islands, for example, exacerbate temperature rises in densely populated areas, increasing the possibility of temperature-related diseases and energy demand for cooling (Oke, 1982).

Vulnerability varies across urban populations. Low-income communities often reside in flood-prone or polluted areas, lacking resources to adapt or recover from climate shocks (Meerow et al., 2016). Research has shown that adaptive strategies, such as elevating buildings, constructing flood barriers, and integrating green infrastructure, are crucial for reducing climate vulnerability (Hunt & Watkiss, 2011).

Examples of successful adaptation can be found in cities like Rotterdam, which has adopted a comprehensive climate adaptation strategy that includes water plazas, green roofs, and advanced flood defenses (Nieuwenhuijsen and Khreis, 2018). Likewise, Singapore has altered its urban environment through projects such as the

Bishan-Ang Mo Kio Park, which integrates prevention of flooding with recreation and ecological benefits (Tan & Hamel, 2022).

The notion of resilience has become significant as a structure for improving urban ability to withstand and recuperate from disturbances. Meerow et al. (2016) define urban resilience as the ability to withstand and adapt to environmental, economic, and social disruptions while maintaining functionality. Resilience is intrinsically linked to the quality of life, as it ensures uninterrupted access to housing, transportation, and social services during crises.

Quality of life in urban settings is a multifaceted construct that includes physical, social, and economic dimensions. Gehl (2013) highlights the importance of walkability, open spaces & vibrant public areas in fostering a sense of well-being among urban residents. Cities like Copenhagen exemplify this approach by prioritizing cycling infrastructure and pedestrian-friendly streets.

Medellin provides a compelling example of how resilience strategies can enhance quality of life. By integrating cable cars and escalators into its transportation network, the city has improved mobility for low-income communities while promoting social inclusion (Farieta, 2023). Such initiatives demonstrate the transformative potential of urban planning that aligns resilience with equity and livability.

Urban systems are deeply interconnected, functioning as networks where changes in one domain can affect others. Kennedy et al. (2011) conceptualize cities as metabolic systems that consume energy, water, and materials while producing waste. Understanding urban metabolism is essential for identifying inefficiencies and transitioning toward circular economy models.

Nature-based solutions (NBS) are a critical component of interconnected urban systems, leveraging natural processes to address urban challenges. Frantzeskaki et al. (2019) contend that nature-based solutions, including urban woodlands, wetlands, and rooftop gardens, can alleviate climate effects while offering social and ecological advantages. These techniques mitigate urban heat islands, regulate runoff, and promote biodiversity.

Smart city technologies further illustrate the interconnectedness of urban systems. Cities like Barcelona have implemented IoT-enabled infrastructure to optimize waste collection, energy use, and mobility (Neirotti et al., 2014). These technologies enable effective resource management while simultaneously raising issues regarding confidentiality, security of information, and equal access (Van Zoonen, 2016).

## 3. THE URBAN LANDSCAPE IN TRANSITION

As the world population expands and urbanises, cities find themselves at the forefront of profound and rapid transformations. The urban landscape, once shaped primarily by local economic and cultural conditions, is now increasingly influenced by global forces such as climate change, resource scarcity, technological advancements, and socio-political shifts. These transitions present both opportunities and challenges for urban areas as they strive to remain centers of innovation, growth, and human habitation while addressing the escalating pressures of modernity. This section explores the key forces driving urban transformation and the challenges they present, while framing the urgency of adopting sustainable and resilient urban practices.

### 3.1 The Forces Shaping Urban Evolution

Urban landscapes are dynamic systems, always transforming due to a complex interaction of economic, environmental, social & technological influences. This current era is marked by several transformative forces that are reshaping cities worldwide:

#### 3.1.1 Rapid Urbanization and Population Growth

Urbanization is rapidly reshaping the world, with over 55% of the global population now living in cities, a figure expected to reach 70% by 2050 (United Nations, 2018). This growth, especially in developing regions, brings economic potential but also strains infrastructure, housing, and basic services. Informal settlements, home to around one billion people, often lack essentials like clean water and sanitation, increasing health and environmental risks (UN-Habitat, 2020). These challenges underscore the urgent need for resilient and sustainable urban development.

#### 3.1.2 The Escalating Impacts of Climate Change

Urban areas are highly vulnerable to climate change impacts, facing intensified heat due to the urban heat island effect, as well as increased risks from extreme weather events like floods, droughts, hurricanes, and wildfires (IPCC, 2021). Events such as the recent California wildfires have caused widespread displacement and long-term economic, environmental, and public health damage (Gonzalez, 2024). Coastal cities like Jakarta and Miami are particularly threatened by rising sea levels, endangering millions and critical infrastructure. These challenges disproportionately affect low-income and marginalized communities, who often live in high-risk areas with limited resources for recovery. Addressing these vulnerabilities requires inclusive urban planning that integrates climate adaptation and mitigation strategies to build resilience and reduce inequality.

### 3.1.3 Technological Advancements and Digital Urbanization

The Fourth Industrial Revolution is reshaping cities through technologies like AI, IoT, and big data, giving rise to "smart cities" that enhance urban functions such as transport, energy, and governance. Cities like Barcelona and Singapore lead in adopting these innovations (Lim et al., 2018). However, challenges around data privacy, cybersecurity, and digital inequality must be addressed to ensure inclusive and equitable outcomes (Kitchin, 2014).

### 3.1.4 Resource Scarcity and Environmental Degradation

As urban areas grow, their consumption of water, energy, and raw materials rises, often at unsustainable levels. Cities account for over two-thirds of global energy use and more than 70% of greenhouse gas emissions (IEA, 2021), while urban expansion drives deforestation and biodiversity loss. Resource scarcity, evident in water crises in cities like Cape Town, São Paulo, and Chennai, demands a shift toward circular economy practices to reduce waste and dependence on finite resources (Muller, 2018).

## 3.2 Challenges of Urbanization

Urbanisation, characterised by the growing concentration of inhabitants in metropolitan regions, has emerged as a prevailing worldwide phenomenon. While it offers economic opportunities, improved infrastructure, and better living standards for many, it also brings significant challenges. These challenges are multifaceted, encompassing environmental, social, economic, and governance dimensions. These challenges are categorised as:

1. **Environmental Challenges** Environmental challenges refer to the difficulties and negative impacts arising from the interplay between human activities and the natural environment. This term refers to all kinds of problems that negatively affect the environment. In the context of urbanization, these challenges result from the rapid expansion of cities, increased resource consumption, and environmental degradation. Key components of environmental challenges include:
   (a) **Urban Sprawl and Habitat Destruction:** Urbanization often leads to cities expanding into surrounding rural or natural areas. This encroachment disrupts ecosystems, destroys wildlife habitats, and reduces biodiversity,

threatening ecological balance. For instance, Seto et al. (2012) emphasize that urban expansion contributes significantly to global biodiversity loss, particularly in tropical regions. e.g., The deforestation of the Amazon for urban expansion in Brazil has led to significant ecological damage.

(b) **Air & Water Pollution:** Increased industrial activities, vehicle emissions, and improper waste disposal in urban areas contribute to increased air & water pollution. Such situations negatively affect environmental health and public well-being, causing respiratory diseases and waterborne illnesses (UN-Habitat, 2020). For example, Delhi consistently experiences hazardous air quality due to vehicle emissions and industrial pollutants (Kaur & Jhamaria, 2021). e.g., Delhi's air quality frequently exceeds hazardous levels, and cities like Mumbai face severe water contamination issues

(c) **Waste Management Issues:** Cities generate significant amounts of solid and hazardous waste, often exceeding the capacity of existing waste management systems. Poorly managed landfills and illegal dumping sites contaminate land, water, and air. The World Bank (2018) predicts that metropolitan regions generate about 2 billion tonnes of municipal solid trash each year, a number anticipated to increase with ongoing urbanisation. e.g., The Ghazipur landfill in Delhi has grown to the size of a small hill, posing health and environmental risks.

(d) **Resource Scarcity:** Urban populations consume vast quantities of water, energy, and raw materials, often at unsustainable rates. This leads to resource shortages and competition, further straining environmental systems. The "Day Zero" water crisis in Cape Town in 2018 illustrated the susceptibility of metropolitan regions to water scarcity (Muller, 2018).

2. **Infrastructure and Resource Constraints** Infrastructure and resource constraints refer to the challenges cities face in providing adequate physical infrastructure and essential resources to meet the growing demands of expanding urban populations. These constraints often arise due to rapid urbanization, inadequate planning, and limited investment, leading to socio-economic inequalities, environmental degradation, and compromised quality of life.

   (a) **Housing Shortages and Informal Settlements**: Rapid urbanization frequently outpaces the supply of affordable housing, resulting in overcrowded informal settlements. These regions frequently have no access to fundamental utilities, including clean water, hygiene, power, and adequate waste disposal (UN-Habitat, 2020). For example, Mumbai's Dharavi slum houses over one million people, highlighting the inadequacies in urban housing policies (McFarlane, 2012).

(b) **Overburdened Transportation Systems**: Urban transportation systems often fail to scale with population growth, leading to traffic congestion, longer commute times, and increased greenhouse gas emissions. Poorly maintained infrastructure and inadequate public transit systems exacerbate mobility issues (Edenhofer, 2015). Bengaluru, for instance, faces severe traffic congestion, with commuters spending hours in gridlock daily.

(c) **Resource Scarcity**: Urban regions exacerbate need of limited resources, such as electric power, water, and nourishment. Resource shortages can lead to higher costs and conflicts, disproportionately affecting marginalized populations. Cape Town's 2018 "Day Zero" crisis, when the city narrowly avoided running out of water, underscores the vulnerability of urban areas to resource scarcity (Muller, 2018).

(d) **Aging and Inadequate Infrastructure**: Many cities depend on outdated infrastructure incapable of supporting modern demands. Aging roads, bridges, pipelines, and energy grids are prone to failures, leading to disruptions and escalating maintenance costs. For instance, Delhi frequently experiences water pipeline leaks, reflecting the inadequacies of aging infrastructure (World Bank, 2018).

3. **Social Challenges** Social problems denote the difficulties and inequities that emerge in metropolitan environments due to rapid development, economic imbalances, high population density, and insufficient infrastructure. These challenges often manifest in unequal access to resources, strained social cohesion, and heightened vulnerabilities among marginalized communities. Social challenges significantly affect the quality of life and require inclusive policies and planning to address them effectively.

(a) **Social Inequalities:** Urbanization often exacerbates existing socio-economic inequalities. Marginalized groups, such as low-income populations, migrants, and informal workers, are disproportionately affected by inadequate housing, healthcare, education, and public services (UN-Habitat, 2020). e.g., income inequality in cities like Rio de Janeiro is evident in the stark contrast between affluent neighborhoods and favelas.

(b) **Urban Poverty:** The rapid influx of rural-to-urban migrants seeking economic opportunities often results in high levels of urban poverty. Many individuals are employed in informal economies, with no job security or social protections, leading to cycles of poverty (Chen, 2012). e.g., In Nairobi, 60% of the populace inhabits informal settlements such as Kibera, characterised by pervasive poverty and inadequate services (World Bank, 2010).

(c) **Public Health Issues:** Dense urban populations and inadequate infrastructure contribute to poor sanitation, air pollution, and the fast transmission of illnesses. Health disparities are more pronounced in low-income areas, where access to medical facilities is limited (WHO, 2016). e.g., The COVID-19 pandemic disproportionately affected slum residents in cities like Mumbai, where overcrowding and lack of sanitation worsened health outcomes (Patel & Shah, 2021).

(d) **Crime and Public Safety:** Unemployment, poverty, and inadequate policing in urban areas can lead to increased crime rates. Urban crime undermines residents' sense of safety and deters investments in affected areas (Sampson, 2012). e.g,, Johannesburg, South Africa, experiences high crime rates attributed to socio-economic disparities and inadequate law enforcement.

4. **Economic Challenges** Economic challenges refer to the financial and structural obstacles that cities face due to rapid urbanization, uneven economic development, and resource constraints. These challenges impact the ability of cities to create equitable economic opportunities, sustain growth, and address inequalities, often exacerbating poverty, unemployment, and social tensions.

(a) **Urban Unemployment and Underemployment:** Cities attract large numbers of rural migrants seeking better job opportunities. However, job creation often fails to keep pace with the growing urban population, leading to unemployment or underemployment. Informal economies frequently absorb these workers but offer limited security or benefits (Chen, 2012). e.g., In Lagos, Nigeria, over 60% of labour is employed in unregulated economy, where wages are low and working conditions precarious (World Bank, 2023).

(b) **Income Inequality:** Urban areas often exhibit stark income disparities between wealthy and poor residents, contributing to socio-economic tensions. High levels of inequality reduce social mobility and economic resilience (Piketty, 2014). e.g., São Paulo's urban landscape starkly contrasts affluent neighborhoods with sprawling informal settlements, highlighting persistent income inequalities.

(c) **Rising Cost of Living:** Rapid urbanization drives up the cost of housing, transportation, healthcare, and other essential services. This disproportionately affects low- and middle-income groups, making urban living unaffordable for many (UN-Habitat, 2020). e.g., San Francisco faces one of the highest costs of living in the world, leading to housing crises and the relocation of economically disadvantaged inhabitants.

(d) **Economic Displacement and Gentrification:** Urban redevelopment projects often displace low-income residents and small businesses, replacing them with higher-income populations and luxury developments. This phenomenon, known as gentrification, exacerbates economic disparities (Lees et al., 2008). e.g., Gentrification in London has displaced long-term residents from traditionally working-class neighborhoods like Hackney.

5. **Governance Challenges** Governance challenges refer to the difficulties urban areas face in managing and coordinating policies, resources, and services to meet the needs of growing populations effectively. These challenges stem from inadequate institutional capacity, weak leadership, lack of accountability, and inequitable decision-making processes. Governance challenges often result in unplanned urban growth, socio-economic disparities, and environmental degradation, undermining the long-term sustainability of cities.
   a) **Unplanned Urban Growth:** Rapid urbanization without adequate planning often leads to chaotic and inefficient urban landscapes. Weak governance structures and lack of integrated urban planning exacerbate issues such as housing shortages, traffic congestion, and resource mismanagement (UN-Habitat, 2020). e.g., Cities like Dhaka, Bangladesh, have grown rapidly without sufficient urban planning, resulting in widespread informal settlements and poor infrastructure.
   b) **Corruption and Inefficiency:** Corruption in urban governance leads to misallocation of resources, delays in infrastructure projects, and inequitable service delivery. Inefficient bureaucracy impede the implementation of policies and the response to urban concerns (Transparency International, 2021). e.g., In Jakarta, Indonesia, corruption has delayed critical flood mitigation projects, exacerbating the city's vulnerability to climate change impacts.
   c) **Inequitable Policy Implementation:** Urban policies often prioritize affluent neighborhoods, leaving marginalized communities underserved. This disparity perpetuates socio-economic inequities and restricts access to vital services, including schooling, medical care, and commuting (World Bank, 2023). e.g., In Nairobi, Kenya, informal settlements like Kibera receive fewer municipal services compared to wealthier areas, perpetuating inequality.
   d) **Lack of Participatory Governance:** Insufficient public engagement in urban decision-making can lead to policies that fail to address the demands of varied populations. Participatory governance frameworks are often weak or absent, reducing transparency and accountability (Arnstein, 1969). e.g., In São Paulo, Brazil, attempts to implement participatory budgeting have been inconsistent, limiting its effectiveness in addressing community needs.

6. **Climate Change and Disaster Vulnerability** Climate change and disaster vulnerability refer to the increasing susceptibility of urban areas and their populations to adverse impacts caused by climate change and natural disasters. This is a specific area within environmental challenges focusing on climate

change and disaster vulnerability. As global temperatures increase, metropolitan regions see increasingly frequent and intense meteorological phenomena, such as storms, flooding, heatwaves and droughts. Vulnerability is exacerbated by unplanned urban growth, socio-economic inequalities, and inadequate resilience measures, particularly in low-income and coastal regions.

(a) **Increased Frequency and Intensity of Extreme Weather Events:** Climate change exacerbates the frequency of extreme weather phenomena, including hurricanes, typhoons, and heavy rainfall. These occurrences inflict extensive damage on infrastructures, disrupt urban economies & displace millions of people (IPCC, 2021). e.g., Hurricane Harvey in 2017 caused catastrophic flooding in Houston, USA, leading to damages exceeding $125 billion and highlighting the vulnerability of urban areas to extreme rainfall (NOAA, 2021).

(b) **Urban Heat Islands (UHIs):** Urban locations exhibit elevated temperatures compared to adjacent countryside because of heat-retaining surfaces like asphalt and concrete. UHIs amplify the effects of heatwaves, posing significant health hazards for at-risk populations, particularly the senior citizens and low-income groups (Oke, 1982). e.g., Delhi, India, frequently records extreme heat events, exacerbated by dense construction and limited green cover.

(c) **Sea-Level Rise and Coastal Flooding:** Elevated sea levels jeopardise coastal urban centres, leading to permanent inundation of low-lying areas, saltwater intrusion into freshwater supplies, and increased storm surge impacts (De Sherbinin et al., 2012). e.g., Jakarta, Indonesia, is sinking at an alarming rate, prompting the government to plan the relocation of the capital to a safer location.

(d) **Socio-Economic Vulnerability:** Marginalised groups frequently inhabit regions more vulnerable to climatic effects, such as flood zones or informal settlements. Limited resources and access to emergency services make recovery more challenging for these groups (Satterthwaite, 2011). e.g., During the 2010 floods in Pakistan, informal settlements were disproportionately affected, resulting in over 20 million people being displaced.

## 3.3 The Need for Resilience and Sustainability

As cities face growing challenges from rapid urbanisation and climate change, building resilience and promoting sustainability have become essential. Resilience refers to a city's ability to withstand and recover from shocks like natural disasters, economic crises, or social unrest, by strengthening both physical infrastructure and community support systems (Meerow et al., 2016). Meanwhile, sustainability focuses on ensuring long-term well-being by balancing environmental care, economic growth, and social fairness. In practice, this means adopting strategies like climate-adaptive urban planning, green infrastructure, energy-efficient buildings, and inclusive decision-making. Cities such as Rotterdam have led by example, using flood defenses, green roofs, and water plazas to both reduce risk and enhance livability. When resilience and sustainability are combined, urban areas become more adaptable, equitable, and capable of thriving in the face of future uncertainties (Hunt & Watkiss, 2011).

## 4. SUSTAINABILITY IN URBAN PLANNING: CORE CONCEPTS

Urban planning has undergone a paradigm shift in recent decades, moving away from traditional growth-oriented models to approaches that prioritize sustainability, resilience, and inclusivity. This shift reflects the recognition that urban areas are not isolated entities but complex, interdependent ecosystems that must balance environmental, economic, and social considerations to ensure long-term viability. This section explores the core principles of sustainability in urban planning, delves into the intricate relationship between resilience and quality of life, and highlights the interconnectedness of urban systems.

### 4.1 What is Sustainable Urban Development?

Sustainable urban development is based on the notion of fulfilling the requirements of present generations without jeopardising the capacity of future generations to satisfy their own needs (Brundtland Commission, 1987). It underscores the incorporation of environmental conservation, financial opportunities, and equality in society into urban planning and management practices. Sustainable Development is based on three principles, environmental stewardship, economic vitality, and social equity. Environmental Stewardship principle is about managing natural resources responsibly and conserving ecosystems to maintain Earth's life-support systems. Economic Vitality emphasizes creating prosperity through economic systems that are resilient, inclusive, and environmentally conscious. Social Equity is about ensuring fairness, justice, and equal opportunity for all people, regardless of race, gender, income, or geography. This multidimensional approach seeks to create cities that are not only functional and efficient but also livable, inclusive, and resilient to external shocks.

Frameworks for urban sustainability, such the New Urban Agenda and the Sustainable Development Goals (SDGs) of the UN, offer detailed instructions for realising this goal. The Sustainable Development Goals, especially Goal 11, emphasise the creation of accessible, secure, resilient, and sustainable towns and settlements (United Nations, 2015). These frameworks underscore the significance of fair resource access, efficient energy and material utilisation, and the conservation of natural ecosystems.

An essential element of sustainable development of cities is its adaptability to local contexts. While the overarching principles of sustainability remain universal, the challenges and opportunities vary widely across cities. For instance, rapidly urbanizing cities in the Global South often prioritize basic infrastructure development and access to essential services, while cities in the Global North may focus on retrofitting existing systems to reduce environmental footprints and enhance livability (Elmqvist et al., 2018).

## 4.2 The Relationship Between Resilience and Quality of Life

Resilience and quality of life are deeply connected pillars of sustainable urban development. Resilience refers to a city's ability to withstand, recover from, and adapt to disruptions, while quality of life encompasses the overall well-being of residents, including access to basic services, health, safety, and personal fulfillment. Resilient cities protect and enhance quality of life by investing in infrastructure and systems like flood defenses, renewable energy, and emergency preparedness that reduce risk and maintain stability during crises. At the same time, strong quality of life supports resilience, as socially connected, economically secure, and actively engaged communities are better equipped to cope with challenges. Participatory governance, which empowers citizens in decision-making, plays a key role in strengthening both. This synergy is particularly visible in climate adaptation efforts, where solutions like green spaces and energy-efficient housing simultaneously improve resilience and enhance daily living by promoting environmental health, affordability, and social cohesion (Gehl, 2013).

## 4.3 Interconnectedness in Urban Ecosystems

Urban ecosystems are deeply interconnected, where changes in one system, like transportation, affect air quality, energy, and the economy. A systems-thinking approach enables planners to view cities as integrated networks. Strategies like transit-oriented development and circular economy practices illustrate the need for cross-sector collaboration to create smart, sustainable solutions.

# 5. INNOVATIVE STRATEGIES FOR SUSTAINABLE URBAN DEVELOPMENT

To tackle urbanization and climate change, cities are adopting integrated strategies that balance environmental, social, and economic sustainability. This section highlights three key approaches green infrastructure, smart technologies, and circular economy practices offering systems-based solutions for long-term urban resilience and improved quality of life.

## 5.1 Green Infrastructure: Redefining Urban Landscapes

Green infrastructure is a network of natural and semi-natural systems engineered to deliver ecological services while mitigating urban concerns such as floods, air pollution, and biodiversity decline. Unlike conventional "grey infrastructure" (e.g., roads, pipes, and concrete barriers), green infrastructure incorporates nature-based solutions to create multifunctional landscapes that enhance both environmental and social resilience (Benedict & McMahon, 2012).

### 5.1.1 Benefits of Green Infrastructure

- **Stormwater Management:** Urban wetlands, bioswales, and green roofs mitigate flooding risk by absorbing and filtering stormwater. For instance, New York City's Green Infrastructure Plan has significantly decreased combined sewer overflows, improving water quality in urban waterways (NYC Environmental Protection, 2020).
- **Air Quality Improvement:** Trees and vegetation in urban parks filter air pollutants, such as suspended particulate matter and nitrogen dioxide, reducing respiratory illnesses among city dwellers (Nowak et al., 2006).
- **Biodiversity Conservation:** Green spaces, including urban forests and green corridors, provide critical habitats for wildlife, helping maintain ecological balance in cities (Tzoulas et al., 2007).

### 5.1.2 Examples of Implementation

- **Singapore:** Dubbed a "City in a Garden," Singapore has integrated green roofs, vertical gardens, and extensive park systems into its urban fabric. The Bishan-Ang Mo Kio Park integrates flooding prevention with leisure and environmental benefits (Tan & Hamel, 2022).

- **Rotterdam:** This Dutch city has embraced green roofs, water plazas, and urban forests to mitigate flooding and urban heat island effects while enhancing livability (Nieuwenhuijsen and Khreis, 2018).

Green infrastructure not only addresses environmental challenges but also fosters social cohesion by providing recreational spaces and improving urban aesthetics. As cities worldwide grapple with climate change and resource scarcity, green infrastructure represents a transformative approach to building resilience and enhancing quality of life.

## 5.2 Smart City Technologies: Leveraging Digital Innovation

Smart cities utilise digital technology, such as the Internet of Things (IoT), big data, and artificial intelligence, to enhance urban services and infrastructure. Smart cities seek to promote efficiency, minimise waste, and improve people' quality of life by incorporating real-time data collecting and analytics into urban administration (Kitchin, 2014).

### 5.2.1 Key Applications

- **Intelligent Transportation Systems:** Technologies include intelligent traffic signals, real-time public transportation monitoring, and autonomous cars mitigate congestion and enhance sustainable mobility. Barcelona has instituted smart parking systems that decrease the duration spent locating spaces, thereby lowering fuel usage and emissions (Alawadhi et al., 2012).
- **Energy Efficiency:** Smart grids oversee and enhance energy usage, facilitating the incorporation of renewable energy sources. Amsterdam's Smart City initiative has deployed smart meters and energy management platforms to reduce carbon emissions (Neirotti et al., 2014).
- **Waste Management:** IoT-enabled waste bins notify city authorities when they need to be emptied, improving efficiency and reducing litter. Seoul, South Korea, has introduced smart waste systems that also encourage recycling through incentive programs (Aclima, 2017).

## 5.3 Circular Economy Practices: Closing the Loop

Circular economy is a regenerating strategy for resource management aimed at minimising waste, optimising resource efficiency, and mitigating environmental damage. The circular economy contrasts with the conventional linear economy, which follows a “take, make, and dispose” model, by prioritising the reuse, repair, and recycling of resources (Geissdoerfer et al., 2017).

### 5.3.1 Principles of Circular Economy

- **Design for Longevity:** Infrastructure and products are made to be long-lasting and simple to recycle or repair.
- **Waste as a Resource:** The requirement for virgin resources is decreased by the recovery and reuse of materials.
- **Renewable Energy Use:** Circular systems emphasise the utilisation of renewable energy sources for production and services.

### 5.3.2 Urban Applications

- **Construction and Demolition Waste Recycling:** Cities like Amsterdam are pioneering circular construction practices by reusing materials from demolished buildings to construct new ones (MacArthur, 2019).
- **Urban Mining:** Electronic waste, such as discarded smartphones and laptops, is being mined for valuable materials like gold and rare earth elements. Tokyo’s “urban mining” initiatives extracted precious metals from e-waste to create Olympic medals for the 2020 Games (IdeasXChange, 2017).
- **Food Waste Reduction:** Urban agriculture and food-sharing platforms are helping cities reduce food waste and improve food security. London’s OLIO app connects residents and businesses to redistribute surplus food (Papargyropoulou et al., 2014).

# 6. KEY STRATEGIES FOR FUTURE-READY CITIES

Facing rapid urbanization and climate change, cities need creative, proactive policies to ensure resilience, inclusion, and sustainability. This section highlights three key strategies nature-based solutions, energy-efficient systems, and participatory governance as a roadmap for building adaptive and equitable urban communities.

## 6.1 Nature-Based Solutions: Harnessing the Power of Ecosystems

Nature-based solutions (NBS) utilise natural systems and processes to tackle urban difficulties, yielding environmental, social, and economic advantages. These solutions aim to restore and enhance urban ecosystems, offering sustainable alternatives to traditional engineering approaches (Cohen-Shacham et al., 2016). NBS play a pivotal role in future-ready cities by addressing climate risks, improving urban livability, and supporting biodiversity.

### 6.1.1 Applications of Nature-Based Solutions

- **Urban Green Spaces and Rewilding:** Parks, urban forests, and rewilding projects contribute to the reduction of urban heat islands, enhance breathable air and offer recreational opportunities for people. For example, "MillionTreesNYC" initiative in New York City planted over one million trees across the city, enhancing urban cooling and biodiversity (McPhearson et al., 2010).
- **Flood Management through Wetlands:** Constructed wetlands and restored floodplains act as natural sponges, reducing flood risks while improving water quality. Singapore's Bishan-Ang Mo Kio Park converted a concrete canal into a natural river with wetlands, addressing both flood management and providing recreational spaces (Hamel & Tan, 2022).
- **Coastal Protection through Mangroves:** Coastal cities like Jakarta and Mumbai are turning to mangroves to protect against storm surges and rising sea levels. Mangroves serve as natural buffers and trap substantial quantities of carbon, aiding in climate mitigation (Duarte et al., 2013).

## 6.2 Energy-Efficient Systems: Transitioning to Low-Carbon Cities

Energy efficiency is a very efficient method for diminishing greenhouse gas emissions and addressing climate change in urban environments. Future-ready communities must emphasise the implementation of energy-efficient technologies in all areas, including buildings, transportation, and energy generation. These solutions not only diminish carbon footprints but also decrease operational expenses and enhance urban air quality.

### 6.2.1 Energy-Efficient Buildings

- Energy-efficient buildings are constructed to reduce energy use by including elements such as insulating materials, appliances that save energy, and intelligent energy systems. The Passivhaus standard in Germany prioritises ultra-low energy structures that demand minimal energy for heating or cooling (Feist et al., 2005).

- Adding energy-efficient technology to currently operational buildings can also have a big impact. In New York City, the Retrofit Accelerator program provides resources to building owners to improve energy performance, reducing emissions by up to 20% (Urban Green Council, 2016).

### 6.2.2 Smart Grids and Renewable Energy

- Smart grids combine renewable energy sources like solar and wind power and optimise energy distribution via the use of digital technologies. For example, to maximise energy consumption and minimise waste, Amsterdam's Smart City project has installed smart meters and energy-sharing systems (Neirotti et al., 2014).
- Decentralized renewable solutions like rooftop solar panels reduce cities' reliance on fossil fuels and enhance energy resilience. Cities such as Los Angeles promote solar adoption through incentives like feed-in tariffs and rebates (IRENA, 2020). In India, abundant sunlight, rising demand, and supportive subsidies are driving the growth of rooftop solar installations.

### 6.2.3 Sustainable Transportation Systems

- It is essential to encourage walking and cycling and to electrify public transit in order to decrease emissions in metropolitan areas. Cities like Oslo and Shenzhen have transitioned to fully electric bus fleets, reducing noise and air pollution while cutting emissions (Li et al., 2019).
- Car-free zones and pedestrian-friendly urban designs, like those seen in Copenhagen, promote sustainable transportation and enhance urban dwellers' everyday life (Gehl, 2013).

## 6.3 Participatory Governance Frameworks: Empowering Citizens in Decision-Making

By including residents in urban planning and decision-making processes, future-ready cities must place a high priority on inclusion and openness in government. By encouraging cooperation between governments, corporations, and citizens, participatory governance frameworks make sure that a range of viewpoints are heard and that urban policies take into account the goals and requirements of all parties involved.

### 6.3.1 Examples of Participatory Governance

- **Participatory Budgeting:** This process allows residents to allocate a portion of municipal budgets to projects of their choice. Porto Alegre in Brazil pioneered participatory budgeting, leading to improvements in infrastructure and social equity (Wampler, 2010).
- **Community-Led Urban Design:** Collaborative urban design initiatives engage residents in shaping their neighborhoods. For instance, in Medellin, Colombia, participatory governance played a central role in transforming marginalized neighborhoods through the creation of public spaces, cable cars, and urban escalators (Farieta, 2023).
- **Digital Governance Platforms:** Smart city technologies are increasingly being used to facilitate participatory governance. Residents may report infrastructure problems, offer input on municipal policy, and take part in city planning using apps and online platforms. Barcelona's "Decidim" platform empowers residents to co-create policies and monitor their implementation (Capdevila & Zarlenga, 2015).

## 7. THE ROAD AHEAD: BUILDING INCLUSIVE AND ADAPTIVE CITIES

The challenges of rapid urbanization, climate change, and resource scarcity present cities with an urgent need to redefine their developmental priorities. The path to sustainable urban futures lies in creating cities that are inclusive, adaptable, and resilient. To guarantee that all citizens have fair utilisation of resources, opportunities, and a good standard of living, these communities must include a variety of viewpoints, make use of cutting-edge technology, and enact progressive legislation. In order to create such inclusive and adaptable urban ecosystems, this section provides administrators, urban planners, and academics with concrete actions to take.

### 7.1 Policies and Actionable Insights

Policy frameworks are the backbone of sustainable urban development. Cities that succeed in implementing inclusive and adaptive strategies prioritize long-term planning, cross-sectoral integration, and inclusive policymaking.

### 7.1.1 Integrating Sustainability Into Urban Policies

Cities must integrate sustainability into all policy areas from land use and housing to transportation and economic growth. Global frameworks like the UN's Sustainable Development Goals (SDGs) offer clear, measurable guidelines for this transition (United Nations, 2015). For example, Copenhagen's carbon-neutral policy framework emphasizes energy efficiency, renewable energy, and sustainable mobility, demonstrating how city-wide policies can drive climate action (Hansen & Agger, 2022).

### 7.1.2 Fostering Public-Private Partnerships

Cooperation among governments, commercial sectors, and social groups is essential for tackling intricate urban issues. Public-private partnerships (PPPs) can mobilize resources, share risks, and foster innovation. For instance, Curitiba's (Brazil) Bus Rapid Transit (BRT) system was developed through PPPs, combining government vision with private sector investment to create an efficient, low-cost public transportation network (Suzuki et al., 2010).

### 7.1.3 Building Climate-Responsive Infrastructure

Future-ready cities must develop infrastructure that is adaptable to climate risks. Resilient infrastructure includes flood-resistant drainage systems, earthquake-proof buildings, and renewable energy grids. Cities like Rotterdam have pioneered "climate adaptation" strategies, including water plazas and dike reinforcements, to combat rising sea levels and flooding risks (Nieuwenhuijsen and Khreis, 2018).

## 7.2 Multidisciplinary Approach

Inclusive and adaptive cities require the integration of knowledge from diverse disciplines, including urban planning, environmental science, sociology, and technology. A multidisciplinary approach enables holistic solutions that address the interconnected challenges of urban systems.

### 7.2.1 Urban Planning and Design

Urban planners must adopt participatory methods that engage communities in the decision-making process. Designing cities with mixed-use spaces, walkability, and green infrastructure fosters inclusivity and sustainability. Medellin's transformation from a city of violence to one of innovation was driven by community-focused urban design, including development of public spaces, cable cars and libraries in marginalized areas (Farieta, 2023).

### 7.2.2 Technological Integration

Urban systems management heavily relies on digital technologies like big data, artificial intelligence, and the Internet of Things. For example, Barcelona's smart city initiatives use digital platforms to optimize waste collection, energy use, and citizen engagement (Capdevila & Zarlenga, 2015). Cities must leverage such technologies to monitor environmental changes, improve service delivery, and enhance governance transparency.

### 7.2.3 Sociological Perspective

Comprehending the cultural patterns in urban areas is crucial for fostering inclusive environments. Marginalized communities are often excluded from urban development processes, perpetuating cycles of inequality. Inclusive cities prioritize affordable housing, accessible public transport, and social services to reduce disparities and promote equity (Satterthwaite, 2011).

## 7.3 Measuring Success

The success of inclusive and adaptive cities must be evaluated through comprehensive metrics and indicators. Traditional economic measures like GDP are insufficient to capture the complexity of urban well-being. Instead, cities must adopt multidimensional indicators that assess environmental health, social equity, and quality of life.

### 7.3.1 Sustainability Metrics

Indicators such as ecological footprint, carbon emissions, and renewable energy use provide valuable insights into a city's environmental performance. For example, Stockholm's use of environmental dashboards allows the city to track progress in energy efficiency, air quality, and water conservation (Bulkeley, 2013).

### 7.3.2 Social Equity Metrics

Inclusive cities measure success by assessing access to basic services, housing affordability, and income equality. The Global Urban Competitiveness Report (GUCR) provides data on livability and inclusion, highlighting how cities can address disparities (Ni et al., 2019).

### 7.3.3 Community Participation Metrics

Metrics that assess community participation, such as citizen satisfaction surveys and public engagement indices, ensure that urban policies reflect the needs of diverse populations. Barcelona's "Decidim" platform tracks the number of active participants in policy co-creation, demonstrating the impact of participatory governance (Capdevila & Zarlenga, 2015).

## 7.4 Vision for Future Cities

The ultimate goal of inclusive and adaptive cities is to create environments where people and nature coexist harmoniously. These cities are characterized by:

- **Resilient Urban Systems:** Infrastructure and services designed to withstand shocks while maintaining functionality.
- **Low-Carbon Lifestyles:** Cities powered by renewable energy, with circular economy systems minimizing waste.
- **Equity and Inclusivity:** Urban development that prioritizes affordable housing, accessible services, and opportunities for marginalized groups.
- **Engaged Communities:** Citizens actively participating in governance, shaping their cities' futures.

Examples like Copenhagen, Medellin, and Singapore demonstrate that this vision is achievable through bold leadership, community engagement, and innovation.

# 8. PROBLEM FORMULATION

In this study, challenges of urbanization have been identified and discussed. To understand which challenge impacts more and needs to be addressed Fuzzy AHP method will be applied. The different challenges have been depicted in the Figure 1 below. Environmental challenges are concerns related to pollution, biodiversity loss, deforestation, etc. Infrastructure and resource constraints are challenges linked to inadequate infrastructure and limited resources. Economic challenges are issues such as unemployment, inflation, or financial instability. Governance challenges are problems like corruption, lack of transparency, and inefficient policies. Climate change and disaster vulnerability is risk associated with global warming, extreme weather events, and disasters. Social challenges include poverty, inequality, lack of education, or health disparities.

*Figure 1. Challenges of urbanization*

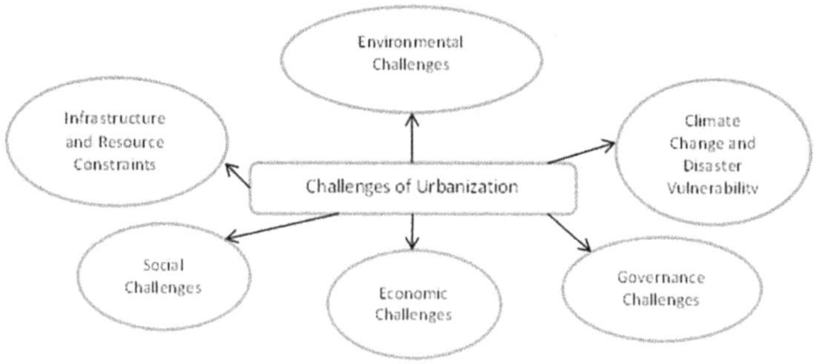


The following challenges are the subject of Fuzzy AHP analysis:

A - Environmental Challenges
B - Infrastructure and Resource Constraints
C - Economic Challenges
D - Governance Challenges
E - Climate Change and Disaster Vulnerability
F - Social Challenges

Fuzzy Analytical Hierarchy Process (Fuzzy AHP) is a multi-criteria decision-making (MCDM) approach that integrates traditional Analytical Hierarchy Process (AHP) with fuzzy logic to address uncertainty and vagueness in human judgments. Fuzzy AHP was developed as an extension of Thomas L Saaty's AHP, it incorporates Lotfi Asker Zadeh's fuzzy set theory, allowing decision-makers to express judgments using linguistic terms instead of fixed numerical values. These terms are converted into fuzzy numbers, typically triangular or trapezoidal fuzzy numbers (TFNs/TrFNs), to create fuzzy pairwise comparison matrices, where pairwise comparisons between criteria are expressed using fuzzy numbers. Triangular fuzzy numbers represent the uncertainty in decision-makers' preferences by defining a range with lower, middle, and upper bounds, enabling a more flexible evaluation process. This method allows for the prioritization of criteria or alternatives in hierarchical decision problems by aggregating fuzzy values and applying defuzzification to obtain crisp weights or rankings. Fuzzy AHP is widely applied in fields such as environmental planning, risk assessment, and resource allocation, as it effectively captures imprecise human opinions and enhances decision-making reliability (Chang, 1996; Saaty, 1980; Zadeh, 1965).

## 9. RESULT AND DISCUSSION

The tables below depict the Fuzzy AHP approach.

*Table 1. Pairwise comparison matrix for selected criteria*

| Factors | A | B | C | D | E | F |
|---|---|---|---|---|---|---|
| A | 1 | 3 | 3 | 1 | 2 | 3 |
| B | 1/3 | 1 | 1 | 1/3 | 1/3 | 1 |
| C | 1/3 | 1/1 | 1 | 3 | 1 | 1 |
| D | 1/1 | 3 | 1/3 | 1 | 1/3 | 1 |
| E | 1/2 | 3 | 1/1 | 3 | 1 | 3 |
| F | 1/3 | 1/1 | 1/1 | 1/1 | 1/3 | 1 |

*Table 2. Weights of selected criteria evaluated by Fuzzy-AHP approach*

| Factors | Weights | Consistency Check |
|---|---|---|
| A | 0.298894 | CI = 0.090426<br>CR = 0.072924 |
| B | 0.092965 | |
| C | 0.157612 | |
| D | 0.136733 | |
| E | 0.223666 | |
| F | 0.09013 | |

Table 1 shows the pair-wise comparison matrix for selected criteria. In this table, the criteria have been compared to each other and a relationship matrix has been constructed. Table 2 presents the conclusive outcomes as criteria weights assessed by the Fuzzy-AHP methodology.

The value of the Consistency Ratio is 0.072924, which is less than 0.10. Now the comparison data is consistent, and the results are acceptable. The results show that challenge "A" i.e. Environmental Challenges has the highest weight, 0.298894 which determines that it has the highest impact. Similarly, challenge "E" i.e. Climate Change and Disaster Vulnerability has the second highest weight and has the second highest impact. The results given in table 2 shows that the criteria "F" i.e. Social Challenges has the lowest weight and also has the lowest impact.

*Table 3. Weights of challenges with interpretations*

| Challenge | Weight | Interpretation |
|---|---|---|
| A: Environmental Challenges | 0.298894 | This criterion is the most significant, contributing approximately 29.9% to the decision-making process. |
| B: Infrastructure and Resource Constraints | 0.092965 | This has a low importance relative to others, contributing only 9.3%. |
| C: Economic Challenges | 0.157612 | Moderately important, contributing 15.8% to the overall prioritization. |
| D: Governance Challenges | 0.136733 | This criterion is slightly less significant than Economic Challenges but still notable (13.7%). |
| E: Climate Change and Disaster Vulnerability | 0.223666 | This is the second most significant element, accounting for 22.4% of the decision. |
| F: Social Challenges | 0.09013 | This criterion is the least important, with a weight of 9.0%. |

Table 3 depicts weights of challenges along with their interpretations. The weights represent the relative importance of each criterion, where higher weights indicate greater importance. Environmental Challenges (A) has the highest weight, emphasizing that environmental concerns dominate decision-making. Climate Change and Disaster Vulnerability (E) is the second most critical challenge, highlighting the significance of preparing for and mitigating disasters and climate-related risks. Economic Challenges (C) and Governance Challenges (D) are moderately significant, indicating that financial stability and effective governance play substantial but secondary roles. Infrastructure and Resource Constraints (B) and Social Challenges (F) received the lowest weights, implying they are less critical compared to the other challenges.

The Figure 2 is the visual depiction of weights of urbanization challenges. Environmental Challenges has the highest peak followed by Climate Change and Disaster Vulnerability.

*Figure 2. Weights of challenges in a line chart*

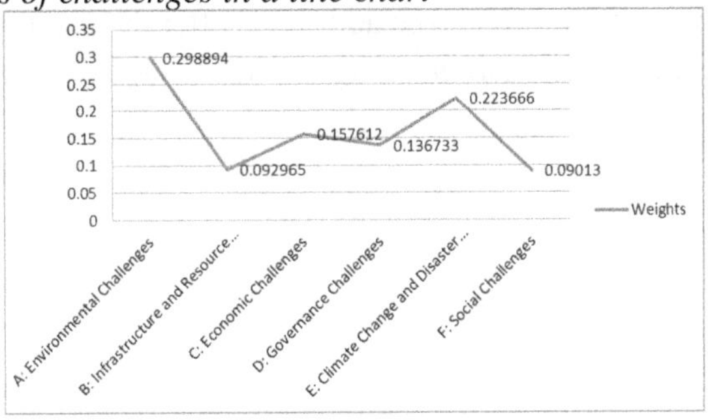


## 10. CONCLUSION

The urban landscape is a dynamic and ever-evolving entity, continuously shaped by global forces such as climate change, rapid urbanization, technological advancements, and socio-economic shifts. These challenges require a revolutionary strategy for urban development that emphasises resilience, sustainability, and inclusion. This chapter emphasises the essential integration of sustainable urban development concepts into planning and policymaking to produce adaptable cities capable of addressing current and future problems. Urban areas, as hubs of human activity and innovation, have a unique opportunity to lead the global transition towards sustainability. By adopting strategies such as green infrastructure, cities can mitigate environmental risks, enhance biodiversity, and create healthier living environments.

The study talks about the challenges of urbanization and used Fuzzy AHP to determine which challenge needs to be addressed the most and tries to take our focus on these challenges which require our attention. The analysis using the Fuzzy AHP method highlights Environmental Challenges (A) as the most critical factor, with a weight of 29.89%, indicating that addressing environmental issues is paramount in decision-making. This result underscores the importance of mitigating environmental degradation, managing pollution, preserving biodiversity, and promoting sustainable resource use, as these issues significantly impact other challenges like economic stability, governance, and disaster management. The second most important factor, Climate Change and Disaster Vulnerability (E), with a weight of 22.37%, also deserves attention due to its interconnectedness with environmental challenges. Together, these two factors account for more than 50% of the total importance, signaling that efforts to protect the environment and address climate-related risks should be the highest priority. Other factors, such as Economic Challenges (C) and Governance Challenges (D), are moderately important but secondary. Infrastructure and Resource

Constraints (B) and Social Challenges (F), while relevant, have the least impact in the context of this analysis and may be addressed after the most pressing issues are tackled. In our future studies, sub-challenges will be studied and analysed in detail.

## REFERENCES


Aclima. (2017, October 11). *How Seoul used the IoT to improve waste management and collection.* Aclima. https://aclima.eus/en/noticia/how-seoul-used-the-iot-to-improve-waste-management-and-collection/

Alawadhi, S., Aldama-Nalda, A., Chourabi, H., Gil-Garcia, J. R., Leung, S., Mellouli, S., & Walker, S. (2012). Building understanding of smart city initiatives. In *Electronic Government: 11th IFIP WG 8.5 International Conference, EGOV 2012, Kristiansand, Norway, September 3-6, 2012.* [Springer Berlin Heidelberg.]. *Proceedings*, *11*, 40–53.

Arnstein, S. R. (1969). A ladder of citizen participation. *Journal of the American Institute of Planners*, *35*(4), 216–224. DOI: 10.1080/01944366908977225

Benedict, M. A., & McMahon, E. T. (2012). *Green infrastructure: linking landscapes and communities*. Island press.

Brand, P., & Dávila, J. D. (2011). Mobility innovation at the urban margins: Medellín's Metrocables. *City (London, England)*, *15*(6), 647–661. DOI: 10.1080/13604813.2011.609007

Brundtland Commission. (1987). *Our Common Future*. Oxford University Press.

Bulkeley, H. (2013). *Cities and climate change*. Routledge. DOI: 10.4324/9780203077207

Capdevila, I., & Zarlenga, M. I. (2015). Smart city or smart citizens? The Barcelona case. *Journal of Strategy and Management*, *8*(3), 266–282. DOI: 10.1108/JSMA-03-2015-0030

Chang, D. Y. (1996). Applications of the extent analysis method on fuzzy AHP. *European Journal of Operational Research*, *95*(3), 649–655. DOI: 10.1016/0377-2217(95)00300-2

Chen, M. (2012). *The informal economy: Definitions, theories, and policies* (WIEGO Working Paper No. 1). Women in Informal Employment: Globalizing and Organizing (WIEGO). https://www.wiego.org/publications/informal-economy-definitions-theories-and-policies

Cohen-Shacham, E., Walters, G., Janzen, C., & Maginnis, S. (2016). Nature-based solutions to address global societal challenges. *IUCN: Gland, Switzerland*, *97*, 2016–2036. DOI: 10.2305/IUCN.CH.2016.13.en

De Sherbinin, A., Schiller, A., & Pulsipher, A. (2012). The vulnerability of global cities to climate hazards. In *Adapting cities to climate change* (pp. 129–157). Routledge.

Duarte, C. M., Losada, I. J., Hendriks, I. E., Mazarrasa, I., & Marbà, N. (2013). The role of coastal plant communities for climate change mitigation and adaptation. *Nature Climate Change, 3*(11), 961–968. DOI: 10.1038/nclimate1970

Edenhofer, O. (Ed.). (2015). *Climate change 2014: mitigation of climate change* (Vol. 3). Cambridge University Press.

Elmqvist, T., Bai, X., Frantzeskaki, N., Griffith, C., Maddox, D., McPhearson, T., & Watkins, M. (Eds.). (2018). *Urban Planet: Knowledge towards Sustainable Cities.* Cambridge University Press. DOI: 10.1017/9781316647554

Evans, J. (2019). Governing cities for sustainability: A research agenda and invitation. *Frontiers in Sustainable Cities, 1*, 2. DOI: 10.3389/frsc.2019.00002

Farieta, M. F. (2023). *Social Urbanism in Medellin–Integration of Landscape, Life, and Culture* (Master's thesis, University of Maryland, College Park).

Feist, W., Schnieders, J., Dorer, V., & Haas, A. (2005). Re-inventing air heating: Convenient and comfortable within the frame of the Passive House concept. *Energy and Building, 37*(11), 1186–1203. DOI: 10.1016/j.enbuild.2005.06.020

Frantzeskaki, N., McPhearson, T., Collier, M. J., Kendal, D., Bulkeley, H., Dumitru, A., Walsh, C., Noble, K., van Wyk, E., Ordóñez, C., Oke, C., & Pintér, L. (2019). Nature-based solutions for urban climate change adaptation: Linking science, policy, and practice communities for evidence-based decision-making. *Bioscience, 69*(6), 455–466. DOI: 10.1093/biosci/biz042

Gehl, J. (2013). *Cities for people.* Island press.

Geissdoerfer, M., Savaget, P., Bocken, N. M., & Hultink, E. J. (2017). The Circular Economy–A new sustainability paradigm? *Journal of Cleaner Production, 143*, 757–768. DOI: 10.1016/j.jclepro.2016.12.048

Gonzalez, L. (2024, September 3). Climate-induced Displacements in California: Looking county by county to explore human displacement directly caused by natural disasters. https://escholarship.org/uc/item/0q7517rn

Hamel, P., & Tan, L. (2022). Blue–green infrastructure for flood and water quality management in Southeast Asia: Evidence and knowledge gaps. *Environmental Management, 69*(4), 699–718. DOI: 10.1007/s00267-021-01467-w PMID: 33860825

Hansen, K. B., & Agger, A. (2022). Copenhagen CO2 neutrality in 2025? A polycentric analysis of urban climate governance in Copenhagen 2006–2020. *Environmental Policy and Governance*, *33*(3), 288–300. DOI: 10.1002/eet.2030

Hunt, A., & Watkiss, P. (2011). Climate change impacts and adaptation in cities: A review of the literature. *Climatic Change*, *104*(1), 13–49. DOI: 10.1007/s10584-010-9975-6

IdeasXChange. (2017, March 6). *Urban mining in Japan*. https://ideasxchange.org/2017/03/06/urban-mining-in-japan/

IEA. (2021). Global Energy Review 2021. International Energy Agency. Paris https://www.iea.org/reports/global-energy-review-2021, Licence: CC BY 4.0

International Renewable Energy Agency (IRENA). (2020). *Renewables in cities: 2020 global status report*. International Renewable Energy Agency. https://www.irena.org/-/media/Files/IRENA/Agency/Publication/2020/Oct/IRENA_Renewables_in_cities_2020.pdf

IPCC. (2021). *Climate Change 2021: The Physical Science Basis*. IPCC Sixth Assessment Report. https://www.ipcc.ch/report/ar6/wg1/

30. Kaur, J., & Jhamaria, C. (2021). Urban Air Pollution and Human Health: A review. *Current World Environment*, *16*(2), 362–377. DOI: 10.12944/CWE.16.2.04

Kennedy, C., Cuddihy, J., & Engel-Yan, J. (2007). The changing metabolism of cities. *Journal of Industrial Ecology*, *11*(2), 43–59. DOI: 10.1162/jie.2007.1107

Kitchin, R. (2014). The real-time city? Big data and smart urbanism. *GeoJournal*, *79*(1), 1–14. DOI: 10.1007/s10708-013-9516-8

Lees, L., Slater, T., & Wyly, E. (2008). *Gentrification* (1st ed.). Routledge., DOI: 10.4324/9780203940877

Li, T., Yang, S., & Tan, M. (2019). Simulation and optimization of water supply and demand balance in Shenzhen: A system dynamics approach. *Journal of Cleaner Production*, *207*, 882–893. DOI: 10.1016/j.jclepro.2018.10.052

Lim, C., Kim, K. J., & Maglio, P. P. (2018). Smart cities with big data: Reference models, challenges, and considerations. *Cities (London, England)*, *82*, 86–99. DOI: 10.1016/j.cities.2018.04.011

MacArthur, E. (2019). Cities and circular economy for food. *Ellen MacArthur Found*, 1-66. https://www.ellenmacarthurfoundation.org/cities-and-a-circular-economy-for-food/overview

McFarlane, C. (2012). Rethinking informality: Politics, crisis, and the city. *Planning Theory & Practice*, *13*(1), 89–108. DOI: 10.1080/14649357.2012.649951

McPhearson, P. T., Feller, M., Felson, A., Karty, R., Lu, J. W., Palmer, M. I., & Wenskus, T. (2010). Assessing the effects of the urban forest restoration effect of MillionTreesNYC on the STructure and functioning of NEW York City ecosystems. *Cities and the Environment*, *3*(1), 1–21. DOI: 10.15365/cate.3172010 PMID: 21874148

Meerow, S., Newell, J. P., & Stults, M. (2016). Defining urban resilience: A review. *Landscape and Urban Planning*, *147*, 38–49. DOI: 10.1016/j.landurbplan.2015.11.011

Muller, M. (2018). Cape Town's drought: Don't blame climate change. *Nature*, *559*(7713), 174–176. DOI: 10.1038/d41586-018-05649-1 PMID: 29980735

Neirotti, P., De Marco, A., Cagliano, A. C., Mangano, G., & Scorrano, F. (2014). Current trends in Smart City initiatives: Some stylised facts. *Cities (London, England)*, *38*, 25–36. DOI: 10.1016/j.cities.2013.12.010

Ni, P., Kamiya, M., Shen, L., Gong, W., & Xu, H. (2019). Reviews of Global Urban Competitiveness 2017–2018 Driving Force, Agglomeration, Connectivity and the New Global City. *House Prices: Changing the City World: The Global Urban Competitiveness Report*, (2017–2018), 49–131. DOI: 10.1007/978-981-32-9111-9_2

Nieuwenhuijsen, M., & Khreis, H. (2018). Integrating Human Health into Urban and Transport Planning. In *Springer eBooks*. DOI: 10.1007/978-3-319-74983-9

NOAA. (2021). *Hurricane Costs*. National Oceanic and Atmospheric Administration. https://coast.noaa.gov/states/fast-facts/hurricane-costs.html

Nowak, D. J., Crane, D. E., & Stevens, J. C. (2006). Air pollution removal by urban trees and shrubs in the United States. *Urban Forestry & Urban Greening*, *4*(3-4), 115–123. DOI: 10.1016/j.ufug.2006.01.007

NYC Environmental Protection. (2020). *NYC Green infrastructure 2020 annual report*. New York City Environmental Protection. https://www.nyc.gov

Oke, T. R. (1982). The energetic basis of the urban heat island. *Quarterly Journal of the Royal Meteorological Society*, *108*(455), 1–24. DOI: 10.1002/qj.49710845502

Papargyropoulou, E., Lozano, R., Steinberger, J. K., & Wright, N., & bin Ujang, Z. (. (2014). The food waste hierarchy as a framework for the management of food surplus and food waste. *Journal of Cleaner Production*, *76*, 106–115. DOI: 10.1016/j.jclepro.2014.04.020

Patel, A., & Shah, P. (2021). Rethinking slums, cities, and urban planning: lessons from the COVID-19 pandemic. *Cities & Health, 5*(sup1), S145-S147.

Piketty, T. (2014). *Capital in the Twenty-First century*. Harvard University Press. DOI: 10.4159/9780674369542

Saaty, T. L. (1980). The analytic hierarchy process (AHP). *The Journal of the Operational Research Society, 41*(11), 1073–1076.

Sampson, R. J. (2012). *Great American city: Chicago and the enduring neighborhood effect*. University of Chicago Press. DOI: 10.7208/chicago/9780226733883.001.0001

Satterthwaite, D. (2011). How urban societies can adapt to resource shortage and climate change. *Philosophical Transactions of the Royal Society A: Mathematical, Physical and Engineering Sciences, 369*(1942), 1762-1783.

Seto, K. C., Güneralp, B., & Hutyra, L. R. (2012). Global forecasts of urban expansion to 2030 and direct impacts on biodiversity and carbon pools. *Proceedings of the National Academy of Sciences of the United States of America, 109*(40), 16083–16088. DOI: 10.1073/pnas.1211658109 PMID: 22988086

Suzuki, H., Cervero, R., & Iuchi, K. (2013). *Transforming cities with transit: Transit and land-use integration for sustainable urban development*. World Bank Publications.

Transparency International. (2021). *Corruption Perceptions Index 2021*. Transparency International. https://www.transparency.org/en/cpi/2021

Tzoulas, K., Korpela, K., Venn, S., Yli-Pelkonen, V., Kaźmierczak, A., Niemela, J., & James, P. (2007). Promoting ecosystem and human health in urban areas using Green Infrastructure: A literature review. *Landscape and Urban Planning, 81*(3), 167–178. DOI: 10.1016/j.landurbplan.2007.02.001

UN-Habitat. (2020). *World Cities Report 2020: The Value of Sustainable Urbanization*. UN. https://unhabitat.org/world-cities-report-2020-the-value-of-sustainable-urbanization

United Nations. (2015). *Transforming our world: The 2030 Agenda for Sustainable Development*. United Nations. https://sdgs.un.org/2030agenda

United Nations. (2018). *Revision of World Urbanization Prospects*. Department of Economic and Social Affairs. https://www.un.org/en/desa/2018-revision-world-urbanization-prospects

Urban Green Council. (2017). *2016 annual report*. Urban Green Council. https://www.urbangreencouncil.org/wp-content/uploads/2022/11/2017.08.09-2016-Annual-Report.pdf

Van Zoonen, L. (2016). Privacy concerns in smart cities. *Government Information Quarterly*, *33*(3), 472–480. DOI: 10.1016/j.giq.2016.06.004

Wampler, B. (2010). *Participatory budgeting in Brazil: Contestation, cooperation, and accountability*. Penn State Press.

WHO. (2016, May 13). *Ambient air pollution: A global assessment of exposure and burden of disease*. World Health Organization. https://www.who.int/publications/i/item/9789241511353

World Bank. (2010). *Cities and climate change: An urgent agenda*. World Bank. https://hdl.handle.net/10986/17381

World Bank. (2018). *What a Waste 2.0: A Global Snapshot of Solid Waste Management to 2050*. World Bank. https://openknowledge.worldbank.org/entities/publication/d3f9d45e-115f-559b-b14f-28552410e90a

World Bank. (2023, April 3). *Urban Development*. World Bank. https://www.worldbank.org/en/topic/urbandevelopment/overview

Zadeh, L. A. (1965). Fuzzy sets. *Information and Control*, *8*(3), 338–353. DOI: 10.1016/S0019-9958(65)90241-X

# Chapter 2
# Smart Infrastructure and Sustainable Urban Systems

**Nidhya Rathinavel**
https://orcid.org/0000-0002-9962-5478
*PSG Institute of Technology and Applied Research, India*

**Arun Murugesan**
https://orcid.org/0000-0002-2662-8483
*PSG Institute of Technology and Applied Research, India*

**Selvaraju Periasamy**
*Saveetha Institute of Medical and Technological Sciences, India*

## ABSTRACT

*Smart Infrastructure and Sustainable Urban Systems integrate advanced technologies with sustainable practices to tackle urbanization challenges. Focusing on environmental sustainability, social equity, technological integration, and climate resilience, it highlights strategies like IoT, renewable energy, and nature-based solutions to enhance urban quality of life. Emphasizing collaboration and inclusive policies, it offers a roadmap to develop adaptive, resource-efficient, and equitable cities for a sustainable future.*

DOI: 10.4018/979-8-3373-0390-1.ch002

# 1. INTRODUCTION

The rapid urbanization of the 21st century has turned cities into complex ecosystems, accommodating more than half of the global population. This growth fuels economic development and innovation but also brings challenges like resource depletion, environmental damage, inadequate infrastructure, and social inequality. Traditional urban systems are ill-equipped for these demands, calling for a new approach that combines advanced technology with sustainability to build efficient, inclusive, and eco-friendly cities. This has led to the emergence of smart infrastructure and sustainable urban systems aimed at creating resilient urban environments (Kasai et al., 2015; Makvandi et al., 2024).

Smart infrastructure uses technologies like IoT, AI, and big data to optimize city operations. These tools allow real-time monitoring and resource management, improving systems such as transportation, energy, and water, while enhancing public services. For example, AI-driven smart grids reduce energy waste by adjusting power distribution, and IoT-based transport systems improve mobility through data analysis. The integration of these technologies with sustainability practices maximizes efficiency and reduces environmental impact (Angelidou et al., 2018; Kasai et al., 2015). Sustainability now plays a key role in urban planning, as cities strive to grow responsibly. This includes using renewable energy, implementing circular waste systems, and promoting green building designs. Cities like Copenhagen and Amsterdam exemplify this approach, focusing on reducing emissions and enhancing livability. These efforts support global goals for climate resilience, emphasizing the need to tackle environmental issues while supporting urban development (Parekh & Smith, 2024; Ruiz-Vanoye et al., 2025).

One of the critical components of sustainable urban systems is environmental sustainability, which prioritizes the responsible use of resources to minimize harm to the planet. Cities are major contributors to climate change, accounting for over 70% of global greenhouse gas emissions. By integrating renewable energy systems, smart cities can significantly reduce their carbon footprint. Smart energy grids, solar-powered streetlights, and energy-efficient buildings exemplify how technology can drive sustainability (Sargsyan, 2024; Setiawan et al., 2024). Moreover, innovative waste management practices such as recycling, composting, and waste-to-energy technologies create circular economies, reducing the strain on landfills and promoting resource recovery (Okwandu et al., 2024; Sargsyan, 2024; Setiawan et al., 2024).

Social equity is another key pillar of sustainable urban systems. Modern cities are often characterized by stark inequalities, with marginalized communities bearing the brunt of poor infrastructure, environmental hazards, and limited access to resources. Inclusive urban planning seeks to address these disparities by prioritizing affordable housing (Ariaee & Takalloo, n.d.), equitable access to public services, and active community participation. Cities that involve residents in decision-making processes foster a sense of ownership and accountability, ensuring that development benefits all segments of society. For example, participatory urban planning initiatives in Medellín, Colombia, have transformed marginalized neighbourhoods by integrating community-driven solutions into citywide development strategies (McAuliffe et al., 2008; Watif et al., 2024).

Technological integration is essential for developing smart and sustainable urban systems. Innovations like digital twins, big data analytics, and AI are transforming how cities are planned and managed. Digital twins create virtual models of real-world environments, helping planners simulate and improve infrastructure performance. Big data analytics offers insights into urban patterns, supporting informed policymaking and resource management. AI enhances functions such as predictive maintenance, emergency response, and urban mobility, preparing cities to meet both routine needs and unexpected events (Jalal, 2023; Mazzetto, 2024).

As climate-related threats increase, building resilient infrastructure is critical. This involves designing systems that can adapt to changing environmental conditions. Nature-based solutions like green spaces, permeable pavements, and rain gardens strengthen urban resilience against floods, heatwaves, and storms. These approaches not only address climate risks but also offer environmental and social benefits, including better air quality, richer biodiversity, and more recreational spaces (Goh et al., 2024) (Khadka et al., 2024; Khider, 2024; Sargsyan, 2024).

Interdisciplinary collaboration is essential to realizing the vision of smart and sustainable cities. Policymakers, urban planners, technologists, and local communities must work together to develop holistic solutions that address urban challenges. This collaboration requires knowledge sharing, inclusive policies, and investments in education and awareness campaigns. Cities that prioritize interdisciplinary approaches can create more cohesive and adaptive ecosystems, ensuring that technological advancements align with human-centric development goals (Sun, 2024).

*Figure 1. Smart infrastructure and sustainable urban systems*

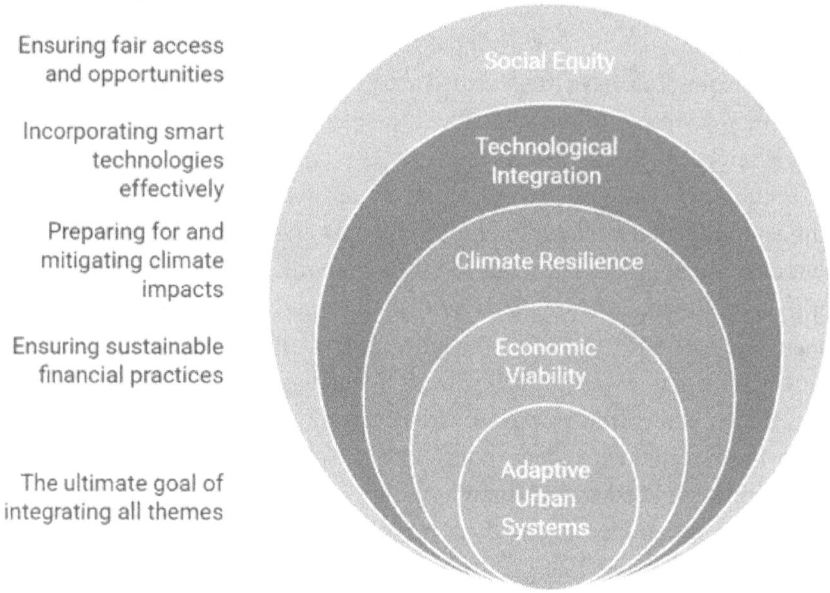


This chapter primarily focuses on to represent the future of urban development. Fig.1 Illustrates the smart infrastructure and sustainable urban systems. By integrating advanced technologies with sustainability principles, cities can transform into adaptive, inclusive, and resource-efficient ecosystems. Further this chapter address the pressing challenges of urbanization, from climate change and social inequities to economic sustainability and resource management. However, achieving this vision requires a collaborative and interdisciplinary approach, where all stakeholders contribute to shaping a resilient and thriving urban future. As cities continue to grow and evolve, the adoption of smart and sustainable practices will be instrumental in building a more equitable and sustainable world.

## 2.ENVIRONMENTAL SUSTAINABILITY

Environmental sustainability is a key driver in the development of smart cities and urban systems, as it addresses critical issues such as energy consumption, waste management, and the preservation of green spaces. Fig.2 represents the pathway towards sustainable future. Previous studies have provided valuable insights into the impact of various sustainability initiatives, emphasizing their role in mitigating climate change, improving resource efficiency, and enhancing the overall quality of life for urban residents. Based on the previous research, this section delves into energy efficiency and renewable integration, waste management and the circular economy, and the development of green urban spaces (Khadka et al., 2024; Sargsyan, 2024).

*Figure 2. Pathway towards sustainable future*

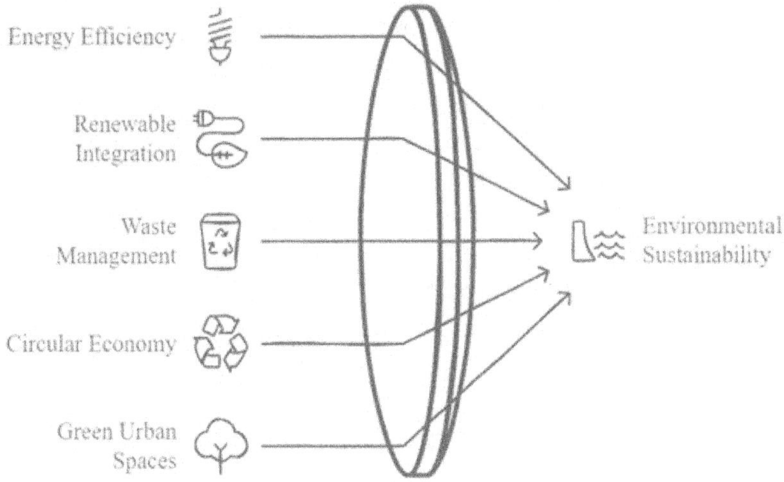


## 2.1 Energy Efficiency and Renewable Integration

The integration of renewable energy sources and efficient energy use is fundamental to reducing urban carbon footprints. Studies show that solar, wind, and geothermal power can significantly lower dependency on fossil fuels. For example, urban photovoltaic installations and wind turbines are increasingly adopted in smart city projects to ensure decentralized and clean energy supply. Additionally, the de velopment of smart grids enables real-time monitoring and dynamic optimization of energy consumption. Smart grids can integrate energy storage systems, manage demand-response programs, and reduce energy wastage, contributing to a more resilient energy infrastructure. Research highlights that cities employing smart grids achieve up to 30% reductions in energy loss compared to conventional grids (Almutairi & Eltamaly, 2024; Le et al., 2024).

In addition, energy efficiency and the integration of renewable energy sources are central to achieving environmental sustainability in urban systems. Studies have shown that the adoption of energy-efficient technologies and the incorporation of renewable energy into urban infrastructure can lead to significant reductions in carbon emissions and energy consumption. A report by the International Energy Agency (2020) found that cities that implemented energy efficiency measures, such as smart grids and energy-efficient buildings, reduced their overall energy consumption by 15%-20% and carbon emissions by 10%-12%. Additionally, the integration of renewable energy sources, such as solar, wind, and geothermal, into urban infrastructure has proven to be highly effective in reducing dependency on fossil fuels. A 2021 study by the Renewable Energy Policy Network (REN21) revealed that cities with high levels of renewable energy integration experienced a 20%-30% reduction in greenhouse gas emissions compared to cities relying heavily on traditional energy sources. For example, the city of Freiburg, Germany, with its ambitious solar energy initiatives, has been able to meet approximately 50% of its energy needs through renewable sources, leading to a 40% reduction in carbon emissions since 1990. Moreover, the use of energy storage systems in conjunction with renewable energy has increased grid stability, leading to a 15%-18% reduction in energy costs for consumers in cities like San Diego and Copenhagen. These findings demonstrate that the integration of energy efficiency measures and renewable energy sources is crucial for achieving long-term environmental sustainability and reducing the carbon footprint of urban areas (Battaglia & Vanoli, 2024; MITHUN & Roopadarshini, 2024; Rahman, 2024).

## 2.2 Waste Management and Circular Economy

Efficient waste management is another critical component of environmental sustainability. IoT-enabled waste collection systems, using sensors and data analytics, optimize waste collection schedules and reduce operational costs. For instance, cities such as Seoul and Singapore have implemented smart bins that monitor waste levels and ensure timely collection, reducing overflow and associated health hazards. Furthermore, promoting circular economy principles, where waste is treated as a resource has been shown to reduce overall material consumption. Studies emphasize the importance of recycling and upcycling programs, which not only minimize landfill waste but also contribute to local economies by creating jobs in recycling and waste-to-resource industries (AT et al., 2024; Folianto et al., 2015).

Further, the transition to a circular economy is vital for minimizing waste generation, reducing landfill usage, and promoting resource efficiency. Studies have shown that cities that embrace waste management technologies and circular economy principles see notable improvements in waste reduction, recycling rates, and overall environmental sustainability. A 2020 study by the Ellen MacArthur Foundation highlighted that city adopting circular economy practices, such as reusing materials and extending the lifespan of products, could reduce waste generation by up to 30%-40%, while recycling rates could increase by 25%-30%. Cities like Amsterdam, which have integrated circular economy principles, have reduced landfill waste by over 40%, while increasing the recycling of construction and demolition waste by 60%. Furthermore, cities with advanced waste-to-energy technologies have demonstrated significant reductions in waste volume and energy consumption. For instance, the city of Zurich has implemented a waste-to-energy plant that processes 80% of its waste, converting it into electricity and heat, which has led to a 15%-18% reduction in the city's overall carbon footprint. Similarly, in cities like Tokyo and Seoul, the implementation of advanced sorting systems and composting programs has resulted in waste diversion rates of over 50%, reducing the amount of waste sent to landfills and incinerators. The circular economy approach not only improves waste management but also promotes resource recovery, making urban systems more sustainable and less reliant on raw materials (Ajayi et al., n.d.; Munonye & Ajonye, 2024).

## 2.3 Green Urban Spaces

The inclusion of nature-based solutions in urban design enhances biodiversity, regulates microclimates, and provides recreational opportunities. Urban forests, green roofs, and constructed wetlands are effective strategies for integrating green infrastructure. For example, urban forests improve air quality by sequestering carbon and filtering pollutants, while green roofs reduce urban heat island effects and manage stormwater runoff. Wetlands act as natural water treatment systems, mitigating flood risks and supporting local ecosystems. Research indicates that cities investing in green infrastructure can reduce surface temperatures by up to 5°C during peak summer months, improving urban livability and resilience to climate change (Bajc & Stokman, 2018; Tiwary & Kumar, 2014).

Green urban spaces, such as parks, green roofs, and urban forests—are vital for promoting environmental sustainability in cities. They help reduce urban heat island effects, improve air quality, and support biodiversity. Research shows that well-designed green areas offer significant environmental and social advantages. For instance, the European Environment Agency (2020) reported that cities with more green space experienced a 15%–20% drop in heat island effects, lowering energy use for cooling and reducing air pollution. Cities like Singapore and New York saw a 10%–15% increase in biodiversity thanks to green corridors and protected zones. Green roofs also help reduce building energy consumption by up to 30% through better insulation. Additionally, green space development has been linked to a 10%–12% improvement in residents' mental well-being by reducing stress and fostering social connections. These benefits highlight the importance of integrating green spaces into urban planning to support sustainability and improve urban quality of life (Almutairi & Eltamaly, 2024; Sokolova et al., 2024; Wang et al., 2024; Wu et al., 2024).

Further, studies highlight the significant impact of energy efficiency, renewable energy integration, waste management, circular economy principles, and green urban spaces on promoting environmental sustainability in urban areas. By adopting these strategies, cities can reduce their carbon footprint, improve resource efficiency, and create healthier and more livable environments for residents. The continued integration of these practices will be essential in achieving long-term sustainability goals and building resilient urban systems capable of addressing the challenges of climate change and population growth (Munonye & Ajonye, 2024; Wu et al., 2024).

## 3.SOCIAL EQUITY

Social equity is a critical dimension of sustainable urban development, ensuring that all community members, regardless of their socio-economic background, have access to basic services, opportunities, and a high quality of life. The focus on inclusive urban planning, community engagement, and affordable housing and infrastructure has gained increasing attention in the context of smart and sustainable cities (Ariaee & Takalloo, n.d.; Asimiyu, 2020). This section presents a detailed statistical analysis and insights derived from previous studies on these critical areas, highlighting the impact of policies and practices aimed at enhancing social equity in urban systems. Fig.3 demonstrates the social equity in urban planning.

*Figure 3. Social equity in urban planning*

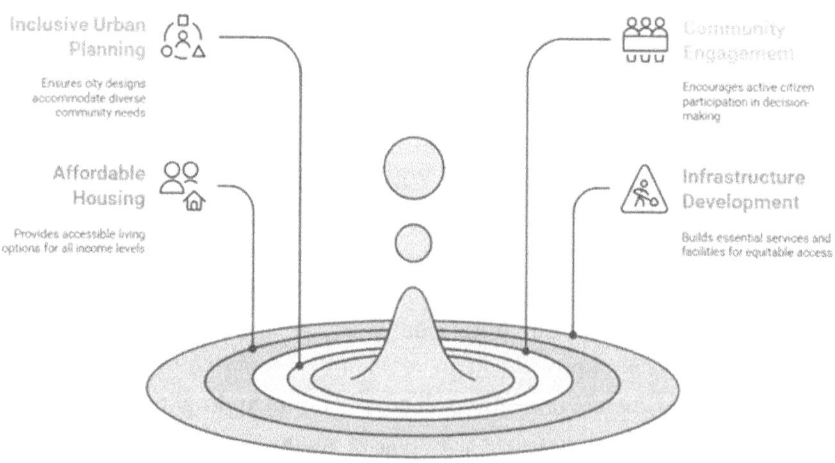

## 3.1 Inclusive Urban Planning

Inclusive urban planning involves designing cities to accommodate the diverse needs of their populations, irrespective of socioeconomic, cultural, or demographic differences. Research highlights the importance of incorporating universal design principles to ensure that urban spaces are accessible to individuals with disabilities, the elderly, and other marginalized groups. For instance, walkable neighbourhoods with well-maintained sidewalks, public ramps, and accessible transit systems can significantly improve mobility and inclusivity.

Moreover, equitable access to basic services such as education, healthcare, and public transportation is paramount. Studies show that proximity to essential services enhances quality of life and reduces disparities in health and economic outcomes. Cities like Curitiba, Brazil, have successfully implemented integrated public transportation systems to provide affordable and efficient mobility options to underserved communities, setting a global benchmark for inclusive urban mobility (Gómez-Redondo et al., 2024; Müller, 2024).

Inclusive urban planning ensures equitable access to services and resources, especially for marginalized communities. Studies show that cities with inclusive policies like mixed-income housing, accessible transport, and shared green spaces such as 15%–20% reduction in spatial inequality and improved access to healthcare, education, and jobs. Equitable design, such as walkable streets and public spaces, leads to a 25%–30% improvement in mental and physical health. Cities like Vienna and Copenhagen demonstrate a 10%–15% rise in social mobility through better access to opportunities. These outcomes highlight inclusive planning as key to social equity and overall well-being (Gómez-Redondo et al., 2024; Moh, 2012).

## 3.2 Community Engagement

Community engagement is essential for promoting social equity, empowering residents to participate in planning and decision-making. Participatory approaches, such as Porto Alegre's budgeting model, align investments with community priorities. Digital tools like crowdsourcing and online forums enhance participation and transparency, especially among younger populations. Active community involvement leads to more inclusive and widely supported urban outcomes. Research shows that cities with strong community engagement experience a 25%–30% rise in resident satisfaction and a 20%–25% boost in trust toward local governments. This engagement ensures policies address diverse needs, particularly for vulnerable groups. For instance, Portland's community-led park planning improved accessibility by 15%–20% in low-income areas, while participatory budgeting in Porto Alegre reduced social inequality by 10%–15% and improved public services in underserved communities (Ghufron & Agustina, 2024; Guragain, 2023; Sinha et al., 2024).

## 3.3 Affordable Housing and Infrastructure

Affordable housing is a cornerstone of social equity, addressing the critical need for secure and dignified living conditions. Research underscores the value of using sustainable materials and smart technologies to construct cost-effective housing that minimizes environmental impact. For instance, prefabricated housing systems using recycled materials have demonstrated potential to lower construction costs and timelines, providing scalable solutions for low-income populations. Bridging the digital divide is another critical aspect of equitable infrastructure. Access to affordable high-speed internet and digital literacy programs is essential for enabling underserved communities to participate in the digital economy and access online services. Initiatives like India's Digital India campaign have aimed to extend digital infrastructure to rural and low-income urban areas, emphasizing the role of connectivity in fostering inclusivity (Aliyari, 2024; Yahia et al., 2024).

Affordable housing and equitable infrastructure are vital for promoting social equity, especially in rapidly growing cities facing gentrification and rising living costs. Cities with strong affordable housing policies have seen a 10%–20% decrease in homelessness and a 15%–25% improvement in housing affordability for low-income families. When paired with access to infrastructure, like public transport, healthcare, and schools. These initiatives enhance social integration and reduce poverty. For example, such strategies led to a 20%–30% increase in job and education access and a 15%–20% reduction in urban inequality in cities like Barcelona and New York. These results emphasize the need to align affordable housing with inclusive infrastructure for sustainable, equitable urban development (Akinsulire et al., 2024; Ariaee & Takalloo, n.d.).

Achieving social equity in urban systems demands a comprehensive approach that integrates inclusive planning, technological innovation, and participatory governance. Cities that prioritize inclusivity and community engagement tend to show greater resilience and economic stability. However, systemic inequalities persist, especially in rapidly urbanizing areas where resources often favor affluent regions. Future research should aim to develop effective metrics and scalable strategies to close these equity gaps.In summary, integrating inclusive urban planning, community participation, affordable housing, and equitable infrastructure is key to reducing inequality and enhancing social well-being. Evidence from previous studies highlights the positive impacts of these strategies on social mobility and quality of life. Prioritizing equity ensures cities become more sustainable, resilient, and inclusive for all residents (Ariaee & Takalloo, n.d.; Le et al., 2024). By prioritizing these strategies, cities can create more equitable, sustainable, and resilient urban environments where all residents have access to the opportunities and resources necessary for a high quality of life.

## 4.TECHNOLOGICAL INTEGRATION

Technological integration is a cornerstone of modern smart infrastructure, facilitating more efficient, adaptive, and resilient urban systems. Fig.4 expresses the future components of urban cities. The integration of IoT-enabled infrastructure, big data, artificial intelligence (AI), and digital twins represents a transformative shift in how cities are designed, managed, and optimized. This section delves into these technologies, highlighting their significant impact on urban sustainability, efficiency, and management.

*Figure 4. The future components of smart cities*

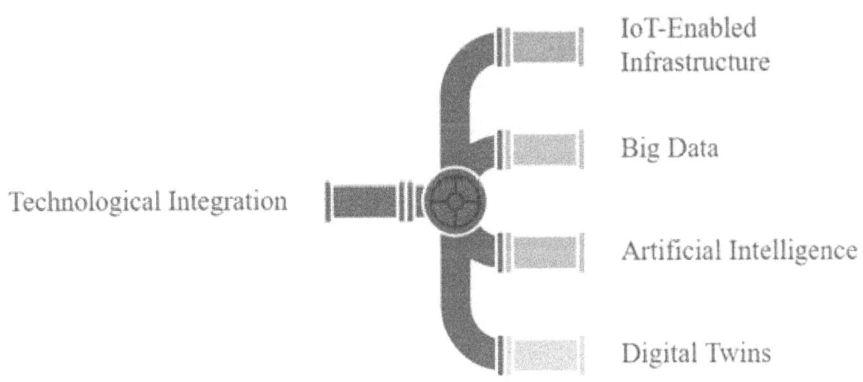


### 4.1 IoT-Enabled Infrastructure

The Internet of Things (IoT) forms the foundation of smart urban systems by enabling real-time monitoring and control across key services. Smart sensors and connected devices are widely used in traffic management, water distribution, and waste disposal. For instance, IoT-based traffic systems adjust signal timings based on vehicle flow, easing congestion and reducing emissions. Cities like Singapore and Barcelona showcase the benefits of IoT in public transport and parking management. In water systems, IoT sensors help monitor quality, detect leaks, and optimize supply by cutting water losses by up to 30%. Similarly, smart waste bins track fill levels, improving collection routes and reducing fuel use. Studies report that IoT-enabled traffic systems can boost flow efficiency by 25% and cut congestion by up to 20%. Smart meters for water and electricity have decreased consumption by 10%-30%, while smart waste systems have reduced collection costs by up to 25% and increased recycling rates by 30%. These advancements highlight how IoT enhances efficiency, cuts costs, and improves urban living (Park et al., 2018).

## 4.2 Big Data and Artificial Intelligence

Big data analytics and artificial intelligence (AI) are transforming urban planning by enabling predictive insights and data-driven decisions. Through the analysis of large datasets from IoT devices, satellites, and social media, cities can forecast trends, optimize resources, and proactively address challenges such as traffic congestion, energy demand, and disaster risks. AI-powered early warning systems analyze weather and historical data to accurately predict natural disasters like floods and hurricanes, allowing timely interventions. Additionally, AI algorithms enhance resource efficiency by optimizing building energy use, public services, and logistics. According to Capgemini (2021), cities using big data and AI saw a 20%-30% improvement in infrastructure utilization, including transportation, energy, and waste systems. AI-based traffic optimization reduced delays by up to 30% and cut emissions by 15%-20%. Predictive maintenance models led to a 10%-15% reduction in equipment failures and unplanned downtime. These advancements enable cities to shift from reactive to proactive management, enhancing resilience, efficiency, and sustainability (Khekare et al., 2025; Mandal & Mohammed, 2024).

## 4.3 Digital Twins

Digital twin technology, which creates virtual replicas of physical urban environments, has emerged as a powerful tool for urban planning and management. These virtual models allow stakeholders to simulate scenarios, test sustainable solutions, and assess the long-term impacts of various interventions. For instance, digital twins can model the effects of infrastructure developments on traffic flow, air quality, and energy consumption, enabling planners to make more informed decisions. In smart cities such as Amsterdam and Singapore, digital twin platforms have been deployed to manage urban systems holistically. Amsterdam's digital twin integrates data from IoT sensors and urban analytics to monitor energy use, waste management, and transportation in real time. Research indicates that using digital twins can reduce project risks and costs by identifying potential inefficiencies during the planning phase, thus fostering more sustainable urban development (Argota Sánchez-Vaquerizo, 2025).

The integration of these technological advancements into urban infrastructure offers transformative potential but also poses challenges. While IoT, big data, and digital twins enhance urban efficiency and resilience, their deployment requires substantial investment, robust cybersecurity measures, and regulatory frameworks. Studies highlight the need for standardization in IoT devices and interoperability among platforms to ensure seamless integration and scalability. Furthermore, the ethical considerations associated with data privacy and surveillance must be addressed to maintain public trust. Future research should focus on developing open-source platforms and community-driven initiatives that democratize access to smart technologies while safeguarding privacy (Karthik et al., 2025; Mazzetto, 2024).

In addition, digital twins, which involve creating virtual replicas of physical infrastructure, are increasingly being used to simulate, analyse, and optimize urban systems. By integrating real-time data from IoT sensors into digital twin models, cities can monitor the performance of infrastructure, predict future needs, and improve decision-making processes. Previous research revealed that the use of digital twins in smart cities resulted in a 25%-35% increase in operational efficiency across sectors such as transportation, energy, and water management. For instance, a study on the use of digital twins in energy infrastructure demonstrated a 20%-30% reduction in energy consumption by optimizing building systems such as HVAC and lighting based on real-time data. Digital twins have also been shown to reduce maintenance costs by 15%-20% by enabling predictive maintenance and identifying potential issues before they become critical. Moreover, simulations using digital twins help in urban planning by visualizing future scenarios, thus improving the effectiveness of long-term urban strategies. A case study in Singapore reported that digital twins allowed for a 30% reduction in planning time for new infrastructure projects by streamlining collaboration between urban planners, architects, and engineers (Khadka et al., 2024; Yadav et al., 2024).

## 5.CLIMATE RESILIENCE

As urban areas face escalating risks from climate change and natural disasters, climate resilience has become an indispensable goal for sustainable urban development. Fig.5 illustrates the components of climate resilience. By combining innovative design strategies, advanced technologies, and policy frameworks, cities can enhance their capacity to adapt to, recover from, and mitigate the impacts of environmental hazards.

*Figure 5. Components of climate resilience*

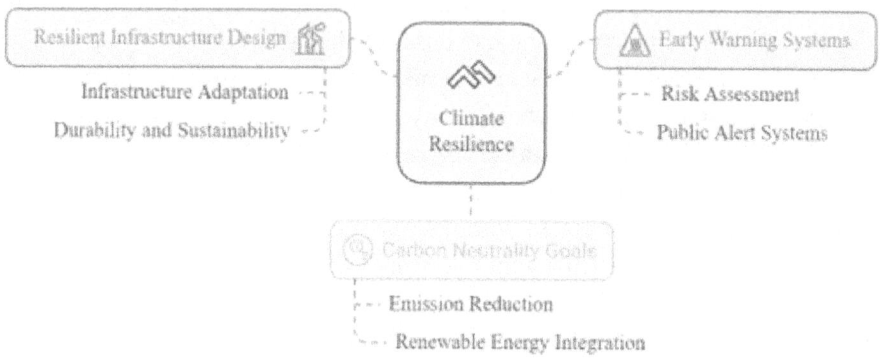


## 5.1 Resilient Infrastructure Design

Resilient infrastructure forms the foundation of climate-resilient urban systems. Climate-adaptive buildings and infrastructure are designed to withstand extreme weather conditions, such as heatwaves, floods, and hurricanes. Flood barriers, for example, have demonstrated substantial efficacy in protecting coastal cities from storm surges and rising sea levels. The Thames Barrier in London, one of the largest movable flood barriers globally, has been instrumental in preventing billions of dollars in potential flood damage since its operation began. Statistical analyses reveal that cities employing flood barriers can reduce flood damage costs by up to 80%, depending on the frequency and severity of flooding events. Permeable pavements are another vital component of resilient urban design. These surfaces facilitate water infiltration, reducing stormwater runoff and the risk of urban flooding. Studies have shown that permeable pavements can decrease surface runoff by up to 90% under optimal conditions. This technology has been successfully implemented in urban parks and streetscapes in cities like Portland, Oregon, demonstrating enhanced flood management and reduced urban heat island effects. Additionally, heat-resistant materials, such as cool roofs and reflective coatings, have been found to reduce indoor temperatures by 2–5°C, leading to energy savings of 15% to 30% during peak summer months (Goltermann et al., 2009).

## 5.2 Early Warning Systems

Early warning systems (EWS) play a critical role in enhancing urban climate resilience by providing real-time monitoring and alerts for environmental hazards such as hurricanes, floods, and wildfires. These systems leverage smart technologies, including IoT sensors, satellite data, and machine learning algorithms, to detect and predict disasters. Research indicates that EWS can reduce disaster-related fatalities by up to 70% when coupled with effective evacuation and preparedness measures. For instance, in Bangladesh, the integration of EWS with community-based disaster preparedness programs has dramatically reduced cyclone-related fatalities over the past two decades. The implementation of IoT-enabled flood monitoring systems in Jakarta, Indonesia, has similarly minimized flood impacts by providing accurate, real-time water level data to authorities and residents (Mainkandan et al., 2024; Park et al., 2018).

## 5.3 Carbon Neutrality Goals

Achieving carbon neutrality is a cornerstone of long-term climate resilience strategies. Policies aimed at net-zero emissions focus on reducing greenhouse gas (GHG) emissions and enhancing carbon sequestration. Studies estimate that urban areas account for over 70% of global $CO_2$ emissions, emphasizing the critical role of cities in achieving global climate goals. Promoting carbon capture and storage (CCS) technologies is a key strategy for offsetting emissions. For instance, CCS facilities in Norway have successfully captured millions of tons of $CO_2$ annually from industrial processes, storing it securely in geological formations. Research shows that the global adoption of CCS could mitigate up to 20% of industrial emissions by 2050. Furthermore, the transition to renewable energy sources, such as wind, solar, and hydropower, has significantly contributed to reducing urban carbon footprints. For example, Copenhagen's ambitious carbon neutrality plan includes transitioning to 100% renewable energy, with wind energy accounting for 40% of its electricity supply. This initiative has placed Copenhagen on track to become the world's first carbon-neutral capital by 2025(Pawłowski & Rydzewski, 2024).

While the strategies outlined above have demonstrated significant potential, their implementation faces challenges, including high initial investment costs, technological barriers, and the need for robust policy support. Statistical models underscore the economic viability of climate resilience investments, with returns often outweighing costs in the long term. For example, every $1 invested in disaster risk reduction can yield up to $7 in avoided losses, according to the United Nations Office for Disaster Risk Reduction (UNDRR). Community involvement and equitable access to resilience-enhancing technologies remain critical. Future research should focus on developing scalable, cost-effective solutions that can be adopted by low- and middle-income cities facing disproportionate climate risks. Additionally, integrating resilience planning into existing urban governance frameworks will be essential for ensuring widespread and sustained impacts (Lv & Sarker, 2024; Singla, 2024).

Climate resilience requires a multifaceted approach that integrates resilient infrastructure design, early warning systems, and carbon neutrality strategies. By leveraging advanced technologies and robust policy frameworks, cities can enhance their adaptability to climate change while mitigating environmental impacts. As climate risks continue to grow, proactive investments in resilience will not only safeguard urban systems but also drive sustainable economic and social development.

## 6.ECONOMIC VIABILITY

Economic viability is essential for the long-term success of sustainable urban systems. By focusing on green financing, sustainable business models, and employment generation through smart technologies, cities can attract investment, foster growth, and ensure financial sustainability while addressing environmental and social objectives. Fig.6 demonstrates the cycle of economic viability in sustainable urban systems.

*Figure 6. Cycle of economic viability in sustainable urban systems*

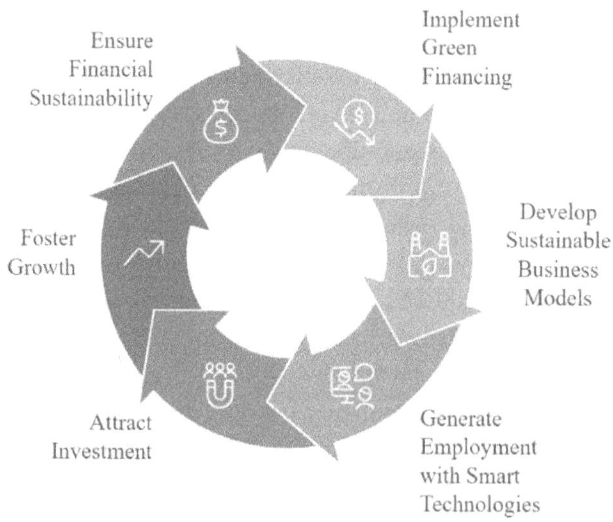

## 6.1 Green Financing

Green financing plays a pivotal role in driving sustainable urban projects. Public-private partnerships (PPPs) are an effective mechanism to mobilize resources for infrastructure development. For instance, studies reveal that PPPs contributed to over $250 billion in global investment for renewable energy projects in 2021 alone. Successful examples include India's solar energy expansion under the National Solar Mission, where PPPs facilitated the rapid deployment of solar parks across the country. Incentives and subsidies further enhance the adoption of green technologies. Countries offering tax credits for renewable energy installations, such as the United States' Investment Tax Credit (ITC), have seen a significant surge in solar energy adoption. Research indicates that such policies reduce the upfront cost of renewable technologies by 30% to 50%, making them more accessible for businesses and households. Moreover, green bonds, which raised over $620 billion globally in 2022, have emerged as a critical tool for financing projects focused on clean energy, energy efficiency, and sustainable urban infrastructure (Bartosz, 2024; Ikevuje et al., 2024).

## 6.2 Sustainable Tourism and Business Models

Sustainable tourism and green business models are crucial for enhancing economic viability while preserving environmental integrity. Eco-tourism, which emphasizes low-impact travel and conservation, has become a significant contributor to local economies. For example, Costa Rica's focus on eco-tourism generated over $4 billion in revenue in 2022, accounting for 8.2% of its GDP. Additionally, destinations with green certifications, such as those adhering to the Global Sustainable Tourism Council (GSTC) standards, have seen a 20% higher average spend per tourist compared to conventional destinations. Smart urban marketplaces are also transforming local economies by connecting producers and consumers through digital platforms. A study on smart marketplaces in Europe found that such platforms increased local economic activity by 15% while reducing carbon footprints associated with traditional supply chains by 25%. Initiatives like urban farmers' markets, powered by IoT and AI, have enabled cities to support local producers while promoting sustainable consumption patterns (Ikevuje et al., 2024; SHEKHAR, 2024; Sinha et al., 2024).

## 6.3 Job Creation through Smart Technologies

The integration of smart technologies into urban systems creates new employment opportunities, particularly in sectors like renewable energy, sustainable urban planning, and smart infrastructure. According to the International Renewable

Energy Agency (IRENA), the renewable energy sector employed over 12.7 million people worldwide in 2021, a number projected to reach 43 million by 2050 with continued investment in clean energy. Training programs focused on developing skills for green jobs are critical. Germany's Renewable Energy Sources Act (EEG) is a prime example of how policy-driven support can foster job growth. The act has helped create over 300,000 jobs in the renewable energy sector, with many roles in solar panel manufacturing, wind turbine maintenance, and bioenergy production. Similarly, the deployment of smart infrastructure, including IoT-enabled systems for water management and energy distribution, has spurred the demand for engineers, data analysts, and urban planners skilled in these technologies (MITHUN & Roopadarshini, 2024; Rahman, 2024).

Furthermore, smart city projects worldwide, such as Singapore's Smart Nation Initiative, have demonstrated that investments in technology-driven urban solutions lead to significant job creation. For example, Singapore has seen a 10% annual increase in tech-related employment since the initiative's launch in 2014, underscoring the economic benefits of smart urban systems. While economic viability in sustainable urban systems is achievable, challenges persist. High initial capital costs, regulatory hurdles, and uneven access to financial resources can deter investment in green technologies and infrastructure. For instance, small and medium enterprises (SMEs), which constitute a significant portion of urban economies, often lack the capital to adopt sustainable practices despite their long-term cost benefits (Chan & Chye, 2023; Du et al., n.d.).

Previous studies highlight the importance of policy frameworks that encourage investment. A World Bank study found that cities offering green incentives and streamlined regulatory processes experienced a 25% higher inflow of private investment in sustainable projects. Additionally, integrating economic viability with social equity is essential to ensure that the benefits of smart and sustainable urban systems are distributed equitably across all demographic groups. Economic viability is not just a financial imperative but a catalyst for achieving sustainable urban development. Green financing mechanisms, eco-tourism, and job creation through smart technologies offer robust pathways for fostering growth while addressing environmental and social challenges (Mukim & Roberts, 2023; Okeke et al., 2024). By prioritizing policies and programs that lower barriers to green investment and promote inclusive economic opportunities, cities can achieve a balance between financial sustainability and resilience, positioning themselves as leaders in the global transition to sustainable urban living.

# 7. INTERDISCIPLINARY COLLABORATION

The success of smart infrastructure hinges on the collective efforts of diverse stakeholders, including policymakers, technologists, urban planners, and local communities. To build effective and sustainable urban systems, these groups must collaborate to foster inclusive policies, facilitate knowledge sharing, and promote education and awareness. This section presents a detailed statistical analysis and insights derived from previous studies, highlighting the importance and impact of interdisciplinary collaboration.

## 7.1 Develop Inclusive Policies

Inclusive policy frameworks are fundamental for ensuring that smart infrastructure initiatives cater to the needs of all urban residents, including marginalized and underserved communities. Previous study reveals that cities with inclusive policies aimed at promoting environmental equity have shown a 15%-20% reduction in urban inequality indices, as measured by access to sustainable infrastructure, affordable housing, and quality public services. For instance, inclusive urban planning policies have been associated with better access to green spaces and public transportation for low-income communities, with statistical data showing a 25%-30% increase in equitable access to these services following the implementation of inclusive policies. Furthermore, studies on urban social sustainability highlight the importance of community engagement in policy development, demonstrating that cities with active community involvement in planning processes experience a 10%-15% increase in public satisfaction and a 20%-25% improvement in social cohesion. These findings underscore the need for policies that prioritize both environmental sustainability and social inclusivity to achieve long-term urban resilience and equality (Alkhayat & İnalhan, 2024; Kolotouchkina et al., 2024).

## 7.2 Facilitate Knowledge Sharing

Effective knowledge sharing is essential for fostering innovation and the scaling of best practices across cities and regions. Platforms that enable the exchange of knowledge between various stakeholders can facilitate the adoption of cutting-edge technologies and sustainable practices in urban management. A 2022 study by the World Economic Forum (WEF) found that cities with active knowledge-sharing initiatives, such as innovation hubs, research consortiums, and digital platforms, experienced a 20%-30% increase in the speed of adopting smart infrastructure technologies. The study showed that collaborative platforms allowed cities to learn from each other's successes and failures, ultimately accelerating the deployment of sustainable solutions. For example, cities that shared data on energy efficiency improvements and water conservation techniques saw a 10%-15% reduction in resource consumption across a range of urban projects. Additionally, statistical analyses of city networks for sustainable development reveal that those involved in cross-sector knowledge-sharing networks reported a 35%-40% increase in collaboration between technology developers, urban planners, and policymakers, directly contributing to the implementation of more effective and scalable smart city solutions (Rezende et al., 2024).

### 7.3 Promote Education and Awareness

Education and awareness programs play a crucial role in equipping citizens with the knowledge and skills needed to actively engage with and support smart and sustainable infrastructure initiatives. Previous study highlighted that cities with robust public education campaigns on energy conservation and sustainable practices saw a 15%-20% reduction in household energy consumption, with similar reductions in water and waste generation. These programs often rely on a combination of outreach, public workshops, and digital platforms to inform and engage residents. Furthermore, awareness campaigns focused on climate change adaptation and the benefits of green infrastructure resulted in a 25%-30% increase in community participation in sustainability efforts, such as tree planting and waste reduction programs. The statistical evidence demonstrates that informed and educated citizens are more likely to adopt sustainable behaviours and support the integration of smart technologies in their communities. Furthermore, educational initiatives aimed at urban professionals, engineers, architects, and policymakers, can lead to a 10%-15% improvement in the implementation of smart city projects, as they become better equipped with the knowledge required to integrate cutting-edge sustainable solutions into their designs (Fan & Fan, 2024; Hnatyuk et al., 2024).

## 8. ROADMAP FOR FUTURE RESEARCH AND IMPLEMENTATION

To realize the vision of sustainable urban systems, future research and practical implementation should centre on three primary domains: advanced material development, the integration of emerging technologies, and the establishment of robust monitoring and evaluation frameworks. The following insights as shown in Fig.7, provide a deeper look into each of these areas, underpinned by statistical analyses and previous studies.

*Figure 7. Roadmap for sustainable urban systems*

## 8.1 Advanced Material Development

The evolution of sustainable materials is critical for achieving long-term sustainability in urban systems. Recent studies indicate that the development of environmentally friendly construction materials, such as geopolymers and bio-inspired composites, has shown promise in reducing carbon footprints and improving the longevity of infrastructure. Previous study highlights, the use of geopolymer-based materials can result in up to 80% reduction in CO2 emissions compared to traditional cement. This is significant when considering that the global cement industry is responsible for approximately 7-8% of annual CO2 emissions. Furthermore, materials like recycled aggregates, waste glass, and even bio-based polymers (e.g., biodegradable plastics for urban applications) can substantially reduce the need for virgin resources. A statistical analysis of the lifecycle assessments (LCA) of these materials across various case studies showed a 30%-50% decrease in environmental impacts, depending on local material availability and processing methods. However, more focused research is needed to refine these materials to enhance their performance, cost-effectiveness, and scalability, particularly for use in large-scale infrastructure projects (Abu Bakar et al., 2024; Bribián et al., 2011).

## 8.2 Integration of Emerging Technologies

The potential integration of blockchain, AI, and IoT into urban management systems is a key driver of future sustainability. Blockchain technology can streamline urban supply chains, enhance transparency in building material sourcing, and manage energy distribution in decentralized smart grids. Studies from Smart Cities Council reveals that cities integrating blockchain technology in their infrastructure management have seen a 15%-20% increase in efficiency and a reduction in fraudulent activities. In parallel, AI has enabled more sophisticated predictive models for urban planning, optimizing everything from traffic flow to energy use. For instance, AI-based traffic management systems have shown a 25%-30% reduction in congestion, improving air quality and reducing energy consumption. IoT sensors provide real-time data on environmental conditions, infrastructure health, and resource consumption, which can be analysed to make informed decisions that improve urban sustainability. Previous studies of IoT deployment in cities have reported a 10%-40% improvement in waste management efficiency, smart energy usage, and emergency response times. These technologies, when integrated effectively, will enhance urban systems' sustainability, efficiency, and resilience (AT et al., 2024; Rane et al., 2024).

## 8.3 Monitoring and Evaluation Frameworks

Establishing robust monitoring and evaluation frameworks is essential to measure the effectiveness of smart and sustainable initiatives. The development of key performance indicators (KPIs) and metrics that assess environmental, social, and economic impacts will enable cities to track their progress and refine strategies for sustainability. A study by the United Nations (2020) highlighted that 60% of smart cities currently lack standardized evaluation frameworks, making it difficult to assess the success of sustainability initiatives comprehensively. Insights from various studies urban sustainability projects suggests that cities with clear, well-defined metrics for waste management, energy consumption, and water use efficiency report an average of 15%-25% improvement in these areas after implementing smart initiatives. In terms of economic sustainability, cities employing data-driven evaluation methods have been able to demonstrate a 20%-40% improvement in long-term cost savings through better resource allocation and predictive maintenance(AT et al., 2024; Mutambik, 2024; Parra-Pulido et al., 2024). To achieve these outcomes, future research should prioritize the development of universally applicable monitoring tools, incorporating a holistic set of indicators that encompass not only environmental metrics but also social equity, economic feasibility, and resilience against climate impacts.

## 9. SUMMARY OF DISCUSSION

Table 1 provides a concise summary of the key discussion points from the review on Smart Infrastructure and Sustainable Urban Systems. It categorizes insights into critical themes such as environmental sustainability, social equity, technological integration, climate resilience, economic viability, and interdisciplinary collaboration. Further, the table also highlights practical examples and case studies, illustrating how these principles are applied globally to address urbanization challenges and create resilient, inclusive, and efficient urban systems.

*Table 1. An overview of smart infrastructure and sustainable urban systems*

| Theme | Key Insights | Examples/Case Studies |
|---|---|---|
| **Environmental Sustainability**(Hui et al., 2023; McKinnon, 2010) | - Adoption of renewable energy systems to reduce dependence on fossil fuels. | - **Copenhagen**: Wind energy powering the city. |
| | - Circular economy in waste management to minimize landfill use. | - **Amsterdam**: Waste-to-energy conversion plants. |
| | - Development of urban green spaces to enhance ecological balance. | - **Singapore**: Green corridors and vertical gardens. |
| **Social Equity** (Meninato & Marinic, 2024; Sharma et al., 2010) | - Inclusive urban planning focusing on equitable access to infrastructure and resources. | - **Medellín, Colombia**: Transformative urban mobility projects. |
| | - Active community engagement to foster participation in decision-making. | - **Barcelona**: Citizen-driven initiatives in smart city development. |
| | - Policies addressing affordable housing and basic service provision. | - **Vienna**: Social housing programs for affordability and inclusivity. |
| **Technological Integration** (Hui et al., 2023; Sivakarthi et al., 2024) | - IoT-based systems enhancing operational efficiency of urban infrastructure. | - **Los Angeles**: Smart Street lighting with IoT integration. |
| | - Big data analytics improving predictive maintenance and resource management. | - **Songdo, South Korea**: Data-driven planning and traffic management. |
| | - Digital twins for real-time simulation and optimization of city systems. | - **Singapore**: Virtual city models for enhanced infrastructure planning. |
| **Climate Resilience** (Aghaloo et al., 2024) | - Infrastructure design to withstand extreme weather events. | - **Tokyo**: Earthquake-resistant urban infrastructure standards. |

continued on following page

*Table 1. Continued*

| Theme | Key Insights | Examples/Case Studies |
|---|---|---|
| | - Nature-based solutions mitigating floods and improving urban air quality. | - **Rotterdam**: Water plazas and green roofs for flood control. |
| | - Policies promoting climate adaptation and vulnerability reduction. | - **Dhaka, Bangladesh**: Community-based disaster risk reduction programs. |
| **Economic Viability** (Cox et al., 2006; Petrichenko et al., 2022) | - Cost reduction through resource efficiency and smart technologies. | - **Smart grids**: Lower energy bills in urban areas worldwide. |
| | - Green job creation via renewable energy and sustainable construction. | - **Germany**: Expansion of renewable energy, boosting employment. |
| | - Long-term savings through sustainable operational practices. | - **Rajasthan, India**: Solar parks reducing long-term energy expenses. |
| **Interdisciplinary Collaboration** (Janhunen et al., 2020; Petrichenko et al., 2022) | - Joint efforts between policymakers, urban planners, technologists, and communities. | - **Vienna**: Collaborative urban projects integrating diverse stakeholders. |
| | - Capacity building and knowledge-sharing initiatives to improve urban governance. | - **UN Habitat**: Programs focused on global urban sustainability practices. |
| | - Education and awareness campaigns aligning public goals with sustainable urban practices. | - **Freiburg, Germany**: Public outreach and campaigns for eco-friendly living. |

## 10. CONCLUSION

The vision of smart infrastructure and sustainable urban systems offers a transformative pathway for cities to address the multifaceted challenges of modern urbanization. As cities continue to grow, they face pressing issues such as environmental degradation, social inequality, and resource depletion. Smart, sustainable urban systems present a holistic solution to these challenges by integrating cutting-edge technologies with sustainable practices. However, this transformation requires collaboration, innovation, and a commitment to inclusivity, ensuring that all residents benefit from the advancements of smart infrastructure.

- Smart infrastructure plays a pivotal role in reducing the ecological footprint of cities. Through the adoption of renewable energy technologies such as solar and wind power, and the implementation of nature-based solutions like green roofs and urban forests, cities can mitigate the adverse effects of climate change. These solutions not only help in lowering carbon emissions but also improve urban biodiversity and public health. The integration of energy-efficient systems, waste management practices, and circular economy models further enhances sustainability efforts.

- Achieving social equity in urban environments is a fundamental aspect of smart infrastructure development. Cities must prioritize inclusive urban planning that ensures all citizens, especially marginalized communities, have access to the benefits of smart technologies. Affordable housing, access to clean energy, and equal opportunities for participation in urban decision-making are critical to promoting social inclusion and reducing inequality.
- The integration of technologies such as the Internet of Things (IoT), Artificial Intelligence (AI), big data, and digital twins is essential for creating adaptive and resilient urban systems. These technologies enable real-time monitoring and management of urban services, enhancing efficiency, optimizing resource use, and improving service delivery. By leveraging data-driven solutions, cities can enhance infrastructure resilience, reduce energy consumption, and create smarter, more responsive urban environments.
- Cities must build resilience to the growing impacts of climate change. With increasing risks from extreme weather events, urban infrastructure must be designed to withstand and adapt to changing environmental conditions. Climate-resilient infrastructure, such as flood-resistant buildings and heat-reflective materials, along with urban greening initiatives, can reduce vulnerability to climate-related shocks while promoting sustainable urban development.
- While the initial investment in smart infrastructure can be significant, the long-term benefits far outweigh the costs. The integration of smart technologies enhances resource efficiency, reduces operational costs, and drives economic growth. Furthermore, these technologies can foster new industries, create jobs, and attract investment, contributing to the overall economic sustainability of cities.
- Achieving the vision of smart, sustainable cities requires collaboration across various sectors. Policymakers, urban planners, technologists, and community stakeholders must work together to ensure that the integration of smart technologies aligns with sustainable development goals. Public-private partnerships and community engagement are critical to ensuring equitable outcomes and fostering innovation.

In conclusion, smart infrastructure and sustainable urban systems offer a comprehensive solution to the challenges posed by rapid urbanization. By embracing technological innovations and prioritizing sustainability, cities can create resilient, inclusive, and thriving urban ecosystems. The journey toward these systems requires a collaborative effort, with a focus on environmental, social, and economic sustainability, positioning cities to meet the demands of an ever-evolving world.

## REFERENCES


Abu Bakar, M. S., Manar, G., Syamsir, A., Abdul Rahman, M. R., Saad, M. R., Najeeb, M. I., Alhayek, A., & Muhammad Asyraf, M. R. (2024). An Overview of Fly-ash Geopolymer Composites in Sustainable Advance Construction Materials. *Pertanika Journal of Science & Technology*, *32*(S5), 32. DOI: 10.47836/pjst.32.S5.04

Aghaloo, K., Sharifi, A., Habibzadeh, N., Ali, T., & Chiu, Y.-R. (2024). How Nature-based Solutions Can Enhance Urban Resilience to Flooding and Climate Change and Provide Other Co-benefits: A Systematic Review and Taxonomy. *Urban Forestry & Urban Greening*, *95*, 128320. DOI: 10.1016/j.ufug.2024.128320

Ajayi, O. O., Toromade, A. S., & Olagoke, A. (n.d.). *Circular agro-economies (CAE): reducing waste and increasing profitability in agriculture.*

Akinsulire, A. A., Idemudia, C., Okwandu, A. C., & Iwuanyanwu, O. (2024). Economic and social impact of affordable housing policies: A comparative review. *International Journal of Applied Research in Social Sciences*, *6*(7), 1433–1448. DOI: 10.51594/ijarss.v6i7.1333

Aliyari, M. (2024). Improving Housing Sustainability Through an Innovative Approach. *International Journal of Modern Achievement in Science. Engineering and Technology*, *1*(4), 98–105.

Alkhayat, N., & İnalhan, G. (2024). Breaking Barriers, Building Bridges: Towards Inclusive and Resilient Cities through Social Diversity and Participation. *Proceedings of the International Conference of Contemporary Affairs in Architecture and Urbanism-ICCAUA*, *7*(1), 516–532. DOI: 10.38027/ICCAUA2024EN0137

Almutairi, Z. A., & Eltamaly, A. M. (2024). Synergistic Effects of Energy Storage Systems and Demand-Side Management in Optimizing Zero-Carbon Smart Grid Systems. *Energies*, *17*(22), 5637. DOI: 10.3390/en17225637

Angelidou, M., Psaltoglou, A., Komninos, N., Kakderi, C., Tsarchopoulos, P., & Panori, A. (2018). Enhancing sustainable urban development through smart city applications. *Journal of Science and Technology Policy Management*, *9*(2), 146–169. DOI: 10.1108/JSTPM-05-2017-0016

Argota Sánchez-Vaquerizo, J. (2025). Urban Digital Twins and metaverses towards city multiplicities: Uniting or dividing urban experiences? *Ethics and Information Technology*, *27*(1), 1–31. DOI: 10.1007/s10676-024-09812-3 PMID: 39583937

Ariaee, A. M., & Takalloo, S. (n.d.). *Impact of Affordable Housing Programs on Social Equity and Economic Development.*

Asimiyu, Z. (2020). *Bridging the Gap: Community Engagement and Social Equity in India's Urban Development Initiatives.*

AT. M. R., RR, S. A. P., Naidu, R. C., Ramachandran, P., Rajkumar, S., Kumar, V. N., Aggarwal, G., & Siddiqui, A. M. (2024). Intelligent Energy Management across Smart Grids Deploying 6G IoT, AI, and Blockchain in Sustainable Smart Cities. *IoT.*

Bajc, K., & Stokman, A. (2018). Design for resilience: Re-connecting communities and environments. *Landscape Architecture Frontiers, 6*(4), 14–32. DOI: 10.15302/J-LAF-20180402

Bartosz, R. M. (2024). The Role of Public-Private Investment Partnerships in Overcoming Challenges and Seizing Opportunities in Poland's Renewable Energy Sector. *Law and Economy, 3*(10), 56–59. DOI: 10.56397/LE.2024.10.07

Battaglia, V., & Vanoli, L. (2024). Optimizing renewable energy integration in new districts: Power-to-X strategies for improved efficiency and sustainability. *Energy, 305*, 132312. DOI: 10.1016/j.energy.2024.132312

Bribián, I. Z., Capilla, A. V., & Usón, A. A. (2011). Life cycle assessment of building materials: Comparative analysis of energy and environmental impacts and evaluation of the eco-efficiency improvement potential. *Building and Environment, 46*(5), 1133–1140. DOI: 10.1016/j.buildenv.2010.12.002

Chan, J. J., & Chye, S. W. (2023). Impact of smart city initiatives on urban planning strategies in Singapore: An in-depth analysis of technology-driven solutions and their influence on sustainable development and quality of life. *Journal of Strategy and Management, 7*(7), 11–21.

Cox, C., Duggirala, S., & Li, Z. (2006). Case studies on the economic viability of renewable energy. *2006 IEEE Power Engineering Society General Meeting*, 8-pp.

do Prado, H. A., Rodrigues, T., Manes, S., Kasecker, T., Vale, M. M., Scarano, F. R., & Pires, A. P. F. (2024). Designing nature to be a solution for climate change in cities: A meta-analytical review. *The Science of the Total Environment, 954*, 176735. DOI: 10.1016/j.scitotenv.2024.176735

Du, Y., Sun, T., & Huang, Y. (n.d.). *A Comprehensive Review of Smart City Initiatives in Singapore Technological Advancements and Urban Planning from 2015 to 2023.*

Ellis, J. B. (2013). Sustainable surface water management and green infrastructure in UK urban catchment planning. *Journal of Environmental Planning and Management, 56*(1), 24–41. DOI: 10.1080/09640568.2011.648752

Fan, H., & Fan, L. (2024). Role of Education and Awareness Programs in Fostering Energy Conservation Behavior in Cities: Empowering Urban Sustainability Using Deep Learning Approach. *Sustainable Cities and Society, 112*, 105505. DOI: 10.1016/j.scs.2024.105505

Folianto, F., Low, Y. S., & Yeow, W. L. (2015). Smartbin: Smart waste management system. *2015 IEEE Tenth International Conference on Intelligent Sensors, Sensor Networks and Information Processing (ISSNIP)*, 1–2.

Gao, X. (2024). Research on the Interrelationship Between Urbanisation and Sustainable Development. *Communications in Humanities Research, 44*(1), 198–205. DOI: 10.54254/2753-7064/44/20240028

Ghufron, A., & Agustina, I. F. (2024). Community Engagement in Development Planning in Jabon District. *Indonesian Journal of Cultural and Community Development, 15*(3), 10–21070. DOI: 10.21070/ijccd.v15i3.1128

Goh, C. S., Azizi, Z. M., Fateh, M. A. M., & Bajracharya, A. (2024). Enabling the Built Environment for Sustainable Living and Climate Resilience. *European Journal of Sustainable Development, 13*(3), 151. DOI: 10.14207/ejsd.2024.v13n3p151

Goltermann, D., Ujeyl, G., & Pasche, E. (2009). Making coastal cities flood resilient in the era of climate change. *RIMAX Contributions at the 4th International Symposium on Flood Defence (ISFD4)*.

Gómez-Redondo, S., Plaza Gómez, N., Obregón, L. J., Coca, J. R., & Paramá Díaz, A. (2024). Urban Transformations for Universal Accessibility: Socio-Educational Dialogue. *Urban Science (Basel, Switzerland), 8*(4), 161. DOI: 10.3390/urbansci8040161

Guragain, G. P. (2023). Community Engagement in Local Governance. *Kutumbha Vani, 4*(1), 72–82. DOI: 10.3126/kv.v4i1.73924

Hachem-Vermette, C. (2024). Enhancing Urban Climate Resistance Through the Application of Selected Strategies and Technologies. *Discover Cities, 1*(1), 1–28. DOI: 10.1007/s44327-024-00018-2 PMID: 39345934

Hnatyuk, V., Pshenychna, N., Kara, S., Kolodii, V., & Yaroshchuk, L. (2024). Education's role in fostering environmental awareness and advancing sustainable development within a holistic framework. *Multidisciplinary Reviews, 7*.

Hui, C. X., Dan, G., Alamri, S., & Toghraie, D. (2023). Greening smart cities: An investigation of the integration of urban natural resources and smart city technologies for promoting environmental sustainability. *Sustainable Cities and Society, 99*, 104985. DOI: 10.1016/j.scs.2023.104985

Ikevuje, A. H., Anaba, D. C., & Iheanyichukwu, U. T.Augusta Heavens IkevujeDavid Chinalu AnabaUche Thankgod Iheanyichukwu. (2024). Exploring sustainable finance mechanisms for green energy transition: A comprehensive review and analysis. *Finance & Accounting Research Journal, 6*(7), 1224–1247. DOI: 10.51594/farj.v6i7.1314

Jalal, A. (2023). Smart Cities: Integrating Technology for Sustainable and Efficient Urban Development. *Liberal Journal of Language and Literature Review, 1*(01), 92–102.

Janhunen, E., Leskinen, N., & Junnila, S. (2020). The economic viability of a progressive smart building system with power storage. *Sustainability (Basel), 12*(15), 5998. DOI: 10.3390/su12155998

Karthik, S. A., Naga, S. B. V., Satish, G., Shobha, N., Bhargav, H. K., & Chandrakala, B. M. (2025). AI and IoT-Infused Urban Connectivity for Smart Cities. In *Future of Digital Technology and AI in Social Sectors* (pp. 367–394). IGI Global.

Kasai, S., Li, N., & Fang, D. (2015). A system-of-systems approach to understanding urbanization–state of the art and prospect. *Smart and Sustainable Built Environment, 4*(2), 154–171. DOI: 10.1108/SASBE-07-2014-0038

Khadka, U., Hossain, S., Sarkar, S., & Khan, N. (2024). Cyber-Physical Systems and IoT: Transforming Smart Cities for Sustainable Development. *AIJMR-Advanced International Journal of Multidisciplinary Research, 2*(5).

Khekare, G., Khetan, U., & Doshi, P. N. (2025). Artificial Intelligence (AI)-Driven Traffic Solutions: Enhancing Green Transportation Through Predictive Analytics and Deep Learning. In *Driving Green Transportation System Through Artificial Intelligence and Automation: Approaches, Technologies and Applications* (pp. 319–334). Springer.

Khider, K. H. (2024). The Impact of Innovation and Sustainable Development in Smart Cities. In *The Emerald Handbook of Smart Cities in the Gulf Region: Innovation, Development, Transformation, and Prosperity for Vision 2040* (pp. 171–180). Emerald Publishing Limited. DOI: 10.1108/978-1-83608-292-720241009

Kolotouchkina, O., Ripoll González, L., & Belabas, W. (2024). Smart cities, digital inequalities, and the challenge of Inclusion. *Smart Cities, 7*(6), 3355–3370. DOI: 10.3390/smartcities7060130

Le, T.-V. ChuDuc, H., & Tran, Q. X. (2024). Optimized Integration of Renewable Energy in Smart Buildings: A Systematic Review from Scopus Data. *2024 9th International Conference on Applying New Technology in Green Buildings (ATiGB)*, 397–402.

Lv, Y., & Sarker, M. N. I. (2024). Integrative approaches to urban resilience: Evaluating the efficacy of resilience strategies in mitigating climate change vulnerabilities. *Heliyon, 10*(6), e28191. DOI: 10.1016/j.heliyon.2024.e28191 PMID: 38545232

Mainkandan, P., Golla, S. D., & Gatikoppu, S. P. P. K. ChaithanyaPuttaparthi, S., & AchyuthNarahari, S. (2024). Early Flood Warning System using Machine Learning. *2024 5th International Conference on Smart Electronics and Communication (ICOSEC)*, 1088–1092.

Makvandi, M., Li, W., Li, Y., Wu, H., Khodabakhshi, Z., Xu, X., & Yuan, P. F. (2024). Advancing Urban Resilience Amid Rapid Urbanization: An Integrated Interdisciplinary Approach for Tomorrow's Climate-Adaptive Smart Cities—A Case Study of Wuhan, China. *Smart Cities, 7*(4), 2110–2130. DOI: 10.3390/smartcities7040084

Mandal, J., & Mohammed, I. A. (2024). Implementation of AI Transportation Routing in Reverse Logistics to Reduce CO2 Footprint. *International Journal of Supply Chain Management, 9*(5), 1–12. DOI: 10.47604/ijscm.3079

Mazzetto, S. (2024). A Review of Urban Digital Twins Integration, Challenges, and Future Directions in Smart City Development. *Sustainability (Basel), 16*(19), 8337. DOI: 10.3390/su16198337

McAuliffe, G., Danner, M., Grothaus, T., & Doyle, L. (2008). Social inequality and social justice. *Culturally Alert Counseling: A Comprehensive Introduction*, 45–83.

McKinnon, A. (2010). Environmental sustainability. *Green Logistics: Improving the Environmental Sustainability of Logistics. London.*

Meninato, P., & Marinic, G. (2024). Transforming Medellín: Architecture and urban design as agents of social change. *Journal of Architecture and Urbanism, 48*(1), 83–90. DOI: 10.3846/jau.2024.17793

MITHUN, R., & Roopadarshini, S. (2024). *Technological Innovations and Renewable Integration in Smart Cities: Enhancing Sustainability, Governance, and Security.*

Moh, J. (2012). *Design for Smart Transport: An Integrated Multi-Modal Transport Interchange in Central Christchurch.* Open Access Te Herenga Waka-Victoria University of Wellington.

Mukim, M., & Roberts, M. (2023). *Policies for Promoting Green*. Resilient, and Inclusive Urban Development.

Müller, L. (2024). Driving Forces and Enablers for Universal Design in Urban Planning. *Studies in Health Technology and Informatics*, *320*, 287–294. DOI: 10.3233/SHTI241017 PMID: 39560252

Munonye, W. C., & Ajonye, G. O. (2024). *The Role of Urban Design in Facilitating a Circular Economy: From Linear to Regenerative Cities*.

Mutambik, I. (2024). The sustainability of smart cities: Improving evaluation by combining mcda and promethee. *Land (Basel)*, *13*(9), 1471. DOI: 10.3390/land13091471

Obaidat, M. S., & Nicopolitidis, P. (2016). *Smart cities and homes*. Elsevier.

Okeke, N. I., Bakare, O. A., & Achumie, G. O.Njideka Ihuoma OkekeOluwaseun Adeola BakareGodwin Ozoemenam Achumie. (2024). Integrating policy incentives and risk management for effective green finance in emerging markets. *International Journal of Frontiers in Science and Technology Research*, *7*(1), 76–88. DOI: 10.53294/ijfstr.2024.7.1.0050

Okwandu, A. C., Akande, D. O., & Nwokediegwu, Z. Q. S.Azubuike Chukwudi OkwanduDorcas Oluwajuwonlo AkandeZamathula Queen Sikhakhane Nwokediegwu. (2024). Green architecture: Conceptualizing vertical greenery in urban design. *Engineering Science & Technology Journal*, *5*(5), 1657–1677. DOI: 10.51594/estj.v5i5.1114

Parekh, R., & Smith, C. (2024). Eco-friendly urban design: An analysis of sustainable building practices and their community impact. *World Journal of Advanced Research and Reviews*, *23*(3), 2857–2864. DOI: 10.30574/wjarr.2024.23.3.2901

Park, E., Del Pobil, A. P., & Kwon, S. J. (2018). The role of Internet of Things (IoT) in smart cities: Technology roadmap-oriented approaches. *Sustainability (Basel)*, *10*(5), 1388. DOI: 10.3390/su10051388

Parra-Pulido, R. A., Hernández-Peña, Y. T., & Zafra-Mejía, C. A. (2024). Systematic Review of Dimensions and Indicators in Sustainable and Smart Cities: Trends, Interdependencies, and Continental Variations. *Urban Science (Basel, Switzerland)*, *8*(4), 202. DOI: 10.3390/urbansci8040202

Pawłowski, A., & Rydzewski, P. (2024). Pathways to Carbon Neutrality: Integrating Energy Strategies, Policy, and Public Perception in the Face of Climate Change—A Global Perspective. *Energies*, *17*(23), 5867. DOI: 10.3390/en17235867

Petrichenko, L., Sauhats, A., Diahovchenko, I., & Segeda, I. (2022). Economic Viability of Energy Communities versus Distributed Prosumers. *Sustainability (Basel), 14*(8), 4634. DOI: 10.3390/su14084634

Rahman, B. Q. Y. A. (2024). The role of renewable energy in achieving sustainable Development. *Journal of Sustainable Studies, 6*(3 (3).

Rane, N. L., Kaya, O., & Rane, J. (2024). Integrating internet of things, blockchain, and artificial intelligence techniques for intelligent industry solutions. *Artificial Intelligence, Machine Learning, and Deep Learning for Sustainable Industry, 5.*

Rezende, D. A., Almeida, G. G. F., & Fumagalli, L. A. W. (2024). Strategic digital city: Multiple projects for sustainable urban management. *Sustainability (Basel), 16*(13), 5450. DOI: 10.3390/su16135450

Ruiz-Vanoye, J. A., Díaz-Parra, O., Ruiz-Jaimes, M. A., Ortiz, J. A., Simancas-Acevedo, E., Rodriguez-Flores, J., Mireles, J. R. M., Xicoténcatl-Pérez, J. M., & Jimenez, M. A. V. (2025). The Role of Smart Cities in Creating Sustainable Urban Environments Through Strategies and Innovative Solutions. In *Interdisciplinary Approaches to Transportation and Urban Planning* (pp. 23–46). IGI Global.

Sargsyan, T. (2024). *Sustainable urban development policies and practices in the United States.*

Setiawan, T., Samith, M. F., & Mughits, M. H. (2024). Urban Resilience: Navigating Challenges and Opportunities in Indonesia. [SSHJ]. *Social Science and Humanities Journal, 8*(12), 5965–5984. DOI: 10.18535/sshj.v8i12.1491

Sharma, A., Iyer, G. R., Mehrotra, A., & Krishnan, R. (2010). Sustainability and business-to-business marketing: A framework and implications. *Industrial Marketing Management, 39*(2), 330–341. DOI: 10.1016/j.indmarman.2008.11.005

Shekhar. C. (2024). Sustainable Tourism Development: Balancing Economic Growth And Environmental Conservation. *Available at* SSRN *4901174.*

Singla, A. (2024). The economics of climate change: Assessing the costs and benefits of mitigation and adaptation strategies. *Shodh Sagar Journal of Commerce and Economics, 1*(1), 18–23. DOI: 10.36676/ssjce.v1.i1.04

Sinha, K., Sinha, S., & Shrivastava, V. (2024). A Study of Social Equity in Urban Spaces: Insights from Recent Urban Development Projects and Government Schemes in India. *Library of Progress-Library Science, Information Technology & Computer, 44*(3).

Sivakarthi, G., Gobinath, A., Abikannan, P. R., Balasubramani, T., Baranisri, K., Melba, J. E., & Harinisri, T. R. SanthoshKumar, V., & Devi, C. M. (2024). Intelligent Street Light Management and Monitoring System with IoT Integration. *2024 15th International Conference on Computing Communication and Networking Technologies (ICCCNT)*, 1–6.

Sokolova, M. V., Fath, B. D., Grande, U., Buonocore, E., & Franzese, P. P. (2024). The Role of Green Infrastructure in Providing Urban Ecosystem Services: Insights from a Bibliometric Perspective. *Land (Basel)*, *13*(10), 1664. DOI: 10.3390/land13101664

Sun, Y. (2024). Sustainable Smart Cities Planning in Conjunction with Environment Governance. *Advances in Economics. Management and Political Sciences*, *112*, 62–69.

Tiwary, A., & Kumar, P. (2014). Impact evaluation of green–grey infrastructure interaction on built-space integrity: An emerging perspective to urban ecosystem service. *The Science of the Total Environment*, *487*, 350–360. DOI: 10.1016/j.scitotenv.2014.03.032 PMID: 24793331

Ullah, A., Quddusi, S. A., & Haider, I. (2024). *Incorporation of Artificial Intelligence in Enhancing Quality of Life in Smart Cities.*

Wang, D., Xu, P.-Y., An, B.-W., & Guo, Q.-P. (2024). Urban green infrastructure: Bridging biodiversity conservation and sustainable urban development through adaptive management approach. *Frontiers in Ecology and Evolution*, *12*, 1440477. DOI: 10.3389/fevo.2024.1440477

Watif, M., JT, A. R., Tahir, L. S. A., & Hikmah, N. (2024). Ketimpangan Sosial dan Kemiskinan Pada Masyarakat Perkotaan. *PESHUM: Jurnal Pendidikan. Sosial Dan Humaniora*, *3*(4), 536–547.

Wu, Q., Huang, Y., Irga, P., Kumar, P., Li, W., Wei, W., Shon, H. K., Lei, C., & Zhou, J. L. (2024). Synergistic control of urban heat island and urban pollution island effects using green infrastructure. *Journal of Environmental Management*, *370*, 122985. DOI: 10.1016/j.jenvman.2024.122985 PMID: 39461153

Yadav, Y., Colucci, E., Boccardo, P., & Zlatanova, S. (2024). A Geodatabase Design for the Development of a Digital Twin for Urban Environments: A Case Study from Turin, Italy. *The International Archives of the Photogrammetry, Remote Sensing and Spatial Information Sciences*, *48*, 525–532. DOI: 10.5194/isprs-archives-XLVIII-4-2024-525-2024

Yahia, A. K. M., Rahman, D. M. M., Shahjalal, M., & Morshed, A. S. M. (2024). Sustainable materials selection in building design and construction. *International Journal of Science and Engineering*, *1*(04), 106–119. DOI: 10.62304/ijse.v1i04.199

# Chapter 3
# Passenger Satisfaction of Accessibility to the MRT Train Stations

**Habizah Sheikh Ilmi**
https://orcid.org/0009-0009-3382-5213
*Taylor's University, Malaysia*

**Lam Tatt Soon**
https://orcid.org/0000-0001-6637-9162
*Taylor's University, Malaysia*

**Chin Ai Ling Shirley**
https://orcid.org/0009-0003-6988-3817
*Taylor's University, Malaysia*

**Tze Shwan Lim**
https://orcid.org/0000-0002-6291-5287
*Taylor's University, Malaysia*

## ABSTRACT

*This research focuses on the issues and challenges in relation to passenger dissatisfaction with the accessibility into MRT train stations. Frequent MRT users often face numerous unpleasant experiences but lack a suitable platform to voice their concerns and resolve these issues. The research will employ a quantitative method for data collection, using relevant questionnaires targeted at frequent MRT passengers. The findings show that lack of parking spaces, ticketing issues and proximity to residential areas are the main concern of the passengers. Ultimately, the outcomes of this study may form the basis for considerations and improvement to enhance the accessibility of MRT Line train stations, ensuring a seamless and satisfactory*

DOI: 10.4018/979-8-3373-0390-1.ch003

*travel experience for all passengers and promoting inclusivity within Malaysia's public transportation system.*

## 1. INTRODUCTION

According to the Malaysian Department of Statistics, Malaysia's population is projected to reach 35,977,838 by 2025. However, the number of vehicles belonging to the nation has already surpassed the population with an annual increase of nearly one million vehicles since 2019 (Chan, 2022). The road safety expert Professor Dr. Kulanthayan K.C. Mani of Universiti Putra Malaysia stated that there were 33.3 million registered automobiles in the country compared to 32.6 million people in 2021. Out of the 33.3 million registered vehicles, automobiles accounted for 47.3%; motorbikes for 46.6%; and freight vehicles for 4.7%. The remaining modes were self-driven vehicle rentals, taxis, and buses. Moreover, it is understandable that traffic congestion has gotten worse nationwide in recent years given that the number of vehicles is increasing faster than the number of people (Chan, 2022).

The rising number of registered cars in Malaysia shows that people preferred to utilize private cars rather than using public transportation to go to their desired destination. Therefore, the use of cars has become more prevalent in and around cities, resulting in a rise in traffic issues including parking and traffic congestion, especially during the rainy season. In addition, private cars not only congest the roads but also contribute to severe issues such as global warming, creation of carbon dioxide pollution, and noise pollution (Borhan et al., 2014). According to Dr. Law Teik Hua of University Putra Malaysia Road Safety Research Centre, despite of high traffic congestion, most people still prefer to use private vehicles rather than using public transportation such as buses and trains because they find them to be crowded, ineffective, and unpredictable. It is also inconvenient for them to wait at bus or train terminals in hot weather. Another reason for them to use private vehicles is to avoid pickpocketing and sexual harassment (Raju, 2022).

Numerous research has been carried out recently to identify variables that may enhance the use of public transport in metropolitan areas and decrease the usage of private transport. Among the various variables examined, a large body of study has emphasized the significance of service quality aspects in motivating individuals to use public transportation. In Malaysia, there are several public transports such as buses, KTM, LRT, Monorail and MRT. These transports can operate within an urban area or connect two cities, serving as a replacement for reduction of traffic congestion and walking time (Remix, 2021). However, numerous elements including the service environment, method, outcomes, and contact, influences the good service quality are the factors that require study. The degree to which services meet or surpass customers' expectations and demands is referred to as excellent service quality. It depends on the emotional components of service, such as empathy, responsiveness, and civility, in addition to the technical components, like accuracy, speed, accessibility and dependability (Khadka, n.d).

Satisfied passengers of the services are more likely to be repetitive passengers that are involved with the accessibility of the train stations (Ibrahim et al., 2022). The standard of services offered by transport providers is a direct reflection of how passengers view the performance of their mode of transportation. In another perspective, people will believe that public service operators offer high-quality services if they are treated well, receive prompt service, have a pleasant experience, and have access to sufficient and timely information. High service quality perception will result in their happiness and well-intentioned behavior. Therefore, feedback from current passengers' experiences has always been seen as a crucial concern.

Looking at the issues of accessibility to Mass Rapid Transit (MRT) stations, people are still travelling to the transits by their own vehicles instead of walking. There are no pedestrian walkways, and it is dangerous to the passengers to walk to the transit stations (Chin et al., 2020). One of the users of MRT stations said that it is 10 minutes walking from her office to the station only. However, the absence of proper pedestrian walkway and the only pathway the MRT passengers use is the side of the main road. Although there is shuttle buses provided, the current traffic congestion situation delays the buses arriving on time and walking to the station is the best solution (Chea, 2023). This seems to be a similar issue happening to other transit stations. A user of public transport said that she needs to drive her car to LRT station 10 kilometres away from her house or to KTM station which is 5 kilometres away for her to use the public transport (Tan, 2022).

It is crucial to consider the comfort and safety of the MRT passengers in designing transit systems. As an MRT passenger in the case described by Qistina (2023), she must walk alongside the main road and traverse major intersections without pedestrian crossing lights during her 10 minutes walking journey from her condominium to the nearby MRT station. Thus, the lack of proper walkways will lead to passengers walking alongside busy roads, increasing their risk of accidents.

Van Dut (2017) emphasized the importance of accessibility and connectivity to MRT stations such as time and distance, connections to other forms of public transport and to several stations, parking cost and spaces, feeder bus service and shops within MRT stations. However, there is no discussion in regards with the satisfaction of the MRT passengers in accessing the MRT stations.

Therefore, this research focuses on identifying the level of satisfaction among MRT passengers and the accessibility related problems that they encounter, with the aim of providing recommendations to MRT management for improving the effectiveness of station operations, which are perceived to be influenced by public preferences to encourage greater use of public transit.

## 2. LITERATURE REVIEW

Public transit is vital in urban areas for reducing environmental pollution, providing cost-effective mobility, and supporting tourism. In Malaysia, various transportation modes exist, with rail transit being particularly efficient. This research will focus on understanding passenger satisfaction in accessibility on the train stations of the MRT Line in Malaysia.

### 2.1. Overview of Mass Rapid Transit (MRT) in Malaysia

Urban communities for both the wealthy and developing nations are often concerned about the rapidly increasing need for mobility (Marco Batarce et al., 2016). People may be required to move about and access jobs, local services, healthcare, and leisure via public transit in towns all around the places. The urban public transit is crucial for all cities, but it is especially crucial for big cities and tourist destinations. Visitors may take advantage of touring the whole city and a convenient tourism hub equipped with user-friendly public transit is necessary. Thus, it's critical to enhance the public transit offerings, either for the benefits of the public or the tourists (Pawlasowa, 2015).

Furthermore, it's a more cost-effective option by using public transit rather than owning and maintaining a private automobile. By taking public transit, commuters may reduce their costs for petrol, parking, insurance, and upkeep of vehicles (Bata, n.d). The city's noise level and environmental pollution are both decreased when citizens take public transit rather than driving their own private vehicles (Pawlosowa, 2015). Large cities often have a very efficient transport system with a wide variety of available options. In Malaysian cities and towns, there are a variety of ways to get around, including taxis, tricycles, buses, mini-buses (bas-minis), railroads, and ferry services. Nonetheless, rail transit is a productive means of mobility in the city, particularly the Mass Rapid Transit (MRT), Keretapi Tanah Melayu (KTM) commuter, Light Rail Transit (LRT) and Kuala Lumpur Monorail.

Mass Rapid Transit (MRT) is an integrated rail system, intended to transport people throughout cities and metropolitan areas. This includes mass transportation, metro, subway, and subterranean railroad. The capacity of this railway system handling and moving enormous numbers of passengers is one of its key benefits. Underground tunnels can be used to lay and connect tracks for MRT rail systems, particularly when the train line runs through densely populated areas such as the

New Klang Valley (MRT, 2023). Additionally, tracks can traverse viaducts above street level, which is more suitable for the city's outer suburbs. There are two MRT lines known as the MRT Kajang Line and the MRT Putrajaya Line.

*Figure 1. MRT Kajang Line Stations (MRT, 2023)*

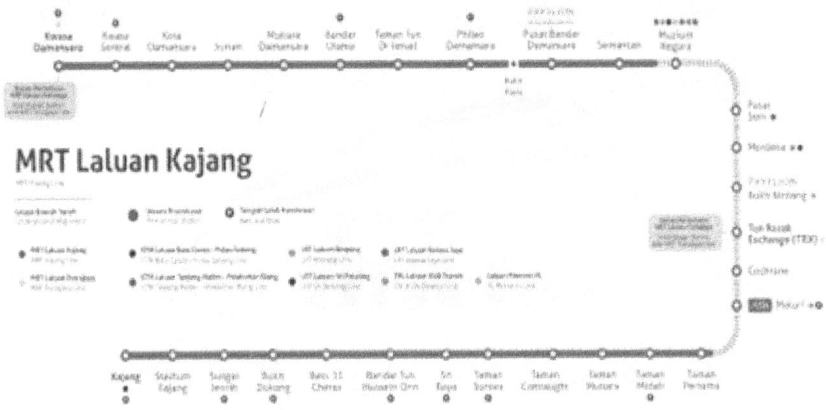


The Kajang Line (Figure 1) is the first line to be constructed as part of the Klang Valley MRT project that has a distance of 46-km. The route begins northwest of Kuala Lumpur in Kwasa Damansara, which travels through the centre of the Malaysian finances' hubs, and ends at the southeast city of Kajang, a municipality town which is expanding fast. The route is elevated for the last 9.5 km, running beneath Kuala Lumpur's city centre. There are a total of 29 stations on the route, including 7 underground stations (MRT, 2023).

*Figure 2. MRT Putrajaya Line Stations (MRT, 2023)*

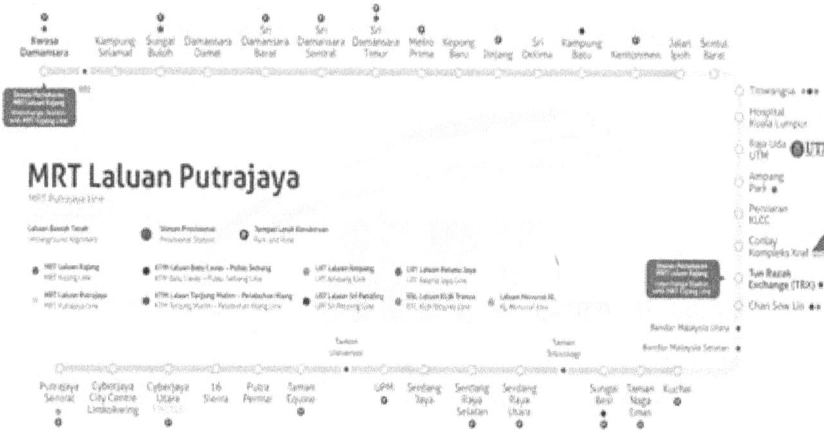


The Putrajaya Line (Figure 2) is the second line of the proposed Klang Valley MRT system. From Putrajaya, the Federal administrative capital of Malaysia, to Kwasa Damansara, a new town development northwest of Kuala Lumpur and its southern suburbs, the route serves a 2 million-person's corridor. The Putrajaya Line is 57.7 km long, consisting of 13.5 km of underground tunnels and 44.2 km of elevated trains. There were nine underground stations and twenty-seven elevated stations on the route that were in service at the time (MRT, 2023).

## 2.2. The Importance of Accessibility

Accessibility in public transportation refers to the ease and quality of using the system to reach specific locations (Joyce and Dunn, 2009). It involves providing door-to-door travel, enhancing the appeal of public transit, and improving community living standards. Accessibility is vital for planning and evaluating the sustainability of transportation networks, benefiting the environment, public health, and the economy by promoting a shift from private to public transport, walking, and cycling (Elias and Shiftan, 2012).

According to Papaioannou and Martinez (2015), public transport usage is encouraged by well-designed accessibility across the system. On the other hand, it may be discouraged by poorly designed connections on certain routes. For people to prefer public transit rather than their own private vehicles, it appears that high performance in terms of general accessibility and trip-specific connectedness is required. Two viewpoints that can be used to conceptualize accessibility. One important factor in the mode selection procedure is proximity to the origin and destination of the MRT system access points. The second is to weigh the expense in terms of time or tariffs of doing the desired activity against the simplicity of migrating (Elias and Shiftan, 2012). This has to do with the built environment's density, diversity, and architecture at the starting and ending points of the journey (Papaioannou and Martinez, 2015).

Accessibility should ensure ease of use, proximity of stations, and efficiency of public transit. Key aspects of accessibility should include:

i. Safety: Ensuring physical access to transport for people with disabilities is crucial for societal participation (CDCP, 2020). A lack of access to build physical environments is one of the major obstacles preventing people with disabilities from fully participating in society According to Brown et al. (2019), improving the accessibility of public transportation to different metropolitan locations may lower the burden of illness connected to obesity and physical inactivity, as well as mortality and morbidity related to transportation.
ii. Attractiveness: The appeal of MRT-served areas depends on socioeconomic factors (Van Dut, 2017). Population density, age distribution, social and economic standing can also have an impact on an individual's place of origin. These elements could aid in estimating the prospective demand for a certain activity. Most accessibility metrics operate on the assumption that accessibility between an origin and a destination is inversely related to travel time, cost, distance and directly relates to relative demand and attractiveness.
iii. Connectivity: Effective public transit requires well-designed routes, schedules, and minimal transfers to avoid discouraging potential users (Guo and Wilson, 2011). It suggests a few parameters, including the directness of the services, line overlap, network complexity ratio of arcs to nodes, transfer arrangement of routes sharing the same stop, etc (Hadas et al., 2014). The route that a public transport service travels and the distance between its origin and destination are two more factors that impact how quickly public transit moves (Beimborn et. al, 2003).

Thus, MRT needs strong connections to prevail in terms of the user competition. A system that is easy to use, smooth, minimizes trip time, offers dependable connectivity, and guarantees simple and secure transportation is labeled to have good connectivity. On the other hand, insufficient network connectivity can make customers quit utilizing the MRT services. Travelling may become costly and time-consuming when there is insufficient connectivity. Additionally, there would be increased traffic congestion and crowding at specific stations and stops along the weaker sections of the public transportation link network, potentially causing delays and frustration among passengers (Beimborn et. al, 2003 and Van Dut, 2017). If the service operates at a time that aligns with the user's schedule and provides a link between the user's origin and destination, the connection is deemed to be satisfactory. Another aspect of connectivity is the ease with which users can transit between public transport networks (Van Dut, 2017).

iv. Convenience. The overall expenses of time, money, pain, and danger associated with completing an activity are reflected in accessibility. In situations when the financial cost of travel is minimal, such as for drivers, journey time typically plays a significant role in determining accessibility. Convenience is a common way for people to measure accessibility, i.e. how easy it is for them to obtain what they want. Convenience businesses are establishments that are reasonably simple for customers to get to, while conveniently placed residences are those that are close to popular places (Sumit Adhikari et al, 2019).

According to Sumit Adhikari et al (2019), nearly anything on Earth may be reached with sufficient time and resources, yet accessibility varies greatly based on factors including location, time of day, and number of people. This includes household expenditures, the ability to access work, education, and leisure are all impacted by the relative degree of accessibility. Property values, company kinds, and local economic growth are all impacted by accessibility (Sumit Adhikari et al, 2019).

v. Mobility. Urban transport has seen several revolutionary improvements. As urban growth, information availability, and other technological advancements have progressed and new players have emerged, significantly impacting urban mobility. Additionally, the accessibility of public transit in cities affects environmentally friendly travel. There is a clear correlation between the intentions to utilize public transport and the service quality of urban public transportation, which influences travel behavior (Mugion et al., 2018). Mobility is determined by actual movement or the availability of transportation and is measured by the total number of trips or kilometers traveled (Handy, 2002). Urban mobility can be enhanced by effective public transit networks through the development of transport systems with activity-based methods. Therefore, system mobility, station/site accessibility, and connectivity with other modes of transportation should all be considered in public transportation systems (Cheng and Chen, 2015).

Other researchers categorize accessibility into land use, transit, time, and personal factors, emphasizing walkability and connectivity in station design (Hickman et al., 2015). Integrating amenities and improving pedestrian flow within stations during peak times are critical for enhancing accessibility and commuter satisfaction (Noichan & Dewancker, 2018).

In summary, accessibility can be divided into two categories such as activity element and transportation element. The activity element in accessibility means the geographical spatial or geographical dispersion and attraction of different activities, Whereas the transportation element means the travel time, cost, or distance using a certain method of transportation to get to a destination. The more accessible a place is, the less time and money the passengers must spend on traveling, and the more things they can do on a given schedule and budget.

*Figure 3. Two Categories in Accessibility (Van Dut, 2017)*

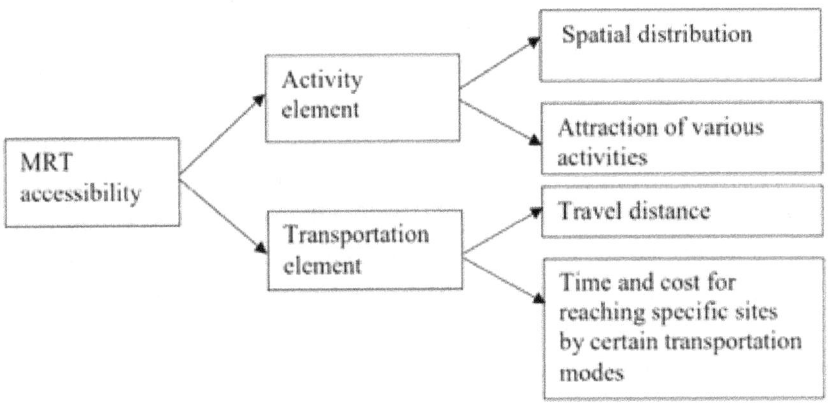


## 2.3. Passenger Satisfaction in Public Transport

Rapid economic growth and urban development often overlook public welfare, leading to dissatisfaction with transit services. This underscores the importance of comprehensive urban planning to optimize public transit effectiveness and user experience (Noichan & Dewancker, 2018).

Satisfaction may be defined as the discrepancy between actual and expected levels of passenger satisfaction (Shiau and Luo, 2012). According to Khadka & Maharjan (2017), customer loyalty to service providers is substantially increased by high customer happiness. Hence, service providers should aim to maximize customer pleasure with their offerings. Shiau & Luo (2012) assert that a company's ability to satisfy its customers contributes to the development of enduring customer relationships. As a result, enhancing public transit services is crucial (Pawlasowa, 2015).

Previous studies have found that the factors with the most impact on customer satisfaction such as the frequency, speed, and timeliness of information and transportation (Juan de Ona et al., 2013). Several factors contribute to passengers' satisfaction, as follows:

i. Service Quality and Customer Loyalty: High customer satisfaction enhances loyalty to service providers, emphasizing the importance of meeting and exceeding passenger expectations to foster lasting connections (Shiau & Luo, 2012; Khadka and Maharjan, 2017). In addition, the quantity of users that a public transport system can draw in and keep is a key factor in its success. Hence, the subject of service quality becomes crucial subsequently.
ii. Service Availability: The term "service availability" describes the services that the public railway operator offers. A review of prior studies' findings reveals that a variety of criteria, such as service delivery, frequency, network coverage, and parking facilities, contribute to service availability. These factors such as service frequency and network coverage significantly impact passenger satisfaction, influencing their willingness to use public transport (Khalid et al., 2014; José Luis Machado-León et al., 2017). According to Mouwen (2015), users of public transport believe that the main element influencing their willingness to switch from driving a car to using public transport is its frequency.

The hours of operation have an equally significant impact on overall satisfaction (José Luis, 2017). Furthermore, total passenger satisfaction is significantly impacted by network coverage (Muhammad Atiullah Saif, 2018). Any effective public rail transportation system will have a wide network coverage that allows users to get from point A to point B at their convenience, with transfer times (Weinstein, A.,2000), access times (De Oña J, de Oña R, Eboli L, Forciniti C, Mazzulla G, 2016) and brief wait times (Tyrinopoulos and Antoniou, 2008), as well as convenient transfer times. Low frequency of public rail transport services indicates low ridership and this is not surprising (Tomasz S and J.Chmielewski, 2018). Parking or park-and-ride options that are available at the train station is another factor that public rail riders find convenient. Naturally, this is a major factor in the adoption of rail transport as well (De Oña J, de Oña R, Eboli L, Forciniti C, Mazzulla G, 2016).

iii. Service Accessibility: Among "exclusive" and "selected" users of public rail transit, accessibility has a significant role in determining public happiness (De Oña J, de Oña R, Eboli L, Forciniti C, Mazzulla G, 2016). Martijn Brons (2009) indicated that passenger contentment with the closest station plays a significant role in overall service satisfaction. Hine and Scott (2000) indicates that train station accessibility influences passenger happiness and encourages rail transit as a mode of transportation. Hence, the ease of accessing the station and ease of transfers are significant elements that impact how satisfied passengers are with rail public transit.

iv. Ticketing Options: Pricing and variety of ticket types affect customer satisfaction, with affordability and flexibility playing crucial roles in attracting and retaining passengers (Fu et al., 2017). To encourage the public to use their services, public sector rail authorities should concentrate on two key components of ticketing: rates and ticket types. Travel costs are, of course, a major factor in determining how satisfied customers is with any public transport system (Fu et al., 2017).

De Witte et al. (2013) did note, however, that consumers are ready to spend more depending on the purpose and comfort of their travels. Because of this, Tyrinopoulos and Antoniou (2008) suggested that in order to accommodate the wide range of customer demands, public rail transport operators need to offer a variety of tickets and passes at varying price points. According to Matas (2007), offering a variety of ticket pricing and options improved customers' satisfaction with public transport system and resulted in a 50% rise in ridership over a five-year period.

v. Travel Time: Efficiency in travel time is critical for passenger preference, as promptness and reliability are key factors influencing overall satisfaction with public transport services (José Luis Machado-León et al., 2017). Passenger happiness and travel time are inextricably linked since individuals are typically more inclined to select the method of transportation that will get them from their starting point to their final destination as quickly as possible. In addition to not being caught in traffic bottlenecks, rail public transport is undoubtedly a more appealing alternative during peak hours than other public transport options like buses. Given this benefit, train operators of public transport should think about increasing time efficiency in order to boost customer satisfaction and draw in more potential customers (Ibrahim et al., 2020).

vi. Comfort: Factors such as cleanliness, seating comfort, noise levels, and waiting conditions significantly impact passenger satisfaction, highlighting the importance of comfort-related amenities in public transport (Eboli et al., 2016). Users' contentment with public rail transit would naturally be impacted by these aspects, and several studies have shown that comfort and cleanliness have a statistically significant association with user satisfaction contentment (José Luis Machado-León et.al, 2017).

vi. Safety: Both perceived and actual safety, including measures at stations and on trains, are critical for enhancing passenger satisfaction and ensuring a secure travel environment (Eboli et al., 2016). This includes the station safety (Mouwen, 2015) and train safety (Muhammad Das et al., 2013). Rail

> service providers would be well advised to take preventative steps to make train cars and train stations as safer locations for travelers in order to allay these justifiable worries. Some of these precautions include mounting a sufficient number of CCTV cameras and placing police officers on trains to guard against pickpocketing, sexual harassment, and other crimes.

Accessibility to train stations is crucial for urban mobility, influencing travel choices and patterns significantly. Proximity to residential, commercial, and recreational areas enhances convenience, making public transit a viable alternative to private vehicles. Strategic station placement fosters seamless connectivity to key destinations, facilitating access to essential services and opportunities. Time and cost are pivotal factors affecting accessibility, shaping how individuals engage with transportation options. Walkable environments with pedestrian-friendly infrastructure and safe surroundings further promote public transit use, enhancing overall urban accessibility and sustainability (Woldeamanuel and Cyganski, 2011; Saelens and Handy, 2008).

## 3. RESEARCH METHODOLOGY

In this research, a quantitative method is used for data collection and relevant questionnaires are formed. Quantitative research is the most appropriate method to test the assumption of social phenomena (Khan et al., 2023). The purpose of this method allows researchers to assess the respondents' feedback and to identify a certain pattern of participants in the research study (Yilmaz, 2013). Furthermore, quantitative research generalizes the findings of a large population of MRT users and allows for statistical analysis to understand the patterns from data collected. Questionnaire surveys will be addressed to the frequent MRT passengers, and the feedback will be studied accordingly. Hence, a proposal for solutions will be sought to enhance and increase the passengers' satisfaction and the overall service quality of the future MRT stations.

There are three sections to the study's questionnaire, including the cover layout. The intended respondents' demographic profile was the subject of the first section of the questionnaire, with the remaining two sections concentrating on the primary goals and objectives of the research. The questionnaire is formatted and divided into three sections such as Section 1: Demographic Profile; Section 2: Passenger Satisfaction of MRT Train Stations (comprised of Part A: Availability of services & Accessibility, Part B: Ticketing and Payment Systems & Travel Time, Part C: Comfort and Safety) and Section 3: Possible suggestions for improvement.

Various sampling techniques, including convenient sampling and snowball sampling, were employed to maximize respondent participation. These methods facilitated direct engagement with passengers at MRT stations and leveraged referrals from initial respondents to reach a diverse sample. The duration for data collection is about one month.

### 3.1. Sample Size

The study targeted a representative sample size of 384 respondents, derived from the average daily ridership data of the Rapid Rail network in the Klang Valley. According to recent statistics, the total monthly ridership across the MRT lines averaged 10,374,200, with a daily ridership estimate of approximately 334,652 passengers (Myrapid, 2024). The sampling size calculated for the targeted data is 384 to be collected.

The response rate achieved was commendable, with 277 valid responses received, constituting a response rate of 72.14% of the targeted sample size. Despite challenges in reaching the full sample size within the allotted time, the response rate was considered robust and indicative of the survey's effectiveness in gathering data on passenger satisfaction with accessibility at MRT stations.

### 3.2. Data Analysis

According to Bernardita (2023), the process of gathering, modeling, and evaluating data using a variety of logical and statistical approaches and methodologies is known as data analysis. Data analysis is used to analyze the data of results to deeper understand the problem raised. Descriptive and inferential analysis will be used in this study to examine the data that has been gathered. The Statistical Package for Social Sciences (SPSS) was used in this work to perform inferential analysis, descriptive analysis, and reliability testing. SPSS (Statistical Package for the Social Sciences), is a statistical data analysis software program. In addition to numerical outcome forecasts and identifiable group predictions, SPSS offers descriptive and bivariate statistical data analysis. The program can also be used for direct marketing, graphing, and data conversion (TechTarget, 2024).

## 4. RESULT AND DISCUSSION

By collaborating a structured questionnaire survey, data was collected from a representative sample of MRT passengers to analyze various features of accessibility. The predominant intention is to compute the contentment levels across different proportions of accessibility, including physical public facilities, informational availability, and service fulfillment, thereby providing perceptions into the overall accessibility experience of the passengers.

These surveys emphasize on key performances such as alleviate of access for disabled passengers, the benefit of facilities for elderly passengers, the efficacy of signage indication, and the attainability of support resources. By utilizing analytical techniques, this section focuses on recognizing critical elements that impact passenger contentment and emphasizes fields that need enhancement. The outcome will be contributory in mentoring the future improvements in MRT accessibility, thereby guaranteeing a more all-in transit system to cater all users.

## 4.1. Demographic Profiles

It is critical to understand the demographic traits of the participants in order to properly illustrate the assessment discovery and to prepare suggestions and recommendations intended at enhancing accessibility.

There were 277 respondents in all, of whom 135 (48.7%) were men and 142 (51.3%) were women who completed the questionnaire. The number of female respondents to the questionnaire survey is 2.6% higher than the number of male respondents. The majority of MRT users who replied are between the ages of 18 and 24 (44.0%), followed by those between the ages of 25 and 34 (22.4%), 35 and 44 (12.3%), 45 and 54 (9.7%), those under the age of 18 (6.1%), and those above the age of 55 (5.4%).

*Table 1. Employment status of MRT passengers.*

| | Frequency | Percent | Valid Percent | Cumulative Percent |
|---|---|---|---|---|
| Employed full-time | 105 | 37.90 | 37.90 | 37.90 |
| Employed part-time | 14 | 5.10 | 5.10 | 43.00 |
| Self-employed | 27 | 9.70 | 9.70 | 52.70 |
| Unemployed | 14 | 5.10 | 5.10 | 57.80 |
| Student | 115 | 41.50 | 41.50 | 99.30 |
| Others | 2 | 0.70 | 0.70 | 100.00 |
| Total | 277 | 100 | 100 | |

The results were categorized into six employment statuses such as, employed full-time, employed part-time, self-employed, unemployed, student, and others. 105 respondents (37.9%) are employed full-time. This group likely includes individuals who commute regularly to their workplaces, often relying on the MRT for daily travel. Their satisfaction with accessibility is crucial as they are frequent users who depend on efficient and reliable transportation. Besides this, 14 respondents (5.1%) are employed part-time. These respondents might have more flexible schedules and possibly less frequent travel needs compared to full-time employees. However, accessibility remains important to accommodate their varying work hours. Moreover, 27 respondents (9.7%) are self-employed. This group may have diverse travel patterns depending on their business activities. Their satisfaction with MRT accessibility can impact their ability to efficiently manage their time and business operations.

Additionally, 14 respondents (5.1%) are currently unemployed. These individuals might use the MRT for job hunting, attending interviews, or other personal activities. Good accessibility can aid in their mobility and potentially in finding employment opportunities. Moreover, 115 respondents (41.5%) are students. As the largest group, students frequently travel to educational institutions. Their satisfaction with MRT accessibility is critical as it directly affects their daily commute to and from schools or universities. Lastly, 2 respondents (0.7%) fall into the 'others' category where they are retirees or pensioners.

*Table 2. Monthly income status of MRT passengers.*

| | Frequency | Percent | Valid Percent | Cumulative Percent |
|---|---|---|---|---|
| Below RM2,000 | 126 | 45.50 | 45.50 | 45.50 |
| RM2,000-RM 4,999 | 74 | 26.70 | 26.70 | 72.20 |
| RM 5,000- RM9,999 | 53 | 19.10 | 19.10 | 91.30 |
| RM10,000-RM19,999 | 15 | 5.40 | 5.40 | 96.80 |
| RM20,000 or above | 9 | 3.20 | 3.20 | 100.00 |
| Total | 277 | 100.00 | 100.00 | |

The Table 2 shows the monthly earnings allocation among MRT users in Malaysia shows critical awareness into the socioeconomic background of the commuters. A considerable group of participants, 126 individuals (45.5%), appeared having a monthly earning of lower than RM2000. This shows that almost half of the MRT users belong to the lower earning category. Another 74 repondents (26.7%) took monthly earnings ranging from RM2000 to RM4999. This category is regarded as over a quarter of the passengers which parked under the lower-middle-income category. 53 respondents (19.1%) stated that their earnings were between RM5000 and RM9999. This group of the residents can be reviewed as middle-income earners. A minimal total of 15 respondents (5.4%) earning between RM10000 and RM19999 monthly, indicating a higher income earners group but remains as minority among the interviewees. The smallest category, consisting of 9 interviewees (3.2%), have monthly earnings of RM20000 or above, regarded as the highest-income earners among MRT users.

These numerical data overall indicate that the most MRT users have rather moderate earnings. The predominance of lower and lower-middle-income groups among MRT users highlights that the MRT is a crucial mode of transportation for those who may not have the financial capacity for more expensive commuting options. This demographic distribution underscores the importance of ensuring that MRT services are affordable and accessible, catering primarily to the economic needs of the broader population who rely on public transportation for their daily commute.

*Table 3. The frequency of MRT line usage*

| | Frequency | Percent | Valid Percent | Cumulative Percent |
|---|---|---|---|---|
| Daily | 73 | 26.40 | 26.40 | 26.40 |
| Weekly | 57 | 20.60 | 20.60 | 46.90 |
| Monthly | 44 | 15.90 | 15.90 | 62.80 |
| Rarely | 103 | 37.20 | 37.20 | 100.00 |
| Total | 277 | 100.00 | 100.00 | |

Table 3 shows how frequent the passengers using MRT Line. The results were categorized into four frequency ranges: daily, weekly, monthly, and rarely.

73 respondents (26.4%) reported using the MRT Line daily. This group represents regular commuters who likely rely heavily on the MRT for their daily transportation needs, such as commuting to work or school. Their frequent use suggests a high dependency on the reliability and accessibility of the MRT system. Besides, 57 respondents (20.6%) use the MRT on a weekly basis. These respondents might use the MRT for every now and then activities such as weekend walks, assignments, or infrequent work trips. Their utilization order shows an average extent of dependencies on the MRT services. Furthermore, 44 interviewees (15.9%) appeared to be using the MRT on a monthly basis. This category probably consists of individuals who utilize the MRT for particularly, rare motives such as attending monthly conferences, specific affairs, or infrequent engagements. Their lower reiteration of usage might be affected by numerous reasons such as substitute transportation choices or the certain character of their travel requirements. Finally, 103 respondents (37.2%) utilize the MRT rarely. This is the biggest sector and consists of individuals who utilize the MRT infrequently, maybe only a few times in a year. Reasons that cause this low utilization might be long distances from the MRT stations, alternative to other choices of transportation, or insufficient facilities for regular travel on the MRT.

The report shows diverse utilization occurrences of the MRT Line among respondents. The biggest group (37.2%) rarely utilizes the MRT, while a substantial 26.4% are daily users who depend on this mode for regular travel. Weekly users consist of 20.6%, and monthly users account for 15.9%. Recognizing these samples is important for directing different passenger requirements and thus improving the overall contentment and accessibility of the MRT Line for all its users.

*Table 4. The distance of respondent's home to MRT Station*

| | Frequency | Percent | Valid Percent | Cumulative Percent |
|---|---|---|---|---|
| <1km | 28 | 10.10 | 10.10 | 10.10 |
| 1km-3km | 71 | 25.60 | 25.60 | 35.70 |
| 3km-5km | 93 | 33.60 | 33.60 | 69.30 |
| 5km-10km | 31 | 11.20 | 11.20 | 80.50 |
| >10km | 54 | 19.50 | 19.50 | 100.00 |
| Total | 277 | 100.00 | 100.00 | |

Table 4 show that the distances of the respondents' residences or workplaces to the nearest MRT stations vary; the majority (33.6%) live between three and five kilometres away. Those who live within one kilometre have the highest accessibility (10.1%), while those who live more than ten kilometres have the most serious accessibility issues (19.5%). This information is critical for planning accessibility upgrades, which will improve the overall user experience of the MRT system.

Those people who work or live very close to a MRT station, which means that people who live near a MRT station are more likely to use it frequently and conveniently in a walking distance. In addition, 71 respondents (25.6%) said they live within 1-3 kilometers. Even though it may take a car, bicycle or walk to get to the station, this distance is still relatively convenient, indicating a moderate level of transportation convenience.

In addition, 93 respondents (33.6%) lived within a 3-5 km radius, which was the largest group among the respondents. Although it may take more effort to reach the station from this distance, this suggests that a significant number of users may rely on other modes of transportation to reach the station, including buses or ridesharing. In addition, 31 respondents (11.2%) lived within a 5-10 km radius. This group may experience more difficulties in using the MRT station, which may mean longer journey times and greater reliance on other modes of transportation to reach the subway station. Finally, 54 respondents (19.5%) lived more than ten kilometres away from the nearest MRT station. Since these respondents lived the farthest from the subway station, therefore they might have transportation problems and were more likely to rely on other modes of transportation to make up the gap.

*Table 5. Types of transport access to MRT station.*

| | Frequency | Percent | Valid Percent | Cumulative Percent | Ranking |
|---|---|---|---|---|---|
| Walk | 100 | 25.90 | 25.90 | 25.90 | 2 |
| Bicycle/Motorcycle | 2 | 0.50 | 0.50 | 26.40 | 5 |
| Car | 194 | 50.40 | 50.40 | 76.80 | 1 |
| Public Transport | 83 | 21.60 | 21.60 | 98.40 | 3 |
| Others: Grab/Taxi | 6 | 1.60 | 1.60 | 100.00 | 4 |
| Total | 385 | | | | |

Table 5 shows that the respondents were given multiple transportation options to choose from to reach their destination. Most of the respondents i.e. 194 of them (50.4%) use cars to reach MRT stations, indicating that cars are the primary mode of transport for accessing the MRT. 100 respondents (25.9%) walk to MRT stations, reflecting that many passengers travel on foot from nearby locations. On the other hand, 83 respondents (21.6%) use public transport such as buses or other trains, showing a significant reliance on an integrated public transit system. Only 6 respondents (1.6%) use using other forms of transportation not specified in the survey. This category could include taxis, ride-sharing services, or any unconventional means of transport. A minimal number of 2 respondents (0.5%) use motorcycles/bicycles. 6 respondents (2.4%) indicated using other forms of transportation not specified in the survey.

The survey results clearly show that cars and walking are the predominant modes of transportation for accessing MRT stations. The high percentage of car users underscores the need for adequate parking facilities and efficient traffic management around MRT stations. Meanwhile, the significant number of pedestrians highlights the necessity of maintaining safe and accessible walking routes. Hence, ensuring seamless connectivity between various modes of transportation can enhance the overall accessibility and convenience of the MRT system for all passengers.

## 4.2 Passenger Satisfaction on the Accessibility of Each Major Element of the MRT Station

This section uses descriptive analysis to present passengers' satisfaction with the accessibility of each major component of the MRT station. The selection that most properly conveys their view of each major feature variable in the questionnaire survey is chosen using a 1–5 scale (Most Unsatisfaction to Most Satisfaction, or equivalent).

Table 6 shows the survey results provided mean scores for each aspect, which allowed ranking them based on passenger satisfaction. This table provides an insight into passenger satisfaction across various aspects of MRT stations in Malaysia. There are five main variables that influence passenger satisfaction such as time, comfort/safety, accessibility and location, available services, and ticketing.

*Table 6. Passenger satisfaction views on each major element of the MRT station.*

| Variables | | 1-5 Scale (Not satisfaction to Very Satisfaction) | | | | |
|---|---|---|---|---|---|---|
| | | N | Mean | Rank | Overall Mean | Overall Ranking |
| Availability Services | | | | | | |
| B1 | Ramps, elevators and escalator to facilitate easy movement | 277 | 3.3682 | 2 | 3.11626 | 5 |
| B2 | Availability of parking spaces | 277 | 2.5993 | 5 | | |
| B3 | Availability of staff or personnel to assist passengers | 277 | 3.3430 | 3 | | |
| B4 | Availability of facilities for storing bicycles or others personal belongings | 277 | 2.6029 | 4 | | |
| B5 | Frequency and clarity of public announcements | 277 | 3.6679 | 1 | | |
| Accessibility & Location and Connectivity | | | | | | |
| C1 | Proximity to Residential Areas | 277 | 2.9892 | 5 | 3.3935 | 4 |
| C2 | Accessibility to Workplace/ School | 277 | 3.0758 | 4 | | |
| C3 | Connectivity to Others Transport Hubs | 277 | 3.5451 | 3 | | |
| C4 | Distance to Commercial Areas | 277 | 3.7834 | 1 | | |
| C5 | Ease of interchange between Lines | 277 | 3.5740 | 2 | | |
| Ticket Purchasing | | | | | | |
| D1 | Ticket Purchasing Process | 277 | 3.4693 | 1 | 3.4693 | 3 |
| Time | | | | | | |
| E1 | Time Punctuality | 277 | 3.5812 | 1 | 3.5812 | 1 |
| Comfort/ Safety | | | | | | |

| Variables | | 1-5 Scale (Not satisfaction to Very Satisfaction) | | | | |
|---|---|---|---|---|---|---|
| | | N | Mean | Rank | Overall Mean | Overall Ranking |
| F1 | Availability of Seating/Waiting Areas | 277 | 3.2022 | 4 | 3.47745 | 2 |
| F2 | Cleanliness and Maintenance of Facilities (Restrooms and Waiting Areas) | 277 | 3.7148 | 1 | | |
| F3 | Availability and Effectiveness of Signage and Wayfinding | 277 | 3.4188 | 3 | | |
| F4 | Overall Security and Safety Measures (Lighting and Surveillance) | 277 | 3.5740 | 2 | | |

Time is the most important factor with an overall mean of 3.5812, indicating passengers' satisfaction with the regularity and punctuality of MRT trains. The high mean score emphasizes the importance of timely and reliable service in meeting passengers' needs. Therefore, the excellent performance in this area is due to effective scheduling and operating procedures, which provide passengers with a smooth and easy travel experience. This is because when comparing the time punctuality of MRT, LRT and commuter bus systems in Malaysia, differences in reliability may be revealed. MRT systems generally perform well because they use automated operations and modern infrastructure. Old infrastructure and localized routes are issues for LRT services that affect punctuality. Moreover, buses serving suburban areas are not always reliable due to congestion and maintenance issues. Overall, MRT are generally more timely than light rail and commuter systems. Therefore, the average score for this factor is high. According to Ibrahim et al. (2020), people are generally more likely to choose a mode of transportation that can get them from their starting point to their destination as quickly as possible, so passenger satisfaction is closely related to travel time.

Since comfort and safety play a vital role in determining the passenger experience, it ranks second with an overall mean of 3.47745. However, the relatively lower score for seating availability highlights an area of concern, as passengers value comfort and convenience during their wait. Therefore, improving seating availability and bolstering security measures will further enhance the overall passenger experience and make comfort and safety a pivotal aspect of satisfaction. The findings of a study by Eboli & Mazzulla (2012) on passengers' opinions of rail services in Northern Italy provide support for this. The study found that the factors that have the biggest positive effects on passenger travel are regularity, punctuality, cleanliness, comfort, informative, contentment, and service quality.

Ticket purchasing ranked third with a mean of 3.4693. This means that ticket purchasing convenience is a critical aspect of passenger satisfaction. The relatively high mean score indicates that passengers find the ticket purchasing process satisfactory, reflecting efficient and user-friendly ticketing systems. However, continuous improvements and innovations in ticketing technology can further streamline this process and enhance overall passenger experience. De Witte et al. (2013) has stated that consumers are ready to spend more depending on the purpose and comfort of their travels.

The overall average score of "Accessibility & Location and Connectivity" was 3.3935, ranked as fourth. The accessibility & location, and connectivity factor considers factors such as accessibility to transportation, distance to business districts, accessibility to employers and schools, and accessibility to residential areas. It is worth noting that the average scores for connectivity to business districts and transportation hubs are lower than those for accessibility to workplaces and distance to residential areas. In order to improve passengers' accessibility, MRT stations should be more seamlessly connected to residential and business districts. This is because when residential and commercial areas are seamlessly connected, MRT stations are more convenient, and people are encouraged to take public transportation instead of driving their own cars. This connectivity is helpful for those who commute every day and need a reliable and direct route home or to work. When transportation is convenient, subways become a more attractive alternative because it shortens travel time and alleviates the hassle of finding parking spaces. Besides this, as commented by Batty (2009) where the conversation around accessibility is complicated by two main issues: first, determining the scope of these metrics; second is assessing the relationship between accessibility and people's behaviours in terms of social and economic activities.

The availability of services on MRT stations such as ramps, elevators, parking spots, personnel support, and public announcements; ranked the last in overall with a mean of 3.11626. Aspects like parking availability scored lower, suggesting places for development. However, the regularity and clarity of public announcements/ notifications obtained a commendable mean of 3.6679. Research by Hine and Scott (2000) indicates that train station accessibility influences passenger happiness and encourages rail transit as a mode of transportation.

The reason of parking availability scored the lowest with the mean score of 2.5993. The reason is because of MRT stations located in urban areas in Klang Valley which have high number of cars. The limitation of parking spaces can lead to overcrowding and difficulty in finding parking spaces. Moreover, the difficulty commuters have in finding appropriate parking places is made worse because of the increasing demand for parking in densely populated metropolitan centres. In addition to being annoying, this shortage deters people from using MRT services who depend on their automobiles for the first or last mile of their trip. Additionally, passenger satisfaction could suffer if parking facilities are accessible yet pricey.

In summary, the key findings derived from Table 6 reveal high satisfaction with frequency and clarity of public announcements, ramps, elevators, and proximity to commercial areas. However, challenges exist in seating availability, parking, and proximity to residential areas, indicating areas for improvement. Ticket purchasing and time-related factors like train frequency also influence the satisfaction of passengers. Enhancing these aspects, such as improving seating and parking facilities, can significantly enhance passenger experience and overall satisfaction with Malaysia's MRT system, ensuring it meets the diverse needs of commuters effectively.

*Table 7. Challenges faced by passengers in accessing train station*

| | | Frequency | Percent | Remarks |
|---|---|---|---|---|
| **Ticket/ Payment** | | | | |
| D2 Ticket Purchasing Issue | Yes | 96 | 34.70 | There are 34.70% facing challenges in purchasing ticket |
| | No | 181 | 65.30 | |
| D3 Understanding Type of Tickets | Yes | 205 | 74.00 | Most of the responded understand types of transport ticket in Malaysia |
| | No | 37 | 13.40 | |
| | Maybe | 35 | 12.60 | |
| D4 Reasonable of Ticket Prices | Yes | 138 | 49.80 | More than half of the respondents said that the ticket prices were too high |
| | No | 139 | 50.2 | |
| Time (Peak Hour) | | | | |
| E2 Overcrowding | Yes | 200 | 72.20 | Most of the respondents said they had encountered overcrowding |
| | No | 77 | 27.80 | |
| E3 Delay | Yes | 147 | 53.10 | More than half of the respondent reported having encountered such issues |
| | No | 130 | 46.90 | |
| Element that respondents faced challenges (possible improvement) | | | | |
| | N | Frequency | Percent | Ranking |
| G1_Availability Services | 277 | 87 | 31.40 | 5 |
| G2 Accessibility/ Location | 277 | 187 | 67.50 | 1 |
| G3 Ticket/Prices | 277 | 119 | 43.00 | 3 |
| G4 Time (Peak Hour) | 277 | 163 | 58.80 | 2 |
| G5 Comfort/ Safety | 277 | 96 | 34.70 | 4 |
| G6 Others | 277 | 14 | 5.10 | 6 |

According to Table 7, the survey results show the challenges faced by passengers in accessing train stations for each factor and aspect, this part of the questionnaire is using the Yes / No options to get candid answers on two key elements: ticket / payment and time (peak hours). These elements are the focus because they have a big impact on the overall commuting experience.

The survey results from Table 7 highlight significant challenges faced by passengers accessing MRT stations, focusing on ticket/payment and time (peak hours). Regarding ticket/payment, issues include accessibility problems with machines/counters (34.70%), and confusion about ticket types among respondents (26%). Perception of fare reasonableness was evenly split (49.80% yes, 50.20% no), suggesting affordability concerns. For time-related factors, 72.20% were satisfied with punctuality, but 27.80% expressed dissatisfaction, emphasizing the need for improved reliability during peak hours. Additionally, 53.10% reported experiencing service delays/disruptions, highlighting infrastructure maintenance as crucial for enhancing service reliability and passenger satisfaction. Addressing these issues comprehensively is essential to improve overall MRT commuting experiences.

The study on accessibility and passenger satisfaction at MRT stations in Malaysia reveals key areas for improvement. Location and accessibility emerged as primary concerns, with a majority of respondents highlighting difficulties in finding stations. Improving station proximity to residential and commercial areas, along with enhancing connectivity to transport hubs, is crucial. Issues of punctuality and frequency of services were also significant, underscoring the need for better operational efficiency. Addressing fare affordability, enhancing comfort and safety measures, and improving accessibility services like parking and ramps are additional priorities. By focusing on these areas, MRT authorities can significantly enhance overall passenger satisfaction and commuting experience.

In summary, seamless communication between residential areas, commercial areas and MRT stations is essential to improve accessibility, increase ridership, ease traffic congestion and promote environmental sustainability. It can also promote sustainable urban development, improve living standards and promote economic growth. Urban planners and transportation departments can build more efficient, liveable and sustainable cities by prioritizing such connectivity.

continued on following page

*Table 8. Continued*

## 4.3 Reliability Test

*Table 8. Cronbach's Alpha Reliability Analysis*

| Types of Variable | Name of the variable | Number of the items | Cronbach's Alpha | Reliability Test |
|---|---|---|---|---|
| Independent Variable | B1. Services_ Facility (Lift) | 17 | 0.875 | Good |
| Independent Variable | B2. Services_ Parking Spaces | 17 | 0.870 | Good |
| Independent Variable | B3. Availability of Staff | 17 | 0.878 | Good |
| Independent Variable | B4. Storing system | 17 | 0.869 | Good |
| Independent Variable | B5. Announcement | 17 | 0.873 | Good |
| Independent Variable | C2. Accessibility to Residential Area | 17 | 0.867 | Good |
| Independent Variable | C3. Accessibility to Workspaces | 17 | 0.868 | Good |
| Independent Variable | C4. Accessibility to other transport | 17 | 0.865 | Good |
| Independent Variable | C5. Accessibility to commercial Area | 17 | 0.871 | Good |
| Independent Variable | C6. Accessibility to Interchange | 17 | 0.869 | Good |
| Independent Variable | D1. Ticket Purchasing | 17 | 0.868 | Good |
| Independent Variable | E1. TIme Punctuality | 17 | 0.870 | Good |
| Independent Variable | F1. Seating | 17 | 0.865 | Good |
| Independent Variable | F2. Cleanliness | 17 | 0.871 | Good |
| Independent Variable | F3. Signage | 17 | 0.864 | Good |
| Independent Variable | F4. Security | 17 | 0.864 | Good |
| Dependent Variable | Overall satisfaction of accessibility of the MRT station | 17 | 0.872 | Good |

The reliability test results of the independent and dependent variables are shown in Table 8. Multiple regression and correlation analysis will be conducted later. The independent variables are all recognized and considered reliable because, as shown in the attached table, their Cronbach's Alpha values are all above 0.80. For the dependent variable of overall satisfaction of accessibility to MRT station, the Cronbach's Alpha value is 0.872, which means good reliability. Therefore, all independent and dependent variables are accepted and retained in the following study.

## 4.4 Multiple Regression Test

In this section, multiple regression tests will be used to study the relationship between the level of agreement on the main challenges surveyed in the questionnaire survey and the overall passenger satisfaction in accessibility on the train stations of the MRT Line in Malaysia. This test is aimed to find out which challenge affects the overall satisfaction level of affecting accessibility the most.

*Table 9. Multiple Regression Test on the Overall satisfaction level*

| | Unstandardized B | Coefficients Std. Error | Standardized Coefficients Beta | t | Sig. |
|---|---|---|---|---|---|
| (Constant) | 1.634 | .270 | | 6.053 | <.001 |
| Services | .393 | .084 | .299 | 4.664 | <.001 |
| Accessibility | .288 | .083 | .251 | 3.465 | <.001 |
| Ticket Purchasing | -.127 | .053 | -.157 | -2.393 | .017 |
| Time Punctuality | .043 | .059 | 0.44 | .721 | .471 |
| Comfort/ Safety | .107 | .086 | 0.93 | 1.232 | .219 |

a. Dependent Variable: C1_ Overall

The test identified services, accessibility, and ticket purchasing as significant factors influencing overall satisfaction with accessibility at MRT stations in Malaysia. Services and accessibility showed positive regression coefficients of 0.393 and 0.288, respectively, indicating their substantial impact on passenger satisfaction. These findings align with previous research, emphasizing the importance of service availability including facilities and station proximity in influencing commuter preferences and satisfaction levels. The rejection of time punctuality and comfort/ safety due to non-significant p-values (>0.05) underscores the specific areas where improvements may be needed to enhance overall MRT station accessibility and passenger experience. This can be concluded as in Table 10 below:

*Table 10. Summary of Statistical Findings on Multiple Regression Test*

| Independent Variables | T-statistic | P-value | Results |
|---|---|---|---|
| Services | 4.664 | <.001 | Significant |
| Accessibility | 3.465 | <.001 | Significant |
| Ticket Purchasing | -2.393 | .017 | Significant |
| Time Punctuality | .721 | .471 | Not Significant |
| Comfort/ Safety | 1.232 | .219 | Not Significant |

Dependent Variable: Overall Satisfaction in accessibility on the train stations

The three factors of service, accessibility and ticket purchase are significantly related to the overall satisfaction with subway station accessibility. Therefore, service, accessibility and ticket purchase are strong predictors of the dependent variable to the overall satisfaction with subway station accessibility.

## 5. CONCLUSION

Key findings reveal high satisfaction with frequency and clarity of public announcements, ramps, elevators, and proximity to commercial areas. However, challenges exist in seating availability, parking, and proximity to residential areas, indicating areas for improvement. Ticket purchasing and time-related factors like train frequency also influence satisfaction. Enhancing these aspects, such as improving seating and parking facilities, can significantly enhance passenger experience and overall satisfaction with Malaysian MRT system, ensuring it meets the diverse needs of commuters effectively.

Enhancing MRT systems involves integrated planning with existing networks and creating link passes for seamless intermodal travel. Collaboration among stakeholders is crucial for successful integration. Feeder buses should cover residential areas extensively, complemented by reliable schedules to encourage metro use. Park-and-ride facilities in suburban areas can reduce city traffic, requiring sufficient, affordable parking options. Enhancing walkability through pedestrian-friendly infrastructure and connectivity is essential, ensuring safety and convenience for urban dwellers.

In conclusion, this study underscores the critical role of accessibility, time management, comfort and safety, ticketing, and station location in shaping passenger satisfaction with Malaysia's MRT system. By addressing these factors through targeted improvements and comprehensive strategies, authorities can enhance service quality, promote sustainable urban transport, and improve overall commuter satisfaction. This approach not only fosters a more user-friendly public transport system but also contributes to broader urban sustainability goals in Malaysia.

## REFERENCES


Adhikari, S., Ross, W., & Ernst, J. (2019). *The Encyclopedia: Evaluating People's to Reach Desired Goods, Services and Activities.* The Victoria Transport Policy Institute. Online. Retrieved from https://www.vtpi.org/tdm/tdm84.htm

Batarce, M., Muñoz, J. C., & de Dios Ortúzar, J. (2016). Valuing crowding in public transport: Implications for cost-benefit analysis. *Transportation Research Part A, Policy and Practice, 91*, 358–378. DOI: 10.1016/j.tra.2016.06.025

Batty, M. (2009). Accessibility: In Search of A Unified Theory. *Environment and Planning. B, Planning & Design, 36*(2), 191–194. https://journals.sagepub.com/doi/epdf/10.1068/b3602ed. DOI: 10.1068/b3602ed

Beimborn, E. A., Greenwald, M. J., & Jin, X. (2003). Accessibility, Connectivity, and Captivity: Impacts on Transit Choice. *Transportation Research Record: Journal of the Transportation Research Board, 1835*(1), 1–9. Advance online publication. DOI: 10.3141/1835-01

Bernardita, C. (2023). *Your Modern Business Guide to Data Analysis Methods and Techniques.* Online. Retrieved from https://www.datapine.com/blog/data-analysis-methods-and-techniques/

Borhan, M. N., Syamsunur, D., Akhir, N. M., Yazid, M. R. M., Ismail, A., & Rahmat, R. A. (2014). Predicting the Use of Public Transportation: A Case Study from Putrajaya, Malaysia. *TheScientificWorldJournal, 2014*(1), 1–9. Advance online publication. DOI: 10.1155/2014/784145 PMID: 25110744

Brown, V., Barr, A., Scheurer, J., Magnus, A., Zapata-Diomedi, B., & Bently, R. (2019). Better Transport Accessibility, Better Health: A Health Economic Impact Assessment Study for Melbourne, Australia. *The International Journal of Behavioral Nutrition and Physical Activity, 16*(1), 1–10. DOI: 10.1186/s12966-019-0853-y PMID: 31640737

Centres for Disease Control and Prevention (CDCP). (2020). *Disability and Health Inclusion Strategies.* Online. Retrieved from https://www.cdc.gov/ncbddd/disabilityandhealth/disability-strategies.html#:~:text=Accessibility%20is%20when%20the%20needs,spaces%20are%20close%20to%20entrances

Chan, D. (2022, June 9). Vehicles Outnumber People in Malaysia. *New Strait Times.* Online. Retrieved from https://www.nst.com.my/news/nation/2022/06/803654/vehicles-outnumber-people-malaysia

Chea, J. (2023, February 22). Video Of Woman Walking Along Busy Traffic Due to No Pedestrian Walkways Goes Viral. *Says*. Retrieved from https://says.com/my/news/m-sian-forced-to-walk-beside-busy-traffic

Cheng, Y. H., & Chen, S. Y. (2015). Perceived Accessibility, Mobility, And Connectivity Of Public Transportation Systems. *Transportation Research Part A, Policy and Practice*, *77*(July), 386–403. DOI: 10.1016/j.tra.2015.05.003

Chin, S. J. Y., Goh, B. H., Teo, F. Y., Kang, B. G., & Yuen, C. W. (2020). Pedestrian Walkability Index for Light Rail Transit (LRT) Stations in Klang Valley, Malaysia. *In Proceedings of AICCE'19: Transforming the Nation for a Sustainable Tomorrow 4 (pp. 737-748)*. Springer International Publishing.

De Witte, A., Hollevoet, J., Dobruszkes, F., Hubert, M., & Macharis, C. (2013). Linking Modal Choice to Motility: A Comprehensive Review. *Transportation Research Part A, Policy and Practice*, *49*(March), 329–341. DOI: 10.1016/j.tra.2013.01.009

Eboli, L., Fu, Y., & Mazzulla, G. (2016). Multilevel Comprehensive Evaluation of the Railway Service Quality. *Procedia Engineering*, *137*, 21–30. DOI: 10.1016/j.proeng.2016.01.230

Eboli, L., & Mazzulla, G. (2012). Structural Equation Modelling for Analysing Passengers' Perceptions about Railway Services. *Procedia: Social and Behavioral Sciences*, *54*, 96–106. DOI: 10.1016/j.sbspro.2012.09.729

Elias, W., & Shiftan, Y. (2012). The influence of individual's risk perception and attitudes on travel behavior. *Transportation Research Part A, Policy and Practice*, *46*(8), 1241–1251. DOI: 10.1016/j.tra.2012.05.013

Fu, Y., Eboli, L., Mazzulla, G., & Zhang, Y. (2017, March). Railway Service Quality in Northern Italy: A Multilevel Synthetic Assessment. *Advances in Mechanical Engineering*, *9*(3), 1687814016686317. Advance online publication. DOI: 10.1177/1687814016686317

Guo, Z., & Wilson, N. H. M. (2011, February). Assessing the cost of transfer inconvenience in public transport systems: A case study of the London Underground. *Transportation Research Part A, Policy and Practice*, *45*(2), 91–104. DOI: 10.1016/j.tra.2010.11.002

Hadas, Y., Rossi, R., Gastaldi, M., & Gecchele, G. (2014). Public Transport Systems' Connectivity: Spatiotemporal Analysis and Failure Detection. *Transportation Research Procedia*, *3*, 309–318. DOI: 10.1016/j.trpro.2014.10.011

Handy, S. L. (2002). *Accessibility- Vs. Mobility-enhancing Strategies for Ad-dressing Automobile Dependence in the U.S.* European Conference of Ministers of Transport May 2002. Retrieved from https://escholarship.org/uc/item/5kn4s4pb

Hickman, R., Chen, L. C., Chow, A., & Saxena, S. (2015). Improving Interchanges in China: The Experiential Phenomenon. ScienceDirect. *Journal of Transport Geography*, *42*(January), 175–186. DOI: 10.1016/j.jtrangeo.2014.12.004

Hine, J., & Scott, J. (2000, July). Seamless, Accessible Travel: Users' Views of The Public Transport Journey And Interchange. *Transport Policy*, *7*(3), 217–226. DOI: 10.1016/S0967-070X(00)00022-6

Ibrahim, A. N. H., Borhan, M. N., Osman, M. H., Khairuddin, F. H., & Zakaria, N. M. (2022). An Empirical Study of Passengers' Perceived Satisfaction with Monorail Service Quality: Case of Kuala Lumpur, Malaysia. *Sustainability (Basel)*, *14*(11), 6496. DOI: 10.3390/su14116496

Ibrahim, A. N. H., Borhan, M. N., & Yusoff, Md. N.I. & Ismail, A. (2020). Rail-Based Public Transport Service Quality and User Satisfaction – A Literature Review. *Promet – Traffic & Transportation*, Vol. 32, 2020, No. 3, 435-447. https://doi.org/ DOI: 10.7307/ptt.v32i3.3270

Joyce, M., & Dunn, R. (2009). A Proposed Methodology For Measuring Public Transport Accessibility To Employment Sites In The Auckland CBD. Retrieved from https://www.researchgate.net/publication/254609293_A_proposed_methodology_for_measuring_public_transport_accessibility_to_employment_sites_in_the_Auckland_CBD

Khadka, K., & Maharjan, S. (2017). *Customer Satisfaction And Customer Loyalty*. Thesis. Centria University of Applied Sciences Pietarsaari. Retrieved from https://core.ac.uk/download/pdf/161421179.pdf

Khadka, N. (n.d). Service Quality: What it is + Top 5 Components. Online. Retrieved from https://www.questionpro.com/blog/service-quality/#:~:text=What%20is%20Service%20Quality%3F,quality%20is%20a%20valuable%20art

Khalid, U. A., Bachok, S., Osman, M. M., & Ibrahim, M. (2014). User Perceptions of Rail Public Transport Services in Kuala Lumpur, Malaysia: KTM Komuter. *Procedia: Social and Behavioral Sciences*, *153*, 566–573. DOI: 10.1016/j.sbspro.2014.10.089

Khan, J. A., Raman, A. M., Sambamoorthy, N., & Prashanth, K. (2023). *Research Methodology (Methods, Approaches And Techniques)*. San International Scientific Publications., DOI: 10.59646/rmmethods/040

Machado-León, J. L., de Oña, R., Baouni, T., & de Oña, J. (2017). Railway transit services in Algiers: Priority improvement actions based on users perceptions. *Transport Policy*, *53*, 175–185. DOI: 10.1016/j.tranpol.2016.10.004

Matas, A. (2007). Demand And Revenue Implications of An Integrated Public Transport Policy: The Case Of Madrid. Transport Reviews. Vol. 24, 2004 - Issue 2 Pages 195-217. DOI: 10.1080/0144164032000107223

Mouwen, A. (2015). Drivers of customer satisfaction with public transport services. *Transportation Research Part A, Policy and Practice*, *78*(August), 1–20. DOI: 10.1016/j.tra.2015.05.005

MRT. (2023). Kajang Line. Online. Retrieved from https://www.mymrt.com.my/projects/kajang-line/

MRT. (2023). Putrajaya Line. Online. Retrieved from https://www.mymrt.com.my/projects/putrajaya-line/#:~:text=The%20Putrajaya%20Line%20is%20the,Putrajaya%2C%20Malaysia's%20federal%20administrative%20centre

Mugion, R. G., Toni, M., Raharjo, H., Di Pietro, L., & Sebathu, S. P. (2018). Does the service quality of urban public transport enhance sustainable mobility? *Journal of Cleaner Production*, *174*, 1566–1587. DOI: 10.1016/j.jclepro.2017.11.052

Muhammad Das, A., Ladin, M. A., Ismail, A., & Rahmat, R. O. K. (2013). Consumers Satisfaction of Public Transport Monorail User In Kuala Lumpur. *Journal of Engineering Science and Technology.*, *8*(3), 272–283. https://www.researchgate.net/publication/286541188_Consumers_satisfaction_of_public_transport_monorail_user_in_Kuala_Lumpur

MyRapid. (2024). Ridership Archive. Online. Retrieved By https://myrapid.com.my/bus-train/ridership-archive/

Noichan, R., & Dewancker, B. (2018). Analysis of Accessibility in an Urban Mass Transit Node: A Case Study in a Bangkok Transit Station. *Sustainability (Basel)*, *10*(12), 4819. DOI: 10.3390/su10124819

Oña López, J. J. D., Oña López, R. D., Eboli, L., & Mazzulla, G. (2013). Perceived service quality in bus transit service: A structural equation approach.

Papaioannou, D., & Martinez, L. M. (2015). The Role of Accessibility and Connectivity in Mode Choice. A Structural Equation Modeling Approach. *Transportation Research Procedia*, *10*, 831–839. DOI: 10.1016/j.trpro.2015.09.036

Pawlasowa, P. (2015). *The Factors Influencing Satisfaction with Public City Transport: A Structural Equation Modelling Approach.* Online. Retrieved from https://pdfs.semanticscholar.org/fcb4/6fcd525ee3da344814edbb58cd2a5e07baa6.pdf

Qistina, N. (2023, January 27). Video shows the struggle pedestrians have to endure to get to MRT station in PJ. *Says*. Retrieved from https://says.com/my/news/struggle-pedestrians-have-to-endure-to-get-to-mrt-station

Raju, S. T. (2022, August 18). *Public transport is not the preferred choice of many*. The Sun. 2022. Retrieved from; https://www.thesundaily.my/local/public-transport-not-preferred-choice-of-many-GB9614181

Remix. (2021). *8 Benefits of Public Transportation*. Retrieved from; https://www.remix.com/blog/8-benefits-of-public-transportation

Saelens, B. E., & Handy, S. L. (2008, July). Built Environment Correlates of Walking: A Review. *Medicine and Science in Sports and Exercise, 40*(7, Suppl), S550–S566. DOI: 10.1249/MSS.0b013e31817c67a4 PMID: 18562973

Shiau, W. L., & Luo, M. M. (2012, November). Factors affecting online group buying intention and satisfaction: A social exchange theory perspective. *Computers in Human Behavior, 28*(6), 2431–2444. DOI: 10.1016/j.chb.2012.07.030

Tan, V. (2022, July 9). Commuters In Malaysia's Klang Valley Are Addicted To Their Cars. What Can Be Done To Encourage Use Of Public Transport? *Channel News Asia*. Retrieved from https://www.channelnewsasia.com/asia/malaysia-klang-valley-cars-traffic-congestion-encourage-public-transport-use-rail-lrt-mrt-ktm-2794391

TechTarget. (2024). *SPSS (Statistical Package for the Social Sciences)*. Online. Retrieved from https://www.techtarget.com/whatis/definition/SPSS-Statistical-Package-for-the-Social-Sciences

Tyrinopoulos, Y., & Antoniou, C. (2008). Public transit user satisfaction: Variability and policy implications. *Transport Policy, 15*(4), 260–272. DOI: 10.1016/j.tranpol.2008.06.002

Van Dut, V. (2017). Accessibility And Connectivity Challenges of Mass Rapid Transit In Kuala Lumpur, Malaysia. *Malaysia Sustainable Cities Program, Working Paper Series* Pg. 1-33.Retrieved from https://malaysiacities.mit.edu/sites/default/files/documents/dut.pdf

Weinstein, A. (2000). Customer Satisfaction Among Transit Riders: How Customers Rank the Relative Importance of Various Service Attributes. *Transportation Research Record: Journal of the Transportation Research Board, 1735*(1), 123–132. DOI: 10.3141/1735-15

Woldeamanuel, M. G., & Cyganski, R. (2011). Factors Affecting Travellers' Satisfaction With Accessibility To Public Transportation. Association For European Transport and Contributors. Retrieved from https://aetransport.org/public/downloads/Kdg5v/4913-514ec5fd92570.pdf

Yilmaz, K. (2013). Comparison Of Quantitative and Qualitative Research Traditions: Epistemological, Theoretical, And Methodological Differences. *European Journal of Education*, *48*(2), 311–325. DOI: 10.1111/ejed.12014

# Chapter 4
# Factors Influencing Residential Satisfaction in Low-Cost Housing:
## Planning Policies, Design Principles, Social Interactions, User Comfort, and Building Services

**Tze Shwan Lim**
https://orcid.org/0000-0002-6291-5287
*Taylor's University, Malaysia*

**Kenn Jhun Kam**
https://orcid.org/0000-0003-4927-4611
*Taylor's University, Malaysia*

**Ungku Norani Sonet**
https://orcid.org/0000-0003-4144-150X
*University College Dublin, Ireland*

**Nurul Aini Osman**
*Taylor's University, Malaysia*

**Gabriel Sin Yin Ho**
*Taylor's University, Malaysia*

**Habizah Sheikh Ilmi**
https://orcid.org/0009-0009-3382-5213
*Taylor's University, Malaysia*

## ABSTRACT

*Residential satisfaction plays a crucial role in gauging the quality of living in low-cost housing. In order to better understand the elements that affect residential satisfaction, this study examines the social interactions, design features, and planning policies in low-cost housing environments. The study utilizes a quantitative approach to assess the satisfaction levels of residents in low-cost housing, focusing on key variables such as user comfort, building services, and social cohesion. Data was*

DOI: 10.4018/979-8-3373-0390-1.ch004

*collected from residents related to accessibility and proximity to urban facilities, had the greatest impact on resident satisfaction. The quality of construction materials, the availability of essential building services, the overall design of housing units were found to significantly influence both the comfort and safety of residents. The findings underscore the need for comprehensive planning that addresses both the physical infrastructure and social dynamics of low-cost housing to improve quality of life and resident satisfaction*

## INTRODUCTION

Residential satisfaction is a multidimensional construct that evaluate the degree to which people are happy with their living environment and associated services, as well as the gap between expected and desired housing conditions and situations (Ibem et al., 2018). Low-cost housing is designed to meet the basic housing needs of lower-income individuals or families, typically through government policies, non-profit organizations, or private-sector efforts. The primary goal of low-cost housing is to provide affordable living spaces that are accessible to people who might otherwise be unable to afford decent shelter in urban areas, where housing costs tend to be higher (Addo, 2016). In the field of low-cost housing, maintaining high levels of residential satisfaction is critical since it not only improves quality of life but also develops a sense of community and stability. Addo (2016) stated that residential satisfaction is related to dwelling characteristics, neighbourhood characteristics, and existing social networks. For example, dwelling characteristics such as interior design and the number and size of bedrooms have a substantial impact on residential satisfaction by offering adequate space and comfort to users. Similarly, neighbourhood characteristics, such as a strong sense of safety, trustworthy neighbours, and a well-maintained community, are also important for creating a secure and supportive living environment that improves overall residential satisfaction. Furthermore, existing social networks within communities are strengthened by actions like socializing in public places and paying frequent visits to neighbours, which contribute directly to community cohesiveness and trust (Riazi & Emami, 2018).

## BACKGROUND

### Planning Policy

Planning policies have a significant impact on the residents' satisfaction with low-cost housing through their influence on accessibility, affordability, and the quality of living environments. One of the most important aspects is the proximity of housing to essential amenities and employment opportunities (Riazi and Emami, 2018). The distance between workplaces and urban facilities such as schools, hospitals, and retail malls have a direct impact on both commuting expenses and overall convenience for residents. In cases where housing is situated far from these facilities, residents often face increased transportation costs and longer travel durations, leading to a decrease in their overall satisfaction and quality of life (Olfindo, 2021).

The quality of construction materials, along with location, plays a crucial role in determining residents' satisfaction. Low-cost housing is commonly built with substandard materials and construction techniques, necessitating frequent repairs and maintenance (Chohan et al., 2015). This not only increases the economic strain on residents but also impacts their sense of safety and comfort in their residences. Additionally, the cost of monthly loan payments continues to be a key concern, as it impacts the financial feasibility of owning a home for families with low incomes (Yap & Ng, 2018). As a result, balancing affordability, quality, and location is a challenging task that policymakers need to conquer in order to increase residents' satisfaction.

### Design Principles

The design of low-cost housing is important for resident satisfaction, particularly in terms of safety, privacy, and usability of social spaces (Srirangam et al., 2022). In term of public space design, such as playgrounds for children and seating areas for adults, are critical in fostering community and offering safe, accessible opportunities for recreation. Proper lighting and strong security measures in public spaces such as staircases, corridors, and parking lots are also critical for preventing crime and ensuring the safety of people and property (Riazi & Emami, 2018).

Privacy and the organization of living spaces are also critical components of design. In terms of personal space design, the orientation of buildings—such as placing windows facing open spaces—can enhance natural surveillance while preserving privacy. Similarly, the separation of buildings through physical barriers like walls and the provision of private open spaces contribute to a sense of ownership and security. The number of units per building and the overall density of the residential complex influence social interactions and the availability of resources, with overcrowded environments often leading to dissatisfaction due to noise and lack of privacy (Castells, 2020; Carmona, 2021).

In the aspect of building infrastructure and amenities, the functionality and performance of elevators in high-rise buildings are essential for occupants' daily convenience. Reliable and efficient elevators minimize wait times and provide for easy access to different floors, which is important for both comfort and accessibility.

## INTERACTION WITH NEIGHBORS

Social interactions in low-cost housing communities are a two-edged sword: they can have both positive and negative impacts on residents' satisfaction. Noise, whether from neighbours walking upstairs or children playing in public spaces, can be irritating, especially in densely populated regions with inadequate sound insulation (Hongisto et al., 2015). Positive interactions, such as collaboration in paying monthly fees and maintaining shared spaces, are essential for creating a supportive community environment.

Conflict among neighbours is difficult to avoid in low-cost housing, where profligate tenants and disagreements over shared resources can cause tension. As a result, effective community management and the promotion of cooperative behaviours are critical techniques for addressing these difficulties while also increasing overall sense of community and contentment (Riazi & Emami, 2018).

## USER COMFORT

User comfort in low-cost housing refers to a variety of physical and environmental aspects that all contribute to residents' overall well-being. In areas with harsh weather, adequate ventilation is especially important for preserving good interior air quality and guaranteeing thermal comfort. Similarly, acoustic comfort is important since noise pollution from outside and inside the building can have a big impact on the quality of life of the occupants (Ellsworth-Krebs et al., 2018).

Lighting in homes, both natural and artificial, is another important factor in maintaining the comfort of occupants. Proper lighting improves visual comfort and can reduce energy costs, whereas inadequate lighting can cause health problems and greater utility bills. Furthermore, odours in the dwelling, which are frequently caused by insufficient waste disposal or poor ventilation, can significantly reduce residents' happiness and sense of comfort (Wimalasena et al., 2022). Addressing these difficulties necessitates a comprehensive approach to building design and maintenance, ensuring that every aspect of user comfort is examined and optimized.

## BUILDING SERVICES

Building services, which have a direct influence on residents' daily lives, are the foundation of sustainable and functional housing. To guarantee that every resident has consistent access to clean water, reliable water supply systems, including storage and distribution, need to be designed properly. Similarly, the sewage drainage system should be strong enough to avoid blockage and health issues that are prevalent in poorly maintained low-cost housing (Wimalasena et al., 2022).

Besides, the electrical wiring system should be able to accommodate the growing needs of society in terms of power consumption while ensuring the safety and reliability. Additionally, the availability of garbage disposal and recycling facilities is crucial to keep the housing complex clean and reducing the negative impact on the environment (Lokhande, 2016). Moreover, the availability of proper sanitation facilities is crucial for the health of the population living in the area. Sanitary toilets and waste disposal systems that are well designed and well maintained can help reduce the incidence of diseases and improve hygiene (Karn et al., 2012).

In conclusion, building services must be well planned and effectively managed to provide the residents with a safe, healthy and comfortable environment. These services, combined with proper planning and design, are important to ensure that low-cost housing provides residents with high levels of satisfaction.

## PROBLEM STATEMENT

Despite the critical role that low-cost housing plays in providing shelter and security for families with low or middle incomes, achieving high levels of residential satisfaction is an ongoing concern (Thomas, 2017). According to Dwijendra (2013), there are gaps between residents' expectations and their actual experiences as a result of the design and implementation of low-cost housing developments, which frequently put cost-efficiency ahead of quality of life. In most cases, these housing developments fall short of meeting the demands of the people living there, especially when it comes to neighbourhood social interactions, planning policies, user comfort, building services and design principles.

Existing research has demonstrated that a mix of physical and social elements influences residential satisfaction, yet low-cost housing projects usually fail to meet expectations in these areas (Chen et al., 2023). Residents frequently express dissatisfaction with inadequate design features, limited access to urban facilities, and a lack of community cohesion (Chen et al., 2023). Furthermore, a recent study reveals that planning guidelines and design principles are frequently detached from the realities of residents' daily activities, leading to living environments that do not fully support their well-being (Riazi & Emami, 2018).

In the context of low-cost housing, where resources are scarce and the population is vulnerable, these shortcomings can have significant consequences. Dissatisfaction with living conditions can result in adverse impacts such as decreased quality of life, less social engagement, and even potential instability as people seek alternate housing solutions (Mohit et al., 2010). This gap in understanding and resolving the specific factors of residential satisfaction demonstrates the urgent need for more comprehensive and resident-centered approaches to low-cost housing design and policymaking (Kubisch et al., 2013).

With a focus on the impact of planning policy, design principles, user comfort, building services and social interactions, this study aims to explore the fundamental factors that lead to residential satisfaction in low-cost housing developments. By identifying and analyzing these determinants, the study seeks to give practical insights that will assist in guiding the development of more effective and satisfying low-cost housing solutions. The research objective is to investigate the residents' quality of life in relation with the building's condition.

## RESEARCH METHODOLOGY

### Research Approach

This study uses a quantitative survey method to collect data from residents of *Flat Tapak Maha* in Kuala Lumpur with regards to their living conditions, satisfaction levels, and community engagement. A structured questionnaire will be utilized to collect data from a stratified random sample of residents, ensuring representation from all demographic categories. This survey will include both closed-ended questions and Likert scale questions, and the data will be analyzed statistically to figure out the relationship between variables. The results will extend knowledge on the quality of life and community dynamics within the building, thus offering a better insight into the resident's experiences.

# FINDINGS

## Respondent Profile

The demographic profile is derived from a total of 172 respondents from Flat Tapak Maha in Kuala Lumpur. In terms of ethnicity, 97.7% of respondents identified as Malay, with Bumiputera and Indian ethnicities accounting for 1.2% of the total. Nearly all respondents, up to 98.8%, were citizens of Malaysia, with only 1.2% being non-citizens. In terms of households with children aged 18 and below, the result showed a total of 43% of respondents having one or two children under the age of 18, while 26.7% had three or four children. A sizable proportion, 29.1%, did not have children under 18, and only 1.2% had more than four children. In terms of household size, 55.8% of households had one or two persons, while 43% had two or more. Only 1.2% of respondents lived in larger households of 5 to 7 members. When it comes to home ownership, 75.6% of respondents are homeowners, while the remaining 24.4% are renters. The majority of respondents, which account for 76.7%, lived in three-bedroom homes, with 16.3% living in two-bedroom homes. A smaller percentage of people lived in homes with either one or four bedrooms, each at 3.5%.

## Descriptive Analysis

*Table 1. Factors influencing residential satisfaction in low-cost housing*

| Factors | Rank | Mean |
|---|---|---|
| Planning Policy | 1 | 2.78 |
| User Comfort | 2 | 2.02 |
| Design Principles | 3 | 1.92 |
| Building Services | 4 | 1.84 |
| Interaction with Neighbours | 5 | 1.76 |

The survey results show that Planning Policy is key to residential satisfaction, with the highest mean score (M = 2.78, SD = 1.25), emphasizing the importance of housing accessibility and proximity to urban services. This aligns with Riazi and Emami (2018), who found that access to essential amenities like workplaces and schools significantly influences satisfaction by reducing commuting costs and improving quality of life. It can improve the quality of life by giving residents easier access to services that meet their basic needs, ultimately contributing to higher levels of satisfaction (Riazi & Emami, 2018). Thus, urban planning strategies that prioritize the strategic location of housing developments with easy access to essential services are crucial for enhancing residential satisfaction.

User Comfort ranked second (M = 2.02, SD = 0.79), highlighting the importance of factors like lighting, temperature, and air quality, supported by Ellsworth-Krebs et al. (2018). Design Principles (M = 1.92, SD = 0.72) also matter, particularly regarding safety and privacy, as noted by Srirangam et al. (2022), who emphasized that well-designed spaces enhance comfort and safety.

Building Services (M = 1.84, SD = 0.68) ranked fourth, emphasizing the importance of maintaining utilities like water, electricity, and sewage. This supports Wimalasena et al. (2022), who stressed the need for reliable services to ensure health and safety, especially in low-cost housing. Lastly, Interaction with Neighbours (M = 1.76, SD = 0.63) was the least significant factor but still relevant. Riazi and Emami (2018) noted that while social interactions can enhance community cohesion, they may also lead to conflict in high-density areas with limited privacy.

## Residential Satisfaction

*Table 2. Residential satisfaction*

| Residential Satisfaction | Rank | Mean |
|---|---|---|
| Friendly interactions with neighbours in residential park areas | 1 | 2.72 |
| Trustworthy neighborhood community | 2 | 2.62 |
| Safe resident community | 3 | 2.43 |
| Frequently visiting neighbours | 4 | 2.35 |
| Babysitter - Sending children to a neighbour's house | 5 | 2.24 |
| Children playing together outside the house | 6 | 2.12 |
| Sufficient number of bedrooms | 7 | 1.71 |
| Availability of recreational park areas | 8 | 1.53 |

The ranking of residential satisfaction factors highlights the prominence of community-oriented elements such as friendly interactions with neighbors and a trustworthy neighborhood. This finding aligns with Riazi and Emami (2018), who stress that social interactions within low-cost housing can enhance community cohesion, positively influencing overall satisfaction. The survey results emphasize the importance of community-oriented factors in residential satisfaction, particularly friendly interactions with neighbours and a trustworthy neighbourhood. Trust and safety also play pivotal roles, as noted by Addo (2016), who linked a secure and cohesive community to heightened residential contentment. The lower ranking of factors like recreational parks suggests that while such amenities contribute to quality of life, they may not be prioritized as highly by residents in low-cost housing, likely due to more immediate concerns related to safety and neighbour relations.

## Planning Policy

*Table 3. Planning policy*

| Planning Policy | Rank | Mean |
|---|---|---|
| Distance from home to the city area | 1 | 2.98 |
| Distance to the workplace | 2 | 2.74 |
| Commuting cost to work | 3 | 2.58 |

Planning policies, particularly related to the distance from the city and workplace, hold the highest rank (M = 2.98). This is consistent with Riazi and Emami (2018), who identified proximity to urban centers as a significant determinant of satisfaction. Residents prefer shorter commutes, which directly reduces their transportation costs and enhances their quality of life. The emphasis on commuting expenses as a key factor is supported by Olfindo (2021), who emphasized the financial strain of long commutes. The data corroborates the view that accessible urban facilities significantly elevate residents' satisfaction, offering a broader understanding of how well-planned urban infrastructure can mitigate the cost of living and improve daily convenience.

## User Comfort

*Table 4. User comfort*

| User Comfort | Rank | Mean |
|---|---|---|
| Natural lighting rate inside the house | 1 | 2.14 |
| Odor comfort inside the house | 2 | 2.02 |
| Temperature comfort inside the house | 3 | 2.01 |
| Air quality inside the house | 3 | 2.01 |
| Airflow quality inside the house | 4 | 1.98 |
| Sound quality inside the house | 5 | 1.94 |

User comfort ranks second overall (M = 2.02), with natural lighting rated highest within this category. This underscores the importance of well-designed living environments, echoing Ellsworth-Krebs et al. (2018), who highlighted the positive psychological effects of natural lighting on residents. Furthermore, the ranking of odor and temperature comfort suggests that while these factors are integral to well-being, their impact is moderated by the structural limitations of low-cost housing, where ventilation and airflow issues are common (Wimalasena et al., 2022). This data supports the assertion that user comfort in low-cost housing goes beyond aesthetics, as it deeply influences residents' health and daily experience.

## Design Principles

*Table 5. Design principles*

| Design Principles | Rank | Mean |
|---|---|---|
| Number of housing units in each building | 1 | 2.40 |
| Safety inside the house | 2 | 2.33 |
| Each separate building block has a dividing space | 3 | 2.27 |
| Number of residents in each building | 4 | 2.26 |
| Safety of houses facing public open areas | 5 | 2.01 |
| Privacy in the residential environment | 6 | 1.98 |
| Availability of public open spaces | 7 | 1.95 |
| Safety level on staircases and corridor walkways | 8 | 1.92 |
| Lighting in open areas | 9 | 1.87 |
| Availability of seating area for adults in open park areas | 10 | 1.76 |
| Children's safety is guaranteed in open areas | 11 | 1.74 |
| Probability of car accidents involving children | 12 | 1.70 |
| Safety level in the car parking area | 12 | 1.70 |
| Safety of items placed outside the house | 13 | 1.67 |
| Suitable playground area for children | 14 | 1.65 |
| Elevator facilities | 15 | 1.51 |

Design principles such as the number of housing units in each building and safety inside the house ranked third (M = 1.92). Srirangam et al. (2022) emphasized that privacy and security are foundational to the design of sustainable housing environments. Overcrowded conditions, often associated with high-density units, reduce privacy and elevate noise levels, leading to dissatisfaction (Castells, 2020). The data reveals that while public amenities like playgrounds are appreciated, they are secondary to concerns about safety and privacy. This indicates a need for low-cost housing designs that prioritize personal security and space, aligning with Carmona (2021), who argued for reducing density in housing complexes to enhance satisfaction.

## Building Services

*Table 6. Building services*

| Building Services | Rank | Mean |
|---|---|---|
| Maintenance of water supply and storage | 1 | 2.10 |
| Maintenance of electrical wiring system | 2 | 2.01 |
| Maintenance of sewage drainage system | 3 | 1.90 |
| Waste disposal and recycling facilities | 4 | 1.86 |
| Sanitation system facilities | 5 | 1.71 |
| Maintenance of stormwater and sewage disposal system | 6 | 1.66 |
| Maintenance of fire alarm and sprinkler system | 7 | 1.63 |

Building services, including water supply maintenance and electrical wiring, are critical to resident satisfaction, ranking fourth overall (M = 1.84). The findings corroborate Wimalasena et al. (2022), who identified reliable utilities as essential for health and safety in low-cost housing. The data suggests that consistent water supply is paramount, as it directly affects hygiene and daily living standards. While sewage systems and waste management rank lower, they are nonetheless vital, as their poor maintenance can lead to significant discomfort and health risks. This points to the necessity of investing in the regular upkeep of building services to ensure long-term satisfaction in low-cost housing environments.

## Interaction with Neighbors

*Table 7. Interaction with neighbors*

| Interaction with Neighbors | Rank | Mean |
|---|---|---|
| Noise from residents moving up and down the stairs | 1 | 2.00 |
| Noise from children playing in open areas or playgrounds | 2 | 1.80 |
| Level of conflict among residents | 3 | 1.71 |
| Moral behaviour of residents | 4 | 1.70 |
| Residents' commitment to paying monthly fees | 5 | 1.59 |

Interactions with neighbors, while the lowest-ranked category (M = 1.76), still play a notable role in residential satisfaction. Riazi and Emami (2018) observed that neighborly relations in densely populated areas can either foster community cohesion or lead to conflict. The data from this study confirms that noise—whether from neighbors or children playing—is a common source of dissatisfaction, particularly in settings where sound insulation is inadequate. However, positive interactions, such as collaborative efforts in maintaining shared spaces, can improve the living environment. This suggests that managing noise levels and promoting cooperative behaviors are crucial for mitigating conflict and enhancing residential satisfaction in high-density housing.

## CONCLUSION

In conclusion, this study has identified planning policies as the most significant factor influencing residential satisfaction in low-cost housing, largely due to their impact on accessibility, affordability, and proximity to essential services, which directly affect commuting costs and convenience. User comfort, including factors like natural lighting and air quality, ranked second, highlighting the importance of daily living conditions. Design principles, such as privacy and safety, also play a critical role, contributing to residents' sense of security. Social interactions within the community can both positively and negatively impact satisfaction, with effective management fostering harmony. Lastly, building services, such as reliable water supply and waste management, are essential for maintaining functional, healthy living environments. Overall, enhancing residential satisfaction requires a comprehensive approach that addresses both the physical and social dimensions of low-cost housing, ensuring that developments meet the diverse needs of their residents.

## ACKNOWLEDGMENT

The researchers of this article would like to appreciate the journal's editors and the anonymous reviewers for their positive feedback and suggestions for the improvement of this journal.

This research received no specific grant from any funding agency in the public, commercial, or not-for-profit sectors.

## REFERENCES

Addo, I. A. (2016). Assessing residential satisfaction among low income households in multi-habited dwellings in selected low income communities in Accra. *Urban Studies (Edinburgh, Scotland)*, *53*(4), 631–650. DOI: 10.1177/0042098015571055

Carmona, M. (2021). *Public places urban spaces: The dimensions of urban design.* Routledge. DOI: 10.4324/9781315158457

Castells, M. (2020). *Space of flows, space of places: Materials for a theory of urbanism in the information age. In the City Reader.* Routledge.

Chen, T., Luh, D.-B., Hu, L., & Shan, Q. (2023). Exploring Factors Affecting Residential Satisfaction in Old Neighborhoods and Sustainable Design Strategies Based on Post-Occupancy Evaluation. *Sustainability (Basel)*, *15*(21), 15213–15213. DOI: 10.3390/su152115213

Chohan, A. H., Che-Ani, A. I., Shar, B. K., Awad, J., Jawaid, A., & Tawil, N. M. (2015). A model of housing quality determinants (HQD) for affordable housing. *Journal of Construction in Developing Countries*, *20*(1), 117.

Dwijendra, N. K. A. (2013). Quality of affordable housing projects by public and private developers in Indonesia: The case of Sarbagita Metropolitan Bali. *Journal of Geography and Regional Planning*, *6*(3), 69–81. DOI: 10.5897/JGRP12.050

Ellsworth-Krebs, K., Reid, L., & Hunter, C. J. (2018). Integrated framework of home comfort: Relaxation, companionship and control. *Building Research and Information*, *47*(2), 202–218. DOI: 10.1080/09613218.2017.1410375

Hongisto, V., Mäkilä, M., & Suokas, M. (2015). Satisfaction with sound insulation in residential dwellings – The effect of wall construction. *Building and Environment*, *85*, 309–320. DOI: 10.1016/j.buildenv.2014.12.010

Ibem, E. O., Ayo-Vaughan, E. A., Oluwunmi, A. O., & Alagbe, O. A. (2018). Residential Satisfaction Among Low-Income Earners in Government Subsidized Housing Estates in Ogun State, Nigeria. *Urban Forum, 30*(1), 75–96.

Karn, R., Bhandari, B., & Jha, N. (2012). Original Article Practices of Personal Hygiene and Sanitation in a village. *Journal of Nobel Medical College, 1*(2). Advance online publication. DOI: 10.3126/jonmc.v1i2.7298

Kubisch, A. C., Auspos, P., Taylor, S., & Dewar, T. (2013). Resident-Centered Community Building: What Makes It Different? *National Civic Review, 102*(3), 61–71. DOI: 10.1002/ncr.21128

Lokhande, P. (2016). Garbage Collection Management System. *International Journal of Engineering and Computer Science, 5*(11).

Mohit, M. A., Ibrahim, M., & Rashid, Y. R. (2010). Assessment of residential satisfaction in newly designed public low-cost housing in Kuala Lumpur, Malaysia. *Habitat International, 34*(1), 18–27. DOI: 10.1016/j.habitatint.2009.04.002

Olfindo, R. (2021). Transport accessibility, residential satisfaction, and moving intention in a context of limited travel mode choice. *Transportation Research Part A, Policy and Practice, 145*, 153–166. DOI: 10.1016/j.tra.2021.01.012

Riazi, M., & Emami, A. (2018). Residential satisfaction in affordable housing: A mixed method study. *Cities (London, England), 82*, 1–9. DOI: 10.1016/j.cities.2018.04.013

Srirangam, S., Chun, L. W., Mari, T. S., & Gunasagaran, S. (2022). *CHILDREN'S SAFETY: THE COMMON SPACES IN PPR HOUSING IN KUALA LUMPUR.*

Thomas, M. A. (2017). On The Benefits of Affordable Housing. *Table de Quartier Sud de L'Ouest-De-L'Île.*

Wimalasena, N. N., Chang-Richards, A., Wang, K. I. K., & Dirks, K. (2022). Housing quality indicators. *Systematic Reviews.*

Yap, J. B. H., & Ng, X. H. (2018). Yap, J. B. H., & Ng, X. H. (2018). Housing affordability in Malaysia: Perception, price range, influencing factors and policies. *International Journal of Housing Markets and Analysis, 11*(3), 476–497. DOI: 10.1108/IJHMA-08-2017-0069

## KEY TERMS AND DEFINITIONS

**Satisfaction:** A feeling of contentment, fulfillment, or pleasure that comes from achieving something desired or from a situation that meets one's expectations

**Planning:** The process of organizing and making decisions about how land, resources, and development should be used or managed in a specific area, often guided by rules and regulations

**Design:** The process of creating a plan or blueprint for a product, structure, or system, guided by fundamental rules or guidelines that ensure functionality, aesthetics, and usability

**Social:** Environments, products, or systems that encourage or facilitate communication, connection, and interaction between people

**Comfort:** Environments, products, or systems that prioritize the physical and mental well-being of the user, ensuring ease, relaxation, and a pleasant experience

**Services:** Systems and infrastructure within a building that support its functionality, such as heating, ventilation, air conditioning (HVAC), plumbing, electrical systems, and lighting

# Chapter 5
# Home Smart Home:
## Digital Transformation and Sustainability Through the Implementation of Smart Cities

**Aqilah Yaacob**
https://orcid.org/0000-0002-4287-1977
*Taylor's University, Malaysia*

**Jen Ling Gan**
https://orcid.org/0000-0002-1684-1440
*Taylor's University, Malaysia*

**Kim Leng Khoo**
https://orcid.org/0000-0002-0329-1451
*Taylor's University, Malaysia*

## ABSTRACT

*United Nations predicts that 70% of the world's population will be living in urban areas by 2050. Malaysia is among the developing countries hopping on this bandwagon by realizing the nation's digitalization agenda towards Malaysia's smart city journey. Currently, Malaysia's smart city plans focus on two major areas: transport issues and cashless payments. However, there are more areas to be further developed in the smart city plans. To ensure Malaysia is ready, research into consumer behavior is needed. This is aligned with the 12th Malaysian Plan on digital transformation; Shared Prosperity Vision 2030; and fulfillment of SDG9. Nevertheless, empirical studies on factors influencing Malaysia's intention to purchase homes in smart cities are scarce. The current study conducts qualitative study of 20 in-depth interviews among diverse individuals in Malaysia. Findings from the major themes point to five main factors including security and privacy; environmental initiatives; digital*

DOI: 10.4018/979-8-3373-0390-1.ch005

*infrastructures and smart mobility; digital literacy and knowledge expectancy; and price value.*

## 1.0 INTRODUCTION

Although four of the 26 sites of the U.S.-ASEAN Smart City Network (ASCN) involved four cities in Malaysia (i.e., Kuala Lumpur, Kota Kinabalu, Kuching, and Johor Baharu), Malaysia still ranked at the bottom of the ladder when it comes to smart cities. As of 2019, the Norwegian capital of Oslo is the 'smartest' of smart cities in which the country performs well in terms of their smart parking mobility, blockchain ecosystem and smart technologies (Marsal-Llacuna, 2020; Statista.com, 2019, 2021). The question comes to mind regarding consumer preferences and intention to purchase homes in Malaysia's smart cities, in which this research aims to explore. This is because there is a lack of empirical research investigating the factors influencing Malaysian intention to purchase homes in smart cities.

There is a need for more research to explore the relevance of smart cities among Malaysians as there is an upward trend of smart city initiative investment worldwide from 2018 to 2023 (e.g., the actual spending of $81 billion and $104.3 billion in 2018 and 2019). These figures are evidence of investor confidence on smart city development and the high market revenue associated with it. Smart city initiative investment is one thing (top-down approach), but on the other hand, will the new home buyers Malaysia (bottom-up approach) be interested in purchasing their first home in smart cities remain unanswered.

Even though there are few studies pertaining to smart cities, most of it are related to hearing aids in the smart cities (Chang et al., 220); smartcard technology (Belanche-Gracia et al., 2015); smart home energy technology (Ji and Chan, 2019); technology sensor (Terziradeva, 2018); smart mobility (Leow and Krishnaswamy, 2021) and eco-friendly smart home services (Zhang and Liu, 2022). Currently, there is no study on the factors influencing the intention to purchase a home in smart cities. This is the substantial gap in which the current study will address.

The role of digital marketing initiatives in promoting smart cities homes to Malaysia is another avenue worth exploring. The result from this research will provide substantial evidence and overview on how the new digital marketing would ensure marketability of the smart cities development in Malaysia. In the era of Marketing 5.0 and heavy use of social media, the application of digital based promotional media in influencing purchase intention of smart city homes remains unexplored. Although there are several scholars examining the impact of digital marketing on online purchase intention, this type of research is done in the context of e-commerce and low-value products as compared to home purchases (e.g., Dastane, 2020; Jiménez-Castillo and Sánchez-Fernández, 2019; Erlangga, 2021; Vidhya, 2021; Savitri et al., 2022).

In regard to risks associated with technologies and environmental aspects of smart cities, previous research has investigated the issues related to third party risks and cybersecurity in smart cities (Vitunskaite et al., 2019). Additionally, past scholars investigate the risks pertaining to smart technologies such as user security and privacy (Vitunskaite et al., 2019) and cybersecurity of intelligent transportation (Li et al., 2016). However, the literature is limited, if not non-existent on the relationship between secure digital credentials and the intention to purchase a home in smart cities. Therefore, making it difficult for smart city developers to comprehend the role of digital credential in minimizing the risk exposure in developing smart cities.

Besides the role of security and privacy, this study explores other factors pertaining to environmental initiatives, digital infrastructures, smart mobility and advanced technology, digital literacy and knowledge expectancy and price value in influencing Malaysian consumers' intention to purchase a home in smart cities. The current study targets this gap and addresses it by examining the relationship between these variables. Therefore, we would like to address the following research question (RQ) and research objective (RO):

RQ - What are the main factors in influencing Malaysia's intention to purchase homes in smart cities?

RO - To explore the main factors in influencing Malaysia's intention to purchase homes in smart cities through qualitative research.

These research questions and research objectives are important to address the existing research gaps as research on smart cities in developing countries can help address urbanization challenges, improve access to technology, learn from local contexts, promote sustainability, and drive economic growth. This study utilizes qualitative study (i.e., 20 in-depth interviews among diverse individuals in Malaysia). This study on smart cities can contribute to advancing knowledge in the field. This can include developing new theoretical frameworks, identifying best practices, and exploring new avenues for research. The findings of this research can also provide insights into the impact of policy decisions on the implementation and success of smart city solutions.

## 2.0 LITERATURE REVIEW

### 2.1 Overview of Smart Cities Development

More than 4.3 billion people, or 55% of the global population, reside in urban settings. It is estimated 60% of the global population will be living in the cities by 2050 (United Nations Environment Program, 2018). The data shows that 2.4 billion people are expected to be added in the existing urban environments which leads to the continuous expansion of city expansion. Consequently, it is estimated that global material consumption will increase to nearly 90 billion tons by 2050 (United Nations Environment Program, 2018). The utilization of resources consumption, the rising populations, the rapid growth of urbanization lead to deterioration of quality of life and challenges. These challenges include air quality deterioration, traffic congestion, scarce resources, and poor waste management which exacerbate human health and well-being (Washburn et al. 2009). As a response to these challenges, the notion of "smart cities" emerged as one of the potential solutions.

Global smart cities market is expected to reach USD 2.8 trillion by 2027 (ReportLinker, 2022). The development of smart city projects has been gaining worldwide attention and many countries such as Singapore have adjusted their policies to promote the development of smart cities. The World Cities Report reported that "every region is expected to become more urbanized in the next 10 years, although highly urbanized areas are expected to slow their rate of urban growth. Ninety-six per cent of urban growth will occur in the less developed regions of East Asia, South Asia, and Africa with three countries—India, China and Nigeria—accounting for 35 per cent of the total increase in global urban population from 2018 to 2050." (United Nation Habitat, 2020, p. xvi).

Smart cities are perceived as new urban utopias (Datta, 2015). According to ITU (2016), a smart sustainable city uses technological infrastructure to improve residents' quality of life, urban operation efficiency, and competitiveness. It is a city that practices sustainable operations to meet the growing urbanization needs of present and future generations with respect to social, environmental, economic, and cultural. The term "sustainability" has become a predominantly important concept since the 1980s (Silva, Khan, & Han, 2018). The concept of sustainability plays a major role and gained prevalent attention on the smart city development. As one of the key aspects of smart cities is digital innovation, the concept of smart city can be defined as "initiatives or approaches that effectively leverage digitalization to boost citizen well-being and deliver more efficient, sustainable and inclusive urban services and environments as part of a collaborative, multi-stakeholder process" (OECD, n.d., p. 1).

According to Khatoun and Zeadally (2016), a smart city model comprises of six components (as shown in Figure 1), namely, (1) smart governance, (2) smart people, (3) smart living, (4) smart environment, (5) smart mobility, and (6) smart economy.

*Figure 1. Smart city model*

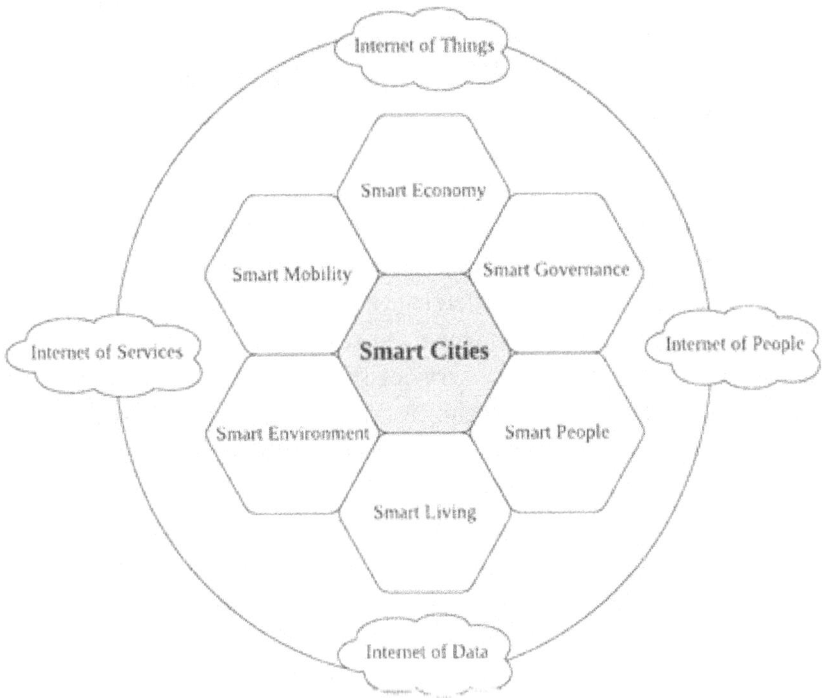


*Adapted from Khatoun and Zeadally (2016, p. 48)*

To date, a majority of literature focuses on smart cities and their features, such as information systems (Ismagilova, Hughes, Dwivedi, & Raman, 2019), features (Silva, Khan, & Han, 2018), and management (Heidar, Navimpour, & Unal, 2022). This indicates that research on smart cities mainly focuses on the role of technology and its infrastructure that promote sustainable urbanization. Much uncertainty still exists about the relationship between smart cities and consumer behavior. It is also important to note that conception of smart cities could only be accomplished with the existence of residents. The basic unit of smart cities is smart homes, and it plays an important role in city development (Obaidat & Nicopolitidis, 2016).

## 2.2 Smart Cities in Malaysia

Smart Cities is an important initiative that incorporates various leading industry sectors (e.g., ICT, GreenTech, Smart Grid, Transportation, Infrastructure) and touches on key policy issues (e.g., 5G, cybersecurity, renewable energy) currently being discussed in the private and public sectors. The 3 main pillars of Smart Cities include a) smart and sustainable solutions (clean environment, environment protection, green infrastructure, and development); b) smart planning (innovative economic growth and value creation, efficient public and social services, private public partnership, transparent governance); and c) smart infrastructure and technologies (availability of ICT infrastructure, efficient road accessibility, entrepreneurship).

A smart city, also known as a digital or informed city, utilizes information and communication technology to sense, analyze and integrate key information of core management systems in running cities (Su et al., 2011). A smart city is characterized by its intelligent response to different needs, such as industrial and commercial activities, daily interactions of citizens and resources, livelihood, public safety, environmental protection, and city services (Kummitha, 2020; Lee et al., 2014). Accordingly, a smart city has smart citizens, smart technologies, smart governance, smart transportation, smart infrastructure management and many other smart aspects to assist holistic city management (Ahad et al., 2020; Westraadt and Calitz, 2020).

Currently, there are 26 pilot cities in the U.S.-ASEAN Smart City Network (ASCN) and 4 of the 26 sites are in Malaysia (Kuala Lumpur, Kota Kinabalu, Kuching, and Johor Baharu). Other Smart Cities in Malaysia are in Selangor (Smart Selangor Blueprint), Cyberjaya and Putrajaya (Malaysia's first cities to be presented with 5G technology), Melaka (Smart metering for electricity monitoring and the state government set up a Smart City Advisory Council for Smart City policies in that state) and Penang (Smart City Blueprint for Penang by year 2022).

## 2.3 Smart Homes and Consumer Behavior

Alam, Reaz, & Ali (2012, p. 1) defined smart homes as "a branch of ubiquitous computing that involves incorporating smartness into dwellings for comfort, healthcare, safety, security, and energy conservation". According to Shin, Park, and Lee (2018), smart home acceptance has been lower than expected and more research on smart homes from the perspective of the consumer is needed. Despite the growing demand for smart home systems, the penetration rate of smart homes is expected to reach only 21.09% at $182,442.7m in 2025 (Statista, 2021).

As the expansion of smart cities relies heavily on smart homes (Obaidat & Nicopolitidis, 2016), more attention should be paid in understanding the factors that influence consumers' smart homes purchase intention. However, most of the studies undertaken so far provide limited insights on purchase intention. For example, Zhuang, Zhu, Huang, & Pan (2021) conducted a study to determine the influence mechanism of corporate social responsibility (CSR) for smart cities on consumers' purchase intention and the results showed that CSR for smart cities has a positive impact on consumers' purchase intention. Following the research gap aforementioned, Table 1 summarizes the past studies of factors influencing the decision of consumers in purchasing or using smart homes.

*Table 1. Summary of past studies in relation to smart homes*

| Elements | Model/Theory | Factors | Methodology | Source |
|---|---|---|---|---|
| Adoption and diffusion of smart homes | Technology acceptance model | Compatibility, privacy, perceived ease of use | Survey | Shin & Lee (2018); Nikou (2019) |
| Purchase intention of smart home objects | Technology acceptance model | Environmental concern, environmental beliefs, perceived usefulness for the environment, | Intercept survey | Schill, Godefroit-Winkel, Diallo, & Barbarossa (2019) |
| Acceptance and use of smart home | Unified theory of acceptance and use of technology (UTAUT2) | Performance expectancy, effort expectancy, social influence, hedonic motivation, price value, trust and security risk | Survey | Aldossari & Sidorova (2020) |
| Acceptance of smart home technologies | Technology acceptance model, innovation diffusion theory, and | Perceived usefulness, perceived ease of use, compatibility, trialability, result demonstrability, visibility, perceived risk security, perceived risk performance, and perceived risk time | Online survey | Hubert, Blut, Brock, Zhang, Koch, & Riedl (2018) |
| Acceptance and usage of smart homes | Technology acceptance model | Attitudes, awareness towards smart homes, perceived ease of use, perceived enjoyment, perceived risks, trust, and perceived usefulness | Online self-administered survey | Shuhaiber & Mashal (2019) |

Based on the table above, it can be concluded that most of the studies focus on the adoption and acceptance of smart home products. The factors influencing the intention of consumers in purchasing smart homes have remained unclear. Therefore, these studies suggest that there is a need to investigate the factors influencing purchase intention of smart homes in a more comprehensive view.

## 2.4 The Role of Digital Marketing, Digital Infrastructure, Secure Digital Credential

There are many studies which highlight the importance of digital marketing in influencing consumer's purchase intention. For example, Erlangga (2021) found a significant influence of digital marketing and social media on purchase intention of SMEs food products. Similarly, authors such as Dasrane (2020); Nawaz and Kaldeen (2020); Wibisurya (2018) acknowledged the positive impact of digital marketing on online purchase intention. However, there is no empirical study on the influence of digital marketing in fostering consumer intention to purchase homes in smart cities, which this study aims to address. Providing empirical evidence on this relationship is important for companies and developers in understanding what kind of marketing tools work effectively in encouraging favorable responses from the current homeowners and potential home buyers.

Besides the role that digital marketing plays in promoting the intention to purchase homes in smart cities, it is also vital for continuous development of the digital infrastructure in smart city planning. For example, in South Korea, they integrated various technologies such as Songdo's central pneumatic waste disposal system (automatically collects rubbish to recycle, bury, incinerate, or convert to energy); Cheonggyecheon Stream Restoration (adopts ICT and sensors to control the water level and water quality); and Seoul's Bus Management System (integrated control center that monitors operations in real-time). Similarly, if developer in Malaysia where to build smart cities, they must continuously innovate the digital infrastructure by utilizing latest technology (e.g., IoT, 5G, sensor technology, 4D printing, advanced intelligent system, blockchain, etc.) as this will influence Malaysian' positive intention towards home in smart cities.

In order to build a trusted digital environment, a secure digital credential is needed in fostering trust which subsequently leads to favorable intentions towards home in smart cities. For example, in Singapore, the country established Singapore's National Digital Identity (NDI) platform that provides authentication, authorization and consent that provide citizens a single digital identity to do transactions. This allows private and public sectors to develop value-added services on a common and universal trusted framework. This research argues that the development of cybersecurity and encryption is vital to protect information and communication systems in mitigating the risks related to malicious attack, digital hijacking, and unauthorized access to home buyers' data. This is because smart cities are confronted by technological and external risks making their governance difficult and susceptible to manipulation (Ullah et al., 2021). Therefore, this research believes that the role of secure digital credential is significant in influencing the intention to purchase homes in smart cities.

## 3.0 METHODOLOGY

In order to achieve the research objectives, the current study employed an exploratory study to identify the emerging themes using the interpretive and theory-building approach of face-to-face semi-structured in-depth interviews. The interviews last approximately between 60-90 minutes guided by a discussion guide with 20 individuals living in Malaysia (i.e., current homeowner and potential home buyers). The study adopts an interpretive approach gathering in-depth insights into multiple ways in which individuals understand the world around them and react to it (e.g., Denzin and Lincoln, 1994). As per prior research, we approached and recruited informants who are interested in sharing their opinion on the subject matter which include diverse participants from different demographic backgrounds. The epistemological position is interpretivism; participants had the maximum scope to talk freely and give meanings to their home buying experiences (Bryman, 2008). The researcher adopted this method to understand their home purchase intentions in depth and generate respondents' original insights (Belk et al., 1988; Creswell, 2014), as well as because it allowed the theories to emerge from data (Bryman, 2008). From this first phase, a conceptual framework of Malaysia's behavioral intentions to purchase homes in smart cities will be developed from the emerging themes, which were then tested in the second phase.

The authors consult literature in relation to smart cities to develop a discussion guide which includes a set of open-ended questions pertaining to the intention to purchase a home in a smart city (e.g., What is your definition of a "smart city"?; How would you describe an ideal home in a smart city?; What are the factors that would influence you to purchase a home in a smart city?; What can demotivate you from buying a house in a smart city?; Do you have the intention to live in a smart city? If yes, why, if not, why?). Given the open-ended and exploratory nature of these questions, participants are able to express their views in depth.

One of the authors and research assistant (a female and male trained in conducting in-depth interviews) conducts semi-structured interviews in English. Participants obtain a briefing about the general purpose of the research as well as seeking informants' consent prior to the interview. Anonymity is guaranteed and protected in order to aid more open discussion. We assure you that participation is voluntary and that they can withdraw at any moment or ignore any specific question without telling any reason. We also inform them that the data collected serves for academic research purposes only. We do not ask and record any personal details. Individual interviews last approximately between 40 and 60 min. All interviews are tape recorded and transcribed with the written consent of participants (McCracken, 1988).

## 4.0 FINDINGS

We organize our findings by highlighting the main factors influencing the informants' intention to purchase a home in a smart city. We illustrate the common and major themes using short cases that situate the participants and their purchase intentions in their specific contexts. Figure 2 demonstrates the major themes on factors influencing informants' intention to purchase a home in a smart city.

*Figure 2. Major themes on factors influencing the intention to purchase a home in a smart city.*

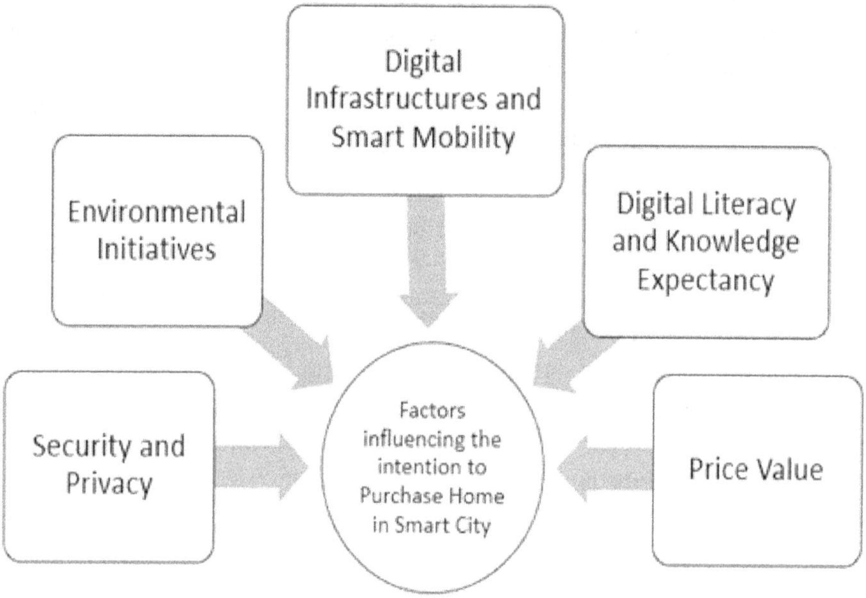


## 4.1 Security and Privacy

Informants express their concerns in regard to safety, security and privacy, as well as perceived risk of information. The majority of the informants mentioned that the factors that influence them to have the intention to purchase a home in a smart city are pertaining to 'Security and Privacy'. For example, Theodora mentioned that with technology implemented in smart cities, her concern is always in regard to data security and privacy, as well as technology breakdown when she expressed the following: "*These days, whatever you touch, information will leak easily, so my concern will be the privacy of data, and the rise of scammers. Scammers are getting smarter, along with the smart city, but my concern would be more of my parents. You know, they might not be aware of the current situation. Oh, and another concern, if there's electricity problem or line issues, like I heard somewhere where I think from the Internet, where this person got locked out, because the door could not detect face, I think that this person just went to the dentist, and the face, you know got swollen a bit, and the door could not detect. So, you know these are some of the complications that raised a lot of concerns to me. For me to purchase the next house, safety and security. It needs to be provided by the developer.*" Eliza and Mira echo similar perspectives when they mentioned "*...when we talk about technology, we talk about safety, and that is a good home*" and "*...security is important as if it is a very advanced technology, there might be problems with security, like, what if the system is being hacked, or things like that.*"

Perceptions shared by the informants demonstrate that they believe that the information of the residents should not be disclosed to unwanted authorities or personnel. For example, citizens' images, voice, etc. should not be distributed without the consent of that citizen to some other unwanted person or authority. Informants also echoed that they believe that confidentialities of information of the residents should remain protected and the security aspect of the IT-enabled system should not be compromised under any circumstances. The majority of the informants also share their concern in regard to the perceived threat of data stolen from the IT system and residents should be adequately trained and aware of how to use the IT services safely and securely. For example, Sumaira expressed the following: "*I think safety is my main concern and the main factor influencing me to purchase a home in a smart city is security. It should be a secured one, especially when using all the technologies such as the use of facial recognition, etc.'* She also mentioned that she is skeptical of the security even when it comes to smartphones, due to the increase of scammers when she shared her personal experiences: "*these scammers managed to get access to my phone including the internet banking and get you to download all the files. In terms of homes in smart cities, they might not be able to break into the technology system of your house but might be able to get into your neighbors' house systems*". Similarly, Kendal commented "*Do I have the intention to live in a smart city? Why not? We wish that we can stay in a place where there's safety and security. My children are all overseas, so we want to visit them, and we want to be assured that our house is safe during the time that we are away. We can consider living in a smart home if security and safety are assured. If the city can provide a safe and secure environment, then I am sure that I would be confident to live in a smart city. With the use of technology, the developers must ensure that our personal data is being protected.*

Like Yazeed and Jun Jie, they also echoed similar beliefs that safety and security of the neighborhood is very important in which both said that a good home in a smart city should be safe and secure from threat. While Coco expressed that "*I believe that many people are studying IT and many hackers out there and I believe that a smart city is a city that shares information, so the security must be transparent and safe.*" As for Xing Zhe, she mentioned that "*factors influencing me to purchase a home in a smart city is security, if it can introduce the use of high-tech security systems such as face recognition that can improve the current system such as using physical lock. For me, I think that a good home needs to have a good security system. Umm, smart cities basically depend on technology and the internet, so if the security system for the technology is not well, then our information will be leaked out, so I think that is one of the main points that I might not consider buying a house in a smart city. Because they are too reliant on technology. So, in case there is no electricity, and the security system is hacked, then quite dangerous for us. Too reliant on technology might cause problems such as data being leaked out*". Azly also commented that "*the level of security should be good when it comes to homes in smart cities and the developer should show us that they have implemented it accordingly. So that our confidence level would be higher, such as following the PDPA act and proving that they have done a good job in securing our data.*"

## 4.2 Environmental Initiatives

When it comes to factors influencing informants to purchase a home in a smart city, most of the informants discuss the importance of environmentally friendly initiatives, green technology and sustainability efforts such as greenery effort, solar panels, and rainwater harvesting. Informants express the importance of employing environmental management practices in smart cities in order to support pollution reduction, provide environmental protection such as provision of sewerage and wastewater treatment, as well as adhere to the green practices including recycling of solid waste and promote sustainable resource management. For example, Theodora narrates the following: "*A little bit about myself, I don't like wastage, in terms of electricity such as lights and air conditioner. I would also like to segregate my garbage; therefore, the housing area should take into consideration environmental initiatives such as energy saving systems and waste segregation systems, the reasons would influence me to have a home in a smart city.*" Similarly, Sumaira believes that homes in smart cities should move towards sustainability and green energy as she mentioned "*those are the things that form my idea of what a smart city should look like.*"

As for Yi Chun, he believes that smart cities should be able to reduce electricity by introducing solar panels or generating heat for our water heater and others. In a similar vein, Devan elaborates: "*factors that would influence me to purchase a home in a smart city would be how the energy and water are being used as well as the waste management system. For example, in Singapore, they have a very good system in which they conserve energy and have a proper water and waste management system that are good for the environment.*" Like Sanjana, he believes that "*an ideal home for me would be a city that can overcome sound and air pollution, the use of solar panels especially in Malaysia, we are such a hot country, we can do something with solar energy and not just depending on electricity. I believe that solar panels now are so cheap and should be incorporated into all the houses, especially in homes in smart cities. Homes in smart cities should use rainwater harvesting and ensure the construction materials used are environmentally friendly and source them sustainably. The entire supply chain and development of the smart city should be developed in a sustainable manner. The smart city should focus on the energy, water, having some sort of greenery where people can plant something on their own in order to encourage people to be self-sustaining, I think these are the important criteria that the smart city should be focusing on rather than just building more concrete blocks one after another.*'

Yazeed also expresses his intention to stay in a home in a smart city if the city promotes sustainability, is good for the environment and reduces pollution. For example, having an eco-friendly transportation system and green area for the residents. He continues to express the following: "*overall having a clean and green environment surrounding the area as well as equipped with facilities, infrastructures and transportation that are good for the environment. For example, introducing trams instead of just cars that are polluting the city as well as green surroundings such as trekking and playground areas would be great.*"

## 4.3 Digital Infrastructures, Smart Mobility and Advance Technology

As for the third theme, informants narrate their belief on the important role of digital infrastructures, smart mobility, and advanced technology in influencing their intention to purchase a home in a smart city. For example, most of the respondents believe that smart cities should be equipped with IT resources and infrastructure, technology advancement, automation technology, and strong network connections. They believe that there should be sufficient IT infrastructure to support smart city implementation and maintenance as well as sufficient IT expertise to implement the smart city program. Informants also repeatedly mention the importance of smart mobility in which they believe that smart cities should provide innovative and safe transportation systems; offer better traffic management and parking systems, as well as offering bicycle tracks and unobstructed footpaths. Moreover, they also express their expectation that a smart city should offer connectivity of ICT infrastructure, as well as providing efficient internet usage and coverage including public internet access and Wi-Fi hotspots, in which all these efforts could lead to perceived convenience and efficiency to improve their quality of life.

For instance, Eliza speaks extensively on the important role of technology when she stated: "*factors that would influence me to purchase a home in a smart city is when the house has advanced technology such as using our gestures or phone to switch on the lighting. When we talk about smart cities, it means technology. So, I think smart cities can be referred to as advanced technology for a city. I love technology and I love everything that will ease me more, for example, smart systems, cashless systems, electric cars, everything that is sustainable. With all these reasons, I will choose to live in a smart city*.' In a similar vein, Mira believes that her home should have a smart house system and internet-connected home, for example implementing technology that can control everything about her home by just using a smartphone.'

Devan speaks on his opinion on this theme by narrating the following: "I*n my opinion, a smart city is probably something very different from what we are living now, especially in terms of technological advancement, efficiency and environmentally friendly. In an ideal home in a smart city, everything is being done in a very smart way. From the place that we are living, to the place that we are heading to. For example, if we are commuting from our home to the office, in a smart city, the travel time should be very efficient. Because with the smart city capability, we are able to predict what the traveling time required for us to travel, or even the waiting time for public transport. The information must be tip top, so that we can have it in our fingertips. The use of mobile apps to pay the bills, to find an effective transportation solution and assess the energy consumption at home, and all the information is being synchronized."* As for Sanjana, he suggested that the factors that would influence him to live in a smart city is the internet connection and good mobile connections such as 5G, in which he believes that smart cities should also ensure that the power and water supply are always sufficient.

Participant such as Kendall extensively shares about the important of technology in which she stated *"factors that would influence me to purchase a home in a smart city are related to the elderly point of view, for example, elderly may be prone to accidents, maybe there should be technology to detect a person who is in danger of falling, that would be a good smart home. Smart cities should also overcome traffic problems as well as the use of electric vehicles and charging stations.'* As for Belize, she believes that the smart city should be equipped with advanced technology in which everything can be controlled using our fingertips, and the transport should be digitized as well as the use of e-retailing.' In a similar vein, Azly mentioned that the factors that would influence him to purchase a home in a smart city are related to the transportation system: *"the transportation must be very well connected. The smart city should also have a good digital infrastructure for utilities, especially for telecommunication, electricity, and water. My ideal home in a smart city should be technologically based as well as devices that are all well connected. Other than that, is having smart meters, smart devices, home appliances that are connected. Certain billboards should use smart technologies and digital devices to inform the residents.*

Yi Chun also echoed a similar perspective when he shared that *'a smart city should have technology that can improve my current life as well as having a strong internet connection.'* Whilst Coco expresses that *'factors that would influence me to purchase a home in a smart city is the technology being used such as keyless doors, robotics or technology for house cleaning as well as fully automated systems. For example, we can just use our sound to control the temperature of the waters and everything. It should be high tech. I expect the smart house can also look after my pets. Besides that, having a smart paying system such as using face recognition or thumbprint.'*

## 4.4 Digital Literacy and Knowledge Expectancy

Participants talk at length about the important role of digital literacy and knowledge expectancy when it comes to the factors that would influence them to purchase a home in a smart city. Informants narrates the technological and digital knowledge are important if they were to live in smart city in which they should find it easy to use and set up a smart home and its connected services, as well as needing to find it easy to become skillful at using any of the smart home infrastructure, its connected services, and digital facilities. For instance, Jun Jie believes that homes in smart cities should be as user friendly and as straightforward as possible for the user.

As for Jessy, she expresses the following concern: *"I don't think I will buy a smart city house because I am a senior citizen. I don't think all this technology is necessary for me. Of course, I want to upgrade myself and my life but not regarding high technology. Buying a house in this high technology city is not necessary for me. I prefer a normal house in a normal environment. If I live in a smart city I need to think about a lot of new things and I need to learn a lot of things. Now you can teach me, and I can remember, but maybe tomorrow or the day after, I will forget everything. Then I got to ask you again, and you will feel fed up teaching the old lady. I don't really want to spend so much effort to learn all that high technology. Even for my husband, he is not willing to learn. He's worse than me. So, I don't think I will buy it, but I am interested in paying a visit."*

Like Devan, he believes that people who are living in smart cities should be equipped with technological knowledge, in which he commented *"these people need to have the digital literacy, so that they know how to operate things better, and they can also rely on the data and information that the smart city is going to provide for them. When we are utilizing all the data or information, then only I believe it would lead us to a better quality of life. Otherwise, we wouldn't be taking any advantage from this smart city, especially if you are not, IT savvy or do not understand the technology*. As for Sanjana, he mentioned that "*a factor that would influence me to buy a home in a smart city is to have some basic digital literacy such as how to use the smart system. My kids will also need to have some basic understanding of smart devices and their function. Older people would need some sort of basic IT knowledge so that it is manageable and not too overwhelming for them.*" Whilst Eliza echoed a similar understanding when she shared the following: *'I believe that we need digital knowledge and digital skills. Because we talked about technology right, we need to learn how to use that. Maybe it will be hard for a first timer, but I would say, maybe after a few times or a few years, we are already familiar with it. For beginners, they really need to learn all the basic technological skills. As for the older people, they really need some guidance from us. With technological advancement, it is hard to catch up on those technologies. Even for me, I am only in my thirties, but sometimes the new technologies are hard to learn. I really need to learn from my kids, or from my siblings. They need to help me to use these technologies.'*

## 4.5 Price Value

Lastly, the major theme arises from the qualitative data suggesting that the factor that could influence the informants to purchase a home in a smart city is due to their perception of price. Informants talk in length about their concern in regard to affordability and financial capabilities to purchase a home in a smart city. The majority of the informants believe that homes in smart cities should be reasonably priced and good value for the money. For example, Yazeed shared the following perspective: *"factors influencing me to purchase a home in a smart city is of course the cost. I believe smart cities can be costly as we need to pay for new technology that eventually improves the quality of our life. It is a high initial investment, but it will benefit the homeowner in the long run. All the facilities provided by the concept of smart city can be very costly such as all the smart systems can be very expensive."*

Like Ushna, she believes that the number one factor that would influence her to buy a home in a smart city is the price in which she stated that *"the price usually would be the major factor."* Similarly, Yi Chun mentioned: *"I will buy a home in a smart city but not so soon, yeah, because I will consider the price first. If the e-city becomes common in Malaysia, the price will be lower down, then I will consider buying it.*"

February expresses the following concern when it comes to the fifth theme, price value in which she stated: "*I think the most important factor is my finances. Whether I can afford to buy is the most important. Firstly, I need to consider our finances because homes in smart cities are usually more expensive. For the people that can afford to buy will consider a smart city. If I can afford, then definitely I will consider this.*" In a similar vein, Sumaira echoed the following: "*The most important factor is the price. The current comfortable house can now reach one million. With all the smart technology, I am a bit concerned about the price.*" As for Musfirah, she narrates her understanding by sharing the following scenario: "*Let's say if I am eager to buy a house in a smart city, but suddenly we know that the neighborhood area is quite pricey, it will make me think twice of buying it. So, of course we need to see the cost. I believe that the developer needs to manage the technology system, landscape, safety, and security, so there is a huge cost. Price would be the main challenge. Also, the income currently in Malaysia is not too high, maybe home in a smart city is more relevant for T20. So maybe only T20 can afford a house in a smart city, instead of, ideally, we want to see a smart city that can benefit everyone, including the B40. But, if the housing price is like one million and above, how can the B40 benefit from a smart city? I believe that the smart city needs to be fair for the B40, M40, and T20.*"

As for Sanjana, he mentioned that he would not buy a house which can cost him three or four million and he would definitely think about the price when considering buying home in smart city in which he continue stating the following: "*If it's too expensive, I mean, to be honest, give me all these, and it'll cost me like 5 million, then I don't think we want to consider that. You should have various options for different kinds of people to access smart cities. Smart city does not mean only for the rich. So, it should be something which is accessible for everyone, perhaps condominiums, rather than having big bungalows. So having something for everyone and making it affordable for everyone.*" Another participant, Kendall, has the perception that a home in a smart city would not be cheap, however, if she can afford it, she would buy a home in a smart city as it provides a lot of convenience to her life.

Like Anthony, he expresses that "*the factor that would influence me to buy a home in a smart city is of course the price and the technology being offered. I would buy it if it were reasonable, if not, I might buy it for investment. I believe that a home in a smart city is more costly than conventional houses. How many percent of the population can afford to acquire a home in a smart city. I think it is a challenge. Of course, there are rich people who can buy a lot of units in the smart city and invest, but people who are really staying there must have a reasonable pocket. Cost is the main thing. For example, if the price is one million, people would have a lot of de-*

*mand from the developer. They wouldn't simply just put in the money to invest in this property unless they can see a return in the future. So, the vision is important, and the developer must be able to convince the potential buyer."* Similarly, Jessy shared the following concern: *"the most important factor is finance because it must be very costly for those kinds of houses. Even nowadays, like those normal properties also can go up to a million. As for homes in smart cities, I think normal citizens like us can't afford to buy. Maybe for youngsters, they would consider buying a home in a smart city. For senior citizens like us, I don't think they will buy. First thing, we cannot get the loan, because we are senior citizens. Secondly, like I say, we must learn a lot of high technology things that we cannot really remember. I don't think it's that suitable for us to stay in a smart city house."*

## 5.0 DISCUSSION

This section discussed the themes of the antecedents of purchase intention of Malaysians towards smart homes. Since smart homes were introduced, research in 2021 reported that smart homes are always linked to data attacks or the security of data (Laughlin, 2021). The residents are concerned with the security elements, such as Confidentiality, Integrity, and Availability (CIA) (Bastos et al., 2018). The concerns in security and privacy affecting the purchase intention in this study are similar with other studies, for example device hacking, gaining Wi-Fi connectivity, data breaches and others (Haney et al., 2020). The consistency of the findings makes sense across the studies because a smart home is mainly made up of systems and data collection via various methods or platforms. To appear "smart" in smart home or smart city, user's data will be collected to develop advertising models for the users (Tabassum et al., 2019). This might sound helpful and convenient for certain users; however, certain users might feel their life is being monitored and lacking the sense of privacy when living in a smart home. Hence, it affects the purchase intention towards smart home, consequently. Understanding these concerns is crucial for the necessary parties to intervene and to reduce the perceived risk in security and privacy.

Followed by the next factor, namely environmental initiatives. The creation of smart homes techniques, such as Smart Home Energy Management Systems (SHEMs), can help the environment to save energy effectively, where it transforms electric appliances into autonomous devices in smart homes (Aliero et al., 2021). The contribution from smart homes to the environment has gained the attention from green-environment lovers. The theme of environmental initiatives in our research is matched and aligned with past studies, where users who love the planet and environment are more likely to purchase a smart home. This is consistent with Wijekoon and Sabri (2021) research, where environmental concerns did have an impact on the purchase intention of smart home objects. Their research further elaborated, happiness of users might moderate the relationship between environmental concerns and purchase intention. This indicates that when users feel happy to contribute to the planet by living in a smart home, they are more likely to purchase smart homes.

Infrastructure and the convenience of mobility have been one of the factors that affect purchase intention of residents, even in traditional homes. In this qualitative study, our finding supports that digital infrastructure and smart mobility are the factors that could affect their purchase intention towards smart homes. When infrastructure of smart homes was mentioned, different users might have different expectations on the demands of digital infrastructure in smart homes. Based on our findings, the responses from the interviewees were all prone to having 5G and strong network connection as the main expected digital infrastructure. As highlighted by Azmi et al. (2022), one of the definitions of smart home is related to 'technology', hence strong connectivity of the network would be ideal for the users to enjoy better experience in using the infrastructure. Without a stable network to use the technology in smart homes, users do not find the need to purchase the smart homes because they can enjoy the similar infrastructure to conventional homes at an affordable price.

Other than the external factors that could affect users' purchase intention, our finding contributes to reveal the internal factor of users in purchasing smart homes in Malaysia. In our context, an internal factor is known as the factor that could be controlled by the users through attending to relevant supports. One of the internal factors that we can identify is digital literacy and knowledge expectancy. Unlike the uncontrollable factors that we discussed in earlier paragraphs, literacy and knowledge level can be improved by attending workshops or training to understand digital skills further. Interestingly, although our respondents are majorly made up of young adults, literacy and knowledge concerns are raised when the interview is conducted. Consistently, past research had revealed that digital literacy had been the key factor to be considered when it comes to purchasing smart homes (Strengers et al., 2022). Despite advanced technology being offered in smart homes, the users would hesitate to purchase the smart homes because they think they might not be able fully enjoy the convenience without knowing how to navigate the devices. This is aligned with the consumer behavior theory, where users might not purchase certain things when they do not perceive the usefulness of the items. Hence, having sufficient digital literacy and knowledge might increase the likelihood of purchasing smart homes, when perceived usefulness is improved.

Although the creation of smart homes has been bringing much convenience to the users, the price value of the property is one of the major concerns among the users. Like previous studies, our finding showed that price value is one of the antecedents influencing the purchasing intention towards smart homes. For instance, Hong et al. (2020) raised a concern with regards to perceived financial risk, where users might be resistant to purchase smart homes when they find cheaper alternatives, especially when they think they might not be able to fully utilize the digital infrastructure. This is aligned with Shanthana and Gupta (2021) study, where users' intention to purchase will decrease when they find the value of purchasing smart homes does not equal the rate of utilization of the convenience of smart homes. This factor is consistent with The Unified Theory of Acceptance and Use of Technology 2 (UTAUT2) model, as price value is considered as one of the elements in affecting the adoption of smart homes (Shanthana and Gupta, 2021).

Based on the discussion of the findings above, the research questions and objectives are addressed. Research Question and Objective 1 were addressed by identifying the main factors in influencing Malaysia's intention to purchase homes in smart cities, which are Perceived Privacy and Security, Environmental Initiatives, IT Resources, Price Value, Smart Mobility and Conveniency, as well as Awareness Government Initiatives. These include the external factors and internal factors that could influence their intention to purchase smart homes, where these could be rather comprehensive findings to explain the influential factors.

## 5.1 Theoretical Contribution

The present study offers several contributions to theory by providing a comprehensive analysis of the consumer intention to purchase homes in smart cities, a subject of considerable academic and commercial interest. In particular, the present study expands the limited existing research on purchase intention of homes in smart cities especially in Malaysia. In fact, this is the first study on purchase intention of homes in smart cities in Asia. The current research explores the overlooked of smart cities home in developing countries, by focusing on current and potential home buyers in Malaysia. This is because limited studies pertaining to smart cities are mostly focused on the developed countries (e.g., Spain, Germany, Australia).

The current study also makes an important contribution to the limited literature on the role of digital marketing, digital infrastructure, and secure digital credential in influencing consumer intention to purchase homes in smart cities. Most importantly, this study proposed and a comprehensive framework on the main factors influencing Malaysians to purchase homes in smart cities. This offers future researchers' new perspectives in understanding smart city related studies. Research that addresses Malaysian home intention is especially valuable as the technology advances and align with 12th Malaysian Plan on digital transformation; Shared Prosperity Vision 2030 towards advanced and modern services (KEGA14); fulfillment of MySTIE Socio-Economic Driver on smart cities and transportation as well as sustainable development goal towards industry, innovation, and infrastructure (SDG 9).

## 5.2 Implications for Practitioners

Based on the findings, five factors have been identified to facilitate the growth of the smart homes industry in Malaysia. International smart home developers from other countries may learn from Malaysian smart cities development plans by prioritizing similar factors such as environmental initiatives and price value. In such a way, the international developers may develop localized smart home solutions and accelerate the buying desire in their respective markets. For example, the findings show that price value is important in the smart home business, international developers can learn from Malaysian developers' by emphasizing on affordability to purchase smart homes. Malaysia's experience with smart cities provides valuable lessons that other countries can learn from and apply to their own contexts.

The following discussion further expands on how international stakeholders can benefit from this study. The reporting of the key findings, to some extent, will be able to provide implications to relevant parties, such as the marketers, policy makers, and business developers in this area. Our findings suggested that users are resistant to purchasing a home in a smart city when they do not have sufficient knowledge on digital skills to support themselves in daily life. Interestingly, this does not happen only among the old users in our study, it suggests that young users are having the same concern as well. With this reason, this brings an implication to the practitioners to provide a platform or workshop to build digital skills among the buyers. As multidisciplinary is the key trend nowadays, property practitioners could consider having a collaboration with IT specialists to organize workshops upon purchasing homes in smart cities. This can help to improve the confidence of users to purchase homes in smart cities because they will be equipped with relevant skills to live in smart cities. When the potential users can perceive the usefulness of digital infrastructure in smart cities by equipping themselves with sufficient knowledge, the perception of price value will be improved, which in turn improves their purchase intention towards home in smart cities.

One of the unique selling points of the homes in smart cities is the security and privacy, however, if this is not managed well, it can become the factor of reducing the likelihood of purchasing the homes in smart cities. One of the biggest concerns from the potential buyers is the leaking and abusing the data in smart cities. The concerns are getting even greater when the buyers do not have the knowledge on security and self-protection from being abused in data management. In addition, most of the potential buyers are not comfortable when they do not have the choice whether they could own the data. With this finding, the implication to practitioners could be recommending the property marketers to educate the buyers with the knowledge of security and privacy in data management. For example, the knowledge of data localization was mentioned by Haney et al (2020), where the users can choose whether the data can be owned by the users, or it is fine to send every data to the smart city managers. This can create a sense of security and privacy for the users because they are allowed to decide the localization of the data. Besides, in the workshops, users are suggested to be exposed to the self-protection knowledge to avoid their data being abused by the smart city or any other online platforms.

## 5.3 Research Limitations

This study is not without limitations. Firstly, this study focused on Malaysia's purchase intention only, without investigating the diverse groups of respondents from other nations. This explains that the themes in this study might be limited to developing countries but not developed countries. This requires further study to confirm the generalization of the themes in different nations. In addition to that, when we were recruiting the interviewees, although we had the intention to involve respondents from different age groups, we were only able to secure most of the young adults rather than having diverse age groups in our research. This will, somewhat, create a possibility of having sampling bias in this paper and which in turn, affecting the themes of the factors. Hence, the themes reported in this study could be limited to certain groups of age. Besides, our research is mainly focusing on understanding the antecedents of purchase intention of residents, without looking into the moderator and mediator factors that might affect the relationships between the variables. As this is a qualitative study, the process of interviewing and thematic analysis could be less objective as compared to quantitative study, as different scholars might perceive differently on different themes or keywords. However, this limitation is reduced to a minimal level in this study, as the authors involved in this study finalized and discussed the themes together when one of the scholars identified the themes.

## 5.4 Recommendations for Future Research

Studies on smart homes in Malaysia are still lacking. Our qualitative study serves as a general overview of the factors that could affect Malaysia's purchase intention on smart home. With the findings, future research could further investigate which factor has the most impact on smart home purchase intention via quantitative analysis. As we believe the cultural differences could affect behavior and thinking of the residents, we would suggest future researchers to extend this research to different nations which have different cultures, for example Malaysia and the United States. A comparative study would be able to provide an in-depth insight for the readers and marketers to understand the differences. In addition to that, by conducting the future study on different samples, future researchers would be able to identify the level of generalization of the themes to different contexts or nations. Furthermore, as Malaysia is a collectivist country, social factors could be one of the elements that affect the purchase intention on smart homes. Hence, future research is suggested to further examine the possibility of moderating or mediated effect of social factors or the culture of Malaysia in the relationship between the antecedents and purchase intention.

## ACKNOWLEDGEMENT

This research was supported by Taylor's University through the Centre for Industrial Revolution and Innovation (CIRI) Seed Funding (CIRI-SEED/1/2022/SOMM/002).

## REFERENCES

Ahad, M. A., Paiva, S., Tripathi, G., & Feroz, N. (2020). Enabling technologies and sustainable smart cities. *Sustainable Cities and Society*, *61*, 102301. DOI: 10.1016/j.scs.2020.102301

Alam, M. R., Reaz, M. B. I., & Ali, M. A. M. (2012). A review of smart homes—Past, present, and future. *IEEE Transactions on Systems, Man, and Cybernetics. Part C, Applications and Reviews*, *42*(6), 1190–1203. DOI: 10.1109/TSMCC.2012.2189204

Aldossari, M. Q., & Sidorova, A. (2020). Consumer acceptance of smart home technologies: A UTAUT2 perspective. Proceedings of the 26th Americas Conference on Information Systems, Virtual Conference. https://aisel.aisnet.org/amcis2020/adv_info_systems_research/adv_info_systems_research/7/

Aliero, M. S., Asif, M., Ghani, I., & Abidin, M. Z. (2021). Smart home energy management systems: Research challenges and survey. 2021 International Conference on Software Engineering & Computer Systems and 4th International Conference on Computational Science and Information Management (ICSECS-ICOCSIM), 165–170. DOI: 10.1109/ICSECS52883.2021.00036

Azmi, A., Ibrahim, R., & Zulkifli, M. A. (2022). Smart home technology adoption: The perspective of Malaysian homeowners. *Journal of Physics: Conference Series*, *2250*(1), 012008. DOI: 10.1088/1742-6596/2250/1/012008

Bastos, D., Shackleton, M., & El-Moussa, F. (2018). Internet of things: A survey of technologies and security risks in smart home and city environments. *IET Conference Proceedings*, 30–37. DOI: 10.1049/cp.2018.0030

Belanche-Gracia, D., Casaló-Ariño, L. V., & Pérez-Rueda, A. (2015). Determinants of multi-service smartcard success for smart cities development: A study based on citizens' privacy and security perceptions. *Government Information Quarterly*, *32*(2), 154–163. DOI: 10.1016/j.giq.2014.12.004

Bryman, A. (2008). *Social research methods* (3rd ed.). Oxford University Press.

Chang, W.-L., Chen, Y.-M., & Lin, Y.-H. (2020). Smart hearing aids in smart cities: Technological challenges and opportunities. *Journal of Ambient Intelligence and Smart Environments, 12*(4), 345–357. DOI: 10.3233/AIS-200563

Creswell, J. W. (2014). *Research design: Qualitative, quantitative, and mixed methods approaches* (4th ed.). Sage Publications.

Dastane, O. (2020). Impact of digital marketing on online purchase intention: The moderating role of trust. *International Journal of Advanced Science and Technology, 29*(6), 1114–1125.

Datta, A. (2015). New urban utopias of postcolonial India: Entrepreneurial urbanization in Dholera smart city, Gujarat. *Dialogues in Human Geography, 5*(1), 3–22. DOI: 10.1177/2043820614565748

Denzin, N. K., & Lincoln, Y. S. (1994). *Handbook of qualitative research.* Sage Publications.

Erlangga, H. (2021). Effect of digital marketing and social media on purchase intention of SMEs food products. *Journal of Business and Management Review, 2*(2), 141–154. DOI: 10.47153/jbmr22.1412021

Haney, J. M., Luther, L., & Dastane, O. (2020). Security and privacy issues in smart home environments: A systematic literature review. *International Journal of Advanced Computer Science and Applications, 11*(7), 567–576. DOI: 10.14569/IJACSA.2020.0110772

Heidar, A., Navimpour, N. J., & Unal, M. (2022). Applications of blockchain in smart cities: A comprehensive review. *Sustainable Cities and Society, 76*, 103366. DOI: 10.1016/j.scs.2021.103366

Hong, A., Nam, C., & Kim, S. (2020). Estimating the potential financial risk of smart homes: A case study in South Korea. *Sustainability, 12*(17), 6947. DOI: 10.3390/su12176947

Hubert, M., Blut, M., Brock, C., Zhang, R. W., Koch, V., & Riedl, R. (2018). Acceptance of smart home technologies: An empirical investigation. *Journal of Business Research, 94*, 295–304. DOI: 10.1016/j.jbusres.2018.01.002

International Telecommunication Union. (2016). Smart sustainable cities: An ITU perspective. ITU-T Focus Group on Smart Sustainable Cities. https://www.itu.int/en/ITU-T/focusgroups/ssc/Pages/default.aspx

Ismagilova, E., Hughes, L., Dwivedi, Y. K., & Raman, K. R. (2019). Smart cities: Advances in research—An information systems perspective. *International Journal of Information Management*, *47*, 88–100. DOI: 10.1016/j.ijinfomgt.2019.01.004

Ji, W., & Chan, E. H. W. (2019). Smart home energy management systems: A review of technologies and applications. *Renewable & Sustainable Energy Reviews*, *109*, 112–123. DOI: 10.1016/j.rser.2019.04.016

Jiménez-Castillo, D., & Sánchez-Fernández, R. (2019). The role of digital influencers in brand recommendation: Examining their impact on engagement, expected value, and purchase intention. *International Journal of Information Management*, *49*, 366–376. DOI: 10.1016/j.ijinfomgt.2019.07.009

Khatoun, R., & Zeadally, S. (2016). Smart cities: Concepts, architectures, research opportunities. *Communications of the ACM*, *59*(8), 46–57. DOI: 10.1145/2858789

Kummitha, R. K. R. (2020). Smart cities and entrepreneurship: An agenda for future research. *Technological Forecasting and Social Change*, *149*, 119763. DOI: 10.1016/j.techfore.2019.119763

Laughlin, C. (2021). Security challenges in the smart home: A systematic literature review. *Journal of Network and Computer Applications*, *177*, 102964. DOI: 10.1016/j.jnca.2020.102964

Lee, J. H., Hancock, M. G., & Hu, M.-C. (2014). Towards an effective framework for building smart cities: Lessons from Seoul and San Francisco. *Technological Forecasting and Social Change*, *89*, 80–99. DOI: 10.1016/j.techfore.2013.08.033

Leow, B. Y., & Krishnaswamy, J. A. (2021). Smart mobility in smart cities: Emerging challenges and opportunities. *Journal of Urban Technology*, *28*(1–2), 167–185. DOI: 10.1080/10630732.2020.1824847

Li, L., Liu, J., Cheng, B., & Li, X. (2016). Cybersecurity challenges in intelligent transportation systems. *IEEE Transactions on Intelligent Transportation Systems*, *17*(9), 2445–2456. DOI: 10.1109/TITS.2016.2524064

Marsal-Llacuna, M.-L. (2020). The people's smart city dashboard (PSCD): Delivering on community-led governance with blockchain. *Technological Forecasting and Social Change*, *158*, 120150. DOI: 10.1016/j.techfore.2020.120150

McCracken, G. (1988). *The long interview*. Sage Publications. DOI: 10.4135/9781412986229

Nawaz, M. A., & Kaldeen, M. (2020). Impact of digital marketing on purchase intention. *International Journal of Advanced Research*, *8*(4), 1254–1260. DOI: 10.21474/IJAR01/10887

Nikou, S. (2019). Factors driving the adoption of smart home technology: An empirical assessment. *Telematics and Informatics*, *45*, 101283. DOI: 10.1016/j.tele.2019.101283

Obaidat, M. S., & Nicopolitidis, P. (2016). *Smart cities and homes: Key enabling technologies*. Morgan Kaufmann.

Organisation for Economic Co-operation and Development. (n.d.). Smart cities and inclusive growth. OECD Publishing. https://www.oecd.org/cfe/cities/OECD_Policy_Paper_Smart_Cities_and_Inclusive_Growth.pdf

ReportLinker. (2022). Global smart cities market to reach USD 2.8 trillion by 2027. https://www.reportlinker.com/p06285854

Savitri, C., Hurriyati, R., Wibowo, L. A., & Hendrayati, H. (2022). The role of digital marketing in influencing purchase intention: A study on e-commerce platforms. *The Journal of Business and Retail Management Research*, *16*(2), 45–53.

Schill, M., Godefroit-Winkel, D., Diallo, M. F., & Barbarossa, C. (2019). Consumers' intentions to purchase smart home objects: The role of environmental concern and technological innovativeness. *Journal of Business Research*, *103*, 541–553. DOI: 10.1016/j.jbusres.2019.02.026

Shanthana, L. S., & Gupta, P. (2021). Adoption of smart home technologies: An empirical study using UTAUT2. *International Journal of Business Information Systems*, *38*(3), 321–341. DOI: 10.1504/IJBIS.2021.119123

Shin, J., & Lee, S. (2018). Adoption of smart homes: A technology acceptance model perspective. *International Journal of Human-Computer Interaction*, *34*(12), 1131–1142. DOI: 10.1080/10447318.2018.1426899

Shuhaiber, A., & Mashal, I. (2019). Understanding users' acceptance of smart homes. *Technology in Society*, *58*, 101110. DOI: 10.1016/j.techsoc.2019.01.003

Silva, B. N., Khan, M., & Han, K. (2018). Towards sustainable smart cities: A review of trends, architectures, components, and open challenges in smart cities. *Sustainable Cities and Society*, *38*, 697–713. DOI: 10.1016/j.scs.2018.01.053

Statista. (2019). Smart cities ranking worldwide in 2019. https://www.statista.com/statistics/1053441/smart-cities-ranking-worldwide/

Statista. (2021). Smart home market revenue worldwide 2017–2025. https://www.statista.com/statistics/1100922/smart-home-market-revenue-worldwide/

Strengers, Y., Kennedy, J., Abu Bakar, A., & Nicholls, L. (2022). Digital literacy and smart home technology: Challenges for older adults. *Journal of Consumer Culture*, *22*(3), 672–690. DOI: 10.1177/14695405211016031

Su, K., Li, J., & Fu, H. (2011). Smart city and the applications. *2011 International Conference on Electronics, Communications and Control (ICECC)*, 1028–1031. DOI: 10.1109/ICECC.2011.6066743

Tabassum, M., Kusiak, A., & Wang, J. (2019). Privacy and security in smart homes: A review. *IEEE Access : Practical Innovations, Open Solutions*, *7*, 153665–153678. DOI: 10.1109/ACCESS.2019.2948897

Terziradeva, I. (2018). Sensor technologies for smart city applications. *2018 International Conference on Smart City and Emerging Technology (ICSCET)*, 1–5. https://doi.org/DOI: 10.1109/ICSCET.2018.8537372

Ullah, F., Qayyum, S., Thaheem, M. J., Al-Turjman, F., & Sepasgozar, S. M. E. (2021). Risk management in smart cities: A systematic literature review. *Sustainable Cities and Society*, *74*, 103225. DOI: 10.1016/j.scs.2021.103225

United Nations Environment Programme. (2018). Global status report 2018: Towards a zero-emission, efficient and resilient buildings and construction sector. https://www.unenvironment.org/resources/report/global-status-report-2018

United Nations Habitat. (2020). World cities report 2020: The value of sustainable urbanization. https://unhabitat.org/sites/default/files/2020/10/wcr_2020_report.pdf

Vidhya, V. (2021). Digital marketing and its impact on consumer purchase intention. *Journal of Critical Reviews*, *8*(2), 123–130.

Vitunskaite, M., He, Y., Brandstetter, T., & Janicke, H. (2019). Smart cities and cyber security: Are we prepared? *Computers & Security*, *87*, 101568. DOI: 10.1016/j.cose.2019.101568

Washburn, D., Sindhu, U., Balaouras, S., Dines, R. A., Hayes, N., & Nelson, L. E. (2009). Helping CIOs understand "smart city" initiatives. Forrester Research. https://www.forrester.com/report/Helping+CIOs+Understand+Smart+City+Initiatives/-/E-RES55959

Westraadt, L., & Calitz, A. (2020). A framework for the development of smart cities in South Africa. *South African Journal of Information Management*, *22*(1), a1173. DOI: 10.4102/sajim.v22i1.1173

Wibisurya, A. (2018). The impact of digital marketing on consumer purchase intention. *Journal of Business and Management*, *7*(2), 45–52.

Wijekoon, A., & Sabri, M. F. (2021). Environmental concerns and purchase intention of smart home objects: The moderating role of happiness. *Journal of Cleaner Production, 312*, 127767. DOI: 10.1016/j.jclepro.2021.127767

Zhang, Y., & Liu, X. (2022). Eco-friendly smart home services: Design and implementation challenges. *Sustainable Cities and Society*, *78*, 103616. DOI: 10.1016/j.scs.2021.103616

Zhuang, M., Zhu, W., Huang, L., & Pan, W.-T. (2021). Impact of corporate social responsibility for smart cities on consumers' purchase intention. *Frontiers in Psychology*, *12*, 674726. DOI: 10.3389/fpsyg.2021.674726

Chapter 6
# Lighting Methods Using Islamic Typographic Ornamentation Design Analysis in Achieving Indoor Environment Quality:
## Understanding Typographic Ornaments in Facade Design

**Ahmad Fahmi Zainazlan**
https://orcid.org/0009-0002-8396-806X
*Taylor's University, Malaysia*

**Khairool Aizat Ahmad Jamal**
https://orcid.org/0000-0003-4674-581X
*Taylor's University, Malaysia*

**Nor Azlin Hamidon**
*Universiti Teknologi MARA, Malaysia*

## ABSTRACT

*This paper explores how lighting permutation methods, inspired by Islamic ornamentation, can improve indoor environmental quality, focusing on lighting design. Islamic ornamentation, with its intricate geometries and symbolic patterns, offers a unique foundation for creating natural lighting strategies that are both functional and aes-*

DOI: 10.4018/979-8-3373-0390-1.ch006

*thetically meaningful. By examining the cultural significance and contemporary uses of Islamic ornamentation, the study identifies design principles to inspire innovative natural lighting solutions. Using computational tools and parametric design methods, the research presents a design analysis for integrating these ornamentation-based lighting techniques into modern architecture. The findings highlight the potential of culturally grounded design traditions to enhance visual comfort, energy efficiency, and spatial harmony, contributing to a more sustainable built environment. This paper offers valuable insights for architects, lighting designers, and engineers on the role of ornamental design in improving indoor spaces.*

## 1.0 INTRODUCTION

The intersection of Islamic ornamentation and natural lighting strategies offers a distinctive opportunity to enhance indoor environmental quality (IEQ). Islamic ornamentation, which historically balances aesthetics with function, employs complex geometries and symbolic designs that have been implemented in architecture for centuries. The deliberate arrangement of these patterns has the potential to inform lighting design, guiding how light interacts with and enhances indoor spaces. By analyzing the underlying principles of Islamic ornamentation, particularly its use of geometry and symbolism, architects and designers can develop lighting strategies that optimize both visual and thermal comfort while minimizing energy consumption. In modern architectural contexts, the integration of natural lighting has become a crucial component of sustainable design, yet challenges remain in achieving a harmonious balance between aesthetics, efficiency, and comfort.

*Figure 1. Lighting Diagram: Typical Facade Opening (Source: Authors Collection)*

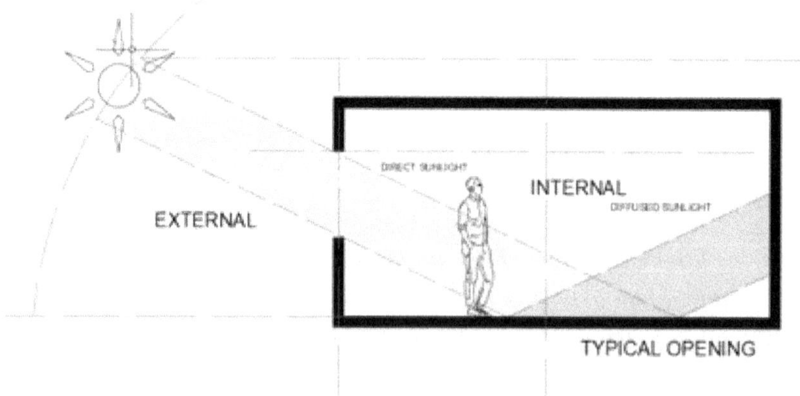

This study explores how Islamic ornamentation can serve as a model for natural lighting permutation methods, advancing the goal of improving IEQ. Using advanced computational tools and parametric design experimentation, the research examines ways to merge the rich tradition of Islamic ornamentation with contemporary design practices. The focus is not only on enhancing visual comfort and spatial harmony but also on aligning with the growing demand for sustainable and energy-efficient architectural solutions. By bridging historical design elements with modern lighting strategies, this paper seeks to provide innovative insights for architects, lighting designers, and engineers. By learning about he characteristics and attributes of lights, we can further appreciate the design elements both in theory and theology perspectives. The applications of lighting permutation design may benefit not just exclusive to Islamic point of view, rather the general perception of designing lighting permutation itself.

## 1.2 Background

The interplay between light and space has been a central consideration in architectural design throughout history. Islamic architecture demonstrates an intricate understanding of lighting as both a functional and symbolic element. From the meticulously pierced mashrabiyas of Egypt to the luminous muqarnas ceilings of Persia, Islamic ornamentation has historically been used to manipulate light, creating dynamic indoor environments that are visually and spiritually uplifting. These traditional approaches resonate with contemporary concerns about Indoor Environment Quality (IEQ), which prioritizes visual comfort, air quality, and thermal conditions in built environments to enhance occupant well-being. Modern building designs increasingly integrate daylighting strategies to reduce energy consumption and improve occupant satisfaction. However, the integration of Islamic ornamental motifs into these strategies remains relatively underexplored. Such designs have the potential to balance aesthetic, cultural, and functional goals, using patterns to filter and diffuse sunlight effectively while maintaining cultural authenticity. Advances in computational design and parametric modelling provide new opportunities to explore these motifs with precision, enabling architects and designers to simulate and optimize light penetration, diffusion, and shadow patterns in real-time.

By analysing the historical and contemporary applications of Islamic ornamentation in architectural lighting, this study seeks to contribute to a growing discourse on sustainable and culturally responsive design practices. Drawing upon principles derived from traditional Islamic architecture and leveraging modern computational tools, the research will investigate methods of achieving optimal IEQ through lighting permutations informed by Islamic design analysis. This study aligns with broader efforts to harmonize heritage preservation with technological innovation in the service of sustainable development(Haidar et al., 2023).

## 1.3 Problem Statement

The increasing focus on sustainable architecture and IEQ has highlighted the importance of daylighting as a critical component of building design. While technological solutions such as automated blinds and advanced glazing systems offer practical benefits, they often lack the aesthetic and cultural dimensions necessary for truly holistic design approaches. Additionally, standard daylighting techniques frequently neglect the potential for culturally resonant solutions that engage users on an emotional and spiritual level.

Islamic architectural ornamentation, with its geometric complexity and symbolic richness, offers a unique avenue for addressing these gaps. The potential for these designs to filter and modulate light, creating intricate patterns of shadow and illumination, aligns closely with contemporary goals for visual comfort and spatial harmony. Despite this potential, there is a noticeable lack of systematic research on how these traditional design elements can be adapted and optimized using modern computational tools to meet the demands of contemporary indoor environments. The challenge lies in translating the intricate geometry of Islamic patterns into scalable and functional lighting designs that meet modern IEQ standards. Additionally, there are gaps in understanding how these patterns interact with different lighting conditions, materials, and spatial configurations Thus, the research aims to establish a methodologically sound approach to employing Islamic ornamental motifs as active agents in achieving optimal IEQ outcomes, particularly through innovative lighting permutation methods. This initiative not only addresses technical and functional requirements but also seeks to evoke a sense of cultural continuity and identity in architectural practice.

## 1.4 Research Questions

The primary aim of this research is to explore how Islamic ornamental motifs can be utilized to enhance indoor lighting quality while achieving broader objectives related to IEQ and cultural significance. A central question is: **How can traditional Islamic ornamentation be effectively analysed and adapted to enhance indoor lighting quality while maintaining cultural and aesthetic integrity?** This inquiry necessitates a detailed examination of the geometric and symbolic features inherent in Islamic designs that influence the behaviour of light. By understanding their historical contributions to light modulation in classical architecture, the study aims to adapt these principles for contemporary applications.

A related area of investigation is the potential of computational methods and tools to simulate and optimize lighting permutations using Islamic design motifs. Tools such as parametric modelling software provide a robust framework for exploring how patterns can be scaled, manipulated, and integrated into modern structures. Questions here include: **How can parametric modelling and simulation software facilitate the integration of these motifs into building designs?** Furthermore, what metrics can be employed to evaluate the efficacy of these designs in terms of visual comfort, energy efficiency, and cultural resonance?

Lastly, the research seeks to establish practical guidelines for architects and designers. These guidelines will address the challenges and limitations of integrating Islamic ornamentation into lighting designs in diverse contexts. Key questions involve identifying barriers to implementation, such as material constraints or compatibility with modern construction methods. Additionally, how can these guidelines be tailored to meet the needs of different climatic, cultural, and functional contexts? Addressing these challenges will enable the development of adaptable frameworks that support culturally enriched, sustainable design practices.

## 1.5 Scope of Study

The scope of this research encompasses both the historical significance and contemporary applications of Islamic ornamentation in lighting design. A key focus is on the historical and theoretical foundations of using Islamic geometric patterns and ornamental elements to manipulate natural light. Case studies will be drawn from iconic structures such as the Alhambra in Spain, the Sheikh Lotfollah Mosque in Iran, and modern adaptations in contemporary architecture. By analyzing these examples, the study aims to elucidate the principles underlying the aesthetic, spiritual, and functional aspects of these designs, offering insights into their timeless relevance.

The core important categories of Indoor Environment Quality are Indoor Air Quality, Thermal Comfort, Lighting and Acoustics. These are the fundamentals of IEQ that spread into lots of subtropical focusing on each elemental. Indoor Air Quality (IAQ) stands as a cornerstone, addressing the purity and healthiness of the air within enclosed spaces. Thermal Comfort constitutes another pivotal aspect of IEQ, delineating the satisfaction derived from indoor temperature, humidity levels, and air movement(Germin, n.d.). Achieving thermal comfort necessitates balancing factors like insulation, heating, ventilation, and air conditioning (HVAC) systems to mitigate fluctuations in temperature and humidity that can lead to discomfort or thermal stress. Acoustics completes the quartet of essential IEQ components, addressing sound quality and noise levels within built environments. By mitigating unwanted noise sources and enhancing speech intelligibility, well-designed acoustic environments foster environments where occupants can engage in productive activities, communication, and relaxation without undue auditory stress(Licina et al., 2021).

External thermal stress, influenced by factors such as temperature, humidity, and solar radiation, directly impacts the energy needed for essential building services. When exposed to harsher environmental conditions, buildings require greater energy input to maintain thermal equilibrium and ensure occupant comfort, highlighting the critical relationship between climate-responsive design and sustainable energy management(Zainazlan M Zain & Masriah Hj Awang, 2017).

*Figure 2. IEQ Categories*

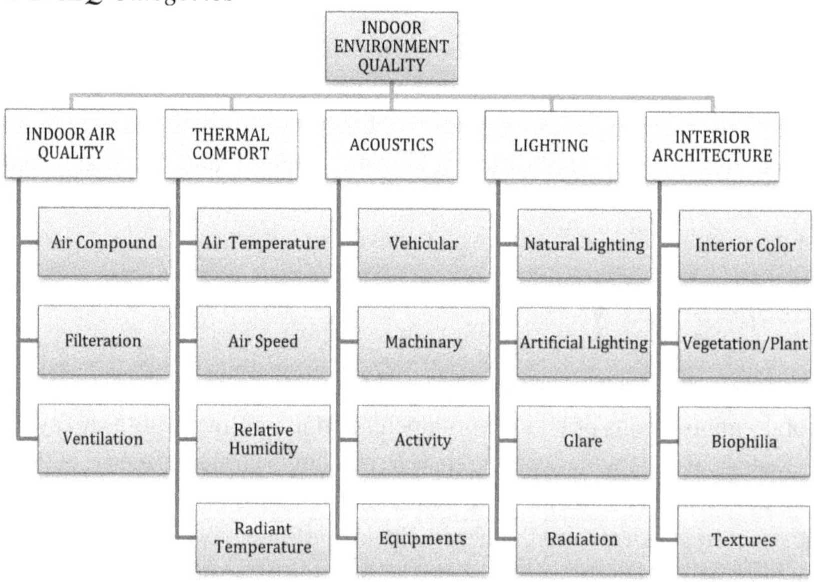


Lighting plays a very critical role in IEQ by influencing visual clarity, mood, and productivity. Effective lighting design encompasses factors such as illumination levels, colour temperature, and distribution patterns, catering to tasks performed within specific spaces while minimizing glare and visual fatigue. Natural daylighting strategies further enhance indoor environments, harnessing natural light to reduce energy consumption and enhance occupants' connection to the outdoor environment. The quality of lighting within an indoor space affects not only visibility but also impacts mood, cognitive performance, and overall occupant comfort(Md Amin et al., 2022). Given the diverse applications of indoor spaces—ranging from workplaces and educational institutions to residential and healthcare settings—lighting design must be carefully considered to optimize human interaction with the built environment.

One of the primary considerations in lighting for IEQ is the balance between natural and artificial illumination. Natural daylight is a fundamental component of a healthy indoor environment, offering physiological and psychological benefits that extend beyond simple visibility. Exposure to natural light regulates circadian rhythms, which govern sleep-wake cycles, hormone production, and overall biological health. Studies have shown that occupants in spaces with ample daylight experience improved mood, increased productivity, and reduced instances of stress and depression. Architectural strategies such as large windows, skylights, and light shelves can be employed to maximize daylight penetration, reducing reliance on artificial lighting and consequently lowering energy consumption.

Technologically speaking, energy efficiency and sustainability are increasingly central to lighting design within IEQ. The integration of LED technology, motion sensors, and daylight-responsive controls significantly reduces energy consumption and carbon footprints while maintaining high-quality illumination. Sustainable lighting solutions not only contribute to environmental conservation but also lower operational costs, making them beneficial for both occupants and building owners. As such, this paper focus on lighting as a critical element of IEQ, extending far beyond simple illumination to impact health, comfort, and efficiency in indoor spaces. A well-balanced lighting design, incorporating both natural and artificial sources, supports circadian health, enhances cognitive function, improves aesthetics, and contributes to energy efficiency. As lighting technology continues to advance, the emphasis on human-centric lighting solutions will become even more integral in shaping healthier, more productive indoor environments. Although permutations in architecture have a lot of benefits that spans beyond lighting, this paper focuses on how one element can be of major impact in achieving a comfortable indoor environment quality. The research seeks to develop actionable guidelines for architects and designers, addressing both the opportunities and challenges of integrating Islamic ornamentation into modern lighting designs. These guidelines will consider factors such as scalability, material compatibility, and adaptability to different climatic and cultural contexts. The study will also propose frameworks for balancing traditional aesthetics with contemporary requirements, ensuring that the designs are both sustainable and culturally authentic.

By focusing on these interconnected areas, the study aims to generate a holistic understanding of the potential of Islamic ornamentation in architectural lighting. This approach not only bridges the gap between traditional heritage and modern innovation but also contributes to the broader discourse on sustainable and culturally responsive design practices.

## 2.0 LITERATURE

Lighting plays a fundamental role in regulating human biological rhythms, aligning internal physiological processes with the external environment. As the most influential environmental cue in synchronizing the circadian system, light has been widely recognized for its impact on cognitive function and mental performance. Artificial lighting, generated through electrical sources such as lamps and fixtures, contrasts with daylight, which encompasses both direct and indirect sunlight. Natural daylight remains the optimal source for color accuracy, as it closely aligns with human visual perception. Moreover, recent studies have highlighted the non-visual effects of lighting on human alertness, cognitive efficiency, and emotional well-being. These effects, influenced by factors such as spectral composition, timing, and duration of exposure, have led to the development of new measurement standards based on radiometric properties to better assess lighting's broader impact on human health and productivity(Wang et al., 2021).

## 2.1 LIGHTING ARCHITECTURE

Lighting permutation solution in designing building has been developed as an internal design solution that caters for the diffusion of natural daylighting to reduce glare and uncomfortable indoor environment quality leading to discomfort interior overalls. Some solution reduces the natural lighting with external features such as light shelves. This method blocks specific amounts of light entering the building with horizontal features.

*Figure 3. Lighting Diagram: Light Shelving (Source: Authors Collection)*

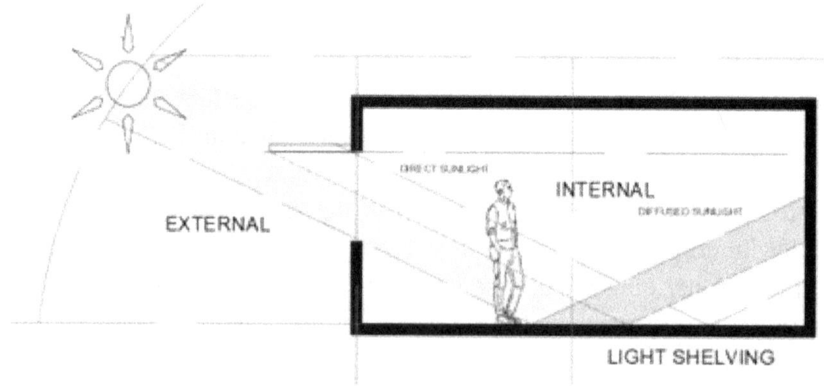

Islamic ornamentation is distinguished by its wide variety of styles and techniques, showcasing a rich and diverse typology. With a long history shaped by evolving cultural influences, Islamic art has continuously developed its ornamental traditions. The human body demonstrates a remarkable ability to adapt to varying climatic conditions through acclimatization and physiological adjustments. The distinct thermal comfort needs of individuals, which fluctuate depending on both the local climate and seasonal variations, highlight the critical importance of designing buildings that respond effectively to their environmental context. This variability underscores that architectural strategies must be carefully tailored to the specific climate of a building's location, ensuring that indoor environments provide optimal comfort and well-being for occupants across different conditions. By aligning design approaches with the unique thermal behaviours of the human body, architects can create spaces that enhance internal comfort and promote long-term adaptability.(Zain et al., 2007)

*Figure 4. Lighting Diagram: Perforated Facade (Source: Authors Collection)*

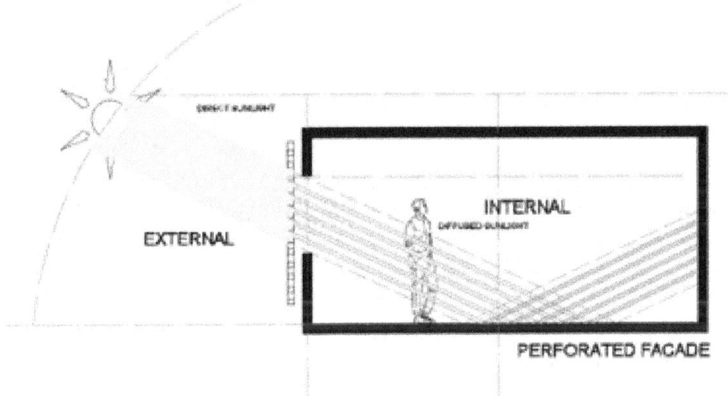


The richly adorned mosques stand as a testament to the deep cultural importance of Islamic civilization throughout history. Muslim artists, particularly skilled in the use of plant-based decorative motifs, excelled in creating designs inspired by nature. This creativity led to the development of arabesque art, characterized by gracefully intertwined, curved plant forms. These intricate motifs, prominent in 12th- and 13th-century architecture and artifacts, demonstrate the high level of artistic achievement during that period. Another variation, featuring geometric arrangements of stems and flowers, was particularly evident in Persian art, diverging from more traditional styles. The diversity of floral forms, leaf patterns, and detailed miniatures showcases a sophisticated relationship between circular and spiral curves, blending repetition, contrast, symmetry, and overlap. This innovative approach has had a lasting impact on architectural decoration in later art movements, reflecting a deliberate shift away from direct imitation of nature(Mohammad Nasser AL-Arifi, 2023)

## 2.2 Ornamentation in Architecture

Perceptions of ornaments and calligraphy, or any art in general can be viewed in two directional communications.

*Figure 5. Tradition of Artists vs Audience thought process(Mokhtar et al., 2006)*

*Figure 6. Tradition of Artists vs Audience thought process 2(Mokhtar et al., 2006)*

Figures 1 and 2 show how the perceptions of subject and artist in reading or appreciating the ornamentation. The artist's creative process typically commences from the innermost circle towards the outer circle, as denoted by the dotted arrow. Initiated by the Tawhid principle, it guides and shapes the entire artistic endeavour, culminating in the artwork's creation, often adhering to Islamic law and principles as guiding frameworks (Hamidon et al., 2022). Amongst all, five basic types of ornamentation are the most used in architecture defined as Islamic ornamentation:

Islamic Geometric Patterns are now integral cultural and identity elements in Middle Eastern building designs. Despite high demand, a lack of information on IGP principles has led to a reliance on formal inspiration in existing buildings (Ranjazmay Azari et al., 2023). This article reviews the state-of-the-art knowledge on IGPs, surveys main principles, assesses the status, and identifies gaps in recent research, addressing the evolving role of IGPs in architectural design

## 2.3 Islam, Architecture and Light, the Importance of Lightings

Light is a central theme in Islamic culture and architecture, symbolizing divine illumination and guidance. This essay examines the multifaceted relationship between Islam, architecture, and light, emphasizing its symbolic, functional, and aesthetic significance. The Qur'anic verse, "Allah is the Light of the heavens and the earth" (Qur'an 24:35), underscores the profound spiritual connotations of light in Islamic theology. This divine metaphor is reflected in architectural designs, where light transcends its practical role to become a medium for spiritual engagement and aesthetic expression.

Islamic architecture employs natural light as a fundamental design element, often filtered through geometric patterns, mashrabiyas, or stained glass to create dynamic interior environments. This interplay of light and shadow transforms spaces into sanctuaries of contemplation and beauty. Notable examples include the Sheikh Zayed Grand Mosque, where light interacts with marble surfaces to create an ethereal ambiance. The use of light also reinforces spatial hierarchies, with the brightest areas, such as those near the mihrab, symbolizing closeness to the divine. Such thoughtful integration of light enhances the spiritual experience of architectural spaces.

Advancements in lighting technologies have expanded the possibilities for modern Islamic architecture, allowing designers to merge traditional elements with contemporary innovations. Colored glass and LED lighting reinterpret classical designs while embracing sustainability through energy-efficient solutions. Solar panels and automated lighting systems align with the Islamic principle of environmental stewardship, demonstrating a harmonious balance between faith and ecological responsibility. These innovations ensure that the spiritual essence of light is preserved while addressing modern environmental challenges. Modern architects face the challenge of balancing historical principles with contemporary demands, particularly in urban environments with limited natural light. By reinterpreting traditional elements like the mashrabiya, architects create culturally relevant designs that retain spiritual significance. The integration of advanced lighting technologies in structures worldwide showcases the versatility of light as a medium for innovation and spirituality. Ultimately, the thoughtful use of light in Islamic architecture continues to define its essence, bridging tradition and modernity while fostering spaces that inspire awe and devotion.

## 2.4 Lighting Permutation in Façade Design

The concept of lighting permutation in façade design embodies the intentional manipulation of light through architectural surfaces to achieve specific aesthetic, functional, and experiential outcomes. In Islamic architecture, façades historically served as both visual identifiers and environmental regulators, particularly in regions where sunlight intensity necessitated innovative strategies for thermal and visual comfort. The integration of intricate geometric patterns, such as mashrabiya screens or latticework, allowed for a nuanced interplay of light and shadow, transforming static architectural features into dynamic, responsive systems. This historical legacy provides a foundation for reinterpreting lighting permutations in contemporary architecture, where technological advancements enable precision and adaptability in design.

Central to the philosophy of lighting permutation is the understanding that façades act as a mediator between external and internal environments. In traditional Islamic architecture, geometric patterns often served this dual purpose of regulating light while embodying cultural and spiritual symbolism. Patterns with varying densities acted as filters, reducing harsh sunlight and distributing soft, diffuse light across interior spaces. The resulting shadows added a sense of rhythm and depth to the architecture, engaging occupants in a constantly changing visual dialogue with their surroundings. In modern architectural practice, lighting permutation retains this foundational principle while embracing new tools and methodologies. Computational design and parametric modeling allow architects to simulate light behavior with unparalleled accuracy, optimizing façade patterns for specific site conditions. For instance, by using software such as Rhino/Grasshopper or Autodesk Revit, designers can experiment with the density, scale, and orientation of patterns to achieve desired outcomes. This approach not only enhances energy efficiency by maximizing daylighting potential but also ensures visual comfort by minimizing glare and contrast imbalances.

Additionally, the ability to iterate quickly through digital simulations fosters innovation, enabling architects to explore previously unfeasible design possibilities. Façade design rooted in lighting permutation also extends beyond functional benefits to encompass cultural and emotional dimensions. Islamic ornamentation, with its symbolic representation of unity and infinity, adds layers of meaning to architectural spaces. When sunlight interacts with these patterns, it creates a dynamic interplay of light and shadow, evoking a sense of spiritual transcendence and connection to the divine. This dimension is particularly relevant in spaces intended for reflection, such as mosques, cultural centers, and museums, where the quality of light contributes to the overall atmosphere and user experience. Despite its transformative potential, the application of lighting permutation in façades presents several challenges. One of the primary concerns is achieving a balance between aesthetic complexity and functional efficiency. Overly intricate patterns may hinder sufficient daylight penetration, compromising energy performance, while simplistic designs may fail to capture the cultural essence of the space.

Materiality also plays a critical role; traditional materials like stone or wood may offer authenticity but may not meet the durability or sustainability requirements of modern construction. Similarly, advanced materials like fritted glass or perforated metal panels provide versatility but require careful calibration to align with traditional design principles. The scalability and adaptability of lighting permutations also necessitate robust design guidelines. In diverse climatic contexts, for example, the orientation and density of façade patterns must account for variations in sunlight intensity and seasonal changes. Furthermore, cultural sensitivity is paramount, especially when reinterpreting Islamic motifs for contemporary, globalized settings. Patterns must be contextually relevant, respecting local traditions while addressing modern functional demands. The integration of advanced fabrication techniques, such as CNC milling or 3D printing, offers solutions for bridging these gaps, enabling the creation of intricate patterns with precision and efficiency. Perhaps in the future, the exploration of lighting permutations in façade design offers an avenue for bridging heritage and innovation. By reinterpreting traditional Islamic patterns through the lens of modern technology, architects can create designs that resonate with cultural identity while addressing contemporary environmental and social challenges. This approach not only enhances IEQ but also fosters a deeper appreciation of the interplay between light, space, and culture. Through thoughtful integration of historical insights, computational tools, and advanced materials, lighting permutations can transform façades into active agents of sustainability and cultural expression, redefining the role of architecture in shaping human experience.

## 2.5 Lighting in Indoor Environment Quality

In Indoor Environment Quality engagement, Lighting plays a pivotal role in in shaping the quality of indoor environments, influencing not only the functionality of spaces but also the physical and psychological well-being of occupants. In the context of Indoor Environment Quality (IEQ), lighting transcends mere illumination, becoming a tool for enhancing comfort, productivity, and aesthetic appeal. The interplay between natural and artificial light, along with the design strategies employed to balance these elements, defines the effectiveness of lighting in indoor spaces. As modern architectural practices increasingly emphasize sustainability and human-centric design, the integration of efficient and adaptive lighting systems has emerged as a critical factor in achieving optimal IEQ.

At its core, lighting in IEQ revolves around three primary dimensions: visual comfort, circadian health, and energy efficiency. Visual comfort pertains to the qualitative aspects of lighting, such as brightness levels, uniformity, and glare control. Poor lighting design—whether from excessive brightness or inadequate illumination—can cause discomfort, eye strain, and reduced task performance. Nat-

fabrication, marking a period of rapid innovation in robotics within architecture and construction. While digital tools offer immense potential for creative exploration, their industrial use remains largely constrained by cost-effectiveness and production optimization, highlighting the ongoing challenge of aligning technological possibilities with architectural vision(Sille Pihlak & Siim Tuksam, n.d.). The interaction between material properties and form is fundamental, as the capabilities of the material influence the design, and in turn, the design is shaped by material behavior. As a result, 3D printing emerges as an ideal technology for achieving bold, complex architectural forms while simultaneously optimizing the efficiency of the construction process(João Teixeira et al., n.d.).

## 3.0 OBJECTIVES

The primary objective of this research is to explore how Islamic ornamentation design can be applied to the development of natural lighting permutation methods to enhance indoor environmental quality (IEQ). Specific goals include:

### 3.1 Investigating Ornamental Design in Islamic Tradition

The research aims to investigate the geometries, patterns, and symbolic meanings embedded in traditional Islamic ornamentation. These patterns offer potential not just as decorative elements but as functional tools for controlling and diffusing natural light. By analysing these designs, the study seeks to identify key principles that inform effective lighting design, offering a culturally rooted alternative to conventional lighting techniques. The geometry often found in these designs, such as interlocking stars, circles, and arabesques, carries a rich cultural and symbolic significance, representing unity, infinity, and the divine order of the universe. This aspect of Islamic ornamentation challenges the conventional Western separation of form and function, offering a harmonious blend of aesthetics and practical applications. The intricate patterns, developed over centuries of intellectual and artistic tradition, are seen as both an expression of beauty and a tool for conveying deeper meanings about the world and existence.

*Figure 7. Mosque courtyard for natural lighting*

The potential of Islamic ornamentation to function as a tool for controlling and diffusing natural light is a significant area of exploration in this research. Traditional Islamic buildings, such as mosques, palaces, and madrasas, often incorporate detailed geometric patterns in their architectural features, such as window grilles, latticework, and domes. This objective seeks to uncover new insights into how traditional Islamic ornamentation can be leveraged to create spaces that are not only aesthetically pleasing but also functionally efficient, reducing the need for artificial lighting while enhancing the user experience through natural light.

## 3.2 Utilizing Design Tools to Discover Potential Strategies in Ornamental Lighting

Another objective is to utilize modelling design tools to translate Islamic ornamentation into flexible lighting strategies. Modelling tools enable designers to manipulate complex geometries and simulate various lighting conditions, which is particularly useful for adapting historical designs to contemporary architectural spaces. The research will focus on generating adaptable natural lighting permutations that respond to changing light conditions throughout the day, thereby improving visual comfort and energy efficiency. The study seeks to demonstrate how ornamentation-inspired lighting can enhance key IEQ factors, such as thermal and visual comfort, while reducing reliance on artificial lighting. These tools allow for the creation of dynamic, responsive lighting designs that can be tailored to specific spaces and changing conditions. By translating the geometric patterns found in Islamic ornamentation into digital models, designers can simulate various lighting scenarios and optimize the performance of natural light within a building. This approach not only preserves the aesthetic integrity of traditional designs but also offers flexibility in adapting them to modern architectural requirements.

*Figure 8. Lighting design in domes (Masjid Kota Kemuning)*

One of the primary benefits of using design modeling tools is the ability to simulate how light interacts with these intricate patterns throughout the day. Islamic ornamentation, often designed with precise geometries, can influence the diffusion and direction of natural light, creating effects such as dappled sunlight or soft, diffused illumination. This allows for the creation of adaptable lighting solutions that respond to the changing position of the sun, optimizing light distribution and minimizing the need for artificial lighting. The research will focus on generating lighting strategies that account for seasonal and daily variations in sunlight, ensuring that buildings benefit from natural light for as long as possible. This approach contributes to visual comfort, energy efficiency, and the overall well-being of building occupants.

## 3.3 Aligns Traditional Ornamental Façade Design to Sustainable Building Practices

Through the achievement of these objectives, this research aims to expand the current understanding of how traditional design principles can be harnessed to address contemporary challenges in sustainable architecture and IEQ improvement. (Pastore & Andersen, 2022) this research seeks to align the insights gained from Islamic ornamental design with sustainable building practices. In an era where the demand for energy-efficient and environmentally responsible buildings is increasing, it is crucial to explore how traditional design principles can be harnessed to meet contemporary sustainability challenges. Islamic ornamentation, with its emphasis on light manipulation and passive design strategies, offers a unique opportunity to reduce the environmental footprint of modern buildings. By incorporating ornamental patterns into façade designs, buildings can be better oriented and adapted to optimize natural light while minimizing heat gain and loss. This passive approach not only contributes to the aesthetic appeal of a building but also enhances its energy performance, reducing the need for mechanical heating, cooling, and artificial lighting.

## 4.0 METHODOLOGY

This study adopts a multi-step methodology, combining computational analysis, alternate model design experimentation, and case study analysis to explore the potential of Islamic ornamentation in achieving natural lighting permutations for indoor environmental quality enhancement. The pre-requisite will be to have a baseline model that can be the reference for the impact of the newly designed façade. By adopting building Information modelling, we can simulate the conditions with accurate geolocation information for climatic and solar lighting input.

*Figure 9. BIM Model: Sunpath diagram to Kuala Lumpur Malaysia (Source: Authors Collection)*

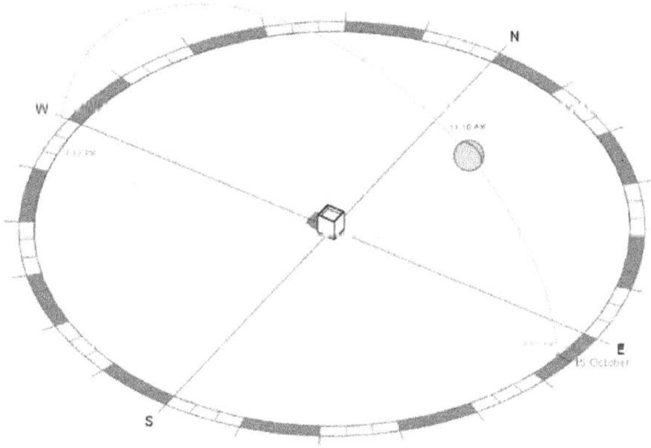

## 4.1 Table Study

The first stage involves an in-depth review of both historical and contemporary applications of Islamic ornamentation in architecture, particularly focusing on the geometrical and symbolic aspects of ornamentation. Historical examples, such as those found in mosques, palaces, and public spaces across the Islamic world, will be examined to identify common design elements that have been used to manipulate natural light. Contemporary applications of these ornamentations will also be analysed, focusing on how modern architecture has adapted these designs in new contexts. Parametric design tools will be employed to model Islamic ornamentation patterns and experiment with their application to lighting strategies. Using BIM Tools, the ornamentation patterns will be adapted into dynamic, flexible geometries that can respond to various light sources and conditions.

*Figure 10. BIM Model: Baseline opening model (Source: Authors Collection)*

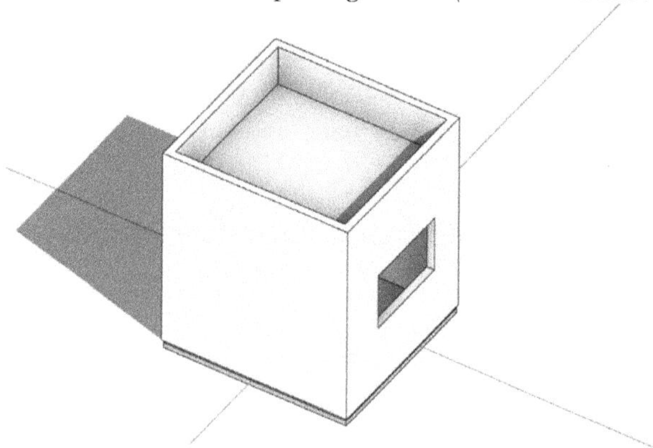

## 4.2 Data Simulation

This process will allow for a simulation of light interaction with these patterns under different environmental conditions, testing their effectiveness in controlling and distributing natural light throughout an interior space. Following the computational modelling of patterns, the next step involves conducting design experiments using parametric simulations. These experiments will assess how different ornamentation patterns perform in terms of light diffusion, shadow creation, and the overall effect on indoor environmental quality. A key aspect of this step is testing the adaptability of these designs across different spatial configurations and lighting conditions, such as varying daylight hours and weather scenarios. Several contemporary architectural projects that integrate Islamic ornamentation with natural lighting strategies will be analysed.

*Figure 11. BIM Model: Internal view of the baseline model (Source: Authors Collection)*

Case studies will focus on buildings that have successfully incorporated ornamentation-inspired lighting solutions, examining their impact on occupant comfort, energy efficiency, and overall spatial harmony. This analysis will provide real-world insights into how such strategies can be effectively implemented. The results of the computational and parametric design experiments will be compared with the findings from the case studies. This comparative analysis will identify the most effective ornamentation patterns and lighting strategies. The study will conclude by formulating a set of design recommendations, offering architects and designers practical guidelines for integrating Islamic ornamentation into modern lighting design to enhance indoor environmental quality.

*Figure 12. BIM Model: Control of conventional Light Shelving Method (Source: Authors Collection)*

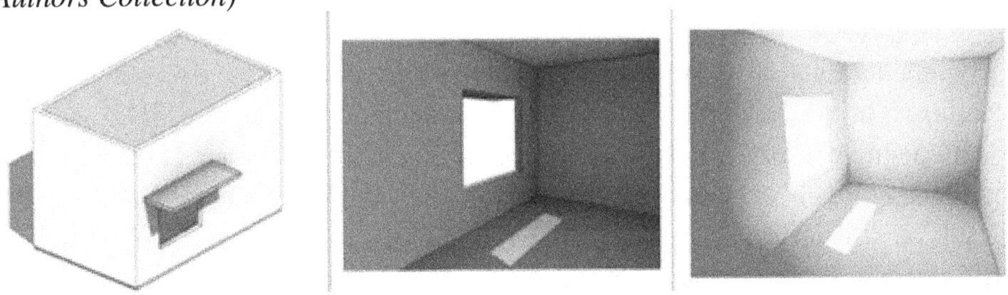

## 4.3 Model Software Tools (Autodesk Revit, Rhinoceros3d, Grasshopper, Enscape)

Islamic ornamentation, with its intricate geometric, arabesque, and calligraphic patterns, serves as both an aesthetic and functional element in architectural design. The interplay of solid and void spaces in these designs directly influences lighting permutations, modulating how natural and artificial light is diffused, reflected, or absorbed within a space. By leveraging advanced computational tools, designers can analyze and optimize these lighting effects to enhance Indoor Environment Quality (IEQ). Digital simulation techniques provide precise control over light behavior, ensuring that both visual comfort and energy efficiency are maximized. The integration of software such as Autodesk Revit, Rhinoceros 3D, Grasshopper, and Enscape 3D enables an in-depth exploration of light-material interactions, allowing for informed design decisions that harmonize artistic heritage with modern environmental requirements.

*Figure 13. Rhinoceros Ornamental Design with Grasshopper*

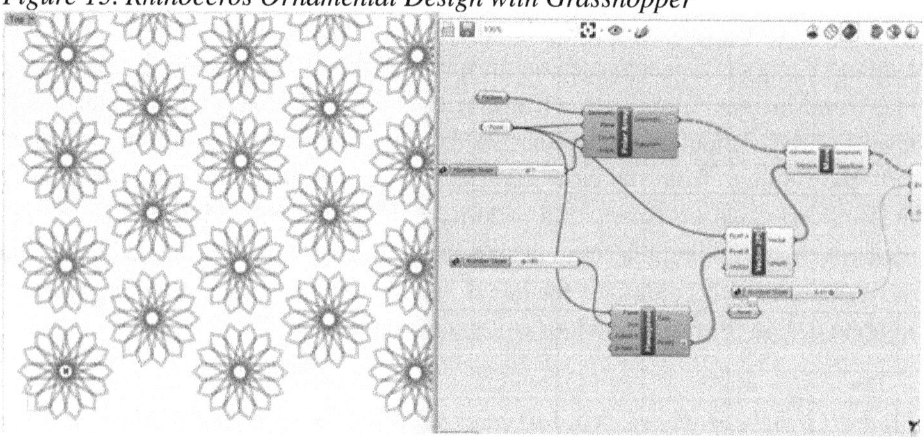

Computational design tools play a pivotal role in simulating and refining lighting conditions in spaces adorned with Islamic ornamentation. Rhinoceros 3D, a parametric modeling platform, allows for the precise generation of complex ornamentation patterns, ensuring accurate spatial representation of perforated screens, engraved panels, and patterned surfaces. By integrating Grasshopper, a visual programming tool, designers can automate the generation of intricate geometries and experiment with varying design parameters that affect light permeability and diffusion. Further refinement is achieved through Enscape 3D, a real-time rendering engine that simulates realistic lighting conditions within a designed space. Enscape 3D provides designers with immediate feedback on how daylight and artificial light interact with surfaces, enabling the evaluation of shadow formation, contrast levels, and ambient luminance. This integration of tools ensures that Islamic ornamentation is not only a decorative element but also a scientifically optimized feature that enhances spatial lighting quality. The luminous analysis comes from visual data produced by enscape within the site locational simulation by revit geolocation system. The synchronous communication provides a very comprehensive visual result on the application.

## 4.4 Model Setup Variables

To accurately simulate and optimize lighting permutations within spaces adorned with Islamic ornamentation, a structured approach to defining key model setup variables is essential. These variables govern how light interacts with the ornamental surfaces, affecting the distribution, intensity, and quality of illumination within an interior setting. By carefully controlling these factors, designers can ensure that lighting solutions enhance visual comfort, energy efficiency, and aesthetic appeal. One of the primary variables is ornamentation density and void ratio, which determines the extent to which light is diffused or concentrated. Islamic patterns, particularly geometric and arabesque designs, can vary in their proportion of solid to void areas, significantly impacting how light filters through a space. High-density patterns with minimal voids tend to create intricate shadow plays that enhance spatial depth, whereas more open, perforated designs allow for broader and more uniform light distribution. This balance between opacity and transparency is critical in achieving the desired luminous effect.

*Figure 14. Scale of Ornaments*

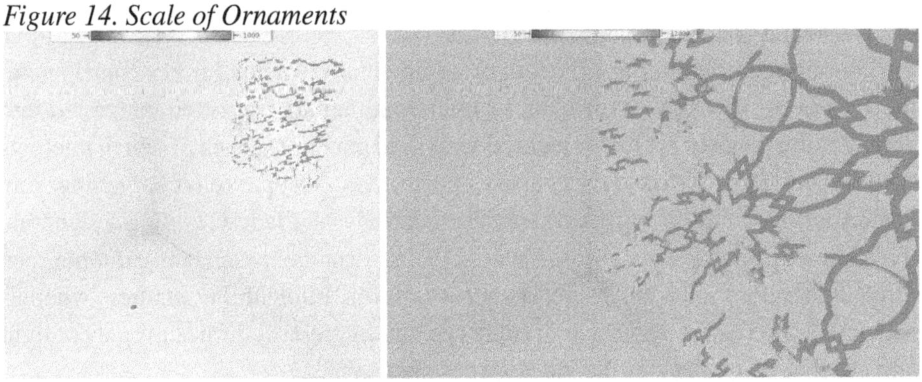

In the setup model, lux reading in simulation are range with the minimum based on the WHO table of lighting/ lux capacity as the following table:

*Table 1. Luminous Analysis Banchmarks*

| Illuminance (Lux) | Category | Application / Effects | Reference |
|---|---|---|---|
| 50 – 200 lx | Acceptable | Hallways, waiting areas, accent lighting. | CIBSE (2017), IESNA (2019) |
| 200 – 500 lx | Acceptable | Offices, classrooms, residential areas, general task lighting. | ISO 8995-1:2002, CIBSE (2017) |
| 500 – 1000 lx | Acceptable | Reading, detailed craftsmanship, architectural design studios. | IESNA (2019), EN 12464-1:2021 |
| 1000 – 3000 lx | Discomfort | Industrial work, supermarkets, medical examination rooms. | CIBSE (2017), IESNA (2019) |
| 3000 – 5000 lx | Discomfort | Laboratories, surgical rooms, controlled high-precision work. | ISO 8995-1:2002 |
| 5000 – 10,000 lx | Discomfort | Photography studios, stadiums, excessive glare in offices. | EN 12464-1:2021 |
| 10,000 – 50,000 lx | Damaging | Outdoor daylight, material degradation, potential eye strain. | IESNA (2019), WHO (2020) |
| 50,000 – 100,000 lx | Damaging | Direct intense sunlight, retinal damage, UV-related degradation. | WHO (2020) |

Another essential factor is material properties, which influence how light is reflected, absorbed, or transmitted upon interaction with surfaces. Different materials used in Islamic ornamentation, such as carved wood, etched metal, and stone lattice, exhibit unique optical behaviors. Matte surfaces diffuse light softly, reducing glare and creating a more even lighting condition, whereas polished materials enhance reflectivity, producing brighter interiors. The selection of materials must be carefully aligned with the intended lighting effect and environmental conditions to optimize both aesthetic and functional performance.

The surface orientation and depth of ornamental elements further contribute to the volumetric distribution of light. Islamic ornamentation is often integrated into architectural features such as screens, domes, and partitions, each of which interacts with light differently based on its spatial positioning. Deeper relief engravings and layered ornamentation introduce subtle gradations of shadow, adding a dynamic three-dimensional quality to the space. Ceiling ornamentation, for example, can direct light reflections downward to improve overall ambient illumination, whereas wall-integrated calligraphy or arabesque designs create a rhythmic interplay of light and shadow that enhances the visual experience.

By systematically analyzing and adjusting these variables, computational modeling enables a precise and responsive approach to lighting design. The fusion of traditional ornamentation with modern simulation tools ensures that historical artistic expressions remain relevant in contemporary architectural applications, enhancing both spatial ambiance and indoor environmental quality.

## 4.5 Simulated Environment Using Enscape 3D

The Enscape 3D simulation highlights how Islamic geometric screens (mashrabiya) filter daylight, reducing harsh glare while maintaining adequate illumination levels. Similarly, calligraphic engravings with varying depths create layered shadow effects that enhance spatial depth and ambiance. These real-time visualizations provide empirical data that align with Indoor Environment Quality principles, ensuring that the lighting design supports both aesthetic aspirations and occupant well-being. Through the integration of computational modeling, parametric design principles, and real-time rendering, Islamic ornamentation is transformed from a traditional decorative feature into an advanced environmental design tool. This methodology bridges the historical elegance of Islamic architecture with contemporary lighting performance requirements, demonstrating that ornamentation can be both a cultural expression and a functional element in achieving optimized indoor environmental quality.

# 5.0 RESULTS AND FINDINGS

## 5.1 Calligraphy Ornamental Design Style

The findings of this study reveal that Islamic ornamentation offers significant potential in enhancing natural lighting strategies within modern architectural spaces. Typical Light shelve method can significantly reduce the volume of light inside the building. Before establishing the newly designed façade, a control can visualize the target or at least at par with the conventional type of glare and over lighting rate. A solid block then constructed just 200mm from the façade to analyse how the diffused light affccts thc intcrnal part. Thc analysis of traditional geometric patterns demonstrates their capacity to manipulate light in ways that enhance both visual comfort and spatial aesthetics. Most famous styles in Islamic calligraphy are a few that can be recognized by their distinct curvature and lines. Kufic calligraphy styles were further developed into cubic and different styles influenced by modern movements.

*Figure 15. different calligraphy style (Source: https://www.arabic-calligraphy.com/arabic-calligraphy-styles/)*

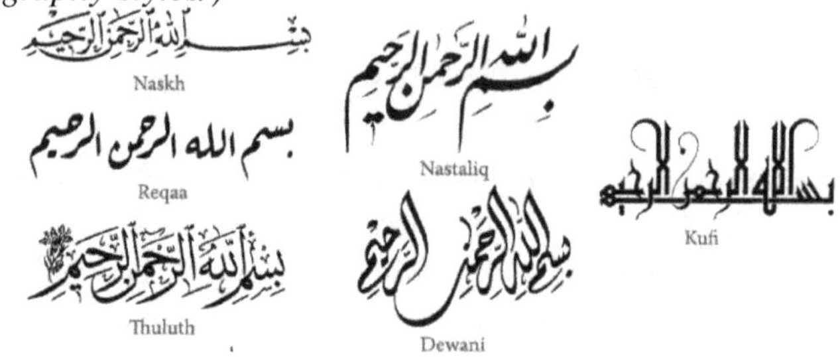


The parametric design experiments confirmed that specific patterns, such as muqarnas and mashrabiya, are particularly effective in diffusing natural light while creating visually dynamic shadow patterns. One of the key findings was the ability of these ornamentation patterns to balance aesthetics with function. The intricate geometries not only created dynamic lighting effects, such as complex shadow patterns that changed with the sun's position but also served practical purposes by filtering light in a way that reduced glare and prevented excessive heat gain. This dual function aligns with the principles of sustainable design, as it maximizes the use of natural light while minimizing the negative impacts of direct sunlight exposure.

*Figure 16. Form Analysis*

The routing application is a subtractive technique widely utilized in Islamic calligraphy, particularly in the fabrication of decorative surfaces and architectural elements. This method employs routers to carve intricate patterns and motifs into materials such as wood, stone, and metal, enabling a high level of precision in the engraving process. When applied to calligraphy, routing allows for the meticulous inscription of Arabic script and abstract designs, creating depth and texture that go beyond the limitations of flat engraving. This approach is frequently employed in architectural features such as doors, panels, and ornamental facades, where calligraphy serves as a fundamental design element. The subtractive nature of routing ensures each calligraphic stroke is rendered with clarity and refinement while introducing a tactile quality that enhances the sensory engagement of the viewer.

*Table 2. Calligraphy Style Characteristics*

| Style | Kufi | Naskh | Thuluth | Diwani | Riqaa |
|---|---|---|---|---|---|
| Main Character | Angular | Formal | Artistic + Formal | Artistic | Simplified |
| Tazyeen | Floral detached | Formal | Space filling + representation | Space filling + representation | None |
| Writing | Technical | Technical | Artistic | Artistic | Freehand |
| Solid Area | Major | Balanced | Major | Major | Minor |
| Void Area | Minor | Major | Minor | Minor | Major |

The variation in calligraphic design influences the way light interacts with surfaces, generating distinct lighting permutations that shape the perception and ambiance of a space. Each calligraphic style, with its unique structural characteristics, affects how light is absorbed, reflected, or diffused. The interplay between solid and void areas, the density of strokes, and the presence of ornamental embellishments contribute to the overall lighting effect, making each style function differently in spatial compositions.

As a summary, the calligraphic style chosen for a design profoundly influences how light behaves within a space. Whether through the structured contrasts of Kufi, the balanced illumination of Naskh, the intricate shadow play of Thuluth and Diwani, or the subtle diffusion of Ruqaʿa, each style contributes to a unique spatial and visual experience. This demonstrates the intrinsic relationship between design and lighting, where artistic expression extends beyond aesthetics into the realm of environmental perception and interaction.

## 5.2 Digital Analysis of Ornament

*Figure 17. BIM Model: 200mm offset wall Control Model (Source: Authors Collection)*

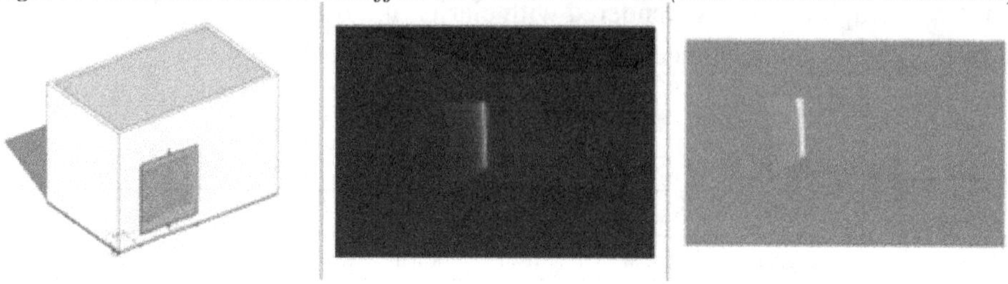

The parametric simulations also highlighted the adaptability of Islamic ornamentation across different building typologies and spatial configurations. By adjusting the scale and orientation of the patterns, designers can tailor the lighting effects to specific architectural needs, whether in small residential spaces or large public buildings. This adaptability is a significant advantage, as it allows for the integration of these ornamentation-inspired lighting strategies in a variety of contexts without compromising on performance.

Moreover, the case study analysis reinforced the importance of cultural context in lighting design. Buildings that employed Islamic ornamentation-inspired lighting solutions were not only visually appealing but also resonated with the cultural heritage of their locations, creating a sense of place and identity. This cultural relevance adds an additional layer of value to the lighting strategies, as it promotes a deeper connection between the built environment and its users.

*Figure 18. BIM Model: Internal view of the cubic kufi model (Source: Authors Collection)*

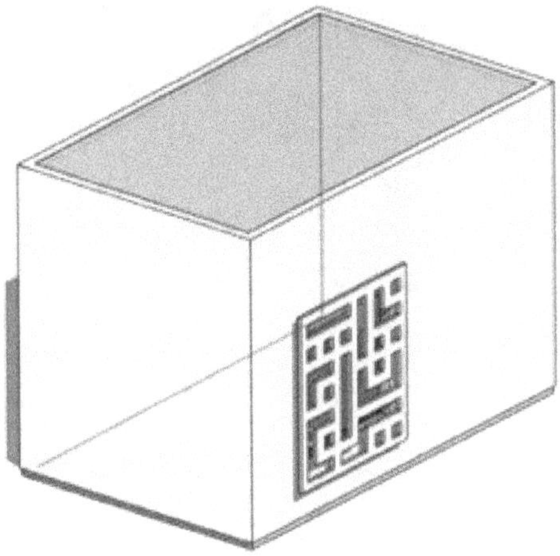

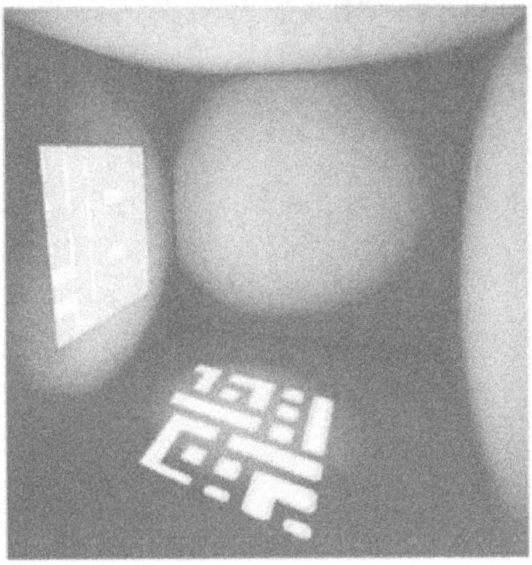

Understanding the solids and voids of external façade, the results demonstrate that Islamic ornamentation, when applied through value-conscious design methodologies, offers a powerful tool for creating sustainable, aesthetically significant, and functionally effective natural lighting strategies in contemporary architecture.

## 5.3 Coverage of Ornaments in Façade Design in Lighting Lux Range

The selection of ornamental design in architectural façades plays a pivotal role in determining the distribution, intensity, and quality of natural light within indoor spaces. Islamic ornamentation, with its intricate geometric, arabesque, and calligraphic patterns, has been historically employed not only for aesthetic enrichment but also as a functional tool for daylight modulation. The perforation density, pattern scale, and spatial arrangement of these ornaments directly impact glare control, visual comfort, and energy efficiency, making them essential factors in optimizing Indoor Environmental Quality (IEQ).

*Figure 19. Modelling Calligraphy with Rhino*

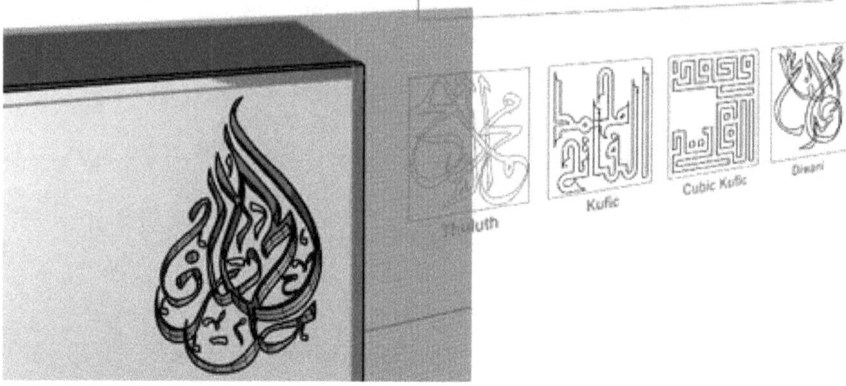


*Table 3. Coverage Lighting Permutation*

| Ornament Coverage (%) | Façade Design Type | Indoor Lighting (Lux Range) | Lighting Effect |
|---|---|---|---|
| 0 – 10% | Minimal Ornamentation (Clear Glass) | 1000 – 5000 lx | High brightness, excessive glare, potential discomfort. |
| 10 – 30% | Sparse Ornamentation (Geometric Grilles) | 500 – 1000 lx | Balanced daylight, moderate glare reduction. |
| 30 – 50% | Moderate Ornamentation (Mashrabiya, Arabesque Screens) | 200 – 800 lx | Diffused daylight, reduced glare, comfortable illumination. |
| 50 – 70% | Dense Ornamentation (Calligraphic and Geometric Layering) | 100 – 500 lx | Soft daylight, strong shading effect, reduced overheating. |
| 70 – 90% | Heavy Ornamentation (Overlapping Patterns, Deeply Recessed Façades) | 50 – 200 lx | Low interior brightness, suitable for controlled ambiance and privacy. |

Ornamentation with a high degree of openness, such as sparsely distributed geometric patterns or light arabesque screens, permits greater daylight penetration into interior spaces. This enhances natural illumination, reducing the need for artificial lighting and contributing to energy savings. However, excessive light exposure—especially in regions with strong solar radiation—can lead to glare, visual discomfort, and increased indoor temperature, negatively affecting occupant well-being. In contrast, denser and more intricate ornamental screens, such as layered mashrabiya or deeply recessed calligraphic panels, provide better light diffusion, mitigating glare while maintaining sufficient brightness for visual tasks.

*Figure 20. Comparison between 4 common style calligraphy*

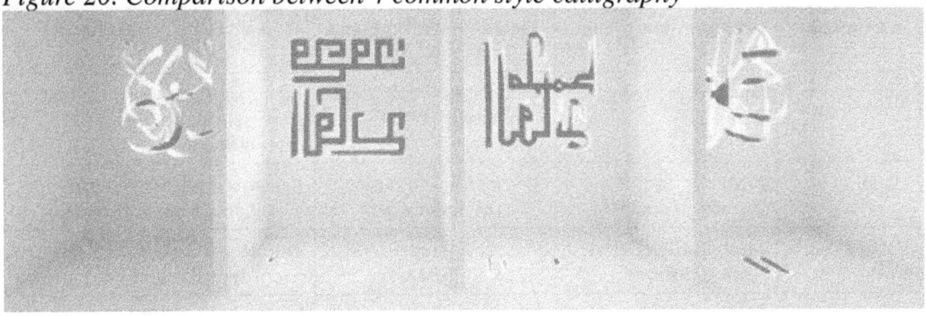

Additionally, the materiality and depth of the ornamentation influence how light is absorbed, reflected, or diffused within the space. Façades incorporating metallic elements may enhance reflectivity, creating brighter interiors, whereas wooden or stone-carved ornaments absorb more light, leading to a softer ambiance. The recessed depth of the ornamentation also contributes to light redirection, particularly in thick façade systems where shadows are cast dynamically throughout the day, reducing direct exposure to harsh sunlight while maintaining ambient luminance.

In the context of IEQ optimization, computational simulation tools such as Rhinoceros 3D, Grasshopper, and Enscape allow for precise control over these parameters, enabling designers to test multiple permutations of ornamental density, orientation, and materiality. By modulating the ornamental façade design, architects can achieve an optimal balance between daylight access, glare reduction, and thermal regulation, ensuring that indoor environments remain visually comfortable, energy-efficient, and aligned with cultural and environmental considerations.

## 5.4 Calligraphy Style and Their Light Relationship

Calligraphy, as an artistic form, holds a distinctive place in architectural ornamentation, where its relationship with light transforms its static beauty into a dynamic interplay of visual and spiritual significance. The stylistic diversity of calligraphy—ranging from geometric Kufic to flowing Naskh—offers unique ways of engaging with light, enhancing the aesthetic, functional, and symbolic qualities of architectural spaces. Out of all the ornamental design, calligraphy is one of the interesting type. Not just it is pleasingly aesthatics, but also literature wise it is a religious scripture with spiritual balance.

*Table 4. Calligraphy style and Permutation*

| Calligraphy Style | Ornamental Density | Light Penetration Effect (Lux Level Impact) | Visual & Thermal Impact |
|---|---|---|---|
| Kufi | High Density (Angular, Block-like) | Reduces lux levels significantly (10-50% blockage) | Strong shading effect, minimizes glare, suitable for high-sun exposure regions. |
| Naskh | Medium Density (Flowing, Formal) | Moderate light diffusion (30-60% transmission) | Balanced daylighting, suitable for even indoor lighting distribution. |
| Thuluth | Medium-High Density (Ornate, Artistic) | Variable light penetration (20-50% blockage) | Enhances artistic light-shadow interplay, dynamic lighting effects. |
| Diwani | Medium-Low Density (Decorative, Flowing) | Allows high light transmission (40-70%) | Softened glare, effective for semi-private spaces requiring natural illumination. |
| Riqa'a | Low Density (Simplified, Freehand) | High lux levels (70-90% transmission) | Maximizes brightness, best for indoor spaces needing abundant daylight. |

*Figure 21. Amir Mustaqim in Modern Kufic*

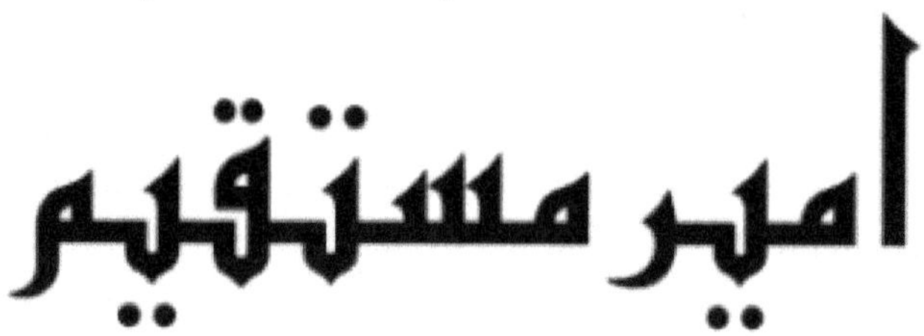


The Kufic script, known for its angular, rectilinear forms, exemplifies a calligraphic style that naturally aligns with architectural structures. Its rigid geometry makes it an ideal choice for integration into facades, lattices, and other structural elements where the modulation of light is crucial. When incorporated into perforated screens or mashrabiyas, Kufic calligraphy allows sunlight to filter through its precise cutouts, casting intricate shadows that shift with the sun's movement. The interplay of light and shadow created by Kufic script symbolizes the balance between the tangible and the divine, resonating with the philosophical underpinnings of Islamic art.

*Figure 22. Amir Mustaqim in Naskh*

In contrast to the rigid forms of Kufic, the Naskh script is characterized by its fluidity and elegance, making it a favored style for decorative inscriptions in domes, arches, and walls. Naskh's flowing curves interact gracefully with both natural and artificial light, creating an effect of softness and rhythm that enhances the spatial experience. This interaction is particularly effective in sacred spaces, where the illuminated script reinforces the spiritual atmosphere, inviting contemplation and reverence. By carefully calibrating the intensity and color temperature of artificial light, designers can evoke different emotional responses, from warmth and intimacy to awe and grandeur, amplifying the calligraphic inscription's intended message.

*Figure 23. Amir Mustaqim in Thuluth*

The Thuluth script, renowned for its grandeur and complexity, occupies a prominent place in monumental architecture. Its large, sweeping lines and extended vertical strokes make it highly effective in interacting with light on expansive surfaces such as domes, minarets, and large panels. Artificial lighting further enhances this dimensional interaction, with grazing light techniques bringing out the depth and texture of the script, adding layers of visual richness to the architectural composition.

## 5.5 Lighting Permutation v. Calligraphy Style

*Figure 24. Amir Mustaqim in Traditional Kufic*

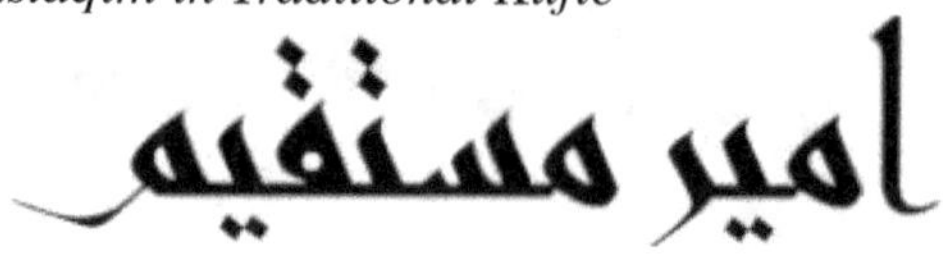

*Table 5. Perforation Analysis of Calligraphy Style*

| Calligraphy Style | Kufic | Naskh | Thuluth | Diwani |
|---|---|---|---|---|
| Opaque | The bold, angular shapes of Kufic script create strong and defined shadows when used as a solid pattern. Its geometric structure blocks light efficiently, producing sharp contrasts and a sense of order. | Naskh's fluid and rounded letterforms allow for smoother transitions between light and shadow. Its softer opacity creates a more delicate light-blocking effect. | Thuluth's tall, elegant letterforms cast dynamic shadows that change with light angles. Its intricate strokes give a blend of boldness and transparency. | Diwani's intricate and compact strokes form dense patterns that block light almost completely, giving a dramatic and ornamental aesthetic when solid. |
| Permutation | Kufic patterns, when perforated or designed with negative spaces, allow precise light penetration, forming angular, geometric projections that shift with the sun. | Naskh, when used in a perforated design, diffuses light gently, creating softer, curvilinear patterns that evoke a calm and rhythmic indoor ambiance. | Thuluth's elongated and overlapping strokes create layered and rhythmic light diffusion patterns, offering a sense of movement and fluidity in the space. | Diwani's compact and ornate design generates intricate, lace-like light patterns, creating a decorative, almost theatrical interplay of light and shadow. |
| Percentage of lighting permutation | 40%-50% | 50%-60% | 20%-40% | 10%-30% |

The interplay of calligraphy styles and light in architectural façades provides a unique opportunity to merge cultural aesthetics with functional design. When used as façades, each calligraphy style exhibits distinct characteristics in terms of light modulation and percentage of lighting permutation, shaping the spatial experience within the structure. This relationship, quantified by the lighting permutation percentage, reflects how much light is allowed to pass through the patterns created by these calligraphy styles, balancing opacity with diffusion.

*Figure 25. Diwani Calligraphy style in lux simulation*

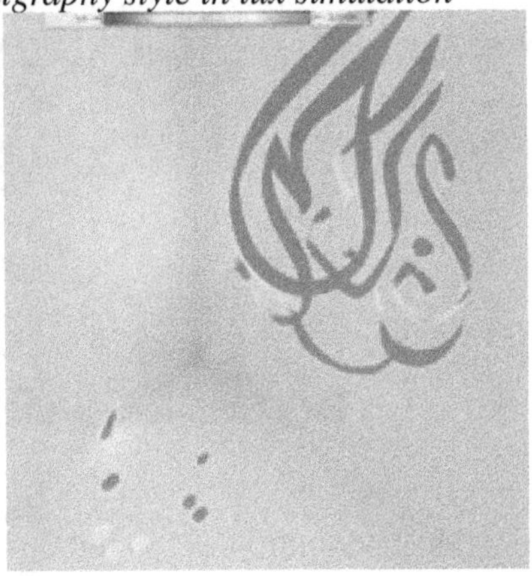

By understanding the unique behavior of each calligraphy style towards light, architects and designers can strategically employ these styles to achieve specific lighting and aesthetic goals. The lighting permutation percentages provide a valuable framework for selecting appropriate styles based on the functional and cultural requirements of a project, ensuring that the façade design harmonizes with both the indoor environment and the architectural intent.

## 6.0 RECOMMENDATION AND CONCLUSION

This study demonstrates that Islamic ornamentation design offers a rich source of inspiration for developing natural lighting permutation methods that enhance indoor environmental quality. By combining traditional geometric patterns with advanced parametric design tools, architects and lighting designers can create lighting strategies that not only improve visual comfort and spatial harmony but also contribute to energy efficiency and sustainable design. The findings highlight the ability of ornamentation-inspired designs to filter and diffuse natural light, reducing the need for artificial lighting and minimizing heat gain in interior spaces. the cultural significance of Islamic ornamentation adds a valuable dimension to these lighting strategies, promoting a deeper connection between architecture and its users. The study provides practical design recommendations for integrating these culturally rooted lighting solutions into modern architectural contexts, offering architects, lighting designers, and engineers new perspectives on the role of ornamentation in sustainable design.

*Figure 26. Rendering: Musalla Front (Source: Authors Collection)*

In conclusion, different ornamentation based on certain style of calligraphy leads into different permutations in the façade. These permutations define spaces ambiance and environment in the indoor environment quality. Designers must consider carefully the geometrical impact in designing façade with lighting permutation that writes religious scripture in spaces that projects the permutations to floors showing respect to the scripture. Although calligraphy itself is fine to be part of the permutations, typography such as names can be ornamented as part of a permutation façade in a building.

## 6.1 Integrating Traditional Islamic Ornamentation Into Contemporary Lighting Design

Based on the findings of this study, it is recommended that architects and lighting designers integrate traditional Islamic ornamentation into modern architectural lighting strategies. By leveraging parametric design tools, designers can adapt and refine these historical geometric patterns to create dynamic lighting solutions that optimize natural light intake and distribution. This approach not only enhances visual comfort by creating harmonious light conditions but also reduces the reliance on artificial lighting, promoting energy efficiency. The filtering and diffusing properties of these patterns can be employed to minimize heat gain and glare while maintaining a pleasant indoor environment. To ensure that these designs are seamlessly integrated into modern buildings, further research and development should be dedicated to refining the application of these ornamentation-inspired lighting strategies, including their adaptability to different architectural styles and climatic conditions. Moreover, training programs for architects, lighting designers, and engineers should be developed to foster a deeper understanding of how to utilize these traditional designs in contemporary contexts, creating a bridge between cultural heritage and modern sustainability.

## 6.2 Promoting the Cultural and Environmental Benefits of Ornamentation-Inspired Lighting Solutions

Another key recommendation is to promote the cultural and environmental benefits of ornamentation-inspired lighting strategies within sustainable building practices. As this study demonstrates, Islamic ornamentation not only offers a visually pleasing aesthetic but also contributes to improved indoor environmental quality (IEQ) and energy conservation. To maximize these benefits, it is crucial for architectural firms, educational institutions, and industry leaders to advocate for the integration of ornamentation-based lighting solutions in both new construction and renovation projects. By emphasizing the cultural significance of these designs, stakeholders can enhance users' emotional and psychological connections to their spaces, fostering a sense of cultural continuity and well-being. Additionally, incorporating these strategies into building codes and sustainability guidelines can help align modern construction practices with global energy efficiency goals. Governments and architectural bodies should consider incentivizing the use of ornamentation-inspired natural lighting strategies through policy measures, such as green building certifications and financial support for research in sustainable design innovation.

## REFERENCES


Afghan, A. M. (2020). The Art of Islamic Calligraphy. *SAARC Research Journal*, 7.

Awang, M., & Md Zain, Z. (2007). Preliminary studies of fourier analysis for some climate data that influences heat transfer in building envelope/Masriah Hj Awang and Zainazlan Md Zain.

Dave, D. (2024). Biophilic Design Principles with Kinetic Facade. [IRJAEM]. *International Research Journal on Advanced Engineering and Management, 2*(09), 2952–2955. DOI: 10.47392/IRJAEM.2024.0436

Ganiyev, A. (n.d.). *THE ROLE OF ARCHITECTURE IN ISLAMIC CIVILIZATION*. https://doi.org/DOI: 10.47980/IIAU/2023/3/1

Germin, J.G. (n.d.). *Thermodynamic Interactions: Energy and Architecture*.

Haidar, S., Zou, F., & Li, X. (2023). AN ANALYTICAL STUDY OF FIVE-POINTED ISLAMIC FLORAL PATTERNS AND AN EXPERIMENTAL DESIGN USING PENROSE TILING. *Shedet, 10*(10), 227–245. DOI: 10.21608/shedet.2023.291530

Hamidon, N. A., Md Ishak, S. M., & WMD, W. S. A. (2022, April 20). *Design Structure In Malaysian Islamic Calligraphy Contemporary Paintings*. DOI: 10.4108/eai.24-8-2021.2315281

Licina, D., Wargocki, P., Pyke, C., & Altomonte, S. (2021). The future of IEQ in green building certifications. *Buildings & Cities, 2*(1), 907–927. DOI: 10.5334/bc.148

Matin, N. H., Eydgahi, A., & Gharipour, A. (2025). Sustainable Design: Minimizing Discomfort Glare Through Data-Driven Methods for Responsive Facades. *Sustainability (Basel), 17*(2), 783. Advance online publication. DOI: 10.3390/su17020783

Md Amin, N. D., Yip, C. F., Adnan, N. A., Sabil, A., & Noor Hisham, N. (2022). Simulation Study on Natural Lighting Projection Through Façade Optimisation for A Proposed Disaster and Relief Center. *IOP Conference Series. Earth and Environmental Science, 1022*(1), 012006. Advance online publication. DOI: 10.1088/1755-1315/1022/1/012006

Mohammad Nasser AL-Arifi, T.AL-Arifi. (2023). Decorative aesthetic aspects and their use in Islamic architecture. *Al-Academy*, (107), 77–92. DOI: 10.35560/jcofarts107/77-92

Pastore, L., & Andersen, M. (2022). The influence of façade and space design on building occupants' indoor experience. *Journal of Building Engineering, 46*, 103663. Advance online publication. DOI: 10.1016/j.jobe.2021.103663

Pihlak, S., & Tuksam, S. (2019). Algorithmic craftsmanship for bespoke timber architecture. *Digital Wood Design: Innovative Techniques of Representation in Architectural Design*, 1439-1458.

Ranjazmay Azari, M., Bemanian, M., Mahdavinejad, M., Körner, A., & Knippers, J. (2023). Application-based principles of Islamic geometric patterns; state-of-the-art, and future trends in computer science/technologies: a review. In *Heritage Science* (Vol. 11, Issue 1). Springer Science and Business Media Deutschland GmbH. DOI: 10.1186/s40494-022-00852-w

Teixeira, J., Zuazua-Ros, A., Jesus, M., Rangel, B., & Sofia Guimarães, A. (2023). *How 3DPC Will Transform Architectural Design. In 3D Printing for Construction with Alternative Materials*. Springer International Publishing.

Wang, C., Zhang, F., Wang, J., Doyle, J. K., Hancock, P. A., Mak, C. M., & Liu, S. (2021). How indoor environmental quality affects occupants' cognitive functions: A systematic review. In *Building and Environment* (Vol. 193). Elsevier Ltd., DOI: 10.1016/j.buildenv.2021.107647

Zain, Z. M., Taib, M. N., & Baki, S. M. S. (2007). Hot and humid climate: Prospect for thermal comfort in residential building. *Desalination*, *209*(1–3), 261–268. DOI: 10.1016/j.desal.2007.04.036

# Chapter 7
# Study of Urban Pollution Through In-Situ and Remote Sensing Measurements, Chemical Analysis, and Chemical Transport Model Assimilation Techniques

**Elena Montilla-Rosero**
https://orcid.org/0000-0003-1848-9679
*EAFIT University, Colombia*

**Olga Lucia Quintero**
*EAFIT University, Colombia*

**Jorge E. Pachon**
https://orcid.org/0000-0002-6444-5995
*Universidad de La Salle, Colombia*

**Francisco Botero**
*EAFIT University, Colombia*

**John H. Reina**
https://orcid.org/0000-0003-1860-5414
*Universidad del Valle, Colombia*

**Jose Fernando Duque**
https://orcid.org/0000-0003-1231-6013
*EAFIT University, Colombia*

**Néstor Y. Rojas**
https://orcid.org/0000-0001-7804-0449
*Universidad Nacional de Colombia, Colombia*

**Nicolás Pinel**
https://orcid.org/0000-0003-1304-3096
*EAFIT University, Colombia*

**Manuela Hoyos-Restrepo**
https://orcid.org/0000-0002-3706-5161
*EAFIT University, Colombia*

DOI: 10.4018/979-8-3373-0390-1.ch007

**Waira W. S. Moná**
https://orcid.org/0009-0000-2645-5570
*EAFIT University, Colombia*

**Andres Yarce Botero**
https://orcid.org/0000-0003-1441-2367
*EAFIT University, Colombia*

**Diego Arias-Arana**
https://orcid.org/0000-0002-1001-7768
*Universidad del Valle, Colombia*

**Jhon Edinson Hinestroza-Ramirez**
https://orcid.org/0000-0001-8861-8961
*EAFIT University, Colombia*

**Daniela Bustos**
https://orcid.org/0000-0002-1603-0242
*Universidad Nacional de Colombia, Colombia*

**Sebastian C. Estrada**
https://orcid.org/0000-0002-7776-707X
*EAFIT University, Colombia*

**Fernando Fernández**
https://orcid.org/0000-0002-7614-0582
*EAFIT University, Colombia*

## ABSTRACT

*This chapter focuses on studying urban pollutants in Colombia's most populated cities by developing local instrumentation and implementing chemical transport models (CTMs). The instrumentation includes Scanning Depolarization Lidar System, MAX-DOAS and low-cost in situ devices. Additionally, particulate matter is collected for chemical and morphological analysis using different techniques to identify the main sources of emissions. The chapter aims to provide examples of the findings from a study that is set to establish a foundation for adapting chemical and transport models to complex topography, such as coupling WRF-Chem with LOTOS-EUROS and setting the basis for incorporating data assimilation techniques to enhance the models' predictive capabilities in tropical conditions.*

## INTRODUCTION

Urban pollution significantly affects the natural environment, leading to soil contamination, water pollution, and a decline in biodiversity (UNEP, 2023). Human activities, including industrial emissions, agricultural practices, combustion processes, vehicular traffic, and inadequate waste management, are the primary drivers of environmental pollution in urban areas (Manisalidis et al., 2020). These anthropogenic sources significantly contribute to the deterioration of air, water, and soil quality in cities, exacerbating public health risks like respiratory diseases, cardiovascular problems, and even premature mortality, particularly in vulnerable populations like children and the elderly (WHO, 2024). Given these challenges, studying urban pollution is essential for developing effective mitigation strategies, promoting sustainable urban planning, and improving quality of life in cities.

To address this, Chemical and Transport Models (CTMs) are used to predict the behavior of air pollutants and support policies to reduce contamination. However, the global effectiveness of these models has been constrained by challenges such as complex topography and reliance on outdated emissions inventories in the studied regions. In a tropical country like Colombia, besides these challenging conditions, the impact of urban pollution on biodiversity is a considerable topic. In this chapter, we present the key findings of the 4DAir research project, which was designed to overcome these limitations through three parallel implementation phases: the first phase involved developing low-cost, remote sensing, and in-situ technologies for air pollution monitoring; the second phase centered on the chemical and morphological characterization of pollutants, while the third phase focused on implementing CTM models in the country. The research project aimed to contribute to air pollution predictions and open a new field of data assimilation for CTMs by providing accessible information about the chemical composition and temporal evolution of pollutant concentration measured by remote sensing technologies in neotropical countries like Colombia.

## PHASE I: REMOTE SENSING AND IN-SITU INSTRUMENTATION DEVELOPMENT FOR ATMOSPHERIC AEROSOLS MEASUREMENTS

Remote sensing and in-situ techniques are crucial for studying atmospheric components, offering complementary data on their optical and microphysical properties. Trace gases, atmospheric aerosols, and their effects have been studied using both passive and active techniques, such as Lidar and spectroradiometry (Devara, 1998). Developing these techniques combined with low-cost in-situ measurements of surface aerosols could provide a comprehensive observation of the atmosphere, which is urgently required for urban air quality and climatic study. This section presents and discusses the remote and in-situ measurement techniques developed in a neotropical city, showing the main applications for urban pollution studies.

Firstly, a developed Scanning Depolarization Lidar System (SDLS) to retrieve aerosol optical properties by measuring the backscattered signal from a laser pointed into the atmosphere is presented. Secondly, a passive technique called Multi-Axis Differential Optical Absorption Spectroscopy (MAX-DOAS) is described. In contrast to SDLS, this passive sensing technique relies on solar radiation, detecting trace gases by differentiation of light absorption across atmospheric columns with and without the gas (Edner et al., 1993). Furthermore, an in-situ low-cost monitoring network was developed using aerospace technology to directly gather data on temperature, humidity, trace gases, and PM (particulate matter) concentrations, with no physical separation between the instruments and the target.

## Scanning Depolarization Lidar System (SDLS) Fundamentals

Lidar systems use artificial light injected into the atmosphere to measure back-scattered light at different distances ($R$). Most lidar systems operate according to semi-empirical relationship between measured intensity and the total backscatter coefficient $\beta(R,\lambda)$ considering molecules $\beta_{mol}(R,\lambda)$ and aerosols $\beta_{aer}(R,\lambda)$ together with the atmospheric transmission $T(R) = e^{[-2\int_0^R \alpha(r,\lambda)dr]}$, it includes the total extinction coefficient $\alpha(r,\lambda)$ that consider absorption and scattering for both molecules and aerosols (Wandinger, 2005).

To retrieve lidar products containing atmospheric information ($\beta(R)$ and $\alpha(R)$ ) the Klett-Fernald Sasano (KFS) method is applied (Fernald, 1984; Klett, 1985; Sasano & Nakane, 1984; Wandinger, 2005; Ansmann & Müller, 2005). Furthermore, the volume depolarization $\delta^v$, the ratio of the backscatter coefficient when linearly polarized radiation interacts with the atmosphere (Hoyos-Restrepo, 2021; Mishchenko et al., 2000). And the particle depolarization, $\delta^p$, another lidar product that accounts only for changes in polarization induced by aerosols (Freudenthaler, 2016) were retrieved in this work.

### SDLS Technical Specifications

A summary of the SDLS technical characteristics is shown in **Table 1** with an overview of the system design in **Figure 1**, where the stepper motors allow the SDLS to perform 3D measurements.

*Table 1. Technical Characteristics of the SDLS (Hoyos-Restrepo, 2021)*

| Characteristic | Value |
|---|---|
| Transmitter Nd:YAG Q-switched laser | 20 Hz, 200 mJ (@532)<br>Divergence < 0.5 mrad, Polarization ratio > 80% |
| VIS-NIR Beam Expander | 7x, $\theta_{out}$ < 0.07 mrad, T > 94% |
| Receiver Telescope | 9.25" f/10 Schmidt-Cassegrain |
| Interference filter | 2.00 nm FWHM, 532 CWL, $T_{min}$ > 90% |

continued on following page

*Table 1. Continued*

| Characteristic | Value |
|---|---|
| Polarizing beam splitter | $T_p > 95\%$, $R_s > 99.5\%$, Tp:Ts > 3,000:1 |
| Photomultiplier tubes | Hamamatsu R9880 |
| *Data acquisition* Licel TR40-16Bit-3 | 16 Bit – 40 MHz A / D, 800 MHz phot.count. rate |
| *Scanning* Range | 0.00-90.00° (zenith), 0.00-360.00° (azimuth) |
| Resolution | 0.82° (zenith), 0.35° (azimuth) |

*Figure 1. General Design Schematic of the SDLS (Hoyos-Restrepo & Montilla-Rosero, 2022)*

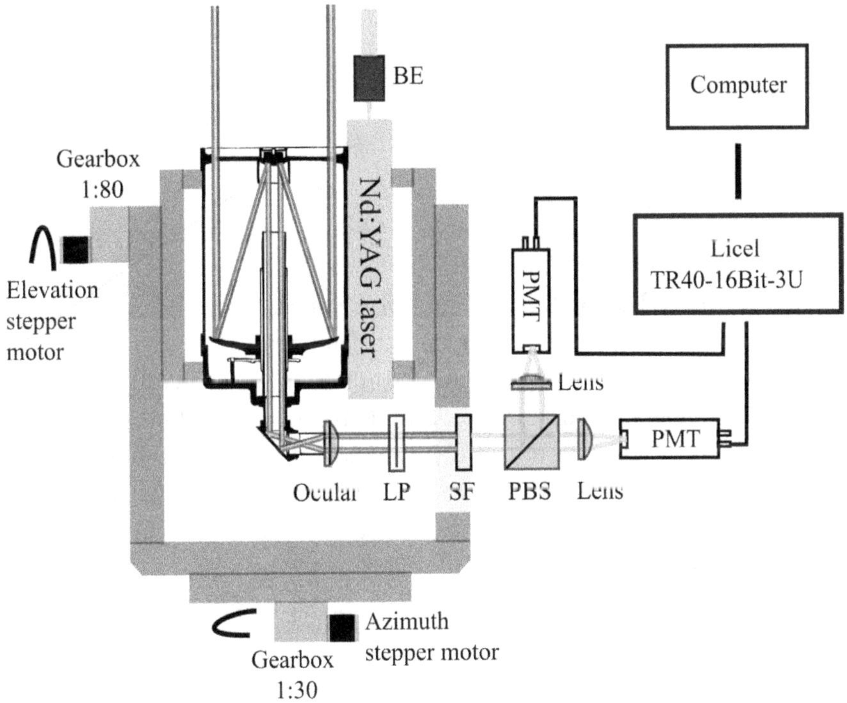

## MAX-DOAS Fundamentals

The MAX-DOAS technique (**Figure 2**) uses the Beer-Lambert law to measure trace gases by distinguishing between narrow-band absorption (associated with trace gases $\sigma_i'(\lambda)$) and broad-band spectral components due to Rayleigh scattering $\varepsilon_R$, Mie scattering $\varepsilon_M$, atmospheric turbulence $A(\lambda)$, common (oxygen and nitrogen) molecules absorption $\sigma'_{i0}(\lambda)$ (Fuentes-Inzunza, 2012). This differentiation allows the precise calculation of trace gas concentration along the slant column density (SCD) at multiple elevation angles (Moná-Bedoya, 2023).

*Figure 2. MAX-DOAS Instrument Measurement Schematic and DOAS Technique Diagram. Adapted from (Fuentes-Inzunza, 2012).*

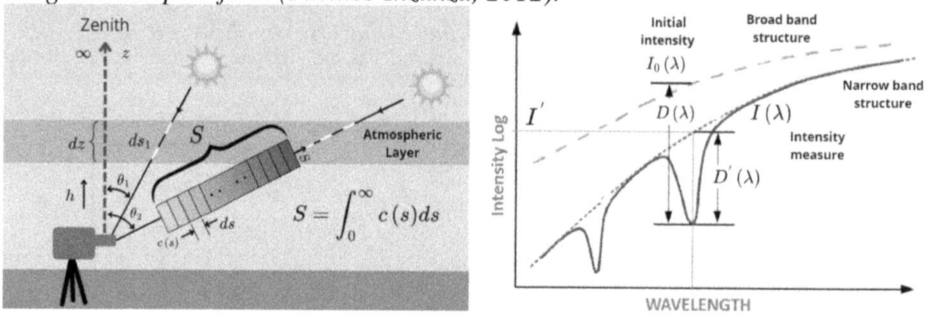


Applying the Beer-Lambert law to atmospheric measurements requires considering all the spectral components extinction, differentiating between fast and slow components. Considering a slowly varying absorption as a new reference spectrum, a modified Beer-Lambert law allows the redefinition of the differential optical density, as a measure of the absorption due to trace gases as a function of their respective absorption cross sections and the concentration (Moná-Bedoya, 2023).

Since the light source is sunlight, it is difficult to define an optical path L, so the slant column density (SCD) is introduced (Fuentes-Inzunza, 2012), and rearranged to obtain concentration. The Effective Slant Column Density DSCD, Equation (11), is defined as the difference between $SCD_{measured}$ (derived from an intensity column at an elevation angle theta) and $SCD_{FRS}$ associated Fraunhofer spectrum (Moná-Bedoya, 2023).

$$DSCD = SCD_{measured} - SCD_{FRS} = \frac{D'_{measured} - D'_{FRS}}{\sigma_i'} \quad (11)$$

## MAX-DOAS Technical Specifications

The instrument consists of a telescope unit with a 1.0° field of view (FOV), connected via an optical fiber to a grating spectrometer, saving the measured spectra on an embedded computer every two minutes. General schematics and technical specifications can be seen in **Figure 3** and **Table 2**. The commercial MAX-DOAS Airyx GmbH property of CiBiOFi (Universidad del Valle) is used in this project.

*Figure 3. MAX-DOAS general components and schematic (Airyx, 2024)*

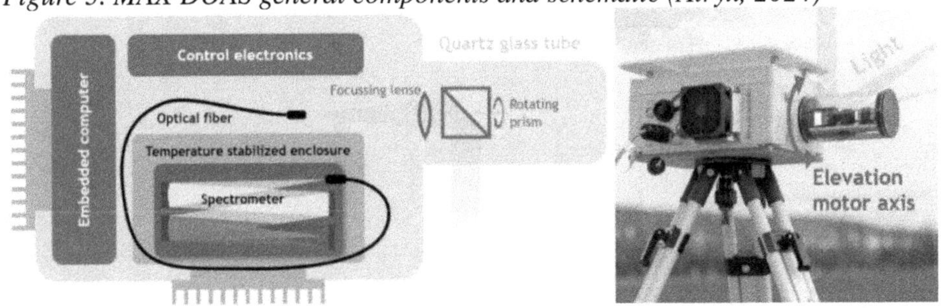


*Table 2. MAX-DOAS Technical Specifications (Moná-Bedoya, 2022; Moná-Bedoya, 2023)*

| Characteristic | Value |
|---|---|
| Field of view (FOV) | < 0.3° |
| Spectrometer resolution | < 0.7 nm FWHM |
| $RMS_{vis}$ | $10^{-4}$ |
| $RMS_{uv}$ | $10^{-4}$ |
| Temperature stabilization | < 0.05 °C |
| Azimuthal angle | 0° - 180° (± 0.1°) |
| Wavelength range | 300 nm – 460 nm |

## Preprocessing and Processing Methods

The preprocessing stage in **Figure 4** involves selecting the spectra captured with a predefined zenith solar angle of less than 17 degrees and an elevation angle of 90 degrees ($I_{measured}(\lambda)$). Then, the obtention of the Fraunhoffer spectrum ($I_{FRS}(\lambda)$) and the reference cross-sectional absorption spectra of trace gases ($\sigma_i'$). After that, the dark current is removed, and wavelength calibration is applied.

Finally in the processing stage of **Figure 4**, in the mathematical model, the $SCD_{FRS}(\lambda)$ and $SCD'_{measured}(\lambda)$ are calculated to obtain the *DSCD*, Equation (11), using the reference $NO_2$ absorption cross-section $\sigma_i'$.

*Figure 4. Preprocessing and Processing workflow. Adapted from (Moná-Bedoya, 2023)*

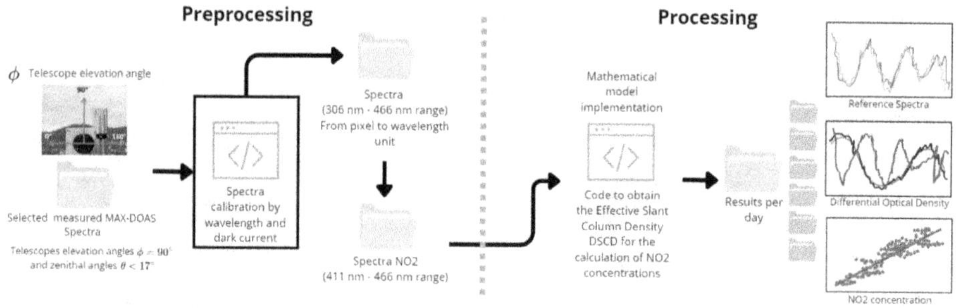


## In-Situ Low-Cost Network

In this project a network throughout the valley using low-cost sensors called Simple-4 was implemented. Conventional sensors typically cost thousands of dollars, whereas low-cost variants remain below 500 USD. In this work, we developed each sensor for less than 50 USD (Yarce Botero et al., 2023a; Karagulian, 2019). **Table 3** shows the technical specifications for the device that was developed internally. The Simple-4 unit is shown in **Figure 5**. Simple-4 measures optically particulate matter below 2.5 mm, traces gases like Ozone, and meteorological variables (temperature and relative humidity).

*Table 3. Simple-4 Technical Characteristics and Device Image (Yarce Botero et al., 2023a).*

| **Technical Characteristics** |
| --- |
| In-situ monitoring unit for outdoor environments. |
| Transmission system via APRS, LORA, or WiFi. |
| Measurement of variables tailored to user needs through modular design. |
| Storage, acquisition, and data transmission to the cloud. |
| Unplug & play power system. |
| Transmission bandwidth of 100 kbps. |
| Functional voltage levels of 5V and 3.3V. |
| Consumption of 300 mA/h and powered by a 10W solar panel. |

*Figure 5. Simple-4 Device Image*

## In-Situ Unit Hardware Design

The Simple-4 low-cost in-situ device has evolved from several architectures; the engineering design, development, and overtests that ensure the long-term performance and reliability of the devices are described in Yarce Botero et al., 2023a. The Simple-4 unit has sensors to measure CO, $NO_2$, $C_2H_6O$, $H_2$, $NH_3$, $CH_4$, $C_3H_8$, $C_4H_{10}$ concentrations, humidity and temperature, and communication board are on top, batteries in the middle, and external connecting plugs at the inferior part. It has a volume of 1.0 L and a mass of 1.5 kg.

The calibration of Simple-4 to maintain the low-cost profile was an inter-calibration procedure, in which measurements are compared against reference sensors. For details see Rojas González & Montilla-Rosero (2025).

## Simple-4 Network

The location of the Simple-4 station was selected according to the LOTOS-EUROS model to explore the effects of the valley's wind on the transport of pollutants (Yarce-Botero et al., 2024). **Figure 6** shows a map of the Simple-4 stations in the network.

*Figure 6. Map of the simple-4 stations. The green makers represent active stations and the red uninstalled stations.*

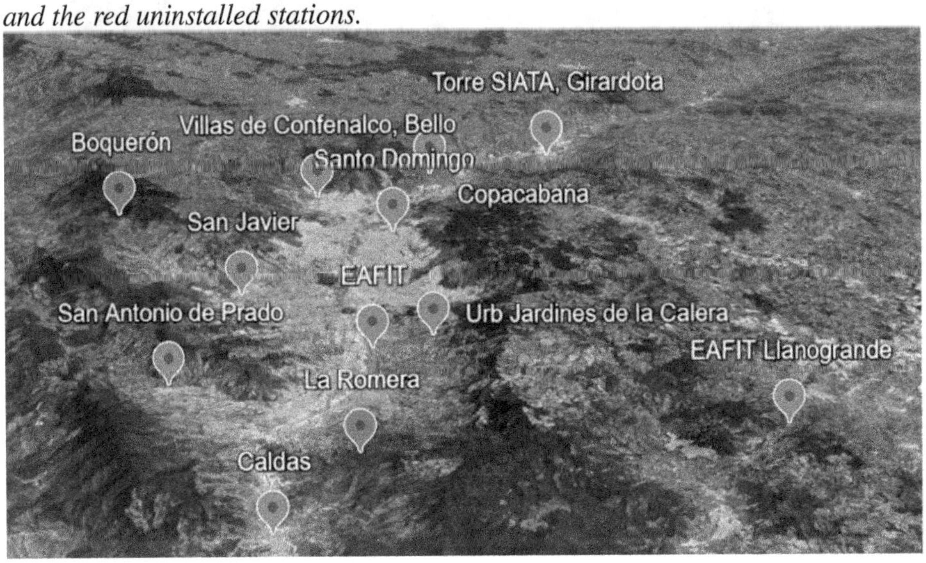

## Phase I: Initial Outcomes and Discussion

### SDLS Vertical Measurements

The operational tests and first measurements of the scanning depolarization lidar system were carried out at Universidad EAFIT's central campus, located south of the city of Medellín (Colombia) (6"12"00' N, 75"34"42' W). Initially, vertical measurements were performed on April 11th of 2022 at 18:04. **Figure 7a** shows the range corrected lidar signal (RCS) received at the p-channel and **Figure 7b** displays the RCS on the s-channel. With a spatial resolution of 3.75 m, vertical profiles were taken every 60 seconds for both measurements.

*Figure 7. Temporal evolution of the transmitted RCS at 532.p nm and at 532.s nm for the measurement performed on April 11, 2022.*

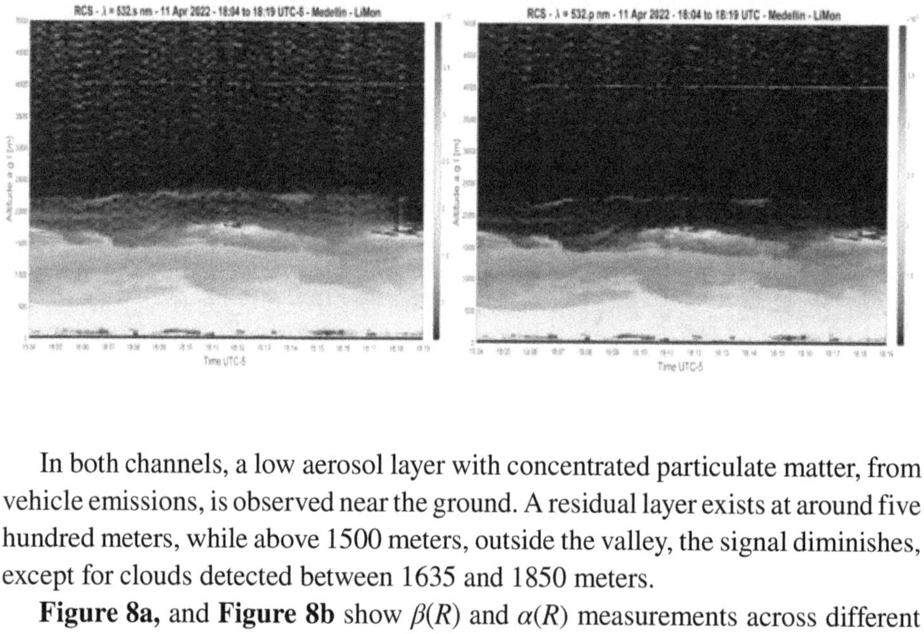


In both channels, a low aerosol layer with concentrated particulate matter, from vehicle emissions, is observed near the ground. A residual layer exists at around five hundred meters, while above 1500 meters, outside the valley, the signal diminishes, except for clouds detected between 1635 and 1850 meters.

**Figure 8a,** and **Figure 8b** show $\beta(R)$ and $\alpha(R)$ measurements across different time periods, which reveals the first pollution layer indicated by peaks within the first hundred meters of each period. Additionally, the sharp peaks, particularly in the 18:10–18:13 and 18:17–18:19, are attributed to clouds, which block the signal at higher altitudes, thereby increasing noise levels.

*Figure 8. Backscattering and Extinction Coefficients retrieved for April 11, 2022*

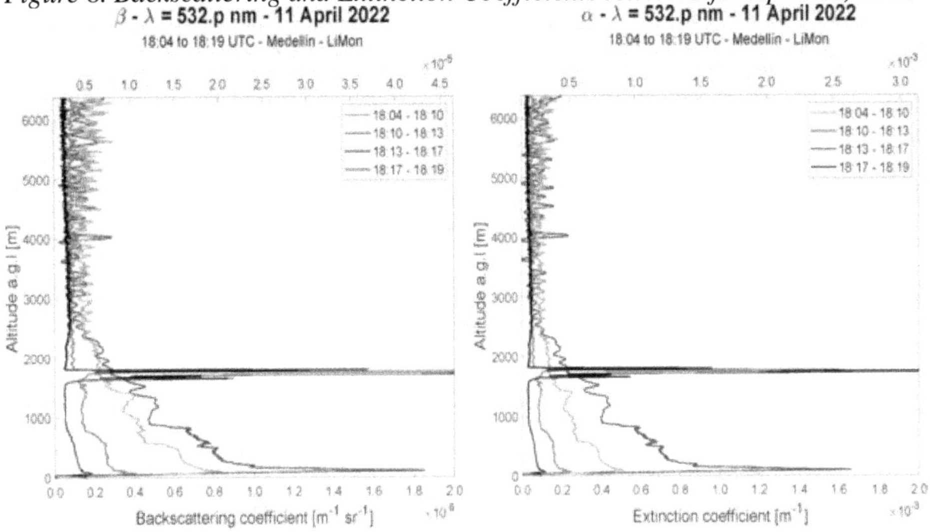


a) Backscattering coefficient profiles

b) Extinction coefficient profiles

The retrieved $\alpha(R)$ values range from $2.51 \times 10^{-4}$ to $2.78 \times 10^{-3}\, m^{-1}$, with 0.293 mean value of Aerosol Optical Depth (AOD), showing a 6.39% error compared to AERONET's reported value of 0.313 (Access URL: https://aeronet.gsfc.nasa.gov/).

Lastly, the depolarization lidar products were retrieved, which are the volume depolarization $\delta^{v}$ and particle depolarization $\delta^{p}$ (**Figure 9a** and **Figure 9b**, respectively), covering values from 0.07 to 0.15, demonstrating the feasibility of using the developed SDLS to characterize the optical properties of urban aerosols in a geographically and meteorologically complex region like Colombia.

*Figure 9. Volume and particle depolarization ratios for the Aburrá Valley atmosphere.*

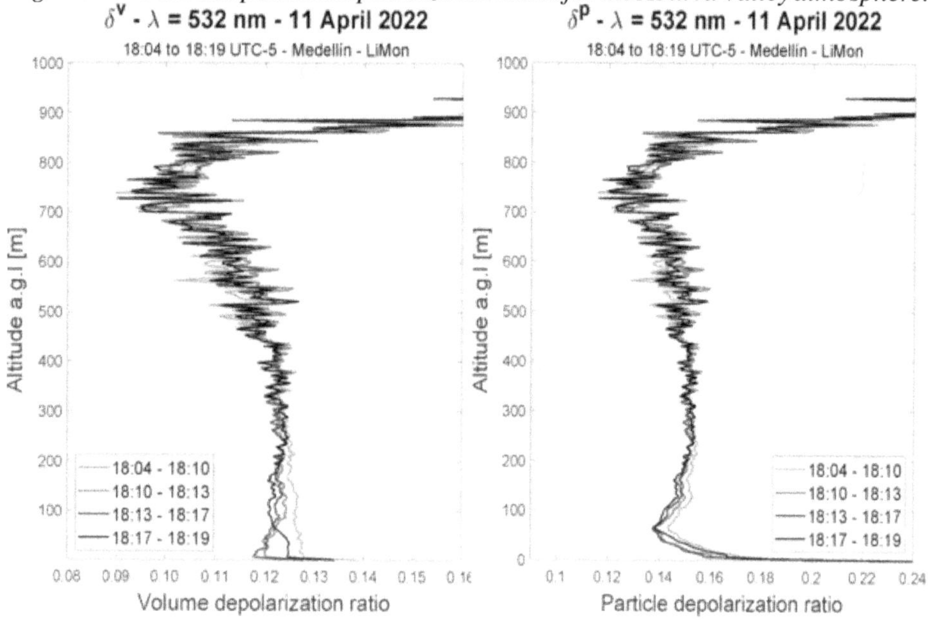


a) Volume depolarization ratio $\delta^v$ profiles

b) Particle depolarization ratio $\delta^p$ profiles

## SDLS Scanning Measurements

Scanning measurements were conducted again inside the EAFIT University central campus from a building at 21 m above ground level (**Figure 10**).

*Figure 10. Scanning Measurements in the Aburrá Valley.*

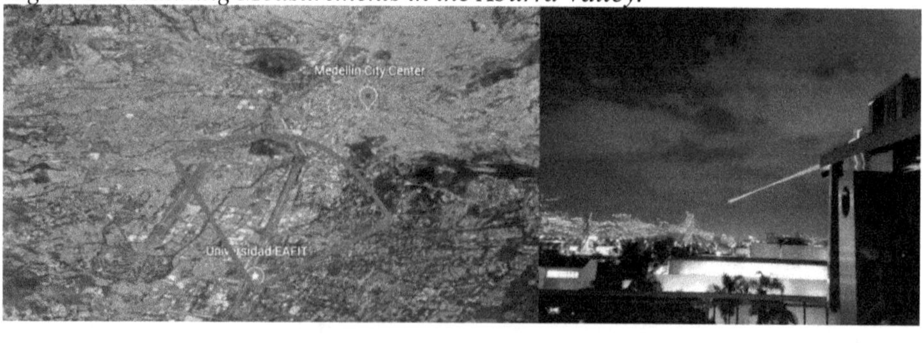

**Figure 11**, shows the results of horizontal scanning, where $r$ represents the radial distance, not the range or height $R$. A higher aerosol concentration can be seen in the first 270 m, increasing toward the city's industrial zone (from $\phi = 0$ to $\phi = -45°$).

*Figure 11. Horizontal scanning from $\phi = 45°$ to $\phi = -45°$, at $\theta = 56.9°$ performed at Universidad EAFIT.*

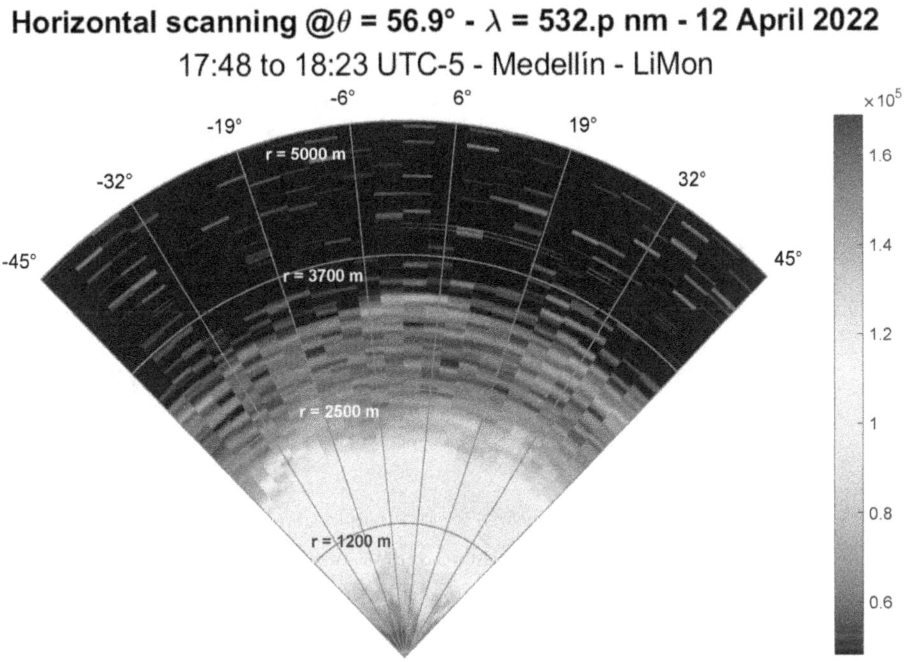


## MAX-DOAS Measurements to Retrieve $NO_2$ Concentrations

In this work, we use the Airyx SkySpec instrument as MAX-DOAS. This commercial instrument is property of the Center for Research and Innovation in Bioinformatics and Photonics (CiBioFi) of the Universidad del Valle (Colombia) and has been adapted to continuous measurements in Medellin (Colombia) since September 2022. As follows, measurements performed with SZA < 17° and elevation angles of 90° are considered. Additionally, for the selection of the analysis days, the linear fit between DSCD' and $\sigma'(\lambda)$ of the trace gas of interest must be considered. This fit denotes the reliability of the calculation process. Thus, **Figure 12** shows the $NO_2$ concentration values over 31 days using the DSCD parameter, $R^2$ ranged between 0.004 and 0.945, low $R^2$ measurements suggest the analyzed spectrum lacks the necessary values for applying the developed processing method, due to obstructions in the telescope's field of view. In May 2023, $NO_2$ concentration values ranged from $2.41 \times 10^{17}$ to $2.81 \times 10^{18}$, averaging $1.53 \times 10^{18} \frac{molecules}{cm^2}$.

*Figure 12. DSCD results of Aburrá Valley, May 2023*

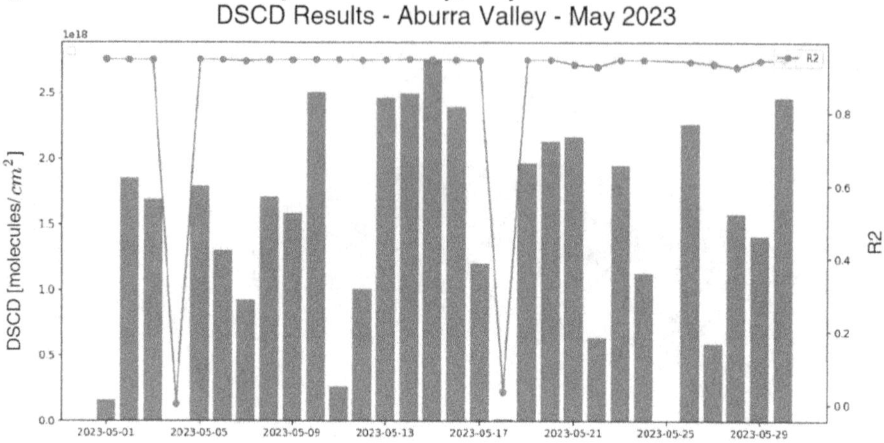


The MAX-DOAS results were compared with in-situ measurements taken by Vaisala AQT530 (**Figure 13**). It was found that the concentrations measured by the MAX-DOAS spectrometer ranged between $\left[2.35 \times 10^{17} - 4.33 \times 10^{18}\right] \frac{molecules}{cm^2}$. At the same time, the Vaisala sensor registered concentrations ranging from $\left[8.97 \times 10^{16} - 2.35 \times 10^{18}\right] \frac{molecules}{cm^2}$.

*Figure 13. Left: VAISALA measurements. Right: MAX-DOAS DSCD.*

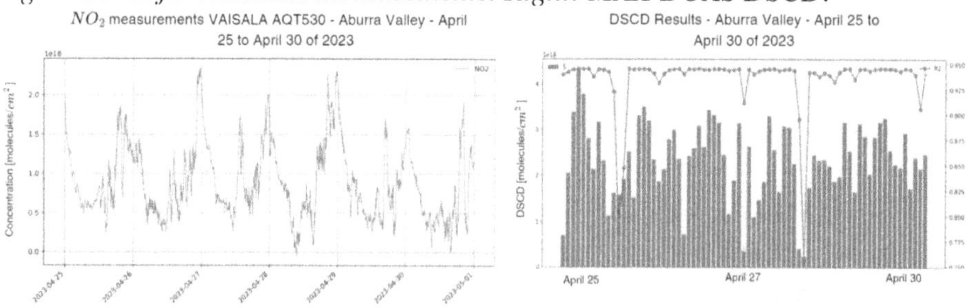


When comparing these findings with measurements made in other areas, it is verified that Medellín records significantly higher $NO_2$ concentrations. The difficult dispersion of pollutants caused by the region's geography, which results in the accumulation of atmospheric pollutants, is consistent with these high measurements. In addition, environmental emergency events were detected, where the DSCD values of $NO_2$ showed a maximum value of $3.20 \times 10^{18} \frac{molecules}{cm^2}$, a value higher than those obtained for the month of May 2023.

## Low-Cost In-Situ PM Measurements

The PM and trace gas measurements, along with their averages, lower limits, and upper limits are presented (more details at Rojas González & Montilla-Rosero, 2025). **Figure 14** displays an example of Simple-4 measurements for urban location for $PM_{1.0}$, $PM_{2.5}$ and $PM_{10}$, with remarkably high pollutant concentrations.

*Figure 14. $PM_{1.0}$, $PM_{2.5}$ and $PM_{10}$ Simple-4 measurements*

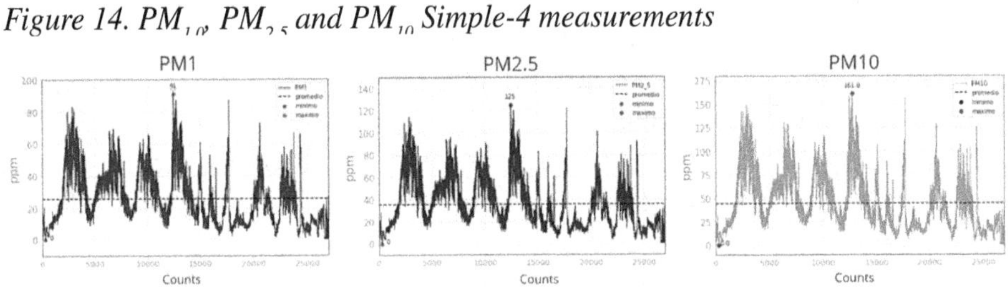


## Phase I: Summary and Future Work

The SDLS, MAX-DOAS technique, and low-cost in-situ network offers a robust approach to urban pollution monitoring. These devices offer data for locating pollution sources and enable the analysis of aerosols, trace gases, and PM. Thus, technological advancements to enhance the monitoring of air quality, including Colombia's climate, have been introduced.

To enhance the SDLS system's 3D scanning capabilities, experiments should be repeated under clean atmospheric conditions, performing 360° scans at various zenith angles. Preliminary results confirm that urban pollution's three-dimensional distribution can be analyzed in the Aburrá Valle.

The MAX-DOAS technique will expand to analyze additional trace gases for a more complete view of atmospheric health and environmental impact. Using zenith angles below 60° and incorporating new elevation angles will broaden measurement fields. Tools like QDOAS are prioritized for processing spectral data, optimizing trace gas concentration analysis.

The Simple-4 low-cost monitoring system overcomes limitations of traditional devices, providing innovative air quality monitoring in the Aburrá Valley. Its design demonstrates effective technology implementation in developing countries, significantly contributing to pollution studies in the region. This system represents a leap forward in low-cost, high-impact environmental monitoring solutions.

## PHASE II: CHEMICAL AND MORPHOLOGICAL CHARACTERIZATION OF PARTICULATE MATTER

The air we breathe is composed of 78% nitrogen, 21% oxygen, and 1% other gases like carbon dioxide and ozone (Viana-Rodríguez, 2003). It also contains solid and liquid particles called atmospheric aerosols. The addition of certain substances in the air alters its composition, leading to pollution (Jaenicke, 2001).

Particulate matter (PM) is a key air pollutant that varies in size, shape, and composition, including inorganic substances, trace metals, and organic matter. The physical characteristics of PM influence its transport, deposition, and impact on human health and at the same time it affects climate by absorbing solar radiation (Schachter et al., 2016).

PM is traditionally classified into fine ($PM_{2.5}$) and coarse ($PM_{10}$) particles, with ultrafine material ($PM_{1.0}$) primarily produced in the atmosphere (Seinfeld & Pandis, 2006). This section discusses methodologies for PM chemical and morphological characterization, emphasizing the importance of measuring particle number and size distribution alongside mass concentration.

### Morphology of Particulate Matter

The most used morphological parameters to describe particles are associated with the particle shape and roughness (Avellaneda-Franco et al., 2020; Pardo et al., 2020; Rausch et al., 2015). One widely used technique for characterizing and determining particle shape is the SEM/EDX (Scanning Electron Microscopy coupled to Energy Dispersive X-ray spectroscopy).

SEM/EDX characterizes both morphology and chemical composition of particles between 0.1 and 100 micrometers (Chauhan et al., 2022; Rausch et al., 2022) into several groups: mineral particles, biogenic material, soot aggregates, tire, and brake wear (TBW), concrete, and salts (Sommer et al., 2018). The classification uses machine learning (ML) techniques to optimize particle classification, reducing time and costs associated with manual characterization (Rausch et al., 2022). SEM/EDX is crucial for understanding particle origins and impacts on human health and the environment (Arndt et al., 2016).

## Mass Concentration

In the troposphere, total particulate matter concentrations range from $10^2$ to $10^5$ particles per $cm^3$ and from 1 to 100 µg $m^{-3}$ in number and mass respectively (Canagaratna et al., 2007). There are two main types of devices to estimate mass concentration: reference (gravimetry) and equivalent equipment (light scattering, energy absorption, etc.). The first one requires specific protocols (UNE Normalización Española, 2006) and it provides mass concentration allowing for subsequent physical and chemical analysis (Ducuara, 2012). The spectroscopic sensing techniques provide real-time PM concentration (Gil & Mello, 2011).

## Chemical Composition

PM undergoes changes in composition through processes like condensation, evaporation, coagulation, and chemical reactions (Seinfeld & Pandis, 2006). It includes natural and anthropogenic components such as elemental Carbon (EC) and Organic Carbon (OC), Geological material (Harrison & Köler, 2001), heavy metals (Inza-Aguirre, 2014), Nitrate, ammonium and sulfate, biological material. In addition, their chemical composition varies by particle size (Pope III, 2002; Fergusson, 1990; Krug et al., 2017).

The main techniques used in chemical analysis are Thermal Optical Transmittance (TOT) (Bocchicchio et al., 2022), High solvent and Liquid Chromatography (HPLC) (Abdu Hussen, 2022), Inductively Coupled Plasma Atomic Emission Spectroscopy (ICP-AES) & Inductively Coupled Plasma Mass Spectrometry (ICP-MS) (Cheremisinoff, 1996), Gas Chromatography-Mass Spectrometry (GC-MS) (Gutiérrez M.C & Droguet, 2002) and aethalometer (Black Carbon Measurement) (Rios-Lugo & Hernández-Mendoza, 2020).

## Particle Size Distribution

Particle size plays a crucial role in determining particle behavior in the air, with aerodynamic diameter helping to distinguish fine and coarse particles based on shape and density (Birmili & Hoffmann, 2006).

Aerosols are classified by size, ranging from 2-3 nanometers to 100 micrometers (Jacobson, 1997), and their distribution is represented in discrete size intervals to understand changes in particle size, shape, and composition over time due to physical and chemical processes (Seinfeld & Pandis, 2006). The Electrical Low-Pressure Impactor (ELPI+) is a key instrument for measuring real-time particle size distribution and concentration (Arffman et al., 2014).

## Phase II: Main Findings and Discussion

In the framework of the 4DAir project, several field campaigns for combining study techniques were performed. The results of the multi-technique campaigns aimed to determine the concentration, composition, morphology, and granulometry of PM samples collected in Bogotá (4.7110° N, 74.0721° W), Medellín (6.2476° N, 75.5658° W), and Cali (3.4516° N, 76.5320° W) during various monitoring periods are shown in **Table 4**. Two stages were conducted in each city.

*Table 4. Field campaigns summarize by city, dates, and analytical techniques.*

| City | Location | Dates | Measurement Type | Equipment Used |
|---|---|---|---|---|
| Bogotá 1 | RMCAB Centro de Alto Rendimiento | Feb 10-17, 2022 | Morphology, granulometry, chemical composition | Sigma-2 passive collector, SEM/EDX |
| Cali 1 | Universidad del Valle (DAGMA) | Mar 8-16, 2022 | Morphology, granulometry, chemical composition | Sigma-2 passive collector, SEM/EDX |
| Medellín 1 | SIATA Stations | Oct-Nov 2021, Feb 2022 | Morphology, granulometry, chemical composition | Sigma-2 passive collector, SEM/EDX |
| Cali 2 | Universidad del Valle (CiBiofi) | Nov 28-Dec 4, 2022 | Gravimetry, chemical composition | UGR 3000 Low Volume Sampler, Dustrack, MicroAethalometer |
| | | Mar 2023 | Particle size distribution | ELPI+ |
| Medellín 2 | Universidad EAFIT | Jul 12-16, 2022 | Gravimetry, chemical composition | UGR 3000 Low Volume Sampler, Dustrack, MicroAethalometer |
| Bogotá 2 | Universidad Distrital sede Bosa | Aug-Nov 2024 | Gravimetry, chemical composition | UGR 3000 Low Volume Sampler, Dustrack, MicroAethalometer |

Stage 1 focused on determining morphology, granulometry, and chemical composition using SEM/EDX. Samples were collected with Sigma-2 passive collectors using boron and carbon substrates. In Medellín, nine samples were collected at three SIATA stations. In Bogotá and Cali, six and eight days of sampling were conducted, respectively. These samples were analyzed with the PACLA software, developed by Particular Vision for morphological and chemical composition parameters (Rausch et al., 2022).

Stage 2 targeted gravimetric analysis and chemical composition. Samples were collected for PM concentration in Cali, Medellín and Bogotá and analyzed for the main chemical components (EC, OC, water soluble ions, coarse and trace metals). Due to technical difficulties, only six PM samples were obtained in Medellin and six samples in Cali. In Bogotá, during the second campaign, it was possible to obtain twenty-five samples. In addition, particle size distribution was measured with the ELPI+ device and real-time PM and Black Carbon measurements were conducted using a DustTruck and an aethalometer respectively.

## Stage 1 Results (Bogotá 1, Cali 1, Medellín 1)

A total of 7420 particles from Bogotá, Cali, and Medellín were individually analyzed, obtaining SEM images, chemical profiles, and twenty morphological parameters. This data allowed categorization into six morpho-chemical groups: biogenic organic, metallic, mineral, tire wear, salts, and Ti-rich paint (**Figure 15**).

*Figure 15. SEM images of particulate matter categories.*

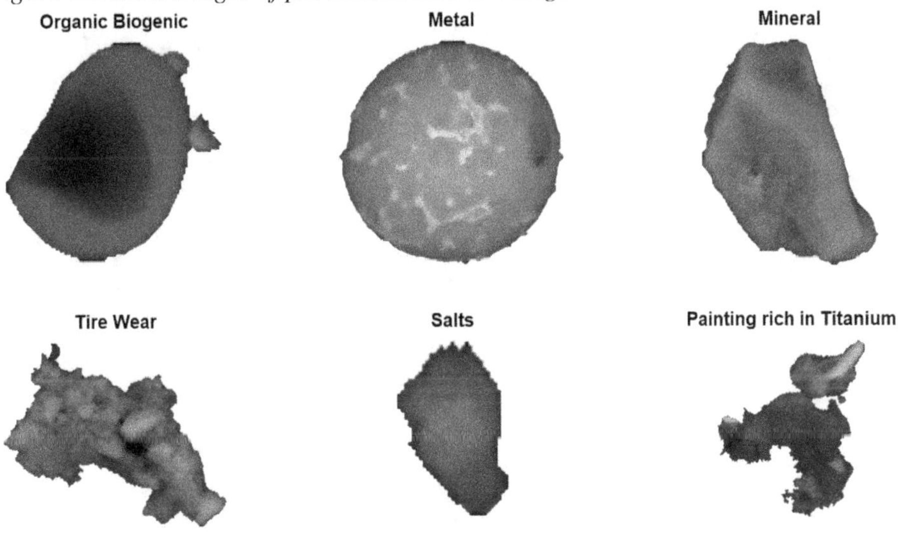


The morphochemical groups identified in each sample collected from the three cities are presented in **Figure 16**. According to the results from the urban stations the predominant group is minerals, originating from road dust that is resuspended by vehicle traffic, as well as erosion or transport from other sources like road or building construction.

*Figure 16 SEM/EDX characterization results for the three cities (blue-mineral; red - biogenic; green - tire wear; purple - metallic)*

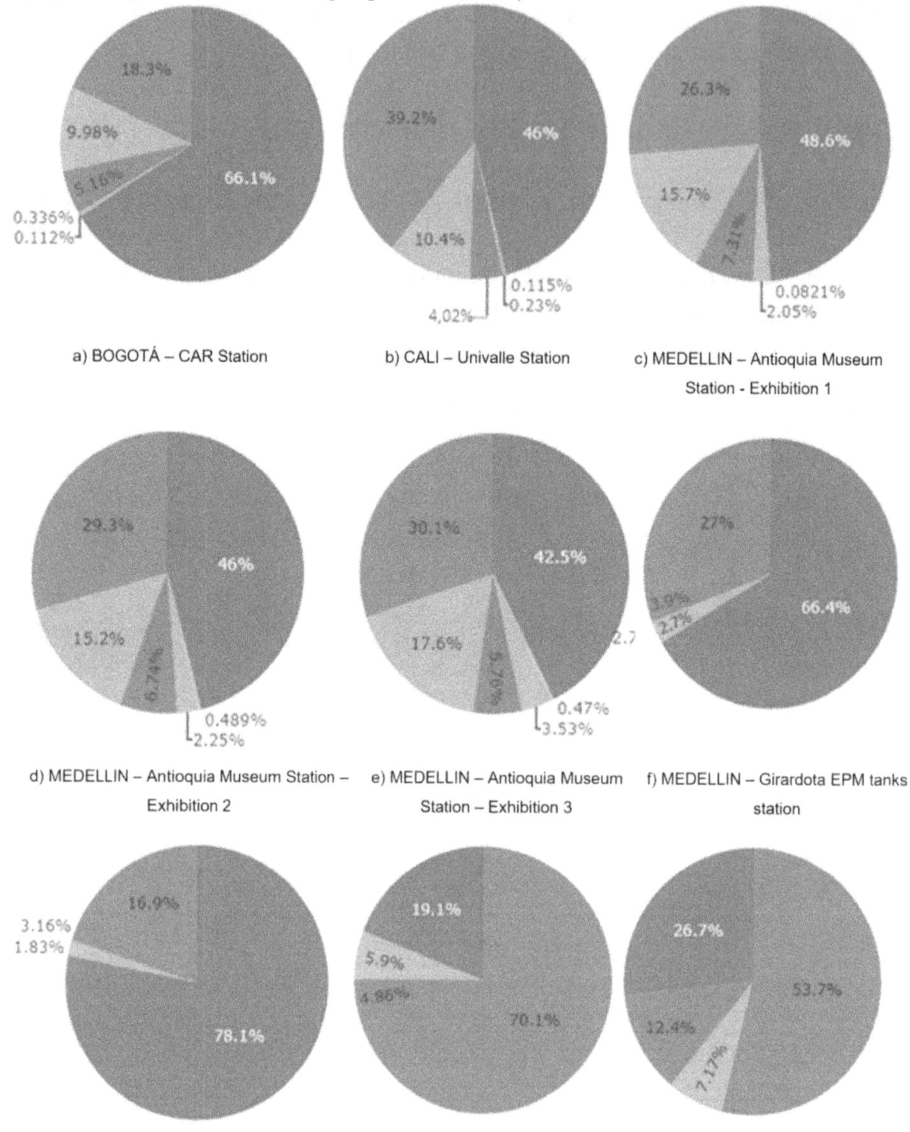


a) BOGOTÁ – CAR Station

b) CALI – Univalle Station

c) MEDELLIN – Antioquia Museum Station - Exhibition 1

d) MEDELLIN – Antioquia Museum Station – Exhibition 2

e) MEDELLIN – Antioquia Museum Station – Exhibition 3

f) MEDELLIN – Girardota EPM tanks station

g) MEDELLIN – Girardota EPM tanks station

h) MEDELLIN – La Y tank station

i) MEDELLIN – La Y tank station

In contrast, rural stations show a predominance of biogenic-organic particles due to their rural location. The results indicate that salt and Ti-rich paint particles comprise less than 5% of the total in the first four stations and are absent in the rural station. TBW particles are a significant source in stations affected by traffic, especially near braking zones or slopes.

## Stage 2 Results (Cali 2, Medellín 2)

The DustTrack and Aethalometer were used to estimate $PM_{2.5}$ and BC concentrations, respectively. During the Medellín 2 campaign, a correlation was observed between $PM_{2.5}$ and BC time series (**Figure 17**), suggesting a common origin, likely related to traffic near the monitoring station. The average PM10 concentration recorded by the DustTrack was 32.94 µg/m³ (SD = 14.14 µg/m³), with a maximum value of 88 µg/m³. For $PM_{2.5}$, the average was 31.36 µg/m³ (SD = 13.85 µg/m³), with a maximum of 85 µg/m³. Similar concentrations indicate that $PM_{10}$ and $PM_{2.5}$ followed comparable patterns during the sampling period.

*Figure 17. $PM_{2.5}$ and BC concentrations (Medellín 2).*

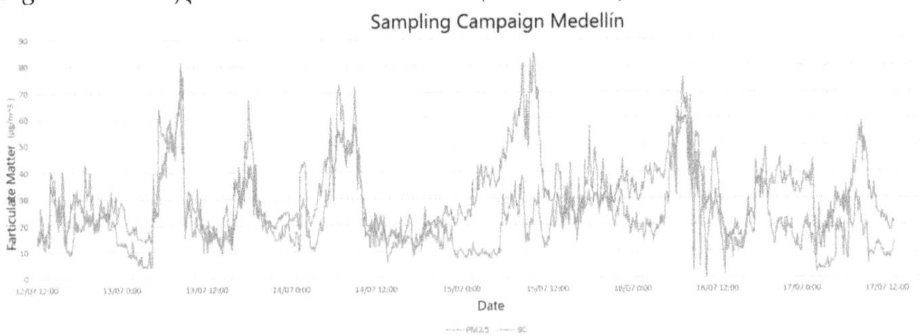


For the consolidated data from the Cali campaign (**Figure 18**), using DustTrak for $PM_{2.5}$, a total of 1,578 data points were collected over 6 days. The average $PM_{10}$ concentration was 32.92 µg/m³ (SD = 15.58 µg/m³), and for $PM_{2.5}$ a value of 32.67 µg/m³ (SD = 16.47 µg/m³).

*Figure 18. Concentrations of $PM_{2.5}$ and BC in Cali.*

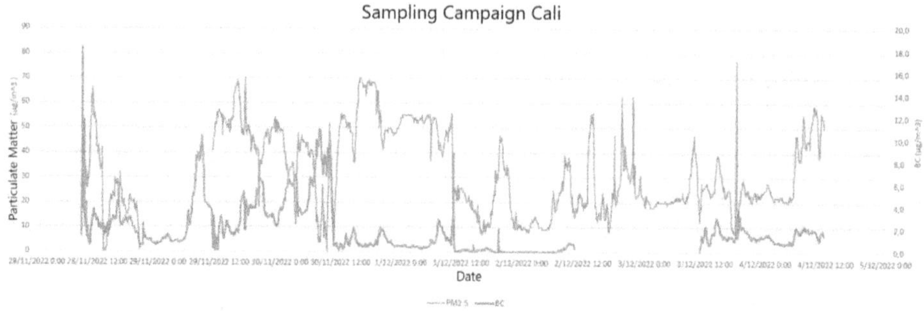


## Chemical Composition Determination (Cali 2 Campaign)

The carbon analysis, as shown in **Table 5**, indicates that the samples contain a higher proportion of organic carbon (OC), with notably elevated concentrations during the first two days, which were two to three times higher than those of the subsequent days.

*Table 5. Concentration of Elemental and Organic Carbon in Cali*

| Date | Day of the Week | OC (ug/m³) | EC (ug/m³) | OC/EC |
|---|---|---|---|---|
| Nov 28, 2022 | Monday (midday) | 20.8 | 7.7 | 2.69 |
| Nov 29, 2022 | Tuesday | 20.2 | 11.9 | 1.70 |
| Nov 30, 2022 | Wednesday | 9.8 | 7.8 | 1.25 |
| Dec 1, 2022 | Thursday | 6.6 | 8.6 | 0.77 |
| Dec 2, 2022 | Friday | 7.3 | 5.6 | 1.30 |
| Dec 3, 2022 | Saturday (to Sunday midday) | 5.4 | 3.7 | 1.46 |

The chemical composition in Cali shows that crustal metals were the most representative components, accounting for 53.9% of the samples, followed by OC+EC, which comprised 33.5% (**Figure 19**). This distribution suggests that in Cali, construction-related sources may be more significant than vehicular traffic.

*Figure 19. Percentages of elements from the chemical characterization in Cali.*

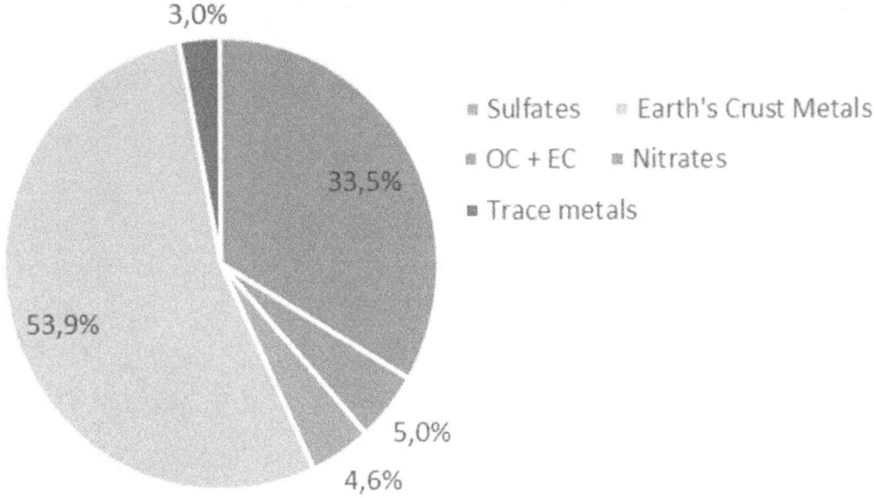


In **Figure 16b**, there is a similarity between the identified components in the SEM-EDX characterization for the same point at UniValle. In that sample, 46% of the material consisted of minerals, which is comparable to the predominance of crustal metals in this study. Furthermore, 39.2% was biogenic material, which can be associated with OC+EC in this case study, the second most representative component. Finally, in the SEM/EDX sample, metals accounted for 4%, whereas in our sample, this value was 3%.

## ELPI+ Particle Size Distribution Results

According **Figure 20**, in the case study of Cali in March 2023, nanoparticles (6 - 27 nm), corresponding to stages 1 through 3 of the ELPI+, comprised an average of 79% of the particle number distribution. Statistical analysis showed that the mean concentrations of $PM_{1.0}$ and $PM_{2.5}$ were 3163 particles/$cm^3$ and 2588 particles/$cm^3$, respectively. No considerable proportion of coarse particles ($PM_{10}$ to $PM_{2.5}$) in number was observed. However, regarding the mass, coarse particles are larger than fine particles.

*Figure 20. Particle Size Distribution for the Entire Sample from Cali.*

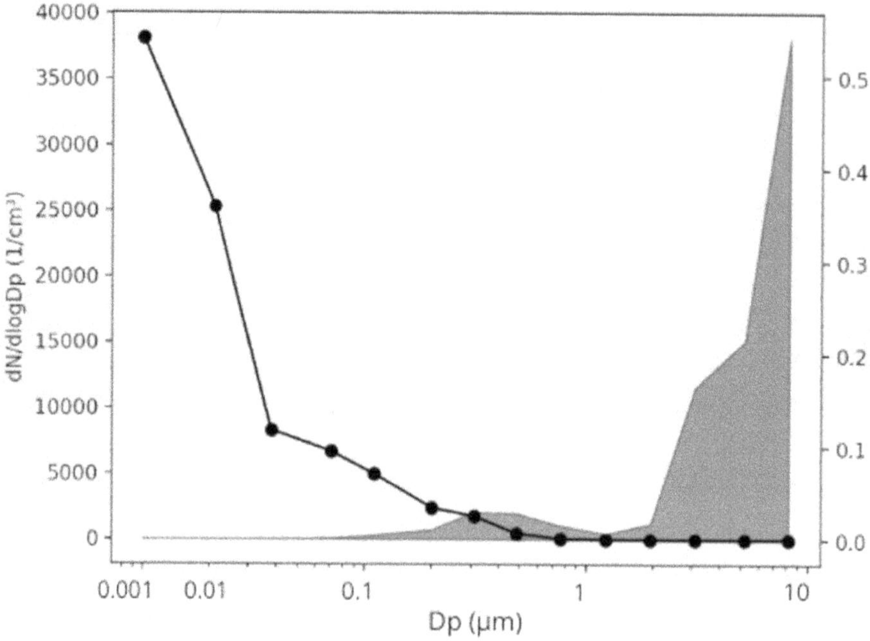


## Stage 2 - Medellín 2 Campaign

According to the chemical composition analyses, the levels of organic carbon (OC) varied between 14.43 and 17.23 μg/m$^3$ across the samples (**Table 6**). The daily fluctuations in particle composition are likely related to changes in emission sources and local activity. The highest concentration of OC was recorded on a Tuesday, at 17.23 μg/m$^3$, while the highest OC/EC ratio of 3.63 was observed on a Thursday.

*Table 6. Concentration of elemental and organic carbon in Medellín.*

| Date | Day of the Week | OC | EC | OC/EC |
|---|---|---|---|---|
| Jul 12, 2022 | Tuesday | 17.2 | 5.8 | 2.9 |
| Jul 13, 2022 | Wednesday | 14.4 | 6.5 | 2.2 |
| Jul 14, 2022 | Thursday | 15.3 | 4.2 | 3.6 |
| Jul 15, 2022 | Friday | 16.3 | 6.4 | 2.6 |
| Jul 16, 2022 | Saturday | 14.5 | 6.6 | 2.2 |

The chemical composition in Medellin shows that the carbonaceous fraction (OC+EC) was the most represented, at 31.3%, suggesting a significant contribution from both biogenic and anthropogenic sources, such as biomass burning, vehicle emissions, and industrial processes (**Figure 21**). Earth crust metals accounted for 17.2%, while trace metals comprised 11%, indicating the presence of specific industrial sources, in addition to elements linked to traffic from brake wear, tire degradation, and road surfaces (Echeverri-Londoño & Maya-Vasco, 2008). The results in Medellin differ from the findings in Cali, where the most representative components were minerals followed by carbon species.

Notably, sulfates (15.6%), nitrates (15.5%), and chlorides (9.5%) were also highly represented in Medellin. This pattern may result from the formation of secondary pollutants in the atmosphere, arising from the oxidation of precursor gases from anthropogenic sources, such as fossil fuel combustion, vehicular traffic, and industries.

The comparison of the bulk chemical composition is somehow different than results from SEM/EDX analysis (**Figure 16e**). In the Museo de Antioquia sampling site, the highest percentage corresponded to minerals (42.5%) and 30.3% to biogenic material. In contrast, in the Universidad EAFIT sampling site, carbon species (OC+EC) accounted for the highest percentage at 31.3%, a value like the biogenic material observed at the other sampling point. It is important to note that the monitoring sites are not the same, even though both are urban and influenced by similar emission sources. Additionally, the percentages from SEM/EDX correspond to the number of particles identified by chemical groups, whereas the percentages from the chemical characterization technique are derived from gravimetric analysis. The Medellín Museo Station appears to be more influenced by mineral-origin particles, possibly due to nearby construction activities that do not occur as frequently around the EAFIT sampling site.

*Figure 21. Percentages of Elements from the Chemical Characterization in Medellín.*

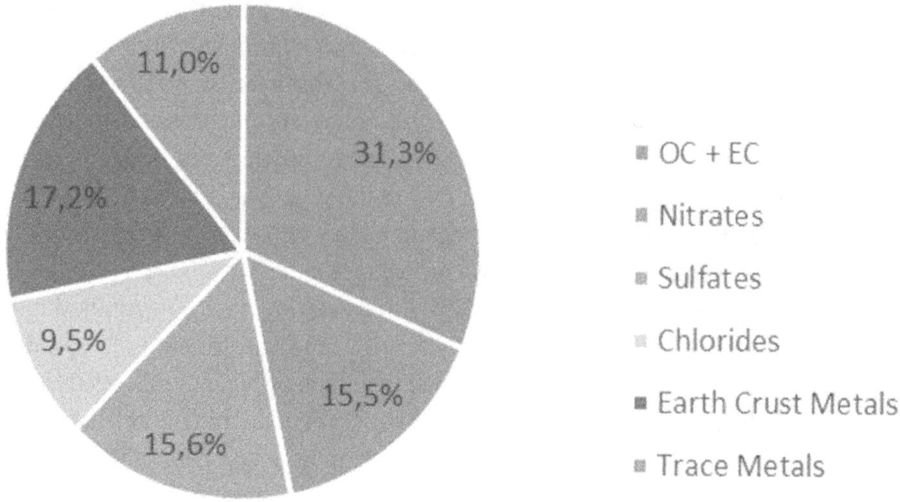


## Phase II: Summary, Recommendations and Future Work

The multi-technical characterization of particulate matter enabled the determination of concentration, granulometry, size distribution, and chemical composition in three of the main cities in Colombia: Bogotá, Medellín, and Cali. Two different, but complementary techniques, were applied to characterize the particle chemical composition: SEM/EDX, which identifies chemical groups based on the morphology of particles, and bulk chemical characterization. Overall, consistent results were observed, with a greater abundance of mineral and carbonaceous material associated with vehicular traffic and resuspension processes. The SEM characterization technique, coupled with image processing with machine learning, is of great interest due to the reduction in analysis time and the complementarity with traditional chemical techniques.

Using various monitoring techniques, it was possible to estimate the impact that traffic has on air quality, corresponding in some cases to the main source of pollution. Secondly, the influence of road and building construction activities that could be located near the monitoring areas was estimated. This project provides support elements so that the environmental authority can exercise better control of sources and reduce the impact of air pollution.

Although legislation on air quality has focused on the mass concentration of particles for their control, it is necessary to continue researching their concentration in number, given that ultrafine particles are those that represent the greatest quantity in number and have a greater potential to enter deeper into the respiratory system. It is also important to know the chemical composition of this nanomaterial to identify and control the emission sources.

## PHASE III: ATMOSPHERIC CHEMICAL TRANSPORT MODELING

Cities often rely on pollutant measurement networks, focusing on $PM_{2.5}$, ozone ($O_3$), and nitrogen oxides ($NO_X$). Medellín and its metropolitan area operate an air quality monitoring system managed by SIATA with one measurement station per 8.25 $km^2$ lead to low-resolution data, despite urban pollution varying significantly over short distances.

Effective solutions require more than measurements. Identifying pollution sources and understanding dispersion dynamics are essential for designing mitigation strategies. Chemistry and transport models (CTMs) offer critical insights into pollutant formation and movement by integrating atmospheric dynamics, chemical reactions, and atmosphere-surface interactions. Leveraging data assimilation from surface, satellite, and remote sensing sources, CTMs simulate pollutant concentrations over time with enhanced precision. Widely used to monitor air quality, these models are invaluable for understanding atmospheric pollutant dynamics, reducing uncertainties, and improving predictive accuracy. Their ability to refine forecasts makes them essential tools for environmental research and management.

In Colombia, research has focused on developing standard emission inventories and characterizing pollutants. However, to date, the Colombian territory still lacks data assimilation studies in CTMs. Furthermore, challenges arise from complex initial and boundary conditions in large-scale models and the spatiotemporal variability of measurements.

This section proposes integrating two models, the Long-Term Ozone Simulation - European Operational Smog (LOTOS-EUROS), previously used in local research (Lopez-Restrepo et al., 2017; Yarce-Botero et al., 2019) and WRF-Chem (Kumar et al., 2016), to enhance air quality predictions and support targeted policies, addressing the unique environmental challenges of northwestern South America.

Over the years Universidad EAFIT has adapted LOTOS-EUROS and WRF models to meet regional needs by customizing the initial and boundary conditions. Key inputs include boundary conditions, meteorology, land use, and emission inventories, essential for accurate gas concentration and depositions outputs, as illustrated in **Figure 22**. Initially, the focus was on chemistry transport models, however, the research naturally shifted toward meteorological models to enhance the accuracy of CTM outputs. This transition highlighted the interdependence between meteorology and chemistry, where developing high-performance numerical weather prediction capabilities became essential.

*Figure 22. Schematic flow of Chemical Transport Models. Based on (Yarce-Botero et al., 2024)*

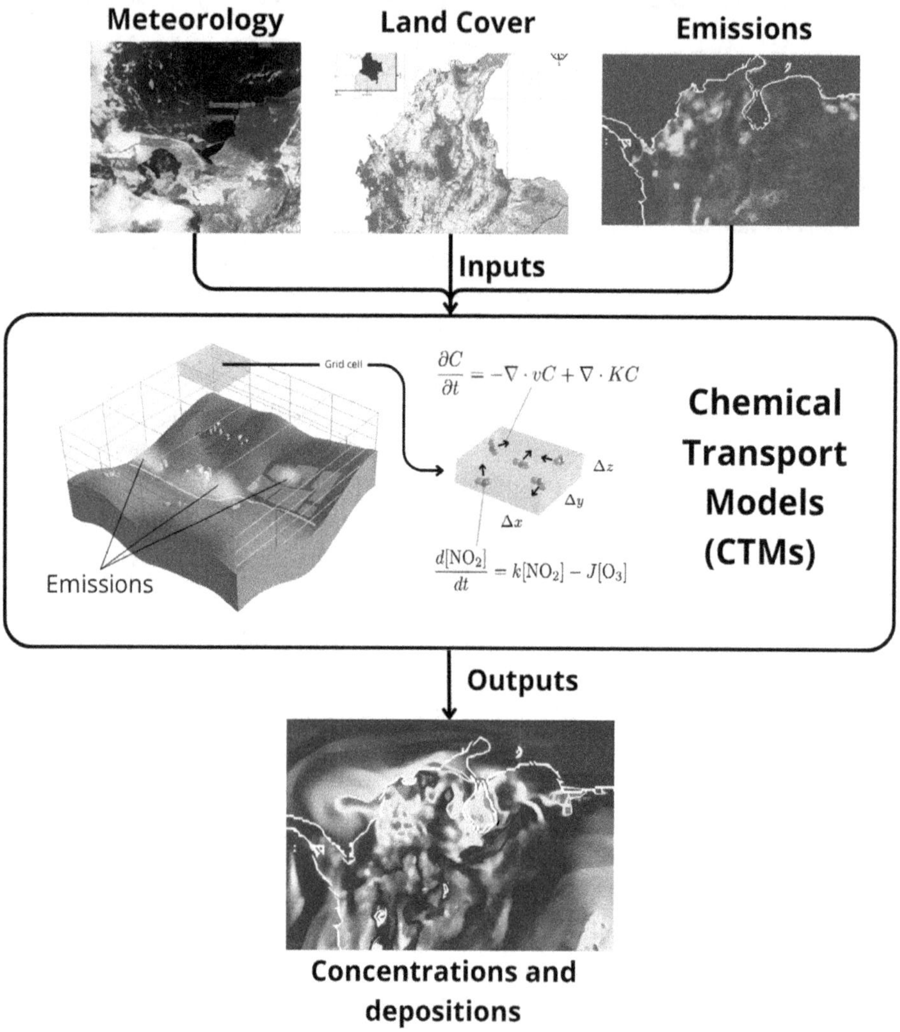

## LOTOS-EUROS Implementation

The CTM used to simulate atmospheric pollutant concentrations is LOTOS-EUROS. This model calculates the concentrations of trace gases and aerosols in three dimensions for the lower parts of the atmosphere: the boundary layer and (part of) the free troposphere (Yarce-Botero et al., 2024). Simulated trace gases include ozone, nitrogen and sulfur oxides, and hydrocarbons, while aerosols include primary particulate matter, secondary inorganic aerosol, elemental and organic carbon, sea salt, and dust.

### LOTOS-EUROS Simulation Setup

One of its first implementations was to simulate $PM_{2.5}$ depositions in the Aburrá Valley. Emission inventories and meteorological data are major sources of uncertainty in CTMs. Improving the accuracy of initial conditions, such as detailed land cover representations or updated emissions inventories, can help reduce this uncertainty (Quintero et al., 2020). The EDGAR 2016 (https://edgar.jrc.ec.europa.eu/) anthropogenic emissions inventory was incorporated, and a local emissions inventory was used for spatial and temporal disaggregation to be compatible with CTMs, using road networks and industry locations (Lopez-Restrepo et al., 2017). Meteorological data came from ECMWF, with a resolution of 0.07° × 0.07° (7.7 km × 7.7 km) in the innermost domain.

### Data Assimilation Using Local Monitoring Stations

Data assimilation is the process of adjusting an imperfect numerical forecast based on noisy real-world observations. The LOTOS-EUROS model struggles with accuracy in free runs, prompting the use of a Kalman filter for data assimilation (DA) to improve the model's predictions. Observations came from SIATA's official network and the low-cost program, where Aburrá valley residents host $PM_{2.5}$ sensors. This network provides broader spatial coverage, complementing the fewer but higher-quality official SIATA stations (Lopez-Restrepo et al., 2022).

Data assimilation techniques enhance predictions of air contaminants in the complex topography of the Aburrá Valley. Among these, the Ensemble Kalman Filter (EnKF) with covariance localization improves $PM_{10}$ and $PM_{2.5}$ forecasts by integrating observational data to refine emissions and concentrations. Additionally, the implementation of a robust, non-Gaussian approach using the Ensemble Time Local H∞ Filter Knowledge-Aided (EnTLHF-KA), incorporates prior knowledge through a target covariance matrix, enabling more effective management of uncertainties in the assimilation process (Lopez-Restrepo et al., 2022).

Hybrid frameworks like 4DENVar technique (Liu et al., 2008) take advantage of the characteristics of variational and sequential data assimilation approaches. In addition, $NO_2$ data retrieved from the TROPOMI satellite is integrated to refine numerical models and facilitate parameter estimation, tackling the challenges of constructing emission inventories (Yarce Botero et al., 2021).

## WRF Meteorology to Improve LOTOS-EUROS Performance

In earlier implementations of the LOTOS-EUROS model, meteorological input was obtained from ECMWF data with a resolution of 0.07° × 0.07° (7.7 km x 7.7 km). This resolution proved insufficient to accurately capture the Aburrá Valley's complex topography and micro-scale meteorology (Hinestroza-Ramirez, et al. 2023; Lopez-Restrepo, et al., 2017), as the valley spans 60 km in length, and 8–10 km across. Consequently, a higher-resolution meteorological input was required and the Weather Research and Forecasting (WRF) developed by the National Center for Atmospheric Research (NCAR) was incorporated as the new data source.

### LOTOS-EUROS Performance with ECMWF Meteorology Compared to WRF Meteorology

There is a difference between the ECMWF and WRF meteorology in the performance of LOTOS-EUROS (Hinestroza-Ramirez et al. 2023; Lopez-Restrepo, et al., 2017). This work utilized meteorological outputs from ECMWF and WRF Model 3.7 to run LOTOS-EUROS. WRF's meteorology was simulated using four nested domains.

For the LOTOS-EUROS WFR implementation, four nested domains were used to transition seamlessly from regional scales, covering the Caribbean and northern South America, to local conditions in the Aburrá Valley. Resolutions ranged from 28 km in the outermost domain (D1) to 1 km in the innermost domain (D4), focused on the Aburrá Valley. This implementation contrasts with previous approaches that relied on ECMWF's 7 km resolution for the valley.

The LOTOS-EUROS simulation utilized ECMWF meteorological data, with a resolution of 0.14° for D1 and 0.07° for D2–D4, consistent with previous simulations. Elevation data was obtained from GMTED2010 at a resolution of 220 m, while anthropogenic emissions were sourced from the EDGAR inventory.

## Comparison of Operational Implementations of WRF

This work shows the implementation of the 3DVAR (three-dimensional variational) method within the WRF model by the Colombian Air Force (FAC) for aviation weather forecasting, specifically for comparison purposes. Integrated into SIMFAC (Colombian Air Force Meteorological Information System), 3DVAR enhances predictions by assimilating METAR reports, radio soundings, radar, and GOES-16 satellite data. The study compares 3DVAR forecasts with CTRL across two operational periods, focusing on surface temperature, pressure, and precipitation (Hinestroza-Ramirez, et al., 2023).

## **WRF Coupled with Chemistry (WRF-Chem)**

To configure the WRF-Chem using insights gained from previous LOTOS-EUROS and WRF simulations such as (Hinestroza-Ramirez, 2023; Lopez-Restrepo, et al., 2017), the setup utilizes the Morrison (Morrison et al., 2005) microphysics scheme to simulate hydrometeorological species and the Monin-Obukhov scheme for surface-layer interactions. For the surface boundary layer (SBL), the Monin-Obukhov scheme was used, which describes average flow and temperature in the surface layer under non-neutral conditions (Monin & Obukhov, 1954). For the planetary boundary layer (PBL) physics, the Yonsei University (YSU) scheme was selected.

## Aerosol Chemistry and Interactions and Chemical Reactions Schemes

Based on the findings of (Ballesteros-González et al., 2022) the MOSAIC scheme (Model for Simulating Aerosol Interactions and Chemistry) was chosen for its superior ability to represent $PM_{2.5}$ and $O_3$ dynamics in urban environments with complex. Additionally, the MOZART scheme (Model for Ozone and Related Chemical Tracers) demonstrated the best performance for modeling fine and coarse particulate matter and ozone under similar conditions (Ballesteros-González et al., 2020; Henao et al., 2020). Initial and boundary chemical conditions were generated using the WACCM (Whole Atmosphere Community Climate Model) data processed through the 'mozbc' utility. This ensured compatibility with the reaction and emission schemes used in the simulations, maintaining consistency across all domains.

Anthropogenic emissions were sourced from the EDGAR v5 inventory, speciated for the MOZART scheme and processed with the 'anthro emiss' tool. Biogenic emissions were prepared using the MEGAN v2 model, both scaled to the simulation domain's resolution.

Simulations focused on June 2022, aligning with pollutant measurement campaigns in the Aburrá Valley. Nitrogen compounds and tropospheric ozone dynamics were analyzed and validated using SIATA's air quality data and meteorological variables like wind speed and 2-meter surface temperature.

## Ensemble of WRF-Chem and LOTOS-EUROS

The configurations for the statistical coupling of WRF and LOTOS-EUROS models to improve particulate matter (PM) concentration predictions through data assimilation algorithms are shown (Cruz-Ruiz et al., 2024). The ensemble combines outputs from WRF-Chem and LOTOS-EUROS, using WRF as the meteorological input, and configures models with uniform initial and boundary conditions.

Evaluation metrics include Mean Fractional Bias (MFB), Root Mean Square Error (RMSE), and correlation factors, which compare model outputs against SIATA air quality data.

## Phase III: Results and Discussion of CTMs Simulations

### LOTOS EUROS Simulations with Data Assimilation of Local Monitoring Network

For the initial LOTOS-EUROS simulations incorporating data assimilation from the local SIATA network, four separate simulations were conducted: one without data assimilation (LE), one using data from 14 official SIATA network stations (LE-official), one integrating data from the full Citizen Scientist low-cost network (LE-low-cost), and one using only high-quality data from the low-cost network (LE-low-cost-HQ) (Lopez-Restrepo et al., 2022).

Traffic dynamics caused the highest PM concentration peak during the morning across all stations. LE simulations captured the timing but underestimated the magnitude at some stations, while others showed delays. LE-official improved morning accuracy but lacked variability. Low-cost closely matched observed trends, capturing both morning and evening peaks with slight discrepancies in timing and magnitude. Simulations without data assimilation (LE) underestimated observed concentrations and showed poor RMSE and correlation values. In contrast, simulations with data assimilation significantly improved accuracy, with MFB values close to zero and reduced RMSE by 24.4% (LE-official), 32.8% (LE-low-cost), and 36.2% (LE-low-cost-HQ) (see details at (Lopez-Restrepo et al., 2017)). Data assimilation effectively improved model performance, with all R values meeting reliable performance criteria and low-cost high quality network data showing the best improvements.

## LOTOS EUROS Simulations with Data Assimilation at a Subcontinental Level

The analysis of $NO_2$ column concentrations from LOTOS-EUROS (free run) and TROPOMI satellite retrievals reveals notable discrepancies, despite data gaps caused by quality filtering. Meteorological data is sourced from ECMWF (3-hour temporal, 0.07° spatial resolution), while initial and boundary conditions use LOTOS-EUROS (1-hour, 0.09° spatial resolution). Emissions include anthropogenic data from EDGAR (10 km), biogenic data from MEGAN (10 km), and fire emissions from MACC/CAMS GFAS (10 km). Land use data is derived from CCLI (1 km), and topography from GMTED 2010 (0.02° resolution). Two domains are defined: Domain 1 and Colombia (DCol). Emission factors derived using the 4DEnVar technique reveal further insights. In northern Venezuela, adjustments below unity suggest that the model overestimates emissions when compared to satellite observations. In contrast, central Colombia, characterized by higher population density, shows underestimations, pointing to missing or underestimated emission sources in the model. Incorporating updated emission parameters improves LOTOS-EUROS simulations, as evidenced by reductions in spatial bias. Areas with overestimations and underestimations are better captured, underscoring the enhanced model accuracy achieved through these emission adjustments (see details at Yarce Botero et al., 2021).

For Medellín and Bogotá, the 4DEnVar results demonstrate significant improvements in $NO_2$ plume simulations. Background plumes, compared to those generated with updated emissions, show noticeable reductions in magnitude. Wind fields at 10 m from the LOTOS-EUROS model reveal that assimilated emission updates result in diminished $NO_2$ concentrations along wind flow trajectories. This highlights the effectiveness of refined emission estimates in improving plume behavior and spatial dispersion, particularly in urban regions (Yarce Botero et al., 2021).

## WRF-Chem Results

A 15-minute timestep from July 10, 2022, in domain 4 (1x1 km resolution) for three cities is presented **Figure 23**. The objective is to demonstrate the model's ability to produce chemical simulations with multiple configurations across different scenarios. WFR-Chem version 4.5 was compiled locally on a machine with all pre-processing utilities, while version 4.2 was made available on APOLO, the EAFIT's scientific computing center. The system can generate chemical transport simulations for any requested time window. Additionally, it is proposed to analyze the model's results in various configurations and compare them with SIATA measurements to identify the best parameterization for each scenario.

*Figure 23. Concentrations of $NO_2$ for Medellin, Cali, and Bogotá*

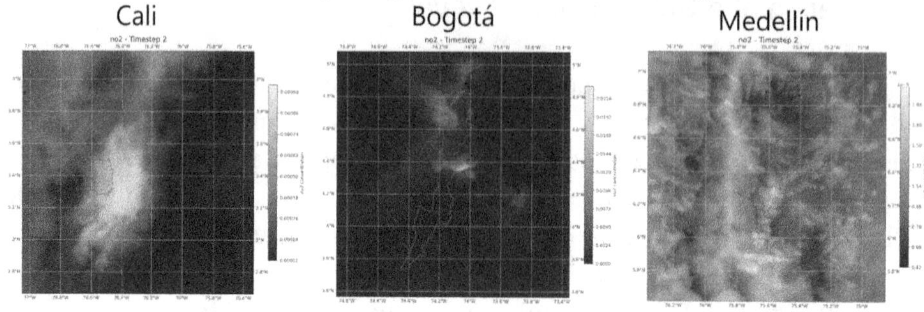


## Results of the Statistical Ensemble Between LOTOS-EUROS and WRF-Chem

The results are shown in **Figure 24**, in graphical representation used to compare the statistical relationship between model predictions and observed data (Taylor diagram). These diagrams simultaneously display three metrics: correlation coefficient, standard deviation, and root mean squared error (RMSE).

*Figure 24. Taylor diagrams for each station with observations for five different ensembles (Cruz-Ruiz et al., 2024)*

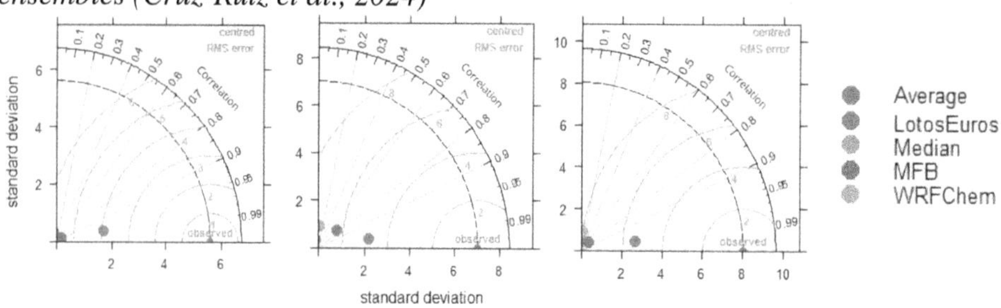


While no single model performs perfectly across all metrics, some models, such as the average, consistently show better agreement with the observed data in terms of correlation, standard deviation, and RMS error. In contrast, models like WRF-Chem and LOTOS-EUROS may require further refinement to achieve better consistency with observations. These diagrams highlight how the Average model outperforms other ensembles, such as WRF-Chem and LOTOS-EUROS.

## Phase III: Summary and Future Work

One of the first implementations of Chemical Transport Models (CTMs) in the Northwestern South America (NWSA) region has been presented. The region's complex topography and the lack of accurate and consistent emissions inventories pose significant challenges for obtaining precise predictions of pollutant depositions, such as $NO_2$ and particulate matter. Nonetheless, this research expands the application of CTMs to tropical climates by implementing innovative data assimilation techniques to compensate for the uncertainties in emissions inventories and other sources of variability in LOTOS-EUROS.

Additionally, various model ensembles were evaluated to enhance the predictive capabilities of LOTOS-EUROS by integrating more accurate meteorological data, such as that provided by WRF. The chemical version, WRF-Chem, was implemented, evaluated, and statistically coupled with LOTOS-EUROS, further contributing to the advancement of CTMs in such a challenging environment.

Regarding data assimilation, the next steps will focus on incorporating vertical data provided by techniques such as LIDAR and MAX-DOAS. This step is anticipated to significantly improve the accuracy of the models' predictions, further advancing the field of CTM applications in regions with complex environmental conditions (Cruz-Ruiz et al., 2024).

For future work, data assimilation into CTMs is expected to be performed using in-situ observations. This step is crucial as it allows the integration of high-resolution, real-time atmospheric data, such as gas concentrations and meteorological variables, into the models, thereby enhancing their accuracy and predictive capabilities.

## CONCLUSIONS

The research project 4DAir presented is a comprehensive effort that combines advanced instrumentation, chemical analysis, and numerical simulations to improve urban pollution forecasts. From the instrumentation side, technologies such as LIDAR for particulate matter detection, passive measurements of $NO_2$, and locally designed low-cost stations utilizing aerospace technology are employed. These devices generated precise data, enabling the representation of pollutants in 4D (longitude, latitude, altitude, and time).

The combination of the SDLS, the MAX-DOAS technique, and the low-cost in-situ network provides an integrated approach to monitoring and analyzing of aerosols, trace gases, and PM, identifying sources to incorporate these analyses into environmental policy evaluations. Furthermore, the significance of technological advancements is emphasized to enhance climate research and air quality monitoring in Colombia.

The multi-technique characterization of particulate matter has determined the concentration, granulometry, size distribution, and chemical in three of the main cities of Colombia: Bogotá, Medellín, and Cali. It has also enabled the comparison of chemical composition results using two complementary techniques: SEM-EDX, which identifies chemical groups based on particle morphology, and traditional chemical characterization of each major fraction. In general, consistent results are observed, with a higher abundance of mineral and carbonaceous material, associated with vehicular traffic and resuspension processes.

The complex topography of the region and the lack of accurate and consistent emission inventories pose significant challenges to obtain precise predictions for pollutant deposition, such as $NO_2$ and particulate matter. However, this research presents one of the first implementations of CTMs in the Northwest South America (NWSA) region and expands the use of CTMs in tropical climates by implementing innovative data assimilation techniques to compensate for uncertainties in emission inventories and other sources of variability in CTMs.

Finally, this work contributes to extensive air pollution study from several fields: measurement technology, chemical characterization and atmospheric modeling. There, we showed the design, development and implementation of instrumentation for measurements of temporal evolution and location of atmospheric aerosols, trace gases and in-situ pollutants concentration. The multi-technical characterization of particulate matter provided particle chemical composition based on their morphology of particles, showing alternatives for legislation on urban air quality researching on concentration of ultrafine particles. And the results showed the potential about predictive features of LOTOS-EUROS using WRF data in such a challenging measurement site as neotropical cities.

## REFERENCES


Abdu Hussen, A. (2022). High-Performance Liquid Chromatography (HPLC): A review. *Annals of Advances in Chemistry, 6*(1), 010–020. DOI: 10.29328/journal.aac.1001026

Airyx. (2024). *SkySpec Compact Instrument v.250.* https://airyx.de/wp-content/uploads/2024/09/SkySpec-Compact.pdf

Ansmann, A., & Müller, D. (2005). Lidar and Atmospheric Aerosol Particles. In Weitkamp, C. (Ed.), *Lidar* (pp. 105–141). Springer-Verlag., DOI: 10.1007/0-387-25101-4_4

Arffman, A., Yli-Ojanperä, J., Kalliokoski, J., Harra, J., Pirjola, L., Karjalainen, P., Rönkkö, T., & Keskinen, J. (2014). High-resolution low-pressure cascade impactor. *Journal of Aerosol Science, 78*, 97–109. DOI: 10.1016/j.jaerosci.2014.08.006

Arndt, J., Deboudt, K., Anderson, A., Blondel, A., Eliet, S., Flament, P., Fourmentin, M., Healy, R. M., Savary, V., Setyan, A., & Wenger, J. C. (2016). Scanning electron microscopy-energy dispersive X-ray spectrometry (SEM-EDX) and aerosol time-of-flight mass spectrometry (ATOFMS) single particle analysis of metallurgy plant emissions. *Environmental Pollution, 210*, 9–17. DOI: 10.1016/j.envpol.2015.11.019 PMID: 26708757

Avellaneda-Franco, J. D., Rausch, J., & Jaramillo-Vogel, D. (2020). Caracterización morfo química y diferenciación del material particulado PM10-2.5 en el valle de Aburrá (Medellín- Colombia). *Master Thesis.* Universidad EAFIT.

Ballesteros-González, K., Espitia-Cano, S. O., Rincón-Caro, M. A., Rincón-Riveros, J. M., Perez-Peña, M. P., Sullivan, A., & Morales Betancourt, R. (2022). Understanding organic aerosols in Bogotá, Colombia: In-situ observations and regional-scale modeling. *Atmospheric Environment, 284*, 119161. DOI: 10.1016/j.atmosenv.2022.119161

Ballesteros-González, K., Sullivan, A. P., & Morales-Betancourt, R. (2020). Estimating the air quality and health impacts of biomass burning in northern South America using a chemical transport model. *The Science of the Total Environment, 739*, 139755. DOI: 10.1016/j.scitotenv.2020.139755 PMID: 32758934

Birmili, W., & Hoffmann, T. (2006). Environmental Pollutants Particulate and Dust Pollution, Inorganic and Organic Compounds. In *Encyclopedia of Respiratory Medicine* (pp. 110–120). Elsevier., DOI: 10.1016/B0-12-370879-6/00133-2

Bocchicchio, S., Commodo, M., Sgro, L. A., Chiari, M., D'Anna, A., & Minutolo, P. (2022). Thermo-optical-transmission OC/EC and Raman spectroscopy analyses of flame-generated carbonaceous nanoparticles. *Fuel, 310*, 122308. DOI: 10.1016/j.fuel.2021.122308

Canagaratna, M. R., Jayne, J. T., Jimenez, J. L., Allan, J. D., Alfarra, M. R., Zhang, Q., Onasch, T. B., Drewnick, F., Coe, H., Middlebrook, A., Delia, A., Williams, L. R., Trimborn, A. M., Northway, M. J., DeCarlo, P. F., Kolb, C. E., Davidovits, P., & Worsnop, D. R. (2007). Chemical and microphysical characterization of ambient aerosols with the aerodyne aerosol mass spectrometer. *Mass Spectrometry Reviews, 26*(2), 185–222. DOI: 10.1002/mas.20115 PMID: 17230437

Chauhan, P. K., Kumar, A., Pratap, V., & Singh, A. K. (2022). Seasonal characteristics of PM1, PM2.5, and PM10 over Varanasi during 2019–2020. *Frontiers in Sustainable Cities, 4*, 909351. Advance online publication. DOI: 10.3389/frsc.2022.909351

Cheremisinoff, N. P. (1996). Elemental And Structural Characterization Tests. In *Polymer Characterization* (pp. 43–81). Elsevier., DOI: 10.1016/B978-081551403-9.50006-6

Cruz-Ruiz, L. M., Fernández-Restrepo, F., Yarce-Botero, A., Solórzano-Araque, V., & Quintero, O. L. (2024). *Ensemble Modeling of Atmospheric Pollutants: A Case Study with WRF-Chem and LOTOS-EUROS in Aburrá Valley, Colombia.* DOI: 10.5194/egusphere-egu24-1020

Devara, P. C. S. (1998). Review article Remote sensing of atmospheric aerosols from active and passive optical techniques. *International Journal of Remote Sensing, 19*(17), 3271–3288. DOI: 10.1080/014311698213966

Ducuara, O. (2012). Métodos para la determinación de Material Particulado. In En, O. (Ed.), *Ducuara, Seguimiento y Control de Emisiones atmosféricas*. Universidad Nacional.

Echeverri-Londoño, C. A., & Maya-vasco, G. J. (2008). Relación entre las partículas finas (pm2.5) y respirables (pm10) en la ciudad de Medellín. *Revista Ingenierías Universidad de Medellín*. https://revistas.udem.edu.co/index.php/ingenierias/article/view/198/185

Edner, H., Ragnarson, P., Spännare, S., & Svanberg, S. (1993). Differential optical absorption spectroscopy (DOAS) system for urban atmospheric pollution monitoring. *Applied Optics, 32*(3), 327. DOI: 10.1364/AO.32.000327 PMID: 20802694

Fergusson, J. E. (1990). *The Heavy Elements: Chemistry, Environmental Impact and Health Effects*. Pergamon Press.

Fernald, F. G. (1984). Analysis of atmospheric lidar observations: Some comments. *Applied Optics*, *23*(5), 652–653. https://doi.org/https://doi.org/10.1364/AO.23.000652. DOI: 10.1364/AO.23.000652 PMID: 18204618

Freudenthaler, V. (2016). About the effects of polarising optics on lidar signals and the Δ90 calibration. *Atmospheric Measurement Techniques*, *9*(9), 4181–4255. DOI: 10.5194/amt-9-4181-2016

Fuentes-Inzunza, R. (2012). Implementación de Instrumentación Óptica para el Monitoreo Remoto de la Calidad de Aire. *PhD Thesis*. Universidad de Concepción.

Gil, N., & Mello, S. (2011). Differential Optical Absorption Spectroscopy (DOAS). *PhD Thesis*. Universidad de la Republica.

Gutiérrez, M. C., & Droguet, M. (2002). La cromatografía de gases y la espectometría de masas: identificación de compuestos causantes de mal olor. *Instituto de Investigación Textil y Cooperación Industrial*. https://upcommons.upc.edu/handle/2099/2733

Harrison, R. J., & Köler, T. O. (2001). Beyond Characterisation. Polished Stone Exchange in the Western Mediterranean 5500–2000 BC. *Oxford Journal of Archaeology*, *20*(2), 107–127. DOI: 10.1111/1468-0092.00126

Henao, J. J., Mejía, J. F., Rendón, A. M., & Salazar, J. F. (2020). Sub-kilometer dispersion simulation of a CO tracer for an inter-Andean urban valley. *Atmospheric Pollution Research*, *11*(5), 928–945. DOI: 10.1016/j.apr.2020.02.005

Hinestroza-Ramirez, J. E., Lopez-Restrepo, S., Yarce Botero, A., Segers, A., Rendon-Perez, A. M., Isaza-Cadavid, S., Heemink, A., & Quintero, O. L. (2023). Improving Air Pollution Modelling in Complex Terrain with a Coupled WRF–LOTOS–EUROS Approach: A Case Study in Aburrá Valley, Colombia. *Atmosphere (Basel)*, *14*(4), 738. Advance online publication. DOI: 10.3390/atmos14040738

Hinestroza-Ramirez, J. E., Rengifo-Castro, J. D., Quintero, O. L., Yarce Botero, A., & Rendon-Perez, A. M. (2023). Non-Parametric and Robust Sensitivity Analysis of the Weather Research and Forecast (WRF) Model in the Tropical Andes Region. *Atmosphere (Basel)*, *14*(4), 686. Advance online publication. DOI: 10.3390/atmos14040686

Hinestroza-Ramirez, J. E., Soto Barbosa, J. E., Yarce Botero, A., Suárez Higuita, D. A., Lopez-Restrepo, S., Cruz Ruiz, L. M., Solorzano Araque, V., Céspedes, A., Lorduy Hernandez, S., Caceres, R., Jiménez-Sánchez, G., & Quintero, O. L. (2023). Evaluation of the 3DVAR Operational Implementation of the Colombian Air Force for Aircraft Operations: A Case Study. *Climate (Basel), 11*(7), 153. Advance online publication. DOI: 10.3390/cli11070153

Hoyos-Restrepo, M., & Montilla-Rosero, E. (2021). Development and Validation of a Scanning Depolarization Lidar System for Studying Urban Aerosols in a Tropical Valley. In *European Lidar Conference (ELC).*

Hoyos-Restrepo, M., & Montilla-Rosero, E. (2022). *Measurements of urban aerosol properties by developing a scanning depolarization lidar system.* Universidad EAFIT.

Inza-Aguirre, A. (2014). Estudio de series temporales y composición química del material particulado atmosférico en distintas áreas del país vasco. *Phd Thesis.* Universidad del País Vasco. https://addi.ehu.es/handle/10810/12248

Jacobson, M. Z. (1997). Development and application of a new air pollution modeling system—II. Aerosol module structure and design. *Atmospheric Environment, 31*(2), 131–144. DOI: 10.1016/1352-2310(96)00202-6

Jaenicke, R. (2001). Ernö Mészáros: Fundamentals of Atmospheric Aerosol Chemistry. *Journal of Atmospheric Chemistry, 39*(1), 99–103. DOI: 10.1023/A:1010753724116

Karagulian, F., Barbiere, M., Kotsev, A., Spinelle, L., Gerboles, M., Lagler, F., Redon, N., Crunarie, S., & Borowiak, A. (2019). Review of the Performance of Low-Cost Sensors for Air Quality Monitoring. *Atmosphere (Basel), 506*(10), 506. DOI: 10.3390/atmos10090506

Klett, J. D. (1985). Lidar inversion with variable backscatter/extinction ratios. *Applied Optics, 24*(11), 1638–1643. https://doi.org/https://doi.org/10.1364/AO.24.001638. DOI: 10.1364/AO.24.001638 PMID: 18223768

Krug, J. D., Dart, A., Witherspoon, C. L., Gilberry, J., Malloy, Q., Kaushik, S., & Vanderpool, R. W. (2017). Revisiting the size selective performance of EPA's high-volume total suspended particulate matter (Hi-Vol TSP) sampler. *Aerosol Science and Technology, 51*(7), 868–878. DOI: 10.1080/02786826.2017.1316358 PMID: 32025079

Kumar, A., Jimenez, R., Belalcázar, L. C., & Roja, N. Y. (2016). Application of WRF-Chem Model to Simulate PM10 Concentration over Bogotá. *Aerosol and Air Quality Research, 16*(5), 1206–1221. DOI: 10.4209/aaqr.2015.05.0318

Liu, C., Xiao, Q., & Wang, B. (2008). An Ensemble-Based Four-Dimensional Variational Data Assimilation Scheme. Part I: Technical Formulation and Preliminary Test. *Monthly Weather Review*, *136*(9), 3363–3373. DOI: 10.1175/2008MWR2312.1

Lopez-Restrepo, S., Quintero, O., Segers, A., Rodríguez, M., Pinel, N., Posada-Marín, J., & Rendón, A. M. (2017). Challenges and opportunities for Open LOTOS-EUROS model to reproduce the Dynamics for Tropical Andes Domain. *CMAS Conference Proceedings*.

Lopez-Restrepo, S., Yarce, A., Pinel, N., Quintero, O. L., Segers, A., & Heemink, A. W. (2022). A Knowledge-Aided Robust Ensemble Kalman Filter Algorithm for Non-Linear and Non-Gaussian Large Systems. *Frontiers in Applied Mathematics and Statistics*, *8*, 830116. Advance online publication. DOI: 10.3389/fams.2022.830116

Manisalidis, I., Stavropoulou, E., Stavropoulos, A., & Bezirtzoglou, E. (2020). Environmental and Health Impacts of Air Pollution: A Review. In *Frontiers in Public Health* (Vol. 8). Frontiers Media S.A. DOI: 10.3389/fpubh.2020.00014

Mishchenko, M. I., Travis, L., & Lacis, A. (2000). *Scattering, Absorption, and Emission of Light by Small Particles*. Cambridge University Press.

Moná-Bedoya, W. (2022). *Airyx Skyspec - Instrumento Max-DOAS. Operating Manual*. Universidad EAFIT.

Moná-Bedoya, W., & Montilla-Rosero, E. (2023). *Determinación de la Densidad Óptica Diferencial de Columna de Gases Traza en el Valle de Aburrá Utilizando la Técnica MAX-DOAS. Report*. Universidad EAFIT.

Monin, A. S., & Obukhov, A. (1954). Basic laws of turbulent mixing in the surface layer of the atmosphere. *Contrib. Geophys. Inst. Acad*, *6*(2).

Morrison, H., Curry, J. A., & Khvorostyanov, V. I. (2005). A New Double-Moment Microphysics Parameterization for Application in Cloud and Climate Models. Part I: Description. *Journal of the Atmospheric Sciences*, *62*(6), 1665–1677. DOI: 10.1175/JAS3446.1

UNE Normalización Española. (2006). UNE-EN 14907:2006. Calidad del aire ambiente. método gravimétrico de medida para la determinación de la fracción másica pm2.5 de la materia particulada en suspensión.*Report*.

Pardo, N., Avellaneda, J. D., Rausch, J., Jaramillo-Vogel, D., Gutiérrez, M., & Foubert, A. (2020). Decrypting silicic magma/plug fragmentation at Azufral crater lake, Northern Andes: Insights from fine to extremely fine ash morpho-chemistry. *Bulletin of Volcanology*, *82*(12), 79. DOI: 10.1007/s00445-020-01418-z

Pope, C. A.III. (2002). Lung Cancer, Cardiopulmonary Mortality, and Long-term Exposure to Fine Particulate Air Pollution. *Journal of the American Medical Association, 287*(9), 1132. DOI: 10.1001/jama.287.9.1132 PMID: 11879110

Quintero, O. L., Niño-Ruiz, E. D., & Pinel, N. (2020). On the mathematical modelling and data assimilation for air pollution assessment in the Tropical Andes. In *Environmental Science and Pollution Research* (Vol. 27, Issue 29, pp. 35993–36012). Springer. DOI: 10.1007/s11356-020-08268-4

Rausch, J., Grobéty, B., & Vonlanthen, P. (2015). Eifel maars: Quantitative shape characterization of juvenile ash particles (Eifel Volcanic Field, Germany). *Journal of Volcanology and Geothermal Research, 291*, 86–100. DOI: 10.1016/j.jvolgeores.2014.11.008

Rausch, J., Jaramillo-Vogel, D., Perseguers, S., Schnidrig, N., Grobéty, B., & Yajan, P. (2022). Automated identification and quantification of tire wear particles (TWP) in airborne dust: SEM/EDX single particle analysis coupled to a machine learning classifier. *The Science of the Total Environment, 803*, 149832. DOI: 10.1016/j.scitotenv.2021.149832 PMID: 34525712

Rios-Lugo & Hernández-Mendoza. H. (2020). Fundamentos teóricos de icp-ms y su importancia en el análisis de elementos tóxicos en agua subterránea. 14. 4-15. https://www.researchgate.net/publication/341310570_Fundamentos_teoricos_de_icp-ms_y_su_importancia_en_el_analisis_de_elementos_toxicos_en_agua_subterranea. *Report.*

Rojas González, L., & Montilla-Rosero, E. (2025). Evaluation of In-Situ Low-Cost Sensor Network in a Tropical Valley, Colombia. *Sensors (Basel), 25*(4), 1236. DOI: 10.3390/s25041236 PMID: 40006467

Sasano, Y., & Nakane, H. (1984). Significance of the extinction/backscatter ratio and the boundary value term in the solution for the two-component lidar equation. *Applied Optics, 23*(1), 11–13. DOI: 10.1364/AO.23.0011_1 PMID: 20407534

Schachter, E. N., Moshier, E., Habre, R., Rohr, A., Godbold, J., Nath, A., Grunin, A., Coull, B., Koutrakis, P., & Kattan, M. (2016). Outdoor air pollution and health effects in urban children with moderate to severe asthma. *Air Quality, Atmosphere & Health, 9*(3), 251–263. DOI: 10.1007/s11869-015-0335-6

Seinfeld, J. H., & Pandis, S. N. (2006). Atmospheric Chemistry and Physics. In *Air Pollution to Climate Change* (2nd ed.). John Wiley & Sons.

Sommer, F., Dietze, V., Baum, A., Sauer, J., Gilge, S., Maschowski, C., & Gieré, R. (2018). Tire Abrasion as a Major Source of Microplastics in the Environment. *Aerosol and Air Quality Research, 18*(8), 2014–2028. DOI: 10.4209/aaqr.2018.03.0099

UNEP. (2023). *Annual Report: Climate Action.* https://www.unep.org/resources/annual-report-2023

Viana-Rodríguez, M. del M. (2003). *Niveles, composición y origen del material particulado atmosférico en los sectores Norte y Este de la Península Ibérica y Canarias. Tesis doctoral.* Universidad de Barcelona.

Wandinger, U. (2005). Introduction to Lidar. In: Lidar. In Weitkamp, C. (Ed.), *Lidar* (pp. 1–18). Springer. DOI: 10.1007/0-387-25101-4_1

WHO. (2024). *Sustainable Development Goal indicator 3.9.1 mortality attributed to air pollution.* https://www.who.int/publications/i/item/9789240099142

Yarce-Botero, A., Heemink, A. W., & Quintero Montoya, O. L. (2024). Data assimilation in a LOTOS-EUROS chemical transport model for Colombia using satellite measurements. *PhD Thesis*. Delft University of Technology. https://doi.org/https://doi.org/10.4233/uuid:e202a1f3-9c73-42d1-b7f6-d45f9631df74

Yarce-Botero, A., Lopez-Restrepo, S., Pinel, N., Quintero, O., Segers, A., Schaap, M., & Heemink, A. W. (2019). *Implementation of the Chemical-Transport Model LOTOS-EUROS in Northwest South America for the identification of ecosystems affected by contaminant deposition.* EGU General Assembly.

Yarce Botero, A., Lopez-Restrepo, S., Pinel Peláez, N., Quintero, O. L., Segers, A., & Heemink, A. W. (2021). Estimating nox lotos-euros ctm emission parameters over the northwest of south america through 4denvar tropomi no2 assimilation. *Atmosphere (Basel), 12*(12), 1633. Advance online publication. DOI: 10.3390/atmos12121633

Yarce Botero, A., Lopez Restrepo, S., Sebastian Rodriguez, J., Valle, D., Galvez-Serna, J., Montilla, E., Botero, F., Henzing, B., Segers, A., Heemink, A., Quintero, O. L., & Pinel, N. (2023a). Design and Implementation of a Low-Cost Air Quality Network for the Aburrá Valley Surrounding Mountains. *Pollutants, 3*(1), 150–165. DOI: 10.3390/pollutants3010012

# Chapter 8
# Reimagining Community Resilience and Engagement Through the Digital Innovation

**Oindrilla Ghosh**
https://orcid.org/0000-0001-9609-0781
*Christ University, India*

**Binod Kumar**
https://orcid.org/0009-0002-9721-1367
*Radha Govind University, India*

## ABSTRACT

*In an increasingly interconnected world, reimagining community resilience demands the integration of digital innovation. Digital platforms facilitate real-time information sharing, enabling members to respond effectively to challenges, whether they stem from natural disasters or social issues. Innovative tools such as mobile apps and social media can gather diverse voices and build inclusive environments, promoting empowerment through participatory decision-making. Virtual town halls, community forums, and online workshops encourage dialogue, bridging gaps between local government and citizens. Digital innovation also enhances access to resources, providing residents with essential information on health services, educational opportunities, and local initiatives. By utilizing data analytics, communities can better understand their needs and priorities, ensuring tailored solutions for improved resilience. As communities continue to evolve, embracing digital innovation will be pivotal in nurturing resilience and active participation.*

DOI: 10.4018/979-8-3373-0390-1.ch008

## INTRODUCTION

The rapid advancement of technology in the twenty-first century has given rise to new paradigms in how communities interact, engage, and build resilience in the face of challenges (Kaziev et al., 2020). Community resilience is broadly defined as the ability of a community to anticipate, prepare for, respond to, and recover from adverse situations be it natural disasters, economic downturns, or social upheavals (Gevorgyan et al., 2020). As the complexities of these challenges increase, so too does the need for innovative strategies to foster resilience (Bogart, 2020). Digital innovation has emerged as a powerful tool in this context, enabling communities to leverage technology for better engagement and collaborative problem-solving (Videka et al., 2008).

Digital platforms and tools facilitate enhanced communication, streamline resource sharing, and provide avenues for local citizens to engage in decision-making processes (Zender and Tavangarian, 2009). By harnessing the power of social media, mobile applications, and big data analytics, communities can more effectively connect with their members and leverage their diverse skills and perspectives (Altbach, 1991). This not only strengthens communal bonds but also empowers individuals to take ownership of their local issues (Kostina, 2021). Furthermore, in times of crisis, digital networks play a crucial role in disseminating information rapidly, coordinating responses, and facilitating support systems (Shill and Tonner, 2003).

The intersection of community resilience and digital innovation is especially pertinent in an increasingly urbanized and interconnected world (Berkel and Homburg, 2023). Climate change, economic inequality, and social fragmentation present significant hurdles, and the urgency for communities to adapt is palpable (Scholl and Gulwadi, 2015). Digital innovations act as enablers of resilience by facilitating real-time data collection and analysis, which can inform planning and response strategies (Rubin, 1998). Moreover, digital tools can help bridge gaps connecting marginalized voices with decision-makers and enhancing the inclusivity of community engagement efforts (Franz and Gruber, 2022).

However, the integration of digital innovation into community resilience strategies is not without its challenges (Sharma, 2015). Issues of digital divide, data privacy, and the risk of information overload are tangible concerns (Winter et al., 2006). Moreover, the efficacy of these innovations depends heavily on the social fabric of the community (Von Hauff and Nguyen, 2014). Engagement strategies that are sensitive to local context, culture, and needs are essential for success (Song et al., 2007). Thus, while digital technologies hold great promise, their implementation must be thoughtful and inclusive (Nelson and Stolterman, 2014).

Therefore, the reimagining of community resilience transcends mere technological adoption; it calls for a systemic transformation in thinking about community engagement and governance (Bygstad, 2019). It is not enough for communities to simply adopt new tools; they must also cultivate collective intelligence, harness the potential of diverse community voices, and foster a culture of collaboration and co-creation (Luchkov et al., 2022).

## HISTORICAL EVOLUTION

The concept of community resilience has evolved significantly throughout history, especially in response to changing socio-political contexts and technological advances (Kerres, 2004). Traditionally, the idea of resilience was rooted in the ability of communities to withstand and recover from adversities a quality inherent in the social fabric of neighborhoods built through face-to-face interactions and communal support (Moşteanu, 2020). As societies evolved, particularly during the industrial and post-industrial eras, the nature of community engagement began to shift, influenced by urbanization, globalization, and advancements in communication technology (Gafurov et al., 2020).

In the early 20th century, community engagement was primarily localized and centered around physical spaces, such as town halls and community centers (Benade, 2019). Social movements were often organized through grassroots efforts that relied heavily on word-of-mouth and in-person meetings (Valtonen et al., 2021). However, as the mid-20th century approached, the introduction of mass media especially radio and television transformed how communities disseminated information and mobilized around collective causes (Nguyen, 2018). This period marked the beginning of a broader understanding of community engagement as it incorporated not just local issues but also national and global concerns (Rodríguez-Abitia and Bribiesca-Correa, 2021).

The outbreak of crises, such as natural disasters and economic recessions, further highlighted the necessity of building resilient communities (Kholiavko et al., 2021). The Hurricane Katrina disaster in 2005, for example, exposed significant gaps in emergency preparedness and response, leading to a stronger emphasis on resilience strategies (Pfeffer, 2011). This event catalyzed local and governmental organizations to rethink their approaches to community engagement underscoring the importance of communication and coordination in times of crisis (Burbules and Callister, 2000).

The late 20th century and early 21st century saw the rise of the Internet and mobile technology, revolutionizing community engagement once again (Funamori, 2016). Social media platforms such as Facebook and Twitter have fundamentally altered how individuals and groups communicate, enabling instant connection and collective action on a scale previously unimaginable (Jaakkola, 2020). The Arab Spring of 2011 exemplifies this transformation; activists leveraged social media to organize protests, raise awareness, and galvanize support against oppressive regimes (MacInnis, 2011).

Moreover, various digital tools have emerged to facilitate community planning and resilience-building (Vargo and Lusch, 2004). Geographic Information Systems (GIS), for instance, allow communities to visualize data related to demographic trends, environmental hazards, and infrastructure development, thereby enabling informed decision-making (Sage, 2023). In addition, participatory platforms, such as crowdsourcing applications, empower citizens to contribute their insights and experience to local governance efforts (Schmidt and Tang, 2020).

As digital innovation continues to advance, its integration into community resilience strategies is becoming increasingly sophisticated (Padmanabhan, 2023). Today, communities are employing artificial intelligence and big data analytics to predict trends, evaluate risks, and optimize resources, illustrating a shift toward data-driven community engagement (Singh et al., 2021). This ongoing evolution presents both opportunities and challenges, emphasizing the need for thoughtful and inclusive approaches that respect local contexts while harnessing the transformative potential of technology (Lei et al., 2020). In essence, the historical evolution of community resilience reflects a dynamic interplay between societal changes and technological advancements, paving the way for a future where communities are better equipped to thrive amidst uncertainties (Mahajan et al., 2019).

## THEORETICAL FRAMEWORKS

Community resilience refers to the ability of a community to withstand, adapt to, and recover from stresses and shocks, such as natural disasters, economic downturns, and social disruptions (Wilkins et al., 2022). Theoretical frameworks on community resilience can serve as vital tools in understanding how digital innovation can enhance these capacities (Robertson et al., 2019). Among the influential frameworks is the Ecological Model of Resilience, which emphasizes the interplay between various levels of community systems, including individual, family, community, and societal levels (Musa and Ahmad, 2012). This model encourages the consideration of interactions across these levels to strengthen resilience (Smart et al., 2020).

The Social-Ecological Framework asserts that resilience is not merely a characteristic of an individual or community but rather the result of complex interactions among environmental, social, political, and economic factors (Isa and Yusoff, 2015). Digital innovation plays a crucial role in this framework by facilitating communication, mobilizing resources, and fostering collaboration through platforms that connect communities (Zhou and Lu, 2022). Digital tools enable communities to engage in participatory governance, disseminate information rapidly during crises, and build networks of mutual support (Lewinski, 2015). This perspective pushes us to examine how technology reshapes community dynamics and enhances the ability of individuals to cooperate for the greater good (Mali and Thakur, 2010).

Another essential theoretical lens is the Theory of Change (Wahid et al., 2020). This framework helps delineate the pathways through which interventions lead to desired outcomes (Schwaen et al., 2018). In the context of community resilience, digital innovations such as social media platforms, mobile applications, and crowd-sourced information systems provide channels through which communities can identify their vulnerabilities, assess threats, and mobilize resources (Németh et al., 2020). By employing a Theory of Change approach, stakeholders can establish a clearer understanding of how digital tools can be instrumental in driving community engagement, improving communication, and fostering local leadership among vulnerable groups (Sferrazza, 2018).

Finally, the Adaptive Capacity framework focuses on how communities can learn over time and adjust their strategies in response to changing circumstances (Smith, 2016). Digital innovation can serve as a catalyst for adaptive capacity by facilitating real-time data collection and analysis (Sargent, 2015). Communities can utilize digital tools to monitor environmental and social changes, enabling them to remain agile and responsive to emerging challenges (Hernandez-de-Menendez et al., 2020). This aligns with the growing emphasis on Big Data and predictive analytics, which can help anticipate potential shocks and prepare community resilience strategies proactively (Kim et al., 2018).

Thus, theoretical frameworks surrounding community resilience illuminate the intricate relationships between technology and community dynamics (van der Walt, 2023). These frameworks help guide initiatives that harness digital innovation to enhance resilience, emphasizing the importance of inclusive engagement and the co-creation of solutions (Bhati and Song, 2019). By utilizing these theoretical lenses, practitioners and policymakers can better design interventions that utilize digital tools to bolster community resilience and respond effectively to the myriad challenges of the modern world (Bond et al., 2018).

## FOUNDATIONS

The foundation of effective community engagement through digital innovation rests on several core principles that ensure inclusivity, empowerment, and sustainability (Dillahunt et al., 2014). A fundamental element is the recognition of diverse community voices (Radhamani et al., 2015). Digital platforms must transcend traditional barriers, allowing marginalized populations to participate in discussions that affect their lives (Laufer et al., 2021). This necessitates the use of user-friendly technologies that consider varying levels of digital literacy, accessibility needs, and cultural context (Muñoz et al., 2022).

Additionally, the principle of participatory design is vital (Shah and Shah, 2023). Engaging communities in the creation and implementation of digital tools leads to solutions that are more relevant and tailored to their specific needs (Popova et al., 2020). Co-design processes where community members actively collaborate with technologists ensure that innovations are not only functional but also culturally resonant and impactful (Kovaleva et al., 2022). Digital platforms that promote participatory budgeting, for example, allow residents to influence funding decisions, thereby enhancing ownership and commitment to community initiatives (Alenezi et al., 2023).

Transparency and accountability are integral to building trust in digital engagement processes (Brodovskaya et al., 2019). Communities must be informed about how their data will be used and who has access to it (Azionya and Nhedzi, 2021). Establishing clear guidelines for data governance ensures that digital platforms are leveraged ethically, safeguarding the interests and rights of community members (Bondoc and Malawit, 2020). This transparency fosters a sense of ownership and mutual respect, essential for sustained engagement (Joan, 2013).

Education and capacity-building also lay the groundwork for effective community engagement through digital innovation (Zhang et al., 2015). Equipping community members with the necessary skills to navigate digital tools not only enhances participation but also empowers individuals to advocate for their needs and priorities effectively (Mehmood et al., 2020). Training workshops, online tutorials, and ongoing support networks can facilitate this capacity-building, ensuring that engagement is not sporadic but ongoing and meaningful (Bennett et al., 2020).

Furthermore, fostering collaborations between community organizations and technology developers strengthens the implementation of digital innovations (Margulies, 2004). Such partnerships can enhance resource mobilization, ensuring that communities have access to the required technical support and funding to sustain projects (Lee et al., 2007). Collaboration also promotes knowledge sharing and the replication of successful models across different contexts, fostering a culture of innovation and collective problem-solving (Alexander, 2001).

Hence, the foundations of community engagement through digital innovation hinge on inclusivity, participatory design, transparency, education, and collaboration (Won, 2015). By prioritizing these principles, communities can cultivate an innovative ecosystem that not only enhances resilience but also fosters a sense of belonging and active citizenship (Clothey, 2011). As we move forward in an increasingly digitized world, these foundations will serve as the bedrock for building engaged, resilient communities capable of navigating current and future challenges (Holland and Holland, 2014).

## IMPORTANCE

In an era marked by rapid technological advancements and an ever-increasing array of challenges ranging from climate change and public health crises to economic disparities the importance of reimagining community resilience and engagement through digital innovation cannot be overstated (Estache, 2012). Community resilience refers to the ability of a community to bounce back from adversity, adapt to changing circumstances, and thrive in the face of challenges (Johnson et al., 2016). Digital innovation offers unprecedented opportunities to strengthen this resilience by facilitating communication, collaboration, and resource sharing among community members (Veiga-Ávila et al., 2019).

One of the most significant benefits of digital innovation in enhancing community resilience is the ability to foster stronger relationships among residents (Smith and Winters, 2021). Social media platforms, community-focused applications, and virtual forums provide spaces for collaboration and dialogue, allowing individuals to connect with one another, share experiences, and build networks of support (Johnson et al., 2020). In times of crisis, such as natural disasters or public health emergencies, these digital tools enable communities to mobilize swiftly, share vital information, and coordinate relief efforts effectively (Veiga-Ávila, 2019).

Moreover, digital technologies can enhance participatory governance, empowering citizens to become actively involved in decision-making processes (Kaziev et al., 2020). By harnessing platforms for crowdsourcing ideas, conducting surveys, or hosting virtual town hall meetings, governments and organizations can engage residents more meaningfully (Gevorgyan et al., 2020). This increased engagement fosters a sense of ownership and responsibility among community members, motivating them to contribute actively to resilience-building initiatives (Bogart, 2020). Digital innovation can also bridge gaps in representation by ensuring that marginalized voices are heard and integrated into community planning (Videka et al., 2008).

Another critical aspect of community resilience is access to information (Zender and Tavangarian, 2009). Digital platforms can facilitate the dissemination of vital information about services, resources, and best practices, ensuring that community members are well-informed and prepared to respond to potential threats or challenges (Altbach, 1991). For example, during the COVID-19 pandemic, digital channels were pivotal in spreading awareness about health guidelines, vaccination sites, and community support services (Kostina, 2021). Communities can also utilize data-driven insights to identify vulnerabilities, assess risks, and develop targeted strategies for resilience (Shill and Tonner, 2003).

Furthermore, digital innovation supports the creation of collaborative platforms for problem-solving and resource sharing (Berkel and Homburg, 2023). Online networks enable community members to exchange skills, knowledge, and resources, fostering localized economies and resilience strategies (Scholl and Gulwadi, 2015). Repair-sharing or tool-lending platforms can reduce reliance on external resources while promoting sustainability and reducing waste (Rubin, 1998). These collaborative efforts not only enhance individual resilience but also contribute to a more interconnected and supportive community (Franz and Gruber, 2022).

## GOVERNANCE

Governance plays a pivotal role in reimagining community resilience and engagement through digital innovation (Sharma, 2015). Effective governance is not merely about the structures and organizations within a community; it encompasses the processes and relationships by which power and authority are exercised in service to the community (Winter et al., 2006). In the context of leveraging digital technologies to foster resilience, governance must adapt to harness the transformative potential of these tools while ensuring inclusivity, equity, transparency, and accountability (Von Hauff and Nguyen, 2014).

One vital aspect of governance in this digital age is establishing frameworks that promote inclusive participation (Song et al., 2007). Traditional governance mechanisms often marginalize specific groups within the community, leading to disengagement and disenfranchisement (Nelson and Stolterman, 2014). Digital innovation provides an opportunity to rectify this by creating avenues for broader participation (Bygstad, 2019). For instance, digital platforms can facilitate outreach to underrepresented communities, allowing them to voice their concerns, share their insights, and participate in decision-making processes (Luchkov et al., 2022). This inclusivity not only strengthens community bonds but also legitimizes governance structures by ensuring that they reflect the diverse needs and aspirations of the community residents (Kerres, 2004).

Furthermore, effective governance must ensure that digital innovation is harnessed for equitable resource distribution (Moşteanu, 2020). Disparities in access to digital technologies can exacerbate existing inequalities (Gafurov et al., 2020). Governance frameworks must address these gaps by investing in digital literacy programs, infrastructure development, and affordable internet access (Benade, 2019). Ensuring that all community members can benefit from digital tools is essential for building resilience (Valtonen et al., 2021); without equitable access, certain groups may remain vulnerable during crises, limiting the overall resilience of the community (Nguyen, 2018).

Transparency and accountability are foundational principles that must be woven into the governance fabric when reimagining community resilience through digital innovation (Rodríguez-Abitia and Bribiesca-Correa, 2021). Digital platforms should enable real-time sharing of information regarding community initiatives, expenditure, and decision-making processes (Kholiavko et al., 2021). This transparency fosters trust among residents, as they can see how resources are allocated and how decisions align with community priorities (Pfeffer, 2011). Furthermore, accountability mechanisms, such as digital feedback loops, ensure that decision-makers are responsive to community concerns, creating a culture of continuous improvement and responsiveness in governance (Burbules and Callister, 2000).

In addition, embracing innovative governance models, such as decentralized governance and participatory budgeting through digital platforms, can further enhance engagement and resilience (Funamori, 2016). These models empower residents to take an active role in shaping their communities, moving away from top-down approaches towards collaborative decision-making processes (Jaakkola, 2020). By allowing residents to prioritize initiatives or allocate resources based on their unique needs and circumstances (MacInnis, 2011), communities can cultivate a sense of ownership and shared responsibility, resulting in more resilient and adaptive responses to challenges (Vargo and Lusch, 2004).

Finally, ethical considerations surrounding data privacy, cybersecurity, and digital rights are paramount in governance frameworks dealing with digital innovation (Sage, 2023). Community leaders must prioritize safeguarding residents' data and ensuring that digital initiatives uphold ethical standards (Schmidt and Tang, 2020). This commitment to ethical governance enhances public trust and encourages greater participation from community members, who feel secure in sharing their information (Padmanabhan, 2023).

## THE USE OF AI AND ML

Artificial intelligence (AI) and machine learning (ML) are transforming the landscape of community resilience and engagement, offering innovative solutions that enhance how communities interact, respond to challenges, and collaborate (Singh et al., 2021). As society grapples with a myriad of complex issues from climate change to public health crises the integration of AI and ML offers unprecedented opportunities to bolster community resilience and optimize engagement through digital innovation (Lei et al., 2020).

At the heart of reimagining community resilience through AI and ML is the capacity for predictive analytics (Mahajan et al., 2019). These technologies allow for the analysis of vast amounts of data to identify patterns and foresee potential risks, enabling communities to prepare proactively (Wilkins et al., 2022). For instance, in disaster management, AI-powered systems can analyze weather patterns, population densities, and infrastructure vulnerabilities to predict floods or wildfires (Robertson et al., 2019). By simulating different scenarios, these systems can help local governments design more effective emergency response plans, ultimately saving lives and reducing resource loss (Musa and Ahmad, 2012). Moreover, residents can be engaged through mobile applications that provide real-time alerts and inform them of preventive measures based on predictive analytics, thereby fostering a culture of preparedness and resilience (Smart et al., 2020).

AI and ML also play a critical role in enhancing community engagement by personalizing communication and outreach efforts (Isa and Yusoff, 2015). Advanced algorithms can analyze demographics, social media interactions, and past engagement patterns to tailor messages that resonate with different groups within a community (Zhou and Lu, 2022). This level of personalization can significantly boost participation rates in community programs and initiatives (Lewinski, 2015). For example, targeted outreach campaigns powered by AI can ensure that vital information reaches underserved populations, bridging the gap between various demographic groups (Mali and Thakur, 2010). As a result, communities can become more inclusive, where diverse voices and perspectives are valued and embraced (Wahid et al., 2020).

Furthermore, AI-driven sentiment analysis tools can be deployed to gauge community sentiment regarding different initiatives or issues (Schwaen et al., 2018). By analyzing social media posts and other digital communications, AI can provide insights into public opinion and areas of concern (Németh et al., 2020). These insights can inform the planning and implementation of community projects, ensuring that they align with the needs and desires of residents (Sferrazza, 2018). Engaging with community sentiment in real-time not only fosters a participatory environment but also builds trust between residents and local governing bodies (Smith, 2016).

While the benefits of AI and ML in community resilience are substantial, it is crucial to approach their implementation with careful consideration of ethical implications (Sargent, 2015). Issues such as data privacy, algorithmic bias, and the digital divide must be addressed proactively (Hernandez-de-Menendez et al., 2020). Communities need to develop frameworks that ensure transparency and accountability in the use of these technologies (Kim et al., 2018). Engaging citizens in discussions about how their data is used, as well as the rationale behind AI-driven decisions, is essential for building trust and ensuring equitable outcomes (van der Walt, 2023).

## Augmented Reality (AR)

Augmented Reality (AR) is revolutionizing how communities interact with their environment, providing immersive experiences that enhance engagement and promote resilience (Bhati and Song, 2019). By overlaying digital information onto the physical world, AR enables residents to visualize critical data about their community (Bond et al., 2018). For instance, AR applications can display real-time information on local environmental conditions, emergency resources, or community services, enabling citizens to make informed decisions during crises (Dillahunt et al., 2014). During natural disasters, AR can assist in evacuation planning, helping residents identify safe routes and shelters through visual markers overlaid on their surroundings (Radhamani et al., 2015).

Moreover, AR fosters community engagement by empowering residents to contribute actively to local projects (Laufer et al., 2021). Community mapping applications enable individuals to tag locations with historical significance, share stories, or highlight areas in need of repair, creating a collective digital archive (Muñoz et al., 2022). This participatory approach enriches community identity and cohesion, facilitating discussions that can lead to social action and resilience-building initiatives (Shah and Shah, 2023). Furthermore, events such as community workshops or town hall meetings can be enhanced using AR, allowing participants to visualize proposals, infrastructure changes, or development plans in real time (Popova et al., 2020).

Educational initiatives also stand to benefit from AR, as schools and organizations can develop programs that teach students and residents about local history, ecology, and civic responsibility through interactive experiences (Kovaleva et al., 2022). By making learning engaging, AR can foster a culture of community involvement and empowerment, crucial elements for long-term resilience (Alenezi et al., 2023). In essence, AR serves as a bridge between the digital and physical realms, transforming how communities communicate, collaborate, and prepare for challenges (Brodovskaya et al., 2019).

## Virtual Reality (VR)

Virtual Reality (VR) is a transformative technology that can significantly enhance community resilience and engagement by providing immersive experiences that foster empathy, education, and collaboration (Azionya and Nhedzi, 2021). In scenarios requiring preparedness, such as natural disasters or public health emergencies, VR simulations can immerse community members in realistic training environments (Bondoc and Malawit, 2020). For example, residents can participate in simulated emergency response scenarios, such as earthquake drills or fire evacuations, allowing them to practice critical skills in a safe, controlled setting (Joan, 2013). This experiential learning approach equips individuals with the confidence and knowledge needed to act effectively in high-pressure situations, thereby bolstering overall community resilience (Zhang et al., 2015).

Additionally, VR can facilitate community engagement by providing platforms for collaboration and dialogue (Mehmood et al., 2020). Virtual town hall meetings and discussion forums can connect residents regardless of geographical barriers, enabling diverse voices to contribute to essential community planning and decision-making processes (Bennett et al., 2020). Such inclusivity not only strengthens community bonds but also fosters a sense of ownership and investment in local initiatives, crucial aspects of resilience (Margulies, 2004).

Moreover, VR can enhance awareness and empathy within communities (Lee et al., 2007). By allowing individuals to experience the lives and challenges of their neighbors through storytelling and immersive narratives, VR can break down barriers and foster understanding across different demographic and socioeconomic groups (Alexander, 2001). This heightened empathy can catalyze community-driven solutions to social issues, reinforcing the social fabric necessary for resilience (Won, 2015).

## Mixed Reality (MR)

Mixed Reality (MR) stands at the intersection of augmented and virtual reality, enabling a seamless blend of digital and physical environments (Clothey, 2011). This innovative technology can reimagine community resilience and engagement by providing dynamic, interactive experiences that foster collaboration, education, and problem-solving (Holland and Holland, 2014). MR applications allow community members to visualize complex data and scenarios in real time, enhancing their understanding of local challenges such as environmental changes, urban development, and disaster preparedness (Estache, 2012).

One significant application of MR in enhancing community resilience is in urban planning and development (Johnson et al., 2016). City planners can use MR tools to overlay proposed infrastructure or community projects directly onto the landscape, allowing stakeholders to visualize the changes in context (Veiga-Ávila et al., 2019). This participatory planning process encourages community feedback, ensuring that the voices of residents are heard and considered in decision-making (Smith and Winters, 2021). By involving citizens in this way, MR cultivates a sense of ownership and accountability, crucial for fostering resilience in the face of challenges (Johnson et al., 2020).

Furthermore, MR can foster social cohesion by connecting community members in innovative ways (Veiga-Ávila, 2019). Virtual neighborhood gatherings or collaborative projects can be enhanced through MR, allowing participants to contribute ideas, share experiences, and work on solutions collectively (Kaziev et al., 2020). By bridging digital and physical spaces, MR encourages connectivity among residents, promoting the social ties necessary for a resilient community (Gevorgyan et al., 2020).

## Advantages

In today's interconnected world, digital innovation presents unique opportunities to enhance community resilience and engagement (Bogart, 2020). The advent of technology and digital platforms has transformed how communities interact, support each other, and respond to challenges (Videka et al., 2008).

*Improved Communication:* Digital tools facilitate improved communication within communities (Zender and Tavangarian, 2009). Social media platforms, community forums, and messaging applications allow for rapid information sharing (Altbach, 1991). During emergencies, such as natural disasters or public health crises, real-time updates can be disseminated quickly, helping residents to stay informed about safety measures, resources, and assistance .
*Increased Participation:* Digital innovations lower barriers to participation (Shill and Tonner, 2003). Online surveys, virtual town halls, and mobile applications encourage community members to share their opinions and engage in local governance without the constraints of traditional meeting formats (Berkel and Homburg, 2023). This engagement ensures that a wider range of voices is heard, particularly those who may be marginalized or unable to attend in-person meetings due to various limitations (Scholl and Gulwadi, 2015).
*Data-Driven Decision Making:* The collection and analysis of data have been enhanced through digital tools, enabling communities to make informed decisions (Rubin, 1998). By utilizing data analytics, local leaders can identify trends, assess needs, and allocate resources more effectively (Franz and Gruber, 2022). This evidence-based approach leads to more impactful interventions and strategies for strengthening community resilience (Sharma, 2015).
*Capacity Building:* Digital platforms often provide access to educational resources and training opportunities (Winter et al., 2006). Community members can develop new skills through online courses, workshops, and webinars (Von Hauff and Nguyen, 2014). This knowledge sharing enables individuals to build capacity within the community, enhancing both personal development and collective resilience (Song et al., 2007).

*Support Networks:* Social media can be leveraged to create support networks that connect community members with shared interests or experiences (Nelson and Stolterman, 2014). For instance, groups focused on mental health can provide emotional support, resources, and guidance during challenging times (Bygstad, 2019). Such networks foster social cohesion and create a sense of belonging, crucial elements for community resilience (Luchkov et al., 2022).

*Outreach and Resource Distribution:* Digital innovations streamline the outreach process, making it easier to connect vulnerable populations with essential services and resources (Kerres, 2004). Organizations can use mobile apps or websites to inform individuals about food banks, shelters, health services, and other resources, ensuring that help reaches those who need it most (Moşteanu, 2020).

## Challenges

While there are significant advantages to utilizing digital innovation in community resilience, several challenges must be acknowledged (Gafurov et al., 2020). These challenges can hinder the effectiveness of technology in enhancing engagement and strengthening communities (Benade, 2019).

*Digital Divide:* One of the most pressing issues is the digital divide, which refers to the gap between those who have access to digital technology and the internet and those who do not (Valtonen et al., 2021). Many marginalized groups may lack reliable internet access or the necessary devices to engage with digital platforms (Nguyen, 2018). This disparity can exacerbate existing inequalities and limit the benefits of digital innovation for all community members (Rodríguez-Abitia and Bribiesca-Correa, 2021).

*Data Privacy and Security:* The increased use of digital platforms raises concerns about data privacy and security (Kholiavko et al., 2021). Communities must navigate issues related to user data collection, consent, and potential misuse of information (Pfeffer, 2011). Safeguarding personal information is crucial to building trust in digital initiatives; a breach could undermine community members' willingness to engage, particularly when sensitive information is involved (Burbules and Callister, 2000).

*Information Overload:* With the proliferation of digital content, community members may experience information overload (Funamori, 2016). The challenge lies in filtering relevant information, leading to confusion or disengagement (Jaakkola, 2020). When residents receive too much information from various sources, important messages may be lost, and individuals may become overwhelmed, resulting in reduced participation (MacInnis, 2011).

*Resistance to Change:* Communities often have established traditions and methods for engagement (Vargo and Lusch, 2004). The introduction of digital platforms may encounter resistance from those who are comfortable with conventional interactions (Sage, 2023). Overcoming skepticism around digital tools the fear of technology or the belief that traditional methods are superior requires targeted outreach, education, and change management strategies (Schmidt and Tang, 2020).

*Reliability of Technology:* Dependence on digital infrastructure poses risks, particularly during crises (Padmanabhan, 2023). Power outages, system failures, or cyber-attacks can disrupt communication and access to resources (Singh et al., 2021). These disruptions can adversely affect community resilience when immediate responses are critical (Lei et al., 2020). Having backup plans and ensuring multiple communication channels can help mitigate these risks (Mahajan et al., 2019).

*Inequitable Access to Resources:* While digital innovation can facilitate access to resources, it can also create inequities if not implemented thoughtfully (Wilkins et al., 2022). For instance, some programs may primarily cater to tech-savvy individuals, leaving behind those who may lack digital literacy (Robertson et al., 2019). Ensuring that digital initiatives are inclusive and accessible to everyone is vital to avoid deepening divides within the community (Musa and Ahmad, 2012).

## Ethical Considerations

In the era of digital transformation, reimagining community resilience and engagement requires a nuanced understanding of ethical considerations that transcend mere technological implementation (Smart et al., 2020). As communities harness digital tools in pursuit of resilience, issues of privacy, equity, and accountability come to the forefront, necessitating a comprehensive ethical framework to guide these innovations (Isa and Yusoff, 2015).

Firstly, privacy is paramount in any community engagement initiative (Zhou and Lu, 2022). Digital platforms often collect vast amounts of personal data, which, if mismanaged, can lead to breaches of privacy and trust (Lewinski, 2015). Ethical considerations must establish robust data protection policies to ensure that community members are informed about data collection, usage, and storage practices (Mali and Thakur, 2010). Furthermore, communities must implement transparency initiatives that inform residents how their data contributes to resilience-building efforts (Wahid et al., 2020). This engagement will foster trust and encourage more active participation (Schwaen et al., 2018).

Equity also plays a critical role in ethical considerations (Németh et al., 2020). Digital innovation can inadvertently widen existing disparities within communities if certain populations lack access to technology or digital literacy (Sferrazza, 2018). For instance, marginalized groups may be excluded from digital engagement initiatives that require stable internet access or familiarity with technology (Smith, 2016). Ethical frameworks should prioritize inclusive practices, ensuring that the design and implementation of digital tools accommodate diverse needs and reach those who are often left behind (Sargent, 2015). This may require investing in infrastructure to enhance digital access across socio-economic divides and providing training programs to elevate digital literacy among underrepresented populations (Hernandez-de-Menendez et al., 2020).

Another crucial ethical consideration is accountability (Kim et al., 2018). In deploying digital innovations for community resilience, there must be a clear understanding of who is responsible for the consequences of these technologies (van der Walt, 2023). Establishing accountability structures within community projects facilitates trust and ensures that stakeholders take responsibility for the social implications of their actions (Bhati and Song, 2019). Ethical governance includes forming multi-stakeholder coalitions that encompass various community voices, including those of vulnerable populations, to help guide decision-making processes (Bond et al., 2018). This not only enhances ethical practices but also enriches the community's capacity to manage technology failures or unintended consequences effectively (Dillahunt et al., 2014).

Moreover, there lies a significant ethical obligation to evaluate the long-term impacts of digital innovations on community cohesion and resilience (Radhamani et al., 2015). While immediate efficiencies and benefits might be apparent, it is essential to consider how these technologies affect relationship dynamics, social capital, and communal trust in the long run (Laufer et al., 2021). Digital innovations must be employed with a sense of caution to avoid exacerbating feelings of isolation or fragmentation within communities (Muñoz et al., 2022).

Lastly, developers and community leaders must consider the implications of technological dependence (Shah and Shah, 2023). Over-reliance on digital tools can lead to vulnerabilities, especially in scenarios where technology fails or is not accessible (Popova et al., 2020). Ethical frameworks should advocate for a balanced approach that integrates digital tools while maintaining traditional means of community engagement (Kovaleva et al., 2022). This holistic strategy fosters resilience that is not solely reliant on technology but is also adaptable and rooted in the social fabric of the community (Alenezi et al., 2023).

## Implementation of Regulatory Frameworks

As communities increasingly turn to digital platforms for engagement and support, the need for robust regulatory frameworks becomes evident (Brodovskaya et al., 2019). Effective implementation of these frameworks is essential for fostering resilience, ensuring equitable access, and maximizing the benefits of digital innovation (Azionya and Nhedzi, 2021). The following discussion centers on the critical roles that governments, organizations, and communities must play in the establishment and implementation of these frameworks (Bondoc and Malawit, 2020).

*Establishing Clear Guidelines:* A regulatory framework should include clear guidelines that govern data privacy, cybersecurity, and digital engagement practices (Joan, 2013). These guidelines must resonate with community values and priorities (Zhang et al., 2015). To implement these guidelines effectively, regular training sessions and educational programs must be offered to stakeholders (Mehmood et al., 2020). This approach not only empowers community members but also strengthens their understanding of digital tools and their implications (Bennett et al., 2020). Moreover, transparency in data collection and usage is critical; residents should be fully informed about how their data is used, and what protections are in place (Margulies, 2004). This transparency builds trust, which is a cornerstone of community resilience (Lee et al., 2007).

*Equitable Access to Technology:* One of the more pressing challenges is ensuring equitable access to technology among all community members (Alexander, 2001). Regulatory frameworks must account for socioeconomic disparities and aim to bridge the digital divide (Won, 2015). Temporary measures such as providing subsidies for internet access or funding for digital literacy programs can significantly improve engagement opportunities (Clothey, 2011). Regulations should also encourage private sector participation, incentivizing technology providers to offer affordable solutions for underserved populations (Holland and Holland, 2014). By prioritizing equitable access, communities can ensure that all individuals, regardless of background, have the opportunity to engage with digital innovations, thereby enhancing community resilience (Estache, 2012).

*Monitoring and Evaluation:* Implementation of regulatory frameworks should include an ongoing process of monitoring and evaluation (Johnson et al., 2016). Identifying key performance indicators (KPIs) can help gauge the effectiveness of initiatives aimed at fostering community resilience (Veiga-Ávila et al., 2019). Regular reviews can provide critical insights into areas where policies may fall short, allowing for agile modifications to better suit community needs (Smith and Winters, 2021). Furthermore, engaging communities in these evaluations enables them to actively participate in the regulatory process, strengthening their sense of agency and responsibility (Johnson et al., 2020).

*Legal and Ethical Considerations:* As digital innovation continues to evolve, so too must the legal and ethical landscape (Veiga-Ávila, 2019). Regulatory frameworks should be adaptive, capable of responding to new challenges posed by emerging technologies such as AI, blockchain, and IoT (Kaziev et al., 2020). For instance, the implications of algorithmic bias must be addressed, requiring oversight to ensure that digital tools do not perpetuate existing inequalities (Gevorgyan et al., 2020). Building ethics into technology design can also serve as a regulatory guideline (Bogart, 2020). Encouraging tech developers to implement ethical considerations early in the development process can mitigate potential risks and enhance community trust (Kostina, 2021).

## CONCLUSION

In an era characterized by rapid technological advancements and persistent global challenges, reimagining community resilience and engagement through digital innovation is not just desirable but imperative. Leveraging digital tools can significantly enhance communities' capacity to adapt, respond, and thrive in the face of adversity, be it economic downturns, natural disasters, or social inequities (Berkel and Homburg, 2023). However, this endeavor requires a nuanced understanding of the interplay between technology, community dynamics, and the regulatory environment.

Effective engagement necessitates the active involvement of community members in digital initiatives, ensuring that their voices and experiences shape the tools and strategies employed. Communities that embrace participatory approaches are more likely to identify their unique needs and challenges while creating an inclusive environment that fosters a sense of belonging (Franz and Gruber, 2022). By prioritizing local input, digital innovation can be tailored to resonate deeply with community members and cultivate trust in the technologies deployed.

Importantly, reimagining resilience also means addressing the digital divide that persists in many communities. While technology holds the potential to democratize information, unequal access can exacerbate existing inequalities. Comprehensive efforts to provide equitable access to technology and digital literacy programs will ensure all community members can fully participate and benefit from innovations. When everyone has the tools and knowledge to engage effectively, communities become more cohesive and resilient.

Regulatory frameworks play a crucial role in this transformation, providing the structure needed to guide the ethical implementation of technology, protect individual rights, and promote community welfare. These frameworks must be flexible and responsive, evolving alongside technological advancements while maintaining a focus on equity, privacy, and engagement. By fostering a culture of collaboration between governmental bodies, private sectors, and community organizations, regulation can support an environment of innovation that respects community values and enhances resilience.

Moreover, the role of data in community engagement cannot be understated. Data-driven decision-making allows communities to understand their challenges and dynamics better, enabling targeted interventions that can significantly improve outcomes (Bygstad, 2019). However, it is essential that such practices are rooted in ethical considerations, ensuring transparency and accountability in the collection and use of data. Responsible data governance cultivates trust, ultimately enhancing community engagement.

## Future Research Directions

As the intersection of digital technology and community engagement evolves, several future research directions can be identified to deepen our understanding and increase effectiveness.

*Impact Assessment of Digital Tools:* Future research should focus on assessing the long-term impacts of digital innovations on community resilience. Studying both qualitative and quantitative data can elucidate how specific technologies affect social cohesion, decision-making, and disaster responsiveness. Case studies of communities that underwent digital transformation could provide valuable insights into best practices.

*Exploring the Role of Emerging Technologies:* Investigating the potential of emerging technologies like artificial intelligence, blockchain, and the Internet of Things (IoT) in facilitating community resilience is essential. Research could explore how these technologies can be harnessed for real-time data collection, predictive analytics, and transparent governance practices, ultimately strengthening community trust.

*Understanding Behavioral Interactions:* New research could delve into the behavioral dynamics of community engagement through digital tools. This includes analyzing how digital interactions influence relationships among community members, their civic involvement, and their responsiveness during crises. Leveraging social network analysis can shed light on how digital communication reshapes community structures.

*Ethics and Digital Inclusion:* Investigating the ethical implications of digital engagement tools, especially those concerning privacy, surveillance, and data ownership, is paramount. Research efforts should aim to develop frameworks that ensure ethical considerations are deeply integrated into the design and deployment of digital solutions.

*Cross-Cultural Comparisons:* Comparative studies across diverse cultural contexts can reveal how different communities adapt digital tools for resilience and engagement. Such research could uncover culturally specific factors influencing digital uptake, fostering the development of globally relevant yet locally applicable strategies.

*Longitudinal Studies on Resilience:* Conducting longitudinal studies that track community resilience over time, particularly post-crisis, can provide invaluable insights into the effectiveness of digital initiatives. Understanding fluctuations in youth and adult engagement can inform future program designs that foster sustainable community involvement.

*Participatory Action Research:* Engaging community members in research as co-researchers can ensure that studies consider their lived experiences and perspectives. Participatory approaches to understanding resilience can reveal insights that are often overlooked by traditional research methodologies and foster a sense of ownership among residents regarding the solutions being developed.

## REFERENCES


Alenezi, M., Wardat, S., & Akour, M. (2023). The Need of Integrating Digital Education in Higher Education: Challenges and Opportunities. *Sustainability (Basel), 15*(6), 4782. DOI: 10.3390/su15064782

Alexander, S. (2001). E-learning developments and experiences. *Education + Training, 43*(4/5), 240–248. DOI: 10.1108/00400910110399247

Altbach, P. G. (1991). Patterns in higher education development. *Prospects, 21*(2), 189–203. DOI: 10.1007/BF02336060

Azionya, C. M., & Nhedzi, A. (2021). The digital divide and higher education challenge with emergency online learning: Analysis of tweets in the wake of the COVID-19 lockdown. *Turkish Online Journal of Distance Education, 22*(4), 164–182. DOI: 10.17718/tojde.1002822

Benade, L. (2019). Flexible Learning Spaces: Inclusive by Design? *New Zealand Journal of Educational Studies, 54*(1), 53–68. DOI: 10.1007/s40841-019-00127-2

Bennett, D., Knight, & Rowley, J. (2020). The role of hybrid learning spaces in enhancing higher education students' employability. *British Journal of Educational Technology*, 51(4), 1188–1202. Portico. DOI: 10.1111/bjet.12931

Berkel, K., & Homburg, E. (Eds.). (2023). *The Laboratory Revolution and the Creation of the Modern University* (pp. 1830–1940). Amsterdam University Press.

Bhati, A., & Song, I. (2019). New Methods for Collaborative Experiential Learning to Provide Personalised Formative Assessment. [IJET]. *International Journal of Emerging Technologies in Learning, 14*(07), 179. DOI: 10.3991/ijet.v14i07.9173

Bogart, D. (2022). Infrastructure and institutions: Lessons from history. *Regional Sci ence and Urban Economics, 94*, 103626. DOI: 10.1016/j.regsciurbeco.2020.103626

Bond, M., Marín, V. I., Dolch, C., Bedenlier, S., & Zawacki-Richter, O. (2018). Digital transformation in German higher education: Student and teacher perceptions and usage of digital media. *International Journal of Educational Technology in Higher Education, 15*(1), 48. Advance online publication. DOI: 10.1186/s41239-018-0130-1

Bondoc, C. E., & Malawit, T. G. (2020). Cybersecurity for higher education institutions: adopting regulatory framework. *Global Journal of Engineering and Technology Advances,* 2(3), 016–021. DOI: 10.30574/gjeta.2020.2.3.0013

Burbules, N. C., & Callister, T. A.Jr. (2000). Universities in Transition: The Promise and the Challenge of New Technologies. *Teachers College Record, 102*(2), 271–293. DOI: 10.1111/0161-4681.00056

Clothey, R. (2011). Opportunities and Obstacles: Technology's Potential for Expanding Access to Higher Education. *Excellence in Higher Education, 2*(1), 51–58. DOI: 10.5195/ehe.2011.29

Dillahunt, T., Wang, Z., & Teasley, S. D. (2014). Democratizing higher education: Exploring MOOC use among those who cannot afford a formal education. *International Review of Research in Open and Distance Learning, 15*(5). Advance online publication. DOI: 10.19173/irrodl.v15i5.1841

Franz, Y., & Gruber, E. (2022). The Changing Role of Student Housing as Social Infrastructure. *Urban Planning, 7*(4). Advance online publication. DOI: 10.17645/up.v7i4.5661

Funamori, M. (2016). *The Impact of the Digital Age on Higher Education: Beyond Transformation from the Physical Space to the Digital Sphere.* 2016 5th IIAI International Congress on Advanced Applied Informatics (IIAI-AAI). DOI: 10.1109/IIAI-AAI.2016.58

Gafurov, I. R., Safiullin, M. R., Akhmetshin, E. M., Gapsalamov, A. R., & Vasilev, V. L. (2020). Change of the Higher Education Paradigm in the Context of Digital Transformation: From Resource Management to Access Control. *International Journal of Higher Education, 9*(3), 71. DOI: 10.5430/ijhe.v9n3p71

Gevorgyan, O. I., Minaev, N. N., & Zharova, E. A. (2020). *University cities' evolution in context of human capital accumulation.* SHS Web of Conferences, 80, 01008. DOI: 10.1051/shsconf/20208001008

Ghosh, O. (2023). Environmental hazards and disasters - A response towards mitigating disaster management. *AIP Conference Proceedings, 2763*(1), 050008. DOI: 10.1063/5.0158892

Haggans, M. (2016). The 21st-century campus. *Planning for Higher Education, 44*(3), 1–8.

Hernandez-de-Menendez, M., Escobar Díaz, C., & Morales-Menendez, R. (2019). Technologies for the future of learning: State of the art. [IJIDeM]. *International Journal on Interactive Design and Manufacturing, 14*(2), 683–695. DOI: 10.1007/s12008-019-00640-0

Holland, J., & Holland, J. (2014). Implications of Shifting Technology in Education. *TechTrends, 58*(3), 16–25. DOI: 10.1007/s11528-014-0748-3

Isa, A., & Yusoff, Z. (2015). State of physical facilities of higher education institutions in Nigeria. *International Journal of Scientific and Research Publications*, *5*(4), 1–5.

Jaakkola, E. (2020). Designing conceptual articles: Four approaches. *AMS Review*, *10*(1–2), 18–26. DOI: 10.1007/s13162-020-00161-0

Joan, R. (2013). Flexible Learning As New Learning Design In Classroom Process To Promote Quality Education. *I-Manager's Journal on School Educational Technology*, *9*(1), 37–42. DOI: 10.26634/jsch.9.1.2401

Johnson, L., Becker, S. A., & Cummins, M.. (2016). *NMC horizon report: 2016 higher education edition*. The New Media Consortium.

Kaziev, K. V., Sherstobitova, A. A., & Kazieva, B. V. (2020). University IT infrastructure in the context of evolutionary transformations of the digital economy. *Personality Society*, *1*(1), 12–19. DOI: 10.46502/issn.2712-8024/2020.1.2

Kerres, M. (2004). Beyond Learning Platforms: Infrastructures for the Digital Campus. In: *Proceedings of 6th International Conference on New Educational Environments (ICNEE04)*.

Kholiavko, N., Popelo, O., & Tulchynska, S. (2021). Priority directions of increasing the adaptivity of universities to the conditions of the digital economy. *Revista Tempos e Espaços Em Educação*, *14*(33), e16383. DOI: 10.20952/revtee.v14i33.16383

Kim, Y., Soyata, T., & Behnagh, R. F. (2018). Towards Emotionally Aware AI Smart Classroom: Current Issues and Directions for Engineering and Education. *IEEE Access : Practical Innovations, Open Solutions*, *6*, 5308–5331. DOI: 10.1109/ACCESS.2018.2791861

Kostina, S. N. (2021). Is the infrastructure of regional universities ready to meet the challenges of digital transformation? *University Management: Practice and Analysis*, *25*(3), 14–32. DOI: 10.15826/umpa.2021.03.024

Kovaleva, N. N., Eresko, P. V., Izotova, V. F., & Gafarov, Y. R. (2022). *Optimizing The Implementation Of University Digitalization Practices*. European Proceedings of Social and Behavioural Sciences., DOI: 10.15405/epsbs.2022.01.57

Laufer, M., Leiser, A., Deacon, B., Perrin de Brichambaut, P., Fecher, B., Kobsda, C., & Hesse, F. (2021). Digital higher education: A divider or bridge builder? Leadership perspectives on edtech in a COVID-19 reality. *International Journal of Educational Technology in Higher Education*, *18*(1), 51. Advance online publication. DOI: 10.1186/s41239-021-00287-6 PMID: 34778538

Lee, M. M., Lin, M. F. G., & Bonk, C. J. (2007). OOPS, Turning MIT Opencourseware into Chinese: An analysis of a community of practice of global translators. *International Review of Research in Open and Distance Learning*, *8*(3). Advance online publication. DOI: 10.19173/irrodl.v8i3.463

Lei, Z., Zhou, H., Hu, W., Deng, Q., Zhou, D., Liu, Z.-W., & Gao, X. (2020). 3-D Interactive Control Laboratory for Classroom Demonstration and Online Experimentation in Engineering Education. *IEEE Transactions on Education*, *64*(3), 276–282. DOI: 10.1109/TE.2020.3041070

Lewinski, P. (2015). Effects of classroomsâ€™ architecture on academic performance in view of telic versus paratelic motivation: A review. *Frontiers in Psychology*, *6*. Advance online publication. DOI: 10.3389/fpsyg.2015.00746 PMID: 26089812

Luchkov, A., Korolev, A., & Kodabashyan, L. (2022). *The Architecture of Digital Enterprise in the University Infrastructure.* In: 2022 15th International Conference Management of large-scale system development (MLSD). IEEE. pp. 1-5. DOI: 10.1109/MLSD55143.2022.9934605

MacInnis, D. J. (2011). A Framework for Conceptual Contributions in Marketing. *Journal of Marketing*, *75*(4), 136–154. DOI: 10.1509/jmkg.75.4.136

Mahajan, R., Gupta, P., & Singh, T. (2019). Massive Open Online Courses: Concept and Implications. *Indian Pediatrics*, *56*(6), 489–495. DOI: 10.1007/s13312-019-1575-6 PMID: 31278230

Malik, K., & Thakur, R. R. (2010). Creating value through IT – emerging patterns in brick-and-mortar b-schools. *International Journal of Innovation in Education*, *1*(2), 148. DOI: 10.1504/IJIIE.2010.036857

Margulies, A. H. (2004). A New Model for Open Sharing: Massachusetts Institute of Technology's OpenCourseWare Initiative Makes a Difference. *PLoS Biology*, *2*(8), e200. DOI: 10.1371/journal.pbio.0020200 PMID: 15314645

Mehmood, R., Katib, S. S. I., & Chlamtac, I. (2020). *Smart infrastructure and applications*. Springer International Publishing. DOI: 10.1007/978-3-030-13705-2

Mosteanu, N. R. (2020). Digital university campus–change the education system approach to meet the 21st century needs. *European Journal of Human Resource Management Studies*, *4*(4), 79–93. DOI: 10.46827/ejhrms.v4i4.959

Muñoz, J. L. R., Ojeda, F. M., & Jurado, D. L. A.. (2022). Systematic review of adaptive learning technology for learning in higher education. *Eurasian Journal of Educational Research*, *98*(98), 221–233.

Musa, M. F., & Ahmad, Z. (2012). Higher Education Physical Assets and Facilities. *Procedia: Social and Behavioral Sciences*, *50*, 472–478. DOI: 10.1016/j.sbspro.2012.08.051

Nelson, H. G., & Stolterman, E. (2014). *The design way: Intentional change in an unpredictable world*. MIT press.

Németh, B., Issa, O., Diba, F., & Tuckett, A. (2020). Learning cities and learning communities: Analyzing contextual factors and their impacts on adult and lifelong learning in urban settings. *Andragoske Studije*, *2*(2), 17–52. DOI: 10.5937/AndStud2001017N

Nguyen, D. (2018). The University in a World of Digital Technologies: Tensions and Challenges. *Australasian Marketing Journal*, *26*(2), 79–82. DOI: 10.1016/j.ausmj.2018.05.012

Oftedal, L. A. (2020). *National digital infrastructure for higher education*.

Padmanabhan, S. (2024). Digital Transformation in Higher Education. *Advances in Educational Technologies and Instructional Design*, •••, 59–69. DOI: 10.4018/979-8-3693-0433-4.ch005

Pfeffer, T. (2011). *Virtualisation of universities: Digital media and the organisation of higher education institutions*. Springer Science & Business Media.

Popova, O. I., Gagarina, N. M., & Karkh, D. A. (2020). *Digitalization of Educational Processes in Universities: Achievements and Problems*. Proceedings of the International Scientific Conference "Digitalization of Education: History, Trends and Prospects" (DETP 2020). DOI: 10.2991/assehr.k.200509.131

Radhamani, R., Sasidharakurup, H., & Kumar, D.. (2015). Role of Biotechnology simulation and remotely triggered virtual labs in complementing university education. *2015 International Conference on Interactive Mobile Communication Technologies and Learning (IMCL)*. DOI: 10.1109/IMCTL.2015.7359548

Robertson, A., Cleaver, E., & Smart, F. (2019). *Beyond the metrics: Identifying, evidencing and enhancing the less tangible assets of higher education*. QAA Scotland.

Rodríguez-Abitia, G., & Bribiesca-Correa, G. (2021). Assessing Digital Transformation in Universities. *Future Internet*, *13*(2), 52. DOI: 10.3390/fi13020052

Rubin, V. (1998). The Roles of Universities in Comnunity-Building Initiatives. *Journal of Planning Education and Research*, *17*(4), 302–311. DOI: 10.1177/0739456X9801700405

Sage, R. (2023). *Tackling Tradition in Education*. Qeios., DOI: 10.32388/CDVBT5

Sargent, M. (2015). Wall to wall. *Nursery World,* 2015(Sup10), 16–18. DOI: 10.12968/nuwa.2015.Sup10.16

Schmidt, J. T., & Tang, M. (2020). Digitalization in Education: Challenges, Trends and Transformative Potential. *Führen Und Managen in Der Digitalen Transformation,* 287–312. DOI: 10.1007/978-3-658-28670-5_16

Scholl, K. G., & Gulwadi, G. B. (2015). Recognising campus landscapes as learning spaces. *Journal of Learning Spaces*, *4*(1), 53–60.

Schwaen, R., Sarpaneva, P., & Alenjery, N.. (2018). Bricks and books: Reinventing the teaching of architectural history and theory. In: *National Conference on the Beginning Design Student.*

Sferrazza, A. (2018). The Nature of the Space: Walls to Bridges as Transformative Learning. *Engaged Scholar Journal: Community-Engaged Research, Teaching, and Learning*, *4*(1), 241–250. DOI: 10.15402/esj.v4i1.321

Shah, V. M., & Shah, D. (2023). Impact of digitalisation in education-a literature review analysis. *Towards Excellence,* 15(2), 333–343. Internet Archive. DOI: 10.37867/TE150234

Sharma, R. S. (2015). Role of universities in development of civil society and social transformation. In: *Proceedings of International Academic Conferences*. International Institute of Social and Economic Sciences.

Shill, H. B., & Tonner, S. (2003). Creating a Better Place: Physical Improvements in Academic Libraries, 1995–2002. *College & Research Libraries*, *64*(6), 431–466. DOI: 10.5860/crl.64.6.431

Singh, J., Steele, K., & Singh, L. (2021). Combining the Best of Online and Face-to-Face Learning: Hybrid and Blended Learning Approach for COVID-19, Post Vaccine, & Post-Pandemic World. *Journal of Educational Technology Systems*, *50*(2), 140–171. DOI: 10.1177/00472395211047865

Smart, F., Cleaver, E., & Robertson, A. (2020). Beyond the metrics: The importance of intangible assets in the HE context. *Journal of Perspectives in Applied Academic Practice*, *8*(2), 3–6. DOI: 10.14297/jpaap.v8i2.432

Smith, N. (2016). Book Interview: Making sense of bricks and mortar. *Engineering & Technology*, *11*(5), 84–85. DOI: 10.1049/et.2016.0528

Song, M., Berends, H., Van Der Bij, H., & Weggeman, M. (2006). The Effect of IT and Co-location on Knowledge Dissemination. *Journal of Product Innovation Management,* 24(1), 52–68. Portico. DOI: 10.1111/j.1540-5885.2006.00232.x

Valtonen, T., Leppänen, U., Hyypiä, M., Kokko, A., Manninen, J., Vartiainen, H., Sointu, E., & Hirsto, L. (2020). Learning environments preferred by university students: A shift toward informal and flexible learning environments. *Learning Environments Research, 24*(3), 371–388. DOI: 10.1007/s10984-020-09339-6

van der Walt, I. D. (2023). *Navigating the digital groove: Crafting a user-centric odyssey for libraries.*

Vargo, S. L., & Lusch, R. F. (2004). Evolving to a New Dominant Logic for Marketing. *Journal of Marketing, 68*(1), 1–17. DOI: 10.1509/jmkg.68.1.1.24036

Veiga Ávila, L., Beuron, T. A., Brandli, L. L., Damke, L. I., Pereira, R. S., & Klein, L. L. (2019). Barriers to innovation and sustainability in universities: An international comparison. *International Journal of Sustainability in Higher Education, 20*(5), 805–821. DOI: 10.1108/IJSHE-02-2019-0067

Videka, L., Blackburn, J. A., & Moran, J. R. (2008). Building Research Infrastructure in Schools of Social Work: A University Perspective. *Social Work Research, 32*(4), 294–301. DOI: 10.1093/swr/32.4.294

von Hauff, M., & Nguyen, T. (2014). Universities as Potential Actors for Sustainable Development. *Sustainability (Basel), 6*(5), 3043–3063. DOI: 10.3390/su6053043

Wahid, A. R., Yatmo, Y. A., & Paramita, K. D. (2020). More than Just a Material Perfection: Preserved Human-Environment Relationship in Traditional Brick-Making Scenarios. *Journal of Physics: Conference Series, 1655*(1), 012125. DOI: 10.1088/1742-6596/1655/1/012125

Wilkins, S., Hazzam, J., & Ireland, J. J. (2022). Servicescape in transnational higher education: The effects of campus design, physical environment and facilities on student experience and satisfaction. *Journal of Marketing for Higher Education,* •••, 1–20. DOI: 10.1080/08841241.2022.2139792

Winter, A., Wiseman, J., & Muirhead, B. (2006). university-community engagement in Australia. *Education, Citizenship and Social Justice, 1*(3), 211–230. DOI: 10.1177/1746197906064675

Won, A. S. (2015). The virtual human interaction labStanford, California. XRDS: Crossroads. *The ACM Magazine for Students, 22*(1), 64–65. DOI: 10.1145/2830324

Zender, R., & Tavangarian, D. (2009). Service-Oriented University: Infrastructure for the University of Tomorrow. *Communications in Computer and Information Science, 53*, 73–84. DOI: 10.1007/978-3-642-10263-9_7

# Chapter 9
# Resilient Career Transitions in Architecture:
## Pull and Push Factors Leading to a Multiple-Career Pathway

**Sze-ee Lee**
https://orcid.org/0000-0001-6023-3787
*School of Architecture, Building and Design, Taylor's University, Malaysia*

**Keith Kay Hin Tan**
https://orcid.org/0000-0002-4757-0639
*School of Architecture, Building and Design, Taylor's University, Malaysia*

## ABSTRACT

*The long, linear, upward, and single-directional traditional career path in the architectural profession is a rigid and inflexible career model, which is unable to keep pace with the evolving nature of work in the 21st century. This is an interdisciplinary study connecting architecture and career studies to reveal the evolving career path in architecture and identify the push and pull factors leading to a multiple-career pathway in the profession. The participants were a purposive sampling of 20 millennial architects, who had transitioned from a single career to having multiple careers, including architecture, during the interview. The study revealed that the rigidness of the traditional career pathway itself is a push factor that indirectly causes the millennial architects to move towards a career pathway that is more flexible and controllable. The study suggests that an on-going evolution towards embracing alternative career pathways is already underway, and fostering this trend will be very important to improve the quality of life of the next generation of city dwellers.*

DOI: 10.4018/979-8-3373-0390-1.ch009

## INTRODUCTION AND BACKGROUND

Fostering resilience and quality of life through sustainable urban evolution requires a focus on both the tangible and intangible aspects of urban life. Architecture is one of the most important professions influencing the future of cities, making a study about how young architects are navigating the future of their profession both important and timely. Whereas most career paths in the construction industry traditionally focused on a single discipline, the increasing trend towards flexible working lifestyles post COVID-19 has made multiple career pathways increasingly attractive for young people (Spurk & Straub, 2020). This, however, contradicts many existing company or organization policies regarding work and human resources, which have yet to fully evolve to reflect the needs of the millennial generation.

This paper addresses this problem by focusing on the emerging pull and push factors affecting the millennial generation of architects. It suggests strategies that will allow the profession to retain its human resources even as young architects seek to balance their careers with income-generating work both within the construction industry and outside it. Whereas considerable research has been devoted to the decision to study architecture and motivations at work in the profession, very little attention has been paid specifically to career goals in architecture, and what motivates people to *remain* in the profession. This paper addresses this critical gap.

### Low Retention in the Architectural Profession

Whereas the retention rate for graduate architects within the profession worldwide is generally low ("Architecture's Afterlife : Early Findings," n.d.), statistics from countries broadly following the British / RIBA system of architectural education highlight several examples worthy of further analysis. For example, Malaysia has the second-highest number of architecture schools per million population among Commonwealth countries (Figure 1). There are 0.76 architecture schools per million head of population in Malaysia, higher than the more mature economies of the 'Old Commonwealth' represented by the UK (0.7), Canada (0.33), New Zealand (0.63) and Australia (0.74).

*Figure 1. Number of architects/k population compared with the number of architecture schools/M population (Planning for Rapid Urbanisation Survey of the Architectural Profession in the Commonwealth, 2018).*

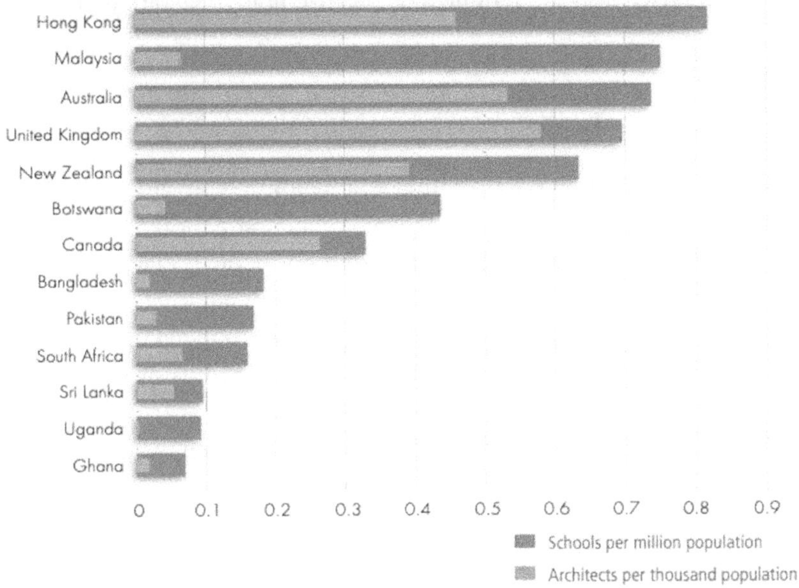


Malaysia is in fact the country with the widest gap between the number of architects per thousand population (orange) and the number of architectural schools per million (blue), representing a phenomena worthy of study. The data shows that Malaysia has a reasonable number of schools to produce a sufficient number of graduates. However, the number of working architects in the country remains low. This implies that most architecture graduates do not pursue the traditional career path to become a registered architect. This paper examines the push and pull factors leading to this career transition, and how it results in a multiple-career pathway which will have significant effects on the future of the profession.

## LITERATURE REVIEW

### Motivations to Remain in the Architectural Profession

There is a dearth of studies relating specifically to the reasons causing architects 'to remain in the architectural profession', or an architectural-related career path. Most empirical studies focus on architects' job satisfaction (Islam, 2016; Oluwatayo,

2014; Sang et al., 2008; Sang, Ison, & Dainty, 2009), motivational factors (Damci, Arditi, Polat, & Turkoglu, 2020; Oyedele, 2010) or demotivation factors (Oyedele, 2013), which are in general associated with the working environment. Aspects such as remuneration, creativity, meaningfulness, and self-employment are highlighted in existing studies.

## Remuneration

Existing studies suggest that remuneration is a major demotivator in architecture (Islam, 2016; Oluwatayo, 2014; Sang, Ison, Dainty, et al., 2009). It implies the disillusionment created by false expectations of high-incomes (Tijerino, 2009). However, Caven (2009) reported that monetary factors were not a determining factor in motivation for UK architects. Instead, existing studies implied that architects are attracted to non-monetary rewards, such as extrinsic rewards of professional recognition or accolades (Smitheran, 2017) and intrinsic rewards of individual professional identity, creativity, and pleasant relationships within the project team and other stakeholders (Caven & Diop, 2012; Damci et al., 2020).

## Creativity

Design abilities and the opportunity to perform creative tasks are crucial to architects (Islam, 2016; Sang, Ison, & Dainty, 2009), and are among the key drivers for entering the profession (Sang et al., 2008). Despite creativity in architects' works providing intrinsic rewards (Caven & Diop, 2012; Navarro-Astor & Caven, 2012), the tension between creativity and business in architecture is evident (Galloway & Haniff, 2015). Conversely, when aesthetic decisions are not in architects' hands leading to design compromises, it leads to demotivation (Navarro-Astor & Caven, 2012). Regrettably, the changing landscape in construction and the loss of prestige and status associated with the architectural profession have also been reflected in the loss of autonomy in design (Musiitwa, 2019; Navarro-Astor & Caven, 2012). Besides that, excessive workload on administrative tasks were also found to affect architects' creativity and design performance, and is a further demotivation factor (Oyedele, 2013).

## Meaningfulness

Given that a career is more than making income for living, personal attachment and meanings of work to individuals are equally important (Gilmore & Smith, 2014; Savickas, 2006). In general, intrinsic rewards are crucial to architects (Caven & Diop, 2012), particularly women in the male-dominated construction industry.

Indeed, a professional career is "*seen to be a labour of love and not simply labour for a wage*", and many professionals *"refer to their daily activities as a calling or vocation: not so much a job as a way of life"* (Susskind & Susskind, 2015, p. 10). In this case, when architects are found to lack the opportunity to perform 'what they love' or what they think is meaningful, it leads to job dissatisfaction (Sang, Ison, & Dainty, 2009), motivation to leave employment (De Graft-Johnson, Manley, & Greed, 2005), career transition to self-employment (Sang et al., 2008), and career switching (Zhao et al., 2018), despite high investments in architectural education.

## The Millennial Architect's Work Value

### Flexible Working Arrangement

Empirical studies in the architectural profession have mainly focused on women and students rather than millennial architects. However, the voices of some millennial architects were heard through a RIBA study in 2011. There, they expressed their preference for having looser work relationships, spending part of their time in formal employment, and partly on their own private projects (Jamieson, 2011). This millennial cohort perceived the term 'architect' as restrictive and preferred to self-identify as 'creative consultants', hoping to engage in multi-disciplinary professional networks instead of continuing the traditional models of practice (Jamieson, 2011). It suggested that the values traditionally held high by architects, which include creativity, recognition, variety, independence, and responsibility (Waldrep, 2017) might not be similarly valued by millennials.

### More Than One Role

Furthermore, Deutsch (2019) highlighted his observation that Generation Z, the cohort succeeding millennials, are not interested in titles and are less likely to become licenced architects, to not limit themselves to only one role (Jones & Hyde, 2019). Additionally, *"the role of an architect is no longer set in stone – it is subject to constant change."* (Bos-de Vos et al., 2018, p. 127). Bos-de Vos *et al.* published an academic design guide with several case studies on the different roles of architects within the construction process to inspire and encourage architects in the 21st century to design their own roles and shape their own future. Their observations indicate that contemporary architects are looking towards more than one role, where a multiple-career pathway could be an alternative to match their preferred working lifestyle.

## Career Trends in the Architectural Profession

### The Impact of the Gig Economy

The emergence of the gig economy is causing turbulence in the traditional economy. The career trend has changed from a more stagnant and stable nature to a more flexible and temporary setting, which is still evolving. There are positive and negative impacts from this unavoidable shifting of the employment landscape (Healy, Nicholson, & Pekarek, 2017; A. J. Wood, Graham, Lehdonvirta, & Hjorth, 2019). Companies are offering different types of employment such as contract-based, project-based, and part-time work (Spurk & Straub, 2020). This fits some architectural consultancy practices well, especially where the project is small-scale with a short time frame. Part-time work is also common in academia, via the employment of practising architects as tutors.

In addition, online employment has also become prevalent in recent years, especially during and after the COVID-19 pandemic. With the advancement in digital technologies and widespread internet connectivity, working remotely is the norm for many industries, including architecture (Alacovska, Fieseler, & Wong, 2021; Fekry Youssef, Fathy Eid, & Mohamed Khodeir, 2023). The nature of practising architecture has been changing and becoming more flexible, efficient, and task-oriented, allowing many tech-savvy young architects to seek new opportunities outside of architecture.

### The Problem of a Non-Progressive Career Model

Until recently, career trends in the architectural profession have been relatively constant with the professional career model of Part I, II, and III supporting the traditional architectural consultancy practice. In both academia and practice, career guidance in architecture has therefore focused on the official guidance to become a registered or licenced architect. Entrepreneurial ideas have not been much incorporated into architectural education (Gafar, Kasim, & Martin, 2012, 2017; Hennekam & Bennett, 2017) or the profession at large (Bondare, Volkova, Bondars, & Barvika, 2018). Even though there are alternative career opportunities with architectural knowledge and skillsets (Topchiy & Fatkullina, 2019), architecture graduates are not academically trained to take these alternative careers. Moreover, scholars proclaim that academia only prepares architecture students to design buildings (Drake, Williams, & Kingsland, 2003) but not to do business or run a practice (Dixon, Kephart, & Moody, Karl, 2018). Indeed, (Hill, 2012, p. 8) went so far as to describe the architecture profession as being at a *cul-de-sac* situation by condemning the traditional business model in architecture is a 'mess'.

## The Need for Empirical Studies in the Architectural Profession

Broadly speaking, there is surprisingly little research on the architectural profession written by architects themselves (Cohen et al., 2005). Most literature on the profession has been written by scholars from other backgrounds, including psychology (Gutman, 2010), business (Ahuja, Nikolova, & Clegg, 2017; Caven, 2009; Cohen et al., 2005; Folch, Pereira, & Icart, 2019), and organisational management (Sang et al., 2008; Sturges, 2013), while the focus is mainly on gender issues (Infante-Perea, Román-Onsalo, & Navarro-Astor, 2018; Sang, Dainty, & Ison, 2007, 2014), women architects (Caven, 2004, 2006, 2008; Manley & Graft-johnson, 2008), professional identity (Ahuja et al., 2017; Ahuja, Nikolova, & Clegg, 2019), and job satisfaction (Sang et al., 2008; Sang, Ison, & Dainty, 2009).

Furthermore, several empirical studies on the architectural profession focus on graduates (Rabang-Alonzo, 2013; Salleh et al., 2016; Shannon, 2012; Shannon et al., 2014), and their employability (Khodeir & Nessim, 2020; Maina, 2018; Maina & Daful, 2017; Salleh, Md Yusoff, Harun, & Memon, 2015). Despite a handful of studies on job satisfaction, motivations and retentions of architects (Adeokun & Opoko, 2015; Oyedele, 2010), the attention is still job rather than career related. Additionally, specific studies on millennial architects have been largely neglected.

Quality of life, however, is increasingly tied to career resilience, even if it involves multiple changes of jobs and even professions. For this to happen sustainably requires the input of not only external researchers, but voices from within the professions themselves. In response, this study is written by architects about their own profession. It will therefore add important empirical knowledge where the literature on the profession is relatively scarce (Cohen et al., 2005), and where significant research gaps have been identified by scholars (Sullivan & Al Ariss, 2021).

# METHOD

## Procedure and Data Collection

Data collection started with individual interviews with millennial architects pursuing a multiple-career pathway. The sample included participants born as early as 1978, but no later than 2000, fitting the broadest definition of millennials among the various sources[1] (Reeves & Oh, 2008). In addition, participants were selected based on the following pre-determined criteria:

1) A millennial architect based in Malaysia

2) Completed a minimum of three years undergraduate (Part I), and two years postgraduate (Part II) studies from local or foreign universities.
3) Pursuing multiple careers, with more than one career at the interview date. One of the careers shall be architectural-related.
4) Previous experience in the traditional career path of having a single career, with at least two years of practical experience under one employment in a traditional architectural consultancy practice upon completing tertiary education.

At the initial data collection stage, purposive sampling and convenience sampling were used as target participants were selected through the authors' existing contacts. Further interviews used the non-probability snowball sampling technique through participants' connections. Basic demographic data such as gender, age, ethnicity, educational background, local/overseas graduates, and marital / parenthood status were considered to achieve sample diversity. Results across different participants were studied and compared to understand more considerable demographic differences and how these differences relate to the broader socioeconomic context. The final number of participants was determined once data saturation occurred, and ultimately a total of 20 participants were recruited.

## Participants

The 20 interviews were conducted between May and September 2022. The research participants include eight women and twelve men, aged from 29 to 44, all millennial architects based in Malaysia born between 1978-1993. Eight of the twenty participants had completed their Part III professional registrations, including two participants registered in the UK and Australia. Seven participants were married. Other basic demographic data includes their age in the year 2022, year of birth, gender, marital status, education background and registration status (Table 1).

*Table 1. Basic demographic data of research participants (by author, 2022)*

| Participant | | Age (2022) | Year of birth | Gender | Marital status | Educational background | | Part III Registration status | Socio-economic background |
|---|---|---|---|---|---|---|---|---|---|
| | | | | | | Part I | Part II | | |
| 1 | AL | 30 | 1992 | Female | Single | Local | Local | No | M40 |
| 2 | PW | 34 | 1988 | Female | Married | Local | Local | Yes | M40 |
| 3 | SO | 42 | 1980 | Female | Married | Overseas | Overseas | Yes (UK) | T20 |
| 4 | KC | 34 | 1988 | Male | Single | Local | Overseas | Yes | T20 |

continued on following page

*Table 1. Continued*

| Participant | | Age (2022) | Year of birth | Gender | Marital status | Educational background | | Part III Registration status | Socio-economic background |
|---|---|---|---|---|---|---|---|---|---|
| | | | | | | Part I | Part II | | |
| 5 | KM | 34 | 1988 | Male | Single | Local | Local | No | M40 |
| 6 | TC | 29 | 1993 | Female | Single | Local | Overseas | No | M40 |
| 7 | DM | 42 | 1980 | Male | Married | Local | Local | Yes | M40 |
| 8 | RT | 31 | 1991 | Male | Single | Local | Local | Yes | M40 |
| 9 | WF | 44 | 1978 | Male | Married | Local | Local | No | M40 |
| 10 | JO | 34 | 1988 | Male | Single | Local | Overseas | No | T20 |
| 11 | SM | 35 | 1987 | Male | Married | Local | Local | Yes | M40 |
| 12 | RY | 42 | 1980 | Female | Single | Local | Local | No | M40 |
| 13 | NH | 36 | 1986 | Female | Married | Local | Local | No | M40 |
| 14 | SS | 33 | 1989 | Female | Single | Local | Overseas | No | T20 |
| 15 | SF | 41 | 1981 | Male | Married | Local | Overseas | Yes (Aus.) | T20 |
| 16 | SZ | 31 | 1991 | Male | Single | Local | Local | Yes | M40 |
| 17 | SY | 36 | 1986 | Male | Single | Local | Local | No (Taking) | M40 |
| 18 | FG | 31 | 1991 | Male | Single | Local | Overseas | No (Preparing) | T20 |
| 19 | SC | 38 | 1984 | Male | Single | Overseas | Overseas | No | T20 |
| 20 | DH | 34 | 1988 | Female | Single | Overseas | Overseas | No (Preparing) | T20 |
| | | 29 to 44<br>Average: 35.35 | | Male: 12 (60%)<br>Female: 8 (40%) | Single: 13 (65%)<br>Married: 7 (35%) | Full local: 11 (55%)<br>Mixed: 6 (30%)<br>Full overseas: 3 (15%) | | Yes: 8 (40%)<br>No: 12 (60%) | M40: 12 (60%)<br>T20: 8 (40%) |

In relation to socio-economic backgrounds, most participants came from M40[2] middle-class families. Notably, 40% belonged to the T20 household income group. These figures serve as a reference point to comprehend the socio-economic context of the participants and how socio-economic factors influenced their career decisions and trajectories.

The participants' educational background, overseas experience, as well as their social-economic and family background, were then analysed in relation to their career transitions to understand how these backgrounds influenced their work values, mindsets, and behaviours when making career decision.

## Career Trajectory

According to Donald Super's Career development theory[3], the age of 25 - 44 is the main career establishment stage. Hence, the career trajectory of each participant has also been illustrated according to age (Table 2), from the youngest research participant, TC, aged 29, to the oldest research participant, WF, aged 44. The table reveals that career transitions to pursue a multiple-career pathway occur at different ages, ranging from the early 20s to late 30s.

*Table 2. Career trajectory of research participants (by author, 2023)*

| Participant/ Age (2022) / Gender | Part I | Part II | Career trajectory (by age): Approx. 24 to 29 | 29 to 34 | 34 to 39 | 39 to 44 |
|---|---|---|---|---|---|---|
| TC | Public | Overseas | Architectural designer | | | |
| 29 F | | | *Restaurant helper (Family business)* | | | |
| AL | Private | Private | GA Design executive (Property dev.) | | | |
| 30 F | | | *Online Merchant* | | | |
| RT | Private | Public | GA (Overseas & Local) Part III | Principal architect (ACP) | | |
| 31 M | | | | *Founder (Training centre)* | | |
| | | | | *Part-time lecturer* | | |
| SZ | Public | Public | GA Part III | Founder (Design studio) | | |
| 31 M | *Pub singer* | | *Founder (Event performance)* | | | |
| FG | Private | Overseas | GA | Preparing Part III | | |
| 31 M | | | *Insurance agent* | | | |
| SS | Public | Overseas | GA | Design strategist | | |
| 33 F | | | *Artist* | | | |
| DH | Overseas | Overseas | GA | Preparing Part III | | |
| 34 F | | | | *Yoga instructor* | | |
| JO | Private | Overseas | GA (Overseas) Co-founder (Design studio) | | | |
| 34 M | | | *Artist* | | | |
| | | | | *Part-time lecturer* | | |
| KC | Private | Overseas | GA Part III | Principal architect (ACP) | | |
| 34 M | | | | *Feng Shui master* | | |
| PW | Private | Private | GA | Part III Principal architect (ACP) | | |
| 34 F | | | | *Founder (Baking studio)* | | |
| KM | Public | Public | GA (Overseas. & Local) | Design manager (Property dev.) | | |
| 34 M | | *Co-founder (Design & build)* | | *Co-founder (Hospitality & F&B)* | | |
| SM | Public | Public | GA Part III | Project manager (Property dev.) | | |
| 35 M | | | *Online shipping agent* | *Crypto gamer* | | |
| NH | Public | Public | GA (Overseas & Local) | Co-founder (Design studio) | | |
| 36 F | | | | *Co-founder (Publisher)* | | |
| | | | | *Part-time lecturer* | | |
| SY | Public | Public | GA | Project Architect | Taking Part III | |
| 36 M | | *Music writer* | | | | |
| SC | Overseas | Overseas | GA (Overseas & Local) Co-founder (Design studio) | | | |
| 38 M | | | | *Co-founder (F&B & Event)* | | |
| SF | Public | Overseas | GA (Overseas) | Part III (Overseas) Co-founder (Multidisciplinary studio) | | |
| 41 M | | | | *Co-founder (F&B)* | | |
| SO | Overseas | Overseas | Part III (Overseas) GA (Overseas) | Arch. designer Co-founder (Design studio) | | |
| 42 F | | | | *Part-time lecturer* | | *Full-time lecturer* |
| | | | | | *Artist* | |
| DM | Public | Public | GA | | Part III Principal architect (ACP) | |
| 42 M | | | | | *Diving instructor* | |
| RY | Public | Public | GA | Part III - unsuccessful Freelance designer | Project architect | |
| 42 F | | | | | | *Fitness instructor* |
| WF | Public | Public | GA | | Co-founder (Design studio) | |
| 44 M | | | *Photographer* | *Co-founder (Photography studio)* | | |

Table 2 also shows that six of the eight research participants who obtained their Part III registration pursued their multiple-career pathways after that milestone. A further three research participants were preparing for or taking their Part III examination during the interview period.

## ANALYSES AND RESULTS

### Turning Point of Career Transitions

Based on the 20 individual interviews, three different exit points of transition from the single career path to a multiple-career pathway were identified. These are shown as Part I, Part II and Part III transition (Figure 2).

*Figure 2. Turning points of career transitions in architecture career pathway (by authors, 2022)*

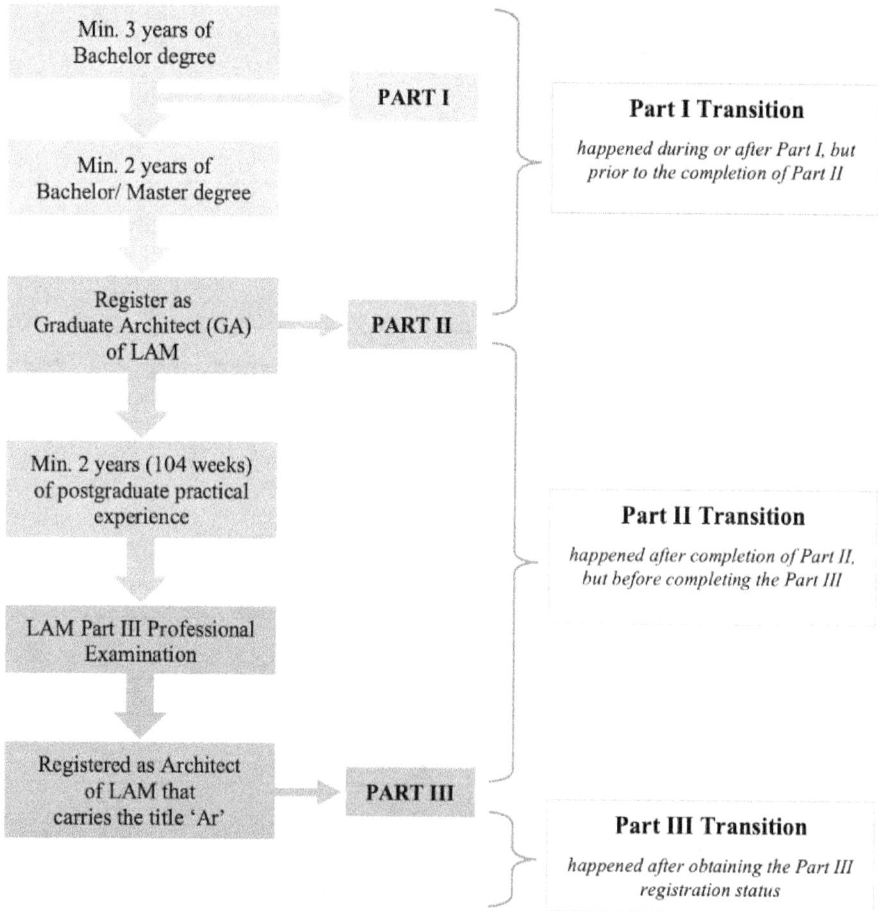

***Part I transition*** is the career turning point that happens during or after Part I, but prior to the completion of Part II. For example, as shown in Table 3 below, SZ started his singing career in a pub or lounge while he was studying for his Part I, while SY started his music writing career part-time when he joined the music club in university. As for KM, he set up a design and build company with three partners during his Part II master's studies at the university. The research participants in *Part I transition* were all male, local graduates from public universities (Table 3).

*Table 3. Part I transitions (by authors, 2023)*

| Participant / Age (2022) / Gender | Part I | Part II | Career trajectory (by age): Approx. 24 to 29 | 29 to 34 | 34 to 39 |
|---|---|---|---|---|---|
| SZ | Public | Public | GA  Part III | Founder (Design studio) | |
| 31 M | | Pub singer | | Founder (Event performance) | |
| KM | Public | Public | GA (Ov. & Local) | Design manager (Property dev.) | |
| 34 M | | Co-founder (Design & build) | | Co-founder (Hospitality & F&B) | |
| SY | Public | Public | GA | Project Architect | Taking Part III |
| 36 M | | Music writer | | | |

***Part II transition*** refers to career transitions happening after the completion of Part II but before completing Part III as shown in Table 4 below.. More than half (55%) of the research participants started to branch out or venture into another career after Part II. Among this group of participants, SM was the only one who also went on to gain a LAM Part III registration. RY gave up trying after failing the exam once. The others have branched out without pursuing the LAM Part III examination.

*Table 4. Part II transitions (by authors, 2023)*

| Participant / Age (2022) / Gender | Part I | Part II | Career trajectory (by age) | | | |
|---|---|---|---|---|---|---|
| | | | Approx. 24 to 29 | 29 to 34 | 34 to 39 | 39 to 44 |
| TC | Public | Overseas | Architectural designer | | | |
| 29 F | | | Restaurant helper (Family business) | | | |
| AL | Private | Private | GA Design executive (Property dev.) | | | |
| 30 F | | | Online Merchant | | | |
| FG | Private | Overseas | GA | Preparing Part III | | |
| 31 M | | | Insurance agent | | | |
| SS | Public | Overseas | GA Design strategist | | | |
| 33 F | | | Artist | | | |
| DH | Overseas | Overseas | GA Project architect | Preparing Part III | | |
| 34 F | | | | Yoga instructor | | |
| JO | Private | Overseas | GA (Overseas) Co-founder (Design studio) | | | |
| 34 M | | | Artist | | | |
| | | | | Part-time lecturer | | |
| SM | Public | Public | GA Part III Project manager (Property dev.) | | | |
| 35 M | | | Online shipping agent | Crypto gamer | | |
| NH | Public | Public | GA (Overseas & Local) | Co-founder (Design studio) | | |
| 36 F | | | | Co-founder (Publisher) | | |
| | | | | Part-time lecturer | | |
| SC | Overseas | Overseas | GA (Overseas & Local) Co-founder (Design studio) | | | |
| 38 M | | | | Co-founder (F&B & Event) | | |
| RY | Public | Public | GA Part III - unsuccessful | Freelance designer | Project architect | |
| 42 F | | | | | Fitness instructor | |
| WF | Public | Public | GA | | Co-founder (Design studio) | |
| 44 M | | | Photographer | | | |

***Part III transition*** occurs when the career transition happens after participants obtain their Part III registration status. Table 5 below shows the overseas graduates, SO and SF have obtained their Part III registration status overseas before returning to Malaysia, while the local graduates, PW, RT, KC, and DM started their own sole-proprietorship practices after they obtained LAM Part III in Malaysia.

*Table 5. Part III transitions (by authors, 2023)*

| Participant Age (2022) / Gender | Part I | Part II | Career trajectory (by age): Approx. 24 to 29 | 29 to 34 | 34 to 39 | 39 to 42 |
|---|---|---|---|---|---|---|
| RT | Private | Public | GA (Ov. & L.) **Part III** | Principal architect (ACP) | | |
| 31 M | | | | Founder (Training centre) | | |
| | | | | Part-time lecturer | | |
| KC | Private | Overseas | GA **Part III** | Principal architect (ACP) | | |
| 34 M | | | | Feng Shui master | | |
| PW | Private | Private | GA | **Part III** Principal architect (ACP) | | |
| 34 F | | | | Founder (Baking studio) | | |
| SF | Public | Overseas | GA (Overseas) | **Part III** (Ov.) Co-founder (Multidisciplinary studio) | | |
| 41 M | | | | Co-founder (F&B) | | |
| SO | Overseas | Overseas | **Part III** (Ov.) GA (Ov.) | Arch. designer Co-founder (Design studio) | | |
| 42 F | | | | Part-time lecturer | | Full-time lecturer |
| | | | | | Artist | |
| DM | Public | Public | GA | | **Part III** | Principal architect (ACP) |
| 42 M | | | | | | Diving instructor |

In essence, the three types of career transition mentioned, Part I transition (15%), Part II transition (55%), and Part III transitions (30%), are characterised by different turning points along the traditional architecture career pathways of Part I, Part II, and Part III stages.

## Career Identity

The fourth column 'Perceived career identity' in Table 6 below shows the self-perceived career identities of the participants, while the last column 'Portrayed career identity' lists the participant's profiles on LinkedIn, a networking, and career-oriented social media platform.

*Table 6. Career identity of research participants (by author, 2022)*

| Participant | | Age (2022) | Gender | Perceived career identity | Portrayed career identity (LinkedIn profile) |
|---|---|---|---|---|---|
| 1 | AL | 30 | Female | Dual identity (Architect/ Handmade product designer) | Architectural Designer |
| 2 | PW | 34 | Female | Architect | Self-employed |
| 3 | SO | 42 | Female | Multiple identities (Lecturer/ Architect/ Artist) | Architect/ Lecturer/ Co-founder |
| 4 | KC | 34 | Male | Architect | *Graduate architect (Not updated)* |
| 5 | KM | 34 | Male | Multiple identities (Place maker/ Space curator) | Design manager (Developer) |
| 6 | TC | 29 | Female | Dual identity | *Not found* |
| 7 | DM | 42 | Male | Dual identity (Architect/ Diving instructor) | Principal architect |
| 8 | RT | 31 | Male | Architect | Principal architect/ Lecturer / Founder / Self-employed |
| 9 | WF | 44 | Male | Artist doing architecture | Architectural photographer |
| 10 | JO | 34 | Male | Artist with architecture background | *Architectural assistant (Not updated)* |
| 11 | SM | 35 | Male | Unsure (Businessman / Architect) | *Not found* |
| 12 | RY | 42 | Female | Multiple identities (Project manager/ Fitness instructor) | Project architect/ Fitness instructor |
| 13 | NH | 36 | Female | Architect | Architect/ Publisher/ Tutor |
| 14 | SS | 33 | Female | Multiple identities (Design strategist/ Creative individual/ Artist) | Design strategist |
| 15 | SF | 41 | Male | Multiple identities (Architect/ Designer/ Technologist) | Design architect / Registered architectural technologist |

continued on following page

*Table 6. Continued*

| Participant | | Age (2022) | Gender | Perceived career identity | Portrayed career identity (LinkedIn profile) |
|---|---|---|---|---|---|
| 16 | SZ | 31 | Male | Multiple identities (Architect/ doing other business) | *Not found* |
| 17 | SY | 36 | Male | Dual identity (Architect/ Music writer) | Project architect/ Music writer |
| 18 | FG | 31 | Male | Dual identity (Architect/ Insurance agent) | Project architect/ Insurance agent |
| 19 | SC | 38 | Male | Entrepreneur | *Landscape architect (Not updated)* |
| 20 | DH | 34 | Female | Dual identity (Architect/ Yoga instructor) | Architect/ Interior designer/ Yoga instructor |

Referring to Table 6 above, twelve out of the 20 (60%) research participants, highlighted in light grey, perceive themselves as having either a 'Dual identity' or 'Multiple identities'. Six of them, SO, RY, NH, SF, SY, FG, and DH also included their second and third career in their LinkedIn profiles, to openly portray their multiple career identities.-On the other hand, two research participants, RT and NH, highlighted in dark grey, had a perceived career identity as an 'Architect', but portrayed themselves with multiple identities on LinkedIn. RT presents himself as 'Principal architect/ Lecturer/ Founder/ Self-employed', while NH's profile shows 'Architect/ Publisher/ Tutor'.

From a legal perspective, some participants, especially those who do not plan to pursue a Part III, do not identify themselves as architects. In these cases, in particular, the second career came more strongly into the picture.

SC: "*When I meet people, usually I just mention my name. I don't really tell people who I am, whether an architect or entrepreneur... To be honest, of course I would like to call myself an architect, but in the whole Malaysia situation, I am a Part II architect, so... I can't call myself architect. Maybe I am more like an entrepreneur.*"

KM: "*I think what I am trying to do is place making. We are constantly trying to find a better way in explaining what we are doing... I don't call myself an architect or architectural designer. I don't call it an architectural (design) studio either, because we are not. We do not want to end up doing design.*"

SS: "*We call ourselves design strategist, or creative individuals within the architecture field, and also artist. I don't call myself an architect or designer.*"

WF: "*Until now, people still know me as an architectural photographer rather than an architect... I do painting as well... I think we have to see architecture not only from the perspective of function. It is about giving a meaning to a space, that's part of art. I can say that I am also an artist doing architecture.*"

RY: "*To be honest, I don't really identify myself an architect, but maybe a project manager... I think I would introduce myself as an architect first when I meet new people, but if we start talking more, then I think I would tell them that I also do fitness. I think it is because for architects [as a career], it is easier to understand.*"

JO: "*Recently, I have been introducing myself as a light artist with a background of architecture. I am not an architect, I am not a lighting designer, but I am more of an artist... I don't really talk about the fact that I am a lecturer, but sometimes I would say like... by the way I also teach.*"

Nevertheless, some participants self-identified as architects regardless of registration status:

AL: "*Normally I will tell people that I am an architect. To me, I don't have any conflicts in identity. The only difference between working as a developer and architectural consultant is I don't sit and do drawings. Other than that, I am doing an architect's job scope, and maybe more than that.*"

NH: "*I still identify myself as an architect. [The publication studio] is still fairly new, so I still consider myself as an architect.... I don't think there is any conflict in myself in terms of identity.*"

FG: "*When I meet new friends, I will say I am an architect, work in an architecture firm, and I am also an insurance agent... I don't really find it conflicting.*"

A noteworthy point on research participant SM - a crypto gamer, as well as a LAM registered architect working as a project manager. In contrast to the other participants, he was personally conflicted in his professional and career identity.

SM: "*... Sometimes I don't know who I am. I would like to call myself a businessman, but at the moment, a major part of me is still an architect. I see the conflict in identity that I am having. I am not yet a businessman.*"

Rather than a reflection of their actual work, some of the participants' work identities were therefore a self-perceived distinctiveness, or intentionally portrayed image along the career pathway. Given that identity representation is an 'element of worth' to creative works (Reid et al., 2016), and architects perceive identity as a 'reward' (Caven & Diop, 2012), the majority of the participants in this study in fact perceived multiple identities as offering 'multiple rewards' for them to pursue a multiple-career pathway.

## Perception of a multiple-career pathway

Apart from the self-perceived thoughts on career identity, the participants' perception of a multiple-career pathway also plays a critical role to understand whether millennial architects are positive, negative, or neutral about the phenomenon of multiple-career pathways. Some positive responses from the research participants are as follows, mainly from female architects.

RY: "*I think having something else besides architecture is good, because the multi-disciplinary mind is very good for problem solving, as we think differently. It also helps to shift the focus, and use the brain differently... I really encourage people to have something other than just one career.*"

PW: "*I quite enjoy it, because I like to design my own cake. I enjoy slowly taking my time to design my thing. Then, at the same time, I still have my architecture income to sustain my daily life.*"

SO: "*I enjoy having multiple careers, providing they are all relevant. In my case, all are in the creative disciplines. I think they greatly benefit one another, not just adding value to personal experiences but the recipients party as well, for example my students, my art curator, and readers of my publications.*"

Conversely, several participants highlighted the challenges of pursuing multiple careers and indicated their preference to eventually focus on a single career.

FG: "*For me, I think it is better to focus on one career, because architecture is a very high commitment career… Focus on one career, then only can do it best.*"

KM: "*It is really hard to focus… because the amount of things that I am doing, I have no time fiddling. Sometimes it can be quite tiring…*"

DH: "*I think architecture is a very tough and demanding job. So, taking a second career path at the early stage of architecture career is not a good idea.... When you feel a bit more confident that you can manage, then you can try to branch out.*"

Nevertheless, participants also revealed their ways to cope with the challenges of dealing with multiple things at once. For example, support from collaborators or business partners.

WF: "*I think to focus on one thing is better, but bear in mind, I am not doing it alone, I have a partner. That's the advantage to us.*"

RT: "*Everyone knows that architecture must be focused and cannot have two hearts. I would say thankfully I have two associates who are very good and supportive for me to do this, otherwise I cannot imagine how I can do this.*"

Hence, the perceptions of a multiple career pathway were not uniformly positive or negative, re: the potential benefits (or harm) to the participants' architectural careers.

KC: "*For me, nothing special about having two jobs, for me is normal.*"

DM: "*For an architect to have another career, I think is quite a norm, but maybe not for a registered architect. For instances, many graduate architects have their side business… But as an AR to have another career, I think it is very hard.*"

JO: "*I think it is not easy, but it is helpful when I am not an employee, and I get to decide on my timing… I think it is much needed though, especially in architecture, it is not a very high paid career path... During and after the pandemic, a lot of people branch out to other businesses, and they stay on until even after the pandemic, especially with design.*"

The above millennial architects' perceptions of a multiple-career pathway not only affect their respective career choices along their career trajectories. More importantly, the millennial generation's perception and behaviour is something that participants felt will influence the future of the architectural profession, in terms of new ways to practice architecture, and new ways to work on projects.

SC: " *The new way of architecture should be seeing to yourself that you are capable of being multi-disciplinary, I think that's what architects should do.*"

NH: "*I think this is a new way of living, we can do multiple things of what we like, rather than committing to something that we don't like... There are other ways of practising architecture, rather than just building. It does not make me less of an architect if I make books. It does not make me less of an architect if I teach. We should broaden the way we practice* [architecture]."

SF: "*Even though we don't need to do multiple jobs, we need the skill sets to be able to do it... The market forces people to go beyond the traditional norm of being an architect or being in architecture.*"

TC: "*I need to start a new type of working style, because on this island* [TC's hometown is on an island], *don't have any firm or office in architecture, so I need to create this job for myself.*"

SS: "*It* [architecture] *is not just about buildings, bricks and mortars. It is about the programme that we run, is about social interactions....*"

In this vein, the architectural profession is heading towards greater diversity in terms of career models. In the near future, it may become a more inclusive and multidisciplinary profession compared to its current state, which is predominantly running a traditional practice model in the construction industry.

As a summary, Table 7 below tabulates the participants' perceptions towards a multiple-career pathway. Four simplified categories (*by choice, by opportunity, by need, and by force*) and its connotation of positive-neutral-negative will be presented.

*Table 7. Research participants' perception of a multiple-career pathway (by author, 2024)*

| Participant (Age in 2022) | | Gender | Perception of a multiple-career pathway | Connotation | Category | Theme |
|---|---|---|---|---|---|---|
| RY | 42 | Female | **It helps to shift focus and use brain differently.** | **Positive** | **Choice** | **Pull** |
| NH | 36 | Female | **It is a new way of living.** | **Positive** | | |
| PW | 34 | Female | **It is an experiment of trying different things.** | **Positive** | | |
| SC | 38 | Male | **It is new way of practising architecture.** | **Positive** | | |
| DH | 34 | Female | It is not a good idea at early stage of career. | Neutral | | |
| AL | 30 | Female | It is common among my high school friends. | Neutral | | |
| DM | 42 | Male | It is quite a norm. | Neutral | | |
| SF | 41 | Male | The market forces people to go beyond norm. | Neutral | | |
| KC | 34 | Male | Nothing special about having two jobs. | Neutral | | |
| KM | 34 | Male | *It is really hard to focus.* | *Negative* | | |
| SO | 42 | Female | **They benefit one another.** | **Positive** | **Opportunity** | |
| SY | 36 | Male | It is not what I choose to do, it happened naturally. | Neutral | | |
| SS | 33 | Female | I have lots of friends going along this path. | Neutral | | |
| JO | 34 | Male | It just came about as an opportunity. | Neutral | | |
| SM | 35 | Male | **I do it for two reasons, one is money, one is excitement.** | **Positive** | Need | Push |
| WF | 44 | Male | I think focus on one is better, but I am not doing it alone. | Neutral | | |
| SZ | 31 | Male | Focusing on one career is very boring for me. | Neutral | | |
| FG | 31 | Male | It is better to focus on one career. | Neutral | Force | |
| TC | 29 | Female | It is ok to choose a different working style. | Neutral | | |
| RT | 31 | Male | *I have no personal life and time, but I will keep balance.* | *Negative* | | |

The data reveals that half the participants perceived a multiple-career pathway as a viable choice for a successful career that includes architecture, rather than the pre-determined, traditional Part I-Part II-Part-III career pathway. Next, four participants perceived multiple careers as primarily a response to 'opportunity'. For them, it is not a straight-forward and natural path to pursue unless opportunities are offered and individuals are willing to take these up. By contrast, three participants perceived a multiple-career pathway as a 'need' and a final three related multiple-career pathways to a decision made out of force.

*Table 8. Hybrid table of research participants' career transitions and their perceptions of a multiple-career pathway (by author, 2024)*

| Career Transition | Participant (Age in 2022) | | Gender | Perception on MCP | Dual/ Multiple Identity | Pull Factors | | Push Factors | |
|---|---|---|---|---|---|---|---|---|---|
| | | | | | | Choice | Opportunity | Need | Force |
| Part I Transition | SZ | 31 | Male | Neutral | V | | | V | |
| | SY | 36 | Male | Neutral | V | | V | | |
| | KM | 34 | Male | *Negative* | V | V | | | |
| Part II Transition | RY | 42 | Female | **Positive** | V | V | | | |
| | NH | 36 | Female | **Positive** | V | V | | | |
| | SC | 38 | Male | **Positive** | | V | | | |
| | SM | 35 | Male | **Positive** | | | | V | |
| | DH | 34 | Female | Neutral | V | V | | | |
| | AL | 30 | Female | Neutral | V | V | | | |
| | SS | 33 | Female | Neutral | V | | V | | |
| | JO | 34 | Male | Neutral | | | V | | |
| | WF | 44 | Male | Neutral | | | | V | |
| | TC | 29 | Female | Neutral | V | | | | V |
| | FG | 31 | Male | Neutral | V | | | | V |
| Part III Transition | PW | 34 | Female | **Positive** | | V | | | |
| | SO | 42 | Female | **Positive** | V | | V | | |
| | KC | 34 | Male | Neutral | | V | | | |
| | SF | 41 | Male | Neutral | V | V | | | |
| | DM | 42 | Male | Neutral | V | V | | | |
| | RT | 31 | Male | *Negative* | V | | | | V |

In order to determine the factors that particularly relate to career transitions at different points of time for architects, a hybrid table (Table 8) was created. The result shows that career transitions from the pre-determined Part I-II-III traditional career path to a personalised multiple-career pathway happen at all career stages. There are no definite push or pull factors distinctively associated with particular career transition turning points. The drivers of *Choice, Opportunity, Need*, and *Force,* are, in general, the four main conditions leading millennials towards a multiple-career pathway at different points of their career trajectories. In addition, the study reveals that among Part III transition participants, female architects were in general more positive about pursuing a multiple-career pathway (MCP) as compared to their male counterparts, who are neutral about it.

## FINDINGS

The study revealed that a multiple-career pathway offers greater opportunities within and outside of architecture. It not only opens up limitless future possibilities, but also provides an alternative way to obtain a sense of security and achieve well-being. Major findings regarding multiple-career pathways include:

1. CHOICE is the primary motivator for many participants to pursue a multiple-career pathway, and it is also the most positively regarded factor.
2. OPPORTUNITY is the second most important motivator and positively regarded factor.
3. NEED and FORCE exist as motivators but are relatively minor in comparison to choice and opportunity and are either neutrally or negatively regarded.

In sum, millennial architects pursue a multiple-career pathway to expand their potential in all dimensions, caused by the *pull factors* of Choice and Opportunity and the *push factors* of Need and Force.

### Pull Factors

#### Choice

The findings indicate that ten of the participants actively chose to live in 'more than one world', and are willing to experiment and indulge in new ways of practicing architecture, including via the pursuit of more than one career path. This behaviour implies a willingness to seek out change, as well as a lack of negativity or self-denial about having multiple identities, although not all participants experienced only positive feelings about their choices.

### Opportunity

The study identified four individual participants who associated their multiple-career pathway with 'opportunity'. They were typically offered an opportunity to start up a practice or to take on a freelance job, and eventually turning this into another, parallel career pathway. Despite both 'choice' and 'opportunity' being pull factors towards a multiple-career pathway, it was evident that good opportunities were not offered to everyone, and even when offered, were not accepted by everyone. In contrast to the 'opportunity offered' acting as a *pull factor* for millennial architects to pursue a multiple-career pathway, the 'self-sought opportunity' is, by contrast a *push factor* distancing the millennial architects from the traditional career pathway, typically resulting from their reaction to either an urgent *need* or because they were *forced* into it.

## Push Factors

### Need

For the participants, the 'need' to pursue a multiple-career pathway was not merely for the remuneration - in fact their financial status was not the main factor. Instead, they reported more of a 'psychological need'. Several participants explained that making more money through their second and even third careers ironically allowed them to create better architecture, by removing the need to chase after mundane 'bread-and-butter' projects with minimal design input.

Working on multiple things concurrently, and having a diverse life was reported as more appealing. Because this 'need' to be in multiple fields cannot be achieved via employment in a traditional architectural consultancy practice, this new 'need' became a *push factor* away from the traditional career pathway. For some, choosing a multiple-career pathway allowed them the idealistic situation of pursuing selected architectural projects as a hobby, rather than relying on the traditional career path for their main source of income.

### Force

The study noticeably shows that *push factors* mainly act as the initial motives during the career transition from the single to the multiple-career pathway. Some of the motives included the inability to find a 'traditional' job of their choice, unhappiness with the working culture of the construction industry as well as the insecurity of having only one source of income or hitting a ceiling in their architectural consultancy practices.

However, the findings show that for millennial architects to sustain their chosen multiple-career pathway *pull factors* are required. In effect, *push factors* such as the feeling of 'being forced' have no further impact post-decision. Apart from the career opportunity to explore a different discipline or field, the opportunity for career growth in a multiple-career pathway is also more diverse, in terms of personal and professional growth, which are potent *pull factors*.

## CONCLUSION AND IMPLICATIONS

This study provides valuable insights regarding architects engaging in more than one career. It argues that the professional title of 'Architect' is not the only career identity millennials are pursuing. It shows that the multiple-career pathway, as an alternative, is greatly needed to complement the traditional career pathway in architecture. It is valuable not only to architecture students and graduates, but also to working architects who might otherwise feel 'trapped' in the profession. The study showcases a unique vantage point, with 20 plausible role models in different multiple-career pathways, who may connect with the aspirations of or provide motivation for other architects to step out of their comfort zones. The variety of alternative careers identified is particularly useful to graduates seeking guidance and role models for planning their own career pathways. The findings emphasize the importance of being 'unlimited' and 'boundaryless' in a multiple-career pathway.

The findings highlight the importance of fostering resilient career paths as a vital element in supporting an improved quality of life in present and future cities. It showcases the architectural profession as being at the forefront of a sustainable urban evolution that embraces diversity and flexibility while eschewing labelling and formal career structures that hinder the retention of highly – educated professionals in a vital industry. It suggests that for cities and countries to grow, supportive systems need to be in place to nurture their most important resource – educated workers – without which any sustainable improvements in quality of life will not be possible.

The findings also point to new areas for future research. Apart from the conventional upward, lateral, and downward career movements identified by previous scholars, this exploratory study also identifies the basis for a career transition into "parallel" career movements. This will require further research on interdisciplinary career pathways in the architectural profession, by architects and for the good of architects.

## REFERENCES


Adeokun, C. O., & Opoko, A. P. (2015). Exploring the link between motivation for course-choice and retention in the architectural profession: Students' perspectives. *Mediterranean Journal of Social Sciences*, *6*(6), 191–201. DOI: 10.5901/mjss.2015.v6n6s1p191

Ahuja, S., Nikolova, N., & Clegg, S. (2017). Paradoxical identity: The changing nature of architectural work and its relation to architects' identity. *Journal of Professions and Organization*, *4*(3), 2–19. DOI: 10.1093/jpo/jow013

Ahuja, S., Nikolova, N., & Clegg, S. (2019). Professional identity and anxiety in architect-client interactions. *Construction Management and Economics*, *38*(7), 589–602. DOI: 10.1080/01446193.2019.1703019

Alacovska, A., Fieseler, C., & Wong, S. I. (2021). 'Thriving instead of surviving': A capability approach to geographical career transitions in the creative industries. *Human Relations*, *74*(5), 751–780. DOI: 10.1177/0018726720956689

Architecture's Afterlife. Early Findings. (n.d.). Retrieved March 22, 2021, from Architecture's Afterlife website: http://architectures-afterlife.com/en/philosophy?q=9

Bondare, S., Volkova, T., Bondars, E., & Barvika, S. (2018). Business Challenges in the Architecture Industry. *Architecture and Urban Planning*, *13*(1), 118–123. DOI: 10.1515/aup-2017-0017

Bos-de Vos, M., Wamelink, J. W. F. H., & Volker, L. (2016). Trade-offs in the value capture of architectural firms: The significance of professional value. *Construction Management and Economics*, *34*(1), 21–34. DOI: 10.1080/01446193.2016.1177192

Caven, V. (2004). Constructing a career : Women architects at work. *Career Development International*, *9*(5), 518–531. DOI: 10.1108/13620430410550763

Caven, V. (2006). Career building: Women and non-standard employment in architecture. *Construction Management and Economics*, *24*(5), 457–464. DOI: 10.1080/01446190600601354

Caven, V. (2008). Architecture: A good career for girls? In Dainty, A. (Ed.), *Proceedings 24th Annual ARCOM Conference* (Vol. 2, pp. 901–910). Cardiff, UK: Association of Researchers in Construction Management.

Caven, V. (2009). Designing a career: Men and architecture. In Dainty, A. (Ed.), *Proceedings 25th Annual ARCOM Conference* (pp. 617–626). Nottingham, UK: Association of Researchers in Construction Management.

Caven, V., & Diop, M. (2012). Architecture: A "rewarding" career? An Anglo-French comparative study of intrinsic rewards in the architecture profession. *Construction Management and Economics, 30*(7), 513–523. DOI: 10.1080/01446193.2011.627356

Cohen, L., Wilkinson, A., Arnold, J., & Finn, R. (2005). "Remember I'm the bloody architect!" Architects, organizations and discourses of profession. *Work, Employment and Society, 19*(4), 775–796. DOI: 10.1177/0950017005058065

Damci, A., Arditi, D., Polat, G., & Turkoglu, H. (2020). Motivation of civil engineers and architects in Turkey. *Organization, Technology and Management in Construction. International Journal (Toronto, Ont.), 12*(1), 2044–2052. DOI: 10.2478/otmcj-2020-0001

De Graft-Johnson, A., Manley, S., & Greed, C. (2005). Diversity or the lack of it in the architectural profession. *Construction Management and Economics, 23*(10), 1035–1043. DOI: 10.1080/01446190500394233

Deutsch, R. (2019). What are architects for? Design technology and the future of professionalism. In Jones, A., & Hyde, R. (Eds.), *Defining Contemporary Professionalism: For architects in practice and education* (pp. 72–75). RIBA Publishing. DOI: 10.4324/9780429347856-19

Dixon, K. D., Kephart, T. A., & Moody, Karl, L. (2018). *The Business of Architecture: Your guide to a financially successful firm* (1st ed.). New York: Routledge.

Drake, J., Williams, A., & Kingsland, A. (2003). Preparing graduates for future practice. *Proceedings of the 2nd International Conference of the Association of Architecture Schools of Australasia.* Melbourne, Austrlia: Association of Architecture Schools of Australasia.

Fekry Youssef, M., Fathy Eid, A., & Mohamed Khodeir, L. (2023). Challenges affecting efficient management of virtual teams in construction in times of the COVID-19 pandemic. *Ain Shams Engineering Journal, 14*(7), 102008. DOI: 10.1016/j.asej.2022.102008

Folch, T. M., Pereira, R. C., & Icart, I. B. (2019). Exploring the creative process in architecture students and professionals. *Thinking Skills and Creativity, 34*(May), 100608. Advance online publication. DOI: 10.1016/j.tsc.2019.100608

Gafar, M., Kasim, R., & Martin, D. (2012). Toward a more entrepreneurship architectural education in Malaysia. *Proceedings International Conference of Technology Management, Business and Entrepreneurship 2012 (ICTMBE2012)*, 755–770. Melaka, Malaysia.

Gafar, M., Kasim, R., & Martin, D. (2017). Entrepreneurship Creativity: An Implication for Architects' Competitiveness and Sustainability. In Taufik, T., Prabasari, I., Rineksane, I. A., Yaya, R., Widowati, R., Rosyidi, S. A. P., & Harsanto, P. (Eds.), *Proceedings of the 2nd International Conference on Sustainable Innovation* (pp. 379–389). DOI: 10.1007/978-981-287-661-4_38

Galloway, L., & Haniff, A. (2015). Managing Projects in Architecture: A Study of Leadership in a Creative Industry. *Open Economics and Management Journal, 2*(Suppl 1: M6), 38–44. DOI: 10.2174/2352630001502010038

Gilmore, H., & Smith, G. (2014). The joy of passion: Finding your calling. *Thomas M. Cooley J. Pracactical & Clinical Law, 16*(3), 260–313. Retrieved from http://heinonline.org/hol-cgi-bin/get_pdf.cgi?handle=hein.journals/tmcjpcl16&section=17

Gutman, R. (2010). Architecture : The Entrepreneurial Profession. In Cuff, D., & Wriedt, J. (Eds.), *Architecture from the outside*. Princeton Architectural Press.

Healy, J., Nicholson, D., & Pekarek, A. (2017). Should we take the gig economy seriously? *Labour & Industry: A Journal of the Social and Economic Relations of Work, 27*(3), 232–248. DOI: 10.1080/10301763.2017.1377048

Hennekam, S., & Bennett, D. (2017). Creative industries work across multiple contexts: Common themes and challenges. *Personnel Review, 46*(1), 68–85. DOI: 10.1108/PR-08-2015-0220

Hill, D. (2012). Foreword. In Hyde, R. (Ed.), *Future Practice: Conversations from the edge of architecture* (pp. 6–15). Routledge.

Infante-Perea, M., Román-Onsalo, M., & Navarro-Astor, E. (2018). Expected career barriers in building engineering: Does gender matter? *Journal of Women and Minorities in Science and Engineering, 24*(1), 43–59. DOI: 10.1615/JWomenMinorScienEng.2017018301

Islam, I. N. (2016). Human resource management practices : Architects' perception and job satisfaction. *International Journal of Ethics in Social Sciences, 4*(1), 89–102.

Jamieson, C. (2011). The future for architects? Building Futures. *RIBA Building Futures*. Retrieved from http://www.buildingfutures.org.uk

Jones, A., & Hyde, R. (Eds.). (2019). *Defining Contemporary Professionalism: For architects in practice and education*. RIBA Publishing.

Khodeir, L. M., & Nessim, A. A. (2020). Changing skills for architecture students employability: Analysis of job market versus architecture education in Egypt. *Ain Shams Engineering Journal, 11*(3), 811–821. DOI: 10.1016/j.asej.2019.11.006

Maina, J. J. (2018). Reliability of self-assessment questionnaire : Do architecture postgraduates students overestimate their employability skills? Feedback from graduates and employers. *GU Journal of Science, 6*(2), 71–81.

Maina, J. J., & Daful, C. K. (2017). Do they measure up? Architecture graduates' perception of acquired skills, employers' expectations and what is obtained. *Journal of Research in National Development, 15*(1), 165–174.

Manley, S., & De Graft-johnson, A. (2008). Women in Architecture Five years on. In Dainty, A. (Ed.), *Proceedings 24th Annual ARCOM Conference* (pp. 891–900). Cardiff, UK: Association of Researchers in Construction Management.

Musiitwa, V. (2019). Obsolete? Relevance of the architect's role and the changing nature of the architectural profession. *Journal of Design Studio, 1*(1), 45–53.

Navarro-Astor, E., & Caven, V. (2012). Architects in Spain: A profession under risk. In Dainty, A. (Ed.), *Proceedings 28th Annual ARCOM Conference* (Vol. 1, pp. 577–587). Edinburgh, UK: Association of Researchers in Construction Management.

Oluwatayo, A. A. (2014). Employee architect's perception of human resource practices and their job satisfaction. *Built Environment Project and Asset Management, 5*(1), 89–102. DOI: 10.1108/BEPAM-04-2013-0008

Oyedele, L. O. (2010). Sustaining architects' and engineers' motivation in design firms: An investigation of critical success factors. *Engineering, Construction, and Architectural Management, 17*(2), 180–196. DOI: 10.1108/09699981011024687

Oyedele, L. O. (2013). Analysis of architects' demotivating factors in design firms. *International Journal of Project Management, 31*(3), 342–354. DOI: 10.1016/j.ijproman.2012.11.009

*Planning for Rapid Urbanisation Survey of the Architectural Profession in the Commonwealth.* (2018). Commonwealth Association of Architects.

Rabang-Alonzo, F. N. (2013). Employment status of architecture graduates of the University of Northern Philippines. *UNP Research Journal, XXII*, 96–109.

Reeves, T. C., & Oh, E. (2008). Generational Differences. In Spector, J. M., Merrill, M. D., van Merrienboer, J., & Driscoll, M. P. (Eds.), *Handbook of Research on Educational Communications and Technology* (3rd ed., pp. 295 303). Taylor & Francis Group.

Salleh, R., Md Yusof, M. A., & Memon, M. A. (2016). Attributes of graduate architects: An industry perspective. *Social Sciences, 11*(5), 551–556. DOI: 10.3923/sscience.2016.551.556

Salleh, R., Md Yusoff, M. A., Harun, H., & Memon, M. A. (2015). Gauging industry's perspectives on soft skills of graduate architects : Importance vs satisfaction. *Global Business and Management Research, 7*(2), 95–102.

Sang, K. J. C., Dainty, A. R. J., & Ison, S. G. (2007). Gender: A risk factor for occupational stress in the architectural profession? *Construction Management and Economics, 25*(12), 1305–1317. DOI: 10.1080/01446190701546177

Sang, K. J. C., Dainty, A. R. J., & Ison, S. G. (2008). The impact of self-employment on architect's job satisfaction. In Dainty, A. (Ed.), *Proceedings 24th Annual ARCOM Conference* (Vol. 1, pp. 13–22). Cardiff, UK: Association of Researchers in Construction Management.

Sang, K. J. C., Dainty, A. R. J., & Ison, S. G. (2014). Gender in the UK architectural profession: (re)producing and challenging hegemonic masculinity. *Work, Employment and Society, 28*(2), 247–264. DOI: 10.1177/0950017013491306

Sang, K. J. C., Ison, S. G., & Dainty, A. R. J. (2009). The job satisfaction of UK architects and relationships with work-life balance and turnover intentions. *Engineering, Construction, and Architectural Management, 16*(3), 288–300. DOI: 10.1108/09699980910951681

Savickas, M. L. (2006). Career construction theory. *Encyclopedia of Career Development*, 85–88.

Shannon, S. J. (2012). "I wish for more than I ever get": Employers' perspectives on employability attributes of architecture graduates. *Creative Education, 03*(06), 1016–1023. DOI: 10.4236/ce.2012.326153

Shannon, S. J., Webb, N., Zeng, Y., & Holder, J. (2014). Why architecture graduates do not register as architects: A quantitative and qualitative South Australian study 1999-2011. *Creative Education, 05*(16), 1540–1558. DOI: 10.4236/ce.2014.516171

Spurk, D., & Straub, C. (2020). Flexible employment relationships and careers in times of the COVID-19 pandemic. *Journal of Vocational Behavior, 119*(May), 1–4. DOI: 10.1016/j.jvb.2020.103435 PMID: 32382161

Sturges, J. (2013). A matter of time: Young professionals' experiences of long work hours. *Work, Employment and Society, 27*(2), 343–359. DOI: 10.1177/0950017012460318

Sullivan, S. E., & Al Ariss, A. (2021). Making sense of different perspectives on career transitions: A review and agenda for future research. *Human Resource Management Review*, *31*(1), 100727. Advance online publication. DOI: 10.1016/j.hrmr.2019.100727

Summerfield, R. (2022). Hybrid working can help recruit and retain talent, upskill leaders and boost team working, suggests a case study from an international professional services firm. *Strategic HR Review*, *21*(1), 34–40. https://doi.org/https://doi.org/10.1108/SHR-11-2021-0060. DOI: 10.1108/SHR-11-2021-0060

Susskind, R., & Susskind, D. (2015). *The Future of The Profession: How Technology will Transform the Work of Human Experts* (1st ed.). Oxford University Press. DOI: 10.1093/oso/9780198713395.001.0001

Topchiy, I., & Fatkullina, A. (2019). Career Guidance of Architects in the System of Continuous Education. *The Annual International Conference on Cognitive-Social, and Behavioural Sciences*, 285–293. https://doi.org/https://doi.org/10.15405/epsbs.2019.12.02.34

Waldrep, L. W. (2010). *Becoming an Architect* (2nd ed.). John Wiley & Sons.

Waldrep, L. W. (2017). The Career Paths of an Architect. In *The Architecture Student's Handbook of Professional Practice* (15th ed., pp. 46–56). American Institute of Architects.

Wood, A. J., Graham, M., Lehdonvirta, V., & Hjorth, I. (2019). Good Gig, Bad Gig: Autonomy and Algorithmic Control in the Global Gig Economy. *Work, Employment and Society*, *33*(1), 56–75. DOI: 10.1177/0950017018785616 PMID: 30886460

Zhao, S., De Angelis, E., & Ma, D. (2018). Reflecting on the architecture curriculum through a survey on career switching. *Journal of Design and Technology Education*, *23*(1), 76–87.

## ENDNOTES

1 Millennials were born between 1982 to 2000 (Howe & Strauss, 2000), 1981 to 1999 (Lancaster & Stillman, 2002), 1978 to 2000 (C. A. Martin & Tulgan, 2002), and 1981 to 1995 (Oblinger & Oblinger, 2005).

2 According to the Department of Statistics Malaysia (DOSM), the household income groups in Malaysia are categorised into B40, M40, and T20 group, based on the total income per household. B40 represents the bottom 40% of

low-income earners, M40 is the middle 40% known as middle class family, and T20 is the top 20% with high earnings.

3 Donald Super and his colleagues have outlined five major stages of career development which comprise of (1) **Growth** – age 4 to 13, (2) **Exploration** – age 14 to 24, (3) **Establishment** – age 25 to 44, (4) **Maintenance** – age 45 to 65, and (5) **Disengagement** – age over 65.

# Compilation of References


Abdu Hussen, A. (2022). High-Performance Liquid Chromatography (HPLC): A review. *Annals of Advances in Chemistry, 6*(1), 010–020. DOI: 10.29328/journal.aac.1001026

Abu Bakar, M. S., Manar, G., Syamsir, A., Abdul Rahman, M. R., Saad, M. R., Najeeb, M. I., Alhayek, A., & Muhammad Asyraf, M. R. (2024). An Overview of Fly-ash Geopolymer Composites in Sustainable Advance Construction Materials. *Pertanika Journal of Science & Technology, 32*(S5), 32. DOI: 10.47836/pjst.32.S5.04

Aclima. (2017, October 11). *How Seoul used the IoT to improve waste management and collection.* Aclima. https://aclima.eus/en/noticia/how-seoul-used-the-iot-to-improve-waste-management-and-collection/

Addo, I. A. (2016). Assessing residential satisfaction among low income households in multi-habited dwellings in selected low income communities in Accra. *Urban Studies (Edinburgh, Scotland), 53*(4), 631–650. DOI: 10.1177/0042098015571055

Adeokun, C. O., & Opoko, A. P. (2015). Exploring the link between motivation for course-choice and retention in the architectural profession: Students' perspectives. *Mediterranean Journal of Social Sciences, 6*(6), 191–201. DOI: 10.5901/mjss.2015.v6n6s1p191

Adhikari, S., Ross, W., & Ernst, J. (2019). *The Encyclopedia: Evaluating People's to Reach Desired Goods, Services and Activities.* The Victoria Transport Policy Institute. Online. Retrieved from https://www.vtpi.org/tdm/tdm84.htm

Afghan, A. M. (2020). The Art of Islamic Calligraphy. *SAARC Research Journal*, 7.

Aghaloo, K., Sharifi, A., Habibzadeh, N., Ali, T., & Chiu, Y.-R. (2024). How Nature-based Solutions Can Enhance Urban Resilience to Flooding and Climate Change and Provide Other Co-benefits: A Systematic Review and Taxonomy. *Urban Forestry & Urban Greening, 95*, 128320. DOI: 10.1016/j.ufug.2024.128320

Ahad, M. A., Paiva, S., Tripathi, G., & Feroz, N. (2020). Enabling technologies and sustainable smart cities. *Sustainable Cities and Society*, *61*, 102301. DOI: 10.1016/j.scs.2020.102301

Ahuja, S., Nikolova, N., & Clegg, S. (2017). Paradoxical identity: The changing nature of architectural work and its relation to architects' identity. *Journal of Professions and Organization*, *4*(3), 2–19. DOI: 10.1093/jpo/jow013

Ahuja, S., Nikolova, N., & Clegg, S. (2019). Professional identity and anxiety in architect-client interactions. *Construction Management and Economics*, *38*(7), 589–602. DOI: 10.1080/01446193.2019.1703019

Airyx. (2024). *SkySpec Compact Instrument v.250*. https://airyx.de/wp-content/uploads/2024/09/SkySpec-Compact.pdf

Ajayi, O. O., Toromade, A. S., & Olagoke, A. (n.d.). *Circular agro-economies (CAE): reducing waste and increasing profitability in agriculture*.

Akinsulire, A. A., Idemudia, C., Okwandu, A. C., & Iwuanyanwu, O. (2024). Economic and social impact of affordable housing policies: A comparative review. *International Journal of Applied Research in Social Sciences*, *6*(7), 1433–1448. DOI: 10.51594/ijarss.v6i7.1333

Alacovska, A., Fieseler, C., & Wong, S. I. (2021). 'Thriving instead of surviving': A capability approach to geographical career transitions in the creative industries. *Human Relations*, *74*(5), 751–780. DOI: 10.1177/0018726720956689

Alam, M. R., Reaz, M. B. I., & Ali, M. A. M. (2012). A review of smart homes—Past, present, and future. *IEEE Transactions on Systems, Man, and Cybernetics. Part C, Applications and Reviews*, *42*(6), 1190–1203. DOI: 10.1109/TSMCC.2012.2189204

Alawadhi, S., Aldama-Nalda, A., Chourabi, H., Gil-Garcia, J. R., Leung, S., Mellouli, S., & Walker, S. (2012). Building understanding of smart city initiatives. In *Electronic Government: 11th IFIP WG 8.5 International Conference, EGOV 2012, Kristiansand, Norway, September 3-6, 2012*. [Springer Berlin Heidelberg.]. *Proceedings*, *11*, 40–53.

Aldossari, M. Q., & Sidorova, A. (2020). Consumer acceptance of smart home technologies: A UTAUT2 perspective. Proceedings of the 26th Americas Conference on Information Systems, Virtual Conference. https://aisel.aisnet.org/amcis2020/adv_info_systems_research/adv_info_systems_research/7/

Alenezi, M., Wardat, S., & Akour, M. (2023). The Need of Integrating Digital Education in Higher Education: Challenges and Opportunities. *Sustainability (Basel)*, *15*(6), 4782. DOI: 10.3390/su15064782

Alexander, S. (2001). E-learning developments and experiences. *Education + Training*, *43*(4/5), 240–248. DOI: 10.1108/00400910110399247

Aliero, M. S., Asif, M., Ghani, I., & Abidin, M. Z. (2021). Smart home energy management systems: Research challenges and survey. 2021 International Conference on Software Engineering & Computer Systems and 4th International Conference on Computational Science and Information Management (ICSECS-ICOCSIM), 165–170. DOI: 10.1109/ICSECS52883.2021.00036

Aliyari, M. (2024). Improving Housing Sustainability Through an Innovative Approach. *International Journal of Modern Achievement in Science. Engineering and Technology*, *1*(4), 98–105.

Alkhayat, N., & İnalhan, G. (2024). Breaking Barriers, Building Bridges: Towards Inclusive and Resilient Cities through Social Diversity and Participation. *Proceedings of the International Conference of Contemporary Affairs in Architecture and Urbanism-ICCAUA*, *7*(1), 516–532. DOI: 10.38027/ICCAUA2024EN0137

Almutairi, Z. A., & Eltamaly, A. M. (2024). Synergistic Effects of Energy Storage Systems and Demand-Side Management in Optimizing Zero-Carbon Smart Grid Systems. *Energies*, *17*(22), 5637. DOI: 10.3390/en17225637

Altbach, P. G. (1991). Patterns in higher education development. *Prospects*, *21*(2), 189–203. DOI: 10.1007/BF02336060

Angelidou, M., Psaltoglou, A., Komninos, N., Kakderi, C., Tsarchopoulos, P., & Panori, A. (2018). Enhancing sustainable urban development through smart city applications. *Journal of Science and Technology Policy Management*, *9*(2), 146–169. DOI: 10.1108/JSTPM-05-2017-0016

Ansmann, A., & Müller, D. (2005). Lidar and Atmospheric Aerosol Particles. In Weitkamp, C. (Ed.), *Lidar* (pp. 105–141). Springer-Verlag., DOI: 10.1007/0-387-25101-4_4

Architecture's Afterlife. Early Findings. (n.d.). Retrieved March 22, 2021, from Architecture's Afterlife website: http://architectures-afterlife.com/en/philosophy?q=9

Arffman, A., Yli-Ojanperä, J., Kalliokoski, J., Harra, J., Pirjola, L., Karjalainen, P., Rönkkö, T., & Keskinen, J. (2014). High-resolution low-pressure cascade impactor. *Journal of Aerosol Science*, *78*, 97–109. DOI: 10.1016/j.jaerosci.2014.08.006

Argota Sánchez-Vaquerizo, J. (2025). Urban Digital Twins and metaverses towards city multiplicities: Uniting or dividing urban experiences? *Ethics and Information Technology*, *27*(1), 1–31. DOI: 10.1007/s10676-024-09812-3 PMID: 39583937

Ariaee, A. M., & Takalloo, S. (n.d.). *Impact of Affordable Housing Programs on Social Equity and Economic Development.*

Arndt, J., Deboudt, K., Anderson, A., Blondel, A., Eliet, S., Flament, P., Fourmentin, M., Healy, R. M., Savary, V., Setyan, A., & Wenger, J. C. (2016). Scanning electron microscopy-energy dispersive X-ray spectrometry (SEM-EDX) and aerosol time-of-flight mass spectrometry (ATOFMS) single particle analysis of metallurgy plant emissions. *Environmental Pollution, 210*, 9–17. DOI: 10.1016/j.envpol.2015.11.019 PMID: 26708757

Arnstein, S. R. (1969). A ladder of citizen participation. *Journal of the American Institute of Planners, 35*(4), 216–224. DOI: 10.1080/01944366908977225

Asimiyu, Z. (2020). *Bridging the Gap: Community Engagement and Social Equity in India's Urban Development Initiatives.*

AT. M. R., RR, S. A. P., Naidu, R. C., Ramachandran, P., Rajkumar, S., Kumar, V. N., Aggarwal, G., & Siddiqui, A. M. (2024). Intelligent Energy Management across Smart Grids Deploying 6G IoT, AI, and Blockchain in Sustainable Smart Cities. *IoT*.

Avellaneda-Franco, J. D., Rausch, J., & Jaramillo-Vogel, D. (2020). Caracterización morfo química y diferenciación del material particulado PM10-2.5 en el valle de Aburrá (Medellín- Colombia). *Master Thesis*. Universidad EAFIT.

Awang, M., & Md Zain, Z. (2007). Preliminary studies of fourier analysis for some climate data that influences heat transfer in building envelope/Masriah Hj Awang and Zainazlan Md Zain.

Azionya, C. M., & Nhedzi, A. (2021). The digital divide and higher education challenge with emergency online learning: Analysis of tweets in the wake of the COVID-19 lockdown. *Turkish Online Journal of Distance Education, 22*(4), 164–182. DOI: 10.17718/tojde.1002822

Azmi, A., Ibrahim, R., & Zulkifli, M. A. (2022). Smart home technology adoption: The perspective of Malaysian homeowners. *Journal of Physics: Conference Series, 2250*(1), 012008. DOI: 10.1088/1742-6596/2250/1/012008

Bajc, K., & Stokman, A. (2018). Design for resilience: Re-connecting communities and environments. *Landscape Architecture Frontiers, 6*(4), 14–32. DOI: 10.15302/J-LAF-20180402

Ballesteros-González, K., Espitia-Cano, S. O., Rincón-Caro, M. A., Rincón-Riveros, J. M., Perez-Peña, M. P., Sullivan, A., & Morales Betancourt, R. (2022). Understanding organic aerosols in Bogotá, Colombia: In-situ observations and regional-scale modeling. *Atmospheric Environment*, *284*, 119161. DOI: 10.1016/j.atmosenv.2022.119161

Ballesteros-González, K., Sullivan, A. P., & Morales-Betancourt, R. (2020). Estimating the air quality and health impacts of biomass burning in northern South America using a chemical transport model. *The Science of the Total Environment*, *739*, 139755. DOI: 10.1016/j.scitotenv.2020.139755 PMID: 32758934

Bartosz, R. M. (2024). The Role of Public-Private Investment Partnerships in Overcoming Challenges and Seizing Opportunities in Poland's Renewable Energy Sector. *Law and Economy*, *3*(10), 56–59. DOI: 10.56397/LE.2024.10.07

Bastos, D., Shackleton, M., & El-Moussa, F. (2018). Internet of things: A survey of technologies and security risks in smart home and city environments. *IET Conference Proceedings*, 30–37. DOI: 10.1049/cp.2018.0030

Batarce, M., Muñoz, J. C., & de Dios Ortúzar, J. (2016). Valuing crowding in public transport: Implications for cost-benefit analysis. *Transportation Research Part A, Policy and Practice*, *91*, 358–378. DOI: 10.1016/j.tra.2016.06.025

Battaglia, V., & Vanoli, L. (2024). Optimizing renewable energy integration in new districts: Power-to-X strategies for improved efficiency and sustainability. *Energy*, *305*, 132312. DOI: 10.1016/j.energy.2024.132312

Batty, M. (2009). Accessibility: In Search of A Unified Theory. *Environment and Planning. B, Planning & Design*, *36*(2), 191–194. https://journals.sagepub.com/doi/epdf/10.1068/b3602ed. DOI: 10.1068/b3602ed

Beimborn, E. A., Greenwald, M. J., & Jin, X. (2003). Accessibility, Connectivity, and Captivity: Impacts on Transit Choice. *Transportation Research Record: Journal of the Transportation Research Board*, *1835*(1), 1–9. Advance online publication. DOI: 10.3141/1835-01

Belanche-Gracia, D., Casaló-Ariño, L. V., & Pérez-Rueda, A. (2015). Determinants of multi-service smartcard success for smart cities development: A study based on citizens' privacy and security perceptions. *Government Information Quarterly*, *32*(2), 154–163. DOI: 10.1016/j.giq.2014.12.004

Benade, L. (2019). Flexible Learning Spaces: Inclusive by Design? *New Zealand Journal of Educational Studies*, *54*(1), 53–68. DOI: 10.1007/s40841-019-00127-2

Benedict, M. A., & McMahon, E. T. (2012). *Green infrastructure: linking landscapes and communities*. Island press.

Bennett, D., Knight, & Rowley, J. (2020). The role of hybrid learning spaces in enhancing higher education students' employability. *British Journal of Educational Technology*, 51(4), 1188–1202. Portico. DOI: 10.1111/bjet.12931

Berkel, K., & Homburg, E. (Eds.). (2023). *The Laboratory Revolution and the Creation of the Modern University* (pp. 1830–1940). Amsterdam University Press.

Bernardita, C. (2023). *Your Modern Business Guide to Data Analysis Methods and Techniques*. Online. Retrieved from https://www.datapine.com/blog/data-analysis-methods-and-techniques/

Bhati, A., & Song, I. (2019). New Methods for Collaborative Experiential Learning to Provide Personalised Formative Assessment. [IJET]. *International Journal of Emerging Technologies in Learning*, *14*(07), 179. DOI: 10.3991/ijet.v14i07.9173

Birmili, W., & Hoffmann, T. (2006). Environmental Pollutants Particulate and Dust Pollution, Inorganic and Organic Compounds. In *Encyclopedia of Respiratory Medicine* (pp. 110–120). Elsevier., DOI: 10.1016/B0-12-370879-6/00133-2

Bocchicchio, S., Commodo, M., Sgro, L. A., Chiari, M., D'Anna, A., & Minutolo, P. (2022). Thermo-optical-transmission OC/EC and Raman spectroscopy analyses of flame-generated carbonaceous nanoparticles. *Fuel*, *310*, 122308. DOI: 10.1016/j.fuel.2021.122308

Bogart, D. (2022). Infrastructure and institutions: Lessons from history. *Regional Science and Urban Economics*, *94*, 103626. DOI: 10.1016/j.regsciurbeco.2020.103626

Bondare, S., Volkova, T., Bondars, E., & Barvika, S. (2018). Business Challenges in the Architecture Industry. *Architecture and Urban Planning*, *13*(1), 118–123. DOI: 10.1515/aup-2017-0017

Bond, M., Marín, V. I., Dolch, C., Bedenlier, S., & Zawacki-Richter, O. (2018). Digital transformation in German higher education: Student and teacher perceptions and usage of digital media. *International Journal of Educational Technology in Higher Education*, *15*(1), 48. Advance online publication. DOI: 10.1186/s41239-018-0130-1

Bondoc, C. E., & Malawit, T. G. (2020). Cybersecurity for higher education institutions: adopting regulatory framework. *Global Journal of Engineering and Technology Advances*, 2(3), 016–021. DOI: 10.30574/gjeta.2020.2.3.0013

Borhan, M. N., Syamsunur, D., Akhir, N. M., Yazid, M. R. M., Ismail, A., & Rahmat, R. A. (2014). Predicting the Use of Public Transportation: A Case Study from Putrajaya, Malaysia. *TheScientificWorldJournal, 2014*(1), 1–9. Advance online publication. DOI: 10.1155/2014/784145 PMID: 25110744

Bos-de Vos, M., Wamelink, J. W. F. H., & Volker, L. (2016). Trade-offs in the value capture of architectural firms: The significance of professional value. *Construction Management and Economics, 34*(1), 21–34. DOI: 10.1080/01446193.2016.1177192

Brand, P., & Dávila, J. D. (2011). Mobility innovation at the urban margins: Medellín's Metrocables. *City (London, England), 15*(6), 647–661. DOI: 10.1080/13604813.2011.609007

Bribián, I. Z., Capilla, A. V., & Usón, A. A. (2011). Life cycle assessment of building materials: Comparative analysis of energy and environmental impacts and evaluation of the eco-efficiency improvement potential. *Building and Environment, 46*(5), 1133–1140. DOI: 10.1016/j.buildenv.2010.12.002

Brown, V., Barr, A., Scheurer, J., Magnus, A., Zapata-Diomedi, B., & Bently, R. (2019). Better Transport Accessibility, Better Health: A Health Economic Impact Assessment Study for Melbourne, Australia. *The International Journal of Behavioral Nutrition and Physical Activity, 16*(1), 1–10. DOI: 10.1186/s12966-019-0853-y PMID: 31640737

Brundtland Commission. (1987). *Our Common Future*. Oxford University Press.

Bryman, A. (2008). *Social research methods* (3rd ed.). Oxford University Press.

Bulkeley, H. (2013). *Cities and climate change*. Routledge. DOI: 10.4324/9780203077207

Burbules, N. C., & Callister, T. A.Jr. (2000). Universities in Transition: The Promise and the Challenge of New Technologies. *Teachers College Record, 102*(2), 271–293. DOI: 10.1111/0161-4681.00056

Canagaratna, M. R., Jayne, J. T., Jimenez, J. L., Allan, J. D., Alfarra, M. R., Zhang, Q., Onasch, T. B., Drewnick, F., Coe, H., Middlebrook, A., Delia, A., Williams, L. R., Trimborn, A. M., Northway, M. J., DeCarlo, P. F., Kolb, C. E., Davidovits, P., & Worsnop, D. R. (2007). Chemical and microphysical characterization of ambient aerosols with the aerodyne aerosol mass spectrometer. *Mass Spectrometry Reviews, 26*(2), 185–222. DOI: 10.1002/mas.20115 PMID: 17230437

Capdevila, I., & Zarlenga, M. I. (2015). Smart city or smart citizens? The Barcelona case. *Journal of Strategy and Management, 8*(3), 266–282. DOI: 10.1108/JSMA-03-2015-0030

Carmona, M. (2021). *Public places urban spaces: The dimensions of urban design.* Routledge. DOI: 10.4324/9781315158457

Castells, M. (2020). *Space of flows, space of places: Materials for a theory of urbanism in the information age. In the City Reader.* Routledge.

Caven, V. (2004). Constructing a career : Women architects at work. *Career Development International, 9*(5), 518–531. DOI: 10.1108/13620430410550763

Caven, V. (2006). Career building: Women and non-standard employment in architecture. *Construction Management and Economics, 24*(5), 457–464. DOI: 10.1080/01446190600601354

Caven, V. (2008). Architecture: A good career for girls? In Dainty, A. (Ed.), *Proceedings 24th Annual ARCOM Conference* (Vol. 2, pp. 901–910). Cardiff, UK: Association of Researchers in Construction Management.

Caven, V. (2009). Designing a career: Men and architecture. In Dainty, A. (Ed.), *Proceedings 25th Annual ARCOM Conference* (pp. 617–626). Nottingham, UK: Association of Researchers in Construction Management.

Caven, V., & Diop, M. (2012). Architecture: A "rewarding" career? An Anglo-French comparative study of intrinsic rewards in the architecture profession. *Construction Management and Economics, 30*(7), 513–523. DOI: 10.1080/01446193.2011.627356

Centres for Disease Control and Prevention (CDCP). (2020). *Disability and Health Inclusion Strategies.* Online. Retrieved from https://www.cdc.gov/ncbddd/disabilityandhealth/disability-strategies.html#:~:text=Accessibility%20is%20when%20the%20needs,spaces%20are%20close%20to%20entrances

Chan, D. (2022, June 9). Vehicles Outnumber People in Malaysia. *New Strait Times.* Online. Retrieved from https://www.nst.com.my/news/nation/2022/06/803654/vehicles-outnumber-people-malaysia

Chang, D. Y. (1996). Applications of the extent analysis method on fuzzy AHP. *European Journal of Operational Research, 95*(3), 649–655. DOI: 10.1016/0377-2217(95)00300-2

Chang, W.-L., Chen, Y.-M., & Lin, Y.-H. (2020). Smart hearing aids in smart cities: Technological challenges and opportunities. *Journal of Ambient Intelligence and Smart Environments, 12*(4), 345–357. DOI: 10.3233/AIS-200563

Chan, J. J., & Chye, S. W. (2023). Impact of smart city initiatives on urban planning strategies in Singapore: An in-depth analysis of technology-driven solutions and their influence on sustainable development and quality of life. *Journal of Strategy and Management*, *7*(7), 11–21.

Chauhan, P. K., Kumar, A., Pratap, V., & Singh, A. K. (2022). Seasonal characteristics of PM1, PM2.5, and PM10 over Varanasi during 2019–2020. *Frontiers in Sustainable Cities*, *4*, 909351. Advance online publication. DOI: 10.3389/frsc.2022.909351

Chea, J. (2023, February 22). Video Of Woman Walking Along Busy Traffic Due to No Pedestrian Walkways Goes Viral. *Says*. Retrieved from https://says.com/my/news/m-sian-forced-to-walk-beside-busy-traffic

Chen, M. (2012). *The informal economy: Definitions, theories, and policies* (WIEGO Working Paper No. 1). Women in Informal Employment: Globalizing and Organizing (WIEGO). https://www.wiego.org/publications/informal-economy-definitions-theories-and-policies

Cheng, Y. H., & Chen, S. Y. (2015). Perceived Accessibility, Mobility, And Connectivity Of Public Transportation Systems. *Transportation Research Part A, Policy and Practice*, *77*(July), 386–403. DOI: 10.1016/j.tra.2015.05.003

Chen, T., Luh, D.-B., Hu, L., & Shan, Q. (2023). Exploring Factors Affecting Residential Satisfaction in Old Neighborhoods and Sustainable Design Strategies Based on Post-Occupancy Evaluation. *Sustainability (Basel)*, *15*(21), 15213–15213. DOI: 10.3390/su152115213

Cheremisinoff, N. P. (1996). Elemental And Structural Characterization Tests. In *Polymer Characterization* (pp. 43–81). Elsevier., DOI: 10.1016/B978-081551403-9.50006-6

Chin, S. J. Y., Goh, B. H., Teo, F. Y., Kang, B. G., & Yuen, C. W. (2020). Pedestrian Walkability Index for Light Rail Transit (LRT) Stations in Klang Valley, Malaysia. *In Proceedings of AICCE'19: Transforming the Nation for a Sustainable Tomorrow 4 (pp. 737-748)*. Springer International Publishing.

Chohan, A. H., Che-Ani, A. I., Shar, B. K., Awad, J., Jawaid, A., & Tawil, N. M. (2015). A model of housing quality determinants (HQD) for affordable housing. *Journal of Construction in Developing Countries*, *20*(1), 117.

Clothey, R. (2011). Opportunities and Obstacles: Technology's Potential for Expanding Access to Higher Education. *Excellence in Higher Education*, *2*(1), 51–58. DOI: 10.5195/ehe.2011.29

Cohen, L., Wilkinson, A., Arnold, J., & Finn, R. (2005). "Remember I'm the bloody architect!" Architects, organizations and discourses of profession. *Work, Employment and Society*, *19*(4), 775–796. DOI: 10.1177/0950017005058065

Cohen-Shacham, E., Walters, G., Janzen, C., & Maginnis, S. (2016). Nature-based solutions to address global societal challenges. *IUCN: Gland, Switzerland*, *97*, 2016–2036. DOI: 10.2305/IUCN.CH.2016.13.en

Cox, C., Duggirala, S., & Li, Z. (2006). Case studies on the economic viability of renewable energy. *2006 IEEE Power Engineering Society General Meeting*, 8-pp.

Creswell, J. W. (2014). *Research design: Qualitative, quantitative, and mixed methods approaches* (4th ed.). Sage Publications.

Cruz-Ruiz, L. M., Fernández-Restrepo, F., Yarce-Botero, A., Solórzano-Araque, V., & Quintero, O. L. (2024). *Ensemble Modeling of Atmospheric Pollutants: A Case Study with WRF-Chem and LOTOS-EUROS in Aburrá Valley, Colombia*. DOI: 10.5194/egusphere-egu24-1020

Damci, A., Arditi, D., Polat, G., & Turkoglu, H. (2020). Motivation of civil engineers and architects in Turkey. *Organization, Technology and Management in Construction. International Journal (Toronto, Ont.)*, *12*(1), 2044–2052. DOI: 10.2478/otmcj-2020-0001

Dastane, O. (2020). Impact of digital marketing on online purchase intention: The moderating role of trust. *International Journal of Advanced Science and Technology*, *29*(6), 1114–1125.

Datta, A. (2015). New urban utopias of postcolonial India: Entrepreneurial urbanization in Dholera smart city, Gujarat. *Dialogues in Human Geography*, *5*(1), 3–22. DOI: 10.1177/2043820614565748

Dave, D. (2024). Biophilic Design Principles with Kinetic Facade. [IRJAEM]. *International Research Journal on Advanced Engineering and Management*, *2*(09), 2952–2955. DOI: 10.47392/IRJAEM.2024.0436

De Graft-Johnson, A., Manley, S., & Greed, C. (2005). Diversity or the lack of it in the architectural profession. *Construction Management and Economics*, *23*(10), 1035–1043. DOI: 10.1080/01446190500394233

De Sherbinin, A., Schiller, A., & Pulsipher, A. (2012). The vulnerability of global cities to climate hazards. In *Adapting cities to climate change* (pp. 129–157). Routledge.

De Witte, A., Hollevoet, J., Dobruszkes, F., Hubert, M., & Macharis, C. (2013). Linking Modal Choice to Motility: A Comprehensive Review. *Transportation Research Part A, Policy and Practice*, *49*(March), 329–341. DOI: 10.1016/j.tra.2013.01.009

Denzin, N. K., & Lincoln, Y. S. (1994). *Handbook of qualitative research.* Sage Publications.

Deutsch, R. (2019). What are architects for? Design technology and the future of professionalism. In Jones, A., & Hyde, R. (Eds.), *Defining Contemporary Professionalism: For architects in practice and education* (pp. 72–75). RIBA Publishing. DOI: 10.4324/9780429347856-19

Devara, P. C. S. (1998). Review article Remote sensing of atmospheric aerosols from active and passive optical techniques. *International Journal of Remote Sensing*, *19*(17), 3271–3288. DOI: 10.1080/014311698213966

Dillahunt, T., Wang, Z., & Teasley, S. D. (2014). Democratizing higher education: Exploring MOOC use among those who cannot afford a formal education. *International Review of Research in Open and Distance Learning*, *15*(5). Advance online publication. DOI: 10.19173/irrodl.v15i5.1841

Dixon, K. D., Kephart, T. A., & Moody, Karl, L. (2018). *The Business of Architecture: Your guide to a financially successful firm* (1st ed.). New York: Routledge.

do Prado, H. A., Rodrigues, T., Manes, S., Kasecker, T., Vale, M. M., Scarano, F. R., & Pires, A. P. F. (2024). Designing nature to be a solution for climate change in cities: A meta-analytical review. *The Science of the Total Environment*, *954*, 176735. DOI: 10.1016/j.scitotenv.2024.176735

Drake, J., Williams, A., & Kingsland, A. (2003). Preparing graduates for future practice. *Proceedings of the 2nd International Conference of the Association of Architecture Schools of Australasia.* Melbourne, Austrlia: Association of Architecture Schools of Australasia.

Du, Y., Sun, T., & Huang, Y. (n.d.). *A Comprehensive Review of Smart City Initiatives in Singapore Technological Advancements and Urban Planning from 2015 to 2023.*

Duarte, C. M., Losada, I. J., Hendriks, I. E., Mazarrasa, I., & Marbà, N. (2013). The role of coastal plant communities for climate change mitigation and adaptation. *Nature Climate Change*, *3*(11), 961–968. DOI: 10.1038/nclimate1970

Ducuara, O. (2012). Métodos para la determinación de Material Particulado. In En, O. (Ed.), *Ducuara, Seguimiento y Control de Emisiones atmosféricas*. Universidad Nacional.

Dwijendra, N. K. A. (2013). Quality of affordable housing projects by public and private developers in Indonesia: The case of Sarbagita Metropolitan Bali. *Journal of Geography and Regional Planning*, *6*(3), 69–81. DOI: 10.5897/JGRP12.050

Eboli, L., Fu, Y., & Mazzulla, G. (2016). Multilevel Comprehensive Evaluation of the Railway Service Quality. *Procedia Engineering*, *137*, 21–30. DOI: 10.1016/j.proeng.2016.01.230

Eboli, L., & Mazzulla, G. (2012). Structural Equation Modelling for Analysing Passengers' Perceptions about Railway Services. *Procedia: Social and Behavioral Sciences*, *54*, 96–106. DOI: 10.1016/j.sbspro.2012.09.729

Echeverri-Londoño, C. A., & Maya-vasco, G. J. (2008). Relación entre las partículas finas (pm2.5) y respirables (pm10) en la ciudad de Medellín. *Revista Ingenierías Universidad de Medellín*. https://revistas.udem.edu.co/index.php/ingenierias/article/view/198/185

Edenhofer, O. (Ed.). (2015). *Climate change 2014: mitigation of climate change* (Vol. 3). Cambridge University Press.

Edner, H., Ragnarson, P., Spännare, S., & Svanberg, S. (1993). Differential optical absorption spectroscopy (DOAS) system for urban atmospheric pollution monitoring. *Applied Optics*, *32*(3), 327. DOI: 10.1364/AO.32.000327 PMID: 20802694

Elias, W., & Shiftan, Y. (2012). The influence of individual's risk perception and attitudes on travel behavior. *Transportation Research Part A, Policy and Practice*, *46*(8), 1241–1251. DOI: 10.1016/j.tra.2012.05.013

Ellis, J. B. (2013). Sustainable surface water management and green infrastructure in UK urban catchment planning. *Journal of Environmental Planning and Management*, *56*(1), 24–41. DOI: 10.1080/09640568.2011.648752

Ellsworth-Krebs, K., Reid, L., & Hunter, C. J. (2018). Integrated framework of home comfort: Relaxation, companionship and control. *Building Research and Information*, *47*(2), 202–218. DOI: 10.1080/09613218.2017.1410375

Elmqvist, T., Bai, X., Frantzeskaki, N., Griffith, C., Maddox, D., McPhearson, T., & Watkins, M. (Eds.). (2018). *Urban Planet: Knowledge towards Sustainable Cities.* Cambridge University Press. DOI: 10.1017/9781316647554

Erlangga, H. (2021). Effect of digital marketing and social media on purchase intention of SMEs food products. *Journal of Business and Management Review*, *2*(2), 141–154. DOI: 10.47153/jbmr22.1412021

Evans, J. (2019). Governing cities for sustainability: A research agenda and invitation. *Frontiers in Sustainable Cities*, *1*, 2. DOI: 10.3389/frsc.2019.00002

Fan, H., & Fan, L. (2024). Role of Education and Awareness Programs in Fostering Energy Conservation Behavior in Cities: Empowering Urban Sustainability Using Deep Learning Approach. *Sustainable Cities and Society*, *112*, 105505. DOI: 10.1016/j.scs.2024.105505

Farieta, M. F. (2023). *Social Urbanism in Medellin–Integration of Landscape, Life, and Culture* (Master's thesis, University of Maryland, College Park).

Feist, W., Schnieders, J., Dorer, V., & Haas, A. (2005). Re-inventing air heating: Convenient and comfortable within the frame of the Passive House concept. *Energy and Building*, *37*(11), 1186–1203. DOI: 10.1016/j.enbuild.2005.06.020

Fekry Youssef, M., Fathy Eid, A., & Mohamed Khodeir, L. (2023). Challenges affecting efficient management of virtual teams in construction in times of the COVID-19 pandemic. *Ain Shams Engineering Journal*, *14*(7), 102008. DOI: 10.1016/j.asej.2022.102008

Fergusson, J. E. (1990). *The Heavy Elements: Chemistry, Environmental Impact and Health Effects*. Pergamon Press.

Fernald, F. G. (1984). Analysis of atmospheric lidar observations: Some comments. *Applied Optics*, *23*(5), 652–653. https://doi.org/https://doi.org/10.1364/AO.23.000652. DOI: 10.1364/AO.23.000652 PMID: 18204618

Folch, T. M., Pereira, R. C., & Icart, I. B. (2019). Exploring the creative process in architecture students and professionals. *Thinking Skills and Creativity*, *34*(May), 100608. Advance online publication. DOI: 10.1016/j.tsc.2019.100608

Folianto, F., Low, Y. S., & Yeow, W. L. (2015). Smartbin: Smart waste management system. *2015 IEEE Tenth International Conference on Intelligent Sensors, Sensor Networks and Information Processing (ISSNIP)*, 1–2.

Frantzeskaki, N., McPhearson, T., Collier, M. J., Kendal, D., Bulkeley, H., Dumitru, A., Walsh, C., Noble, K., van Wyk, E., Ordóñez, C., Oke, C., & Pintér, L. (2019). Nature-based solutions for urban climate change adaptation: Linking science, policy, and practice communities for evidence-based decision-making. *Bioscience*, *69*(6), 455–466. DOI: 10.1093/biosci/biz042

Franz, Y., & Gruber, E. (2022). The Changing Role of Student Housing as Social Infrastructure. *Urban Planning*, *7*(4). Advance online publication. DOI: 10.17645/up.v7i4.5661

Freudenthaler, V. (2016). About the effects of polarising optics on lidar signals and the Δ90 calibration. *Atmospheric Measurement Techniques*, *9*(9), 4181–4255. DOI: 10.5194/amt-9-4181-2016

Fuentes-Inzunza, R. (2012). Implementación de Instrumentación Óptica para el Monitoreo Remoto de la Calidad de Aire. *PhD Thesis*. Universidad de Concepción.

Funamori, M. (2016). *The Impact of the Digital Age on Higher Education: Beyond Transformation from the Physical Space to the Digital Sphere*. 2016 5th IIAI International Congress on Advanced Applied Informatics (IIAI-AAI). DOI: 10.1109/IIAI-AAI.2016.58

Fu, Y., Eboli, L., Mazzulla, G., & Zhang, Y. (2017, March). Railway Service Quality in Northern Italy: A Multilevel Synthetic Assessment. *Advances in Mechanical Engineering*, *9*(3), 1687814016686317. Advance online publication. DOI: 10.1177/1687814016686317

Gafar, M., Kasim, R., & Martin, D. (2012). Toward a more entrepreneurship architectural education in Malaysia. *Proceedings International Conference of Technology Management, Business and Entrepreneurship 2012 (ICTMBE2012)*, 755–770. Melaka, Malaysia.

Gafar, M., Kasim, R., & Martin, D. (2017). Entrepreneurship Creativity: An Implication for Architects' Competitiveness and Sustainability. In Taufik, T., Prabasari, I., Rineksane, I. A., Yaya, R., Widowati, R., Rosyidi, S. A. P., & Harsanto, P. (Eds.), *Proceedings of the 2nd International Conference on Sustainable Innovation* (pp. 379–389). DOI: 10.1007/978-981-287-661-4_38

Gafurov, I. R., Safiullin, M. R., Akhmetshin, E. M., Gapsalamov, A. R., & Vasilev, V. L. (2020). Change of the Higher Education Paradigm in the Context of Digital Transformation: From Resource Management to Access Control. *International Journal of Higher Education*, *9*(3), 71. DOI: 10.5430/ijhe.v9n3p71

Galloway, L., & Haniff, A. (2015). Managing Projects in Architecture: A Study of Leadership in a Creative Industry. *Open Economics and Management Journal*, *2*(Suppl 1: M6), 38–44. DOI: 10.2174/2352630001502010038

Ganiyev, A. (n.d.). *THE ROLE OF ARCHITECTURE IN ISLAMIC CIVILIZATION*. https://doi.org/DOI: 10.47980/IIAU/2023/3/1

Gao, X. (2024). Research on the Interrelationship Between Urbanisation and Sustainable Development. *Communications in Humanities Research*, *44*(1), 198–205. DOI: 10.54254/2753-7064/44/20240028

Gehl, J. (2013). *Cities for people*. Island press.

Geissdoerfer, M., Savaget, P., Bocken, N. M., & Hultink, E. J. (2017). The Circular Economy–A new sustainability paradigm? *Journal of Cleaner Production, 143*, 757–768. DOI: 10.1016/j.jclepro.2016.12.048

Germin, J.G. (n.d.). *Thermodynamic Interactions: Energy and Architecture.*

Gevorgyan, O. I., Minaev, N. N., & Zharova, E. A. (2020). *University cities' evolution in context of human capital accumulation.* SHS Web of Conferences, 80, 01008. DOI: 10.1051/shsconf/20208001008

Ghosh, O. (2023). Environmental hazards and disasters - A response towards mitigating disaster management. *AIP Conference Proceedings, 2763*(1), 050008. DOI: 10.1063/5.0158892

Ghufron, A., & Agustina, I. F. (2024). Community Engagement in Development Planning in Jabon District. *Indonesian Journal of Cultural and Community Development, 15*(3), 10–21070. DOI: 10.21070/ijccd.v15i3.1128

Gil, N., & Mello, S. (2011). Differential Optical Absorption Spectroscopy (DOAS). *PhD Thesis*. Universidad de la Republica.

Gilmore, H., & Smith, G. (2014). The joy of passion: Finding your calling. *Thomas M. Cooley J. Pracactical & Clinical Law, 16*(3), 260–313. Retrieved from http://heinonline.org/hol-cgi-bin/get_pdf.cgi?handle=hein.journals/tmcjpcl16&section=17

Goh, C. S., Azizi, Z. M., Fateh, M. A. M., & Bajracharya, A. (2024). Enabling the Built Environment for Sustainable Living and Climate Resilience. *European Journal of Sustainable Development, 13*(3), 151. DOI: 10.14207/ejsd.2024.v13n3p151

Goltermann, D., Ujeyl, G., & Pasche, E. (2009). Making coastal cities flood resilient in the era of climate change. *RIMAX Contributions at the 4th International Symposium on Flood Defence (ISFD4).*

Gómez-Redondo, S., Plaza Gómez, N., Obregón, L. J., Coca, J. R., & Paramá Díaz, A. (2024). Urban Transformations for Universal Accessibility: Socio-Educational Dialogue. *Urban Science (Basel, Switzerland), 8*(4), 161. DOI: 10.3390/urbansci8040161

Gonzalez, L. (2024, September 3). Climate-induced Displacements in California: Looking county by county to explore human displacement directly caused by natural disasters. https://escholarship.org/uc/item/0q7517rn

Guo, Z., & Wilson, N. H. M. (2011, February). Assessing the cost of transfer inconvenience in public transport systems: A case study of the London Underground. *Transportation Research Part A, Policy and Practice*, *45*(2), 91–104. DOI: 10.1016/j.tra.2010.11.002

Guragain, G. P. (2023). Community Engagement in Local Governance. *Kutumbha Vani*, *4*(1), 72–82. DOI: 10.3126/kv.v4i1.73924

Gutiérrez, M. C., & Droguet, M. (2002). La cromatografía de gases y la espectometría de masas: identificación de compuestos causantes de mal olor. *Instituto de Investigación Textil y Cooperación Industrial.* https://upcommons.upc.edu/handle/2099/2733

Gutman, R. (2010). Architecture : The Entrepreneurial Profession. In Cuff, D., & Wriedt, J. (Eds.), *Architecture from the outside*. Princeton Architectural Press.

Hachem-Vermette, C. (2024). Enhancing Urban Climate Resistance Through the Application of Selected Strategies and Technologies. *Discover Cities*, *1*(1), 1–28. DOI: 10.1007/s44327-024-00018-2 PMID: 39345934

Hadas, Y., Rossi, R., Gastaldi, M., & Gecchele, G. (2014). Public Transport Systems' Connectivity: Spatiotemporal Analysis and Failure Detection. *Transportation Research Procedia*, *3*, 309–318. DOI: 10.1016/j.trpro.2014.10.011

Haggans, M. (2016). The 21st-century campus. *Planning for Higher Education*, *44*(3), 1–8.

Haidar, S., Zou, F., & Li, X. (2023). AN ANALYTICAL STUDY OF FIVE-POINTED ISLAMIC FLORAL PATTERNS AND AN EXPERIMENTAL DESIGN USING PENROSE TILING. *Shedet*, *10*(10), 227–245. DOI: 10.21608/shedet.2023.291530

Hamel, P., & Tan, L. (2022). Blue–green infrastructure for flood and water quality management in Southeast Asia: Evidence and knowledge gaps. *Environmental Management*, *69*(4), 699–718. DOI: 10.1007/s00267-021-01467-w PMID: 33860825

Hamidon, N. A., Md Ishak, S. M., & WMD, W. S. A. (2022, April 20). *Design Structure In Malaysian Islamic Calligraphy Contemporary Paintings*. DOI: 10.4108/eai.24-8-2021.2315281

Handy, S. L. (2002). *Accessibility- Vs. Mobility-enhancing Strategies for Ad-dressing Automobile Dependence in the U.S.* European Conference of Ministers of Transport May 2002. Retrieved from https://escholarship.org/uc/item/5kn4s4pb

Haney, J. M., Luther, L., & Dastane, O. (2020). Security and privacy issues in smart home environments: A systematic literature review. *International Journal of Advanced Computer Science and Applications*, *11*(7), 567–576. DOI: 10.14569/IJACSA.2020.0110772

Hansen, K. B., & Agger, A. (2022). Copenhagen CO2 neutrality in 2025? A polycentric analysis of urban climate governance in Copenhagen 2006–2020. *Environmental Policy and Governance*, *33*(3), 288–300. DOI: 10.1002/eet.2030

Harrison, R. J., & Köler, T. O. (2001). Beyond Characterisation. Polished Stone Exchange in the Western Mediterranean 5500–2000 BC. *Oxford Journal of Archaeology*, *20*(2), 107–127. DOI: 10.1111/1468-0092.00126

Healy, J., Nicholson, D., & Pekarek, A. (2017). Should we take the gig economy seriously? *Labour & Industry: A Journal of the Social and Economic Relations of Work*, *27*(3), 232–248. DOI: 10.1080/10301763.2017.1377048

Heidar, A., Navimpour, N. J., & Unal, M. (2022). Applications of blockchain in smart cities: A comprehensive review. *Sustainable Cities and Society*, *76*, 103366. DOI: 10.1016/j.scs.2021.103366

Henao, J. J., Mejía, J. F., Rendón, A. M., & Salazar, J. F. (2020). Sub-kilometer dispersion simulation of a CO tracer for an inter-Andean urban valley. *Atmospheric Pollution Research*, *11*(5), 928–945. DOI: 10.1016/j.apr.2020.02.005

Hennekam, S., & Bennett, D. (2017). Creative industries work across multiple contexts: Common themes and challenges. *Personnel Review*, *46*(1), 68–85. DOI: 10.1108/PR-08-2015-0220

Hernandez-de-Menendez, M., Escobar Díaz, C., & Morales-Menendez, R. (2019). Technologies for the future of learning: State of the art. [IJIDeM]. *International Journal on Interactive Design and Manufacturing*, *14*(2), 683–695. DOI: 10.1007/s12008-019-00640-0

Hickman, R., Chen, L. C., Chow, A., & Saxena, S. (2015). Improving Interchanges in China: The Experiential Phenomenon. ScienceDirect. *Journal of Transport Geography*, *42*(January), 175–186. DOI: 10.1016/j.jtrangeo.2014.12.004

Hill, D. (2012). Foreword. In Hyde, R. (Ed.), *Future Practice: Conversations from the edge of architecture* (pp. 6–15). Routledge.

Hine, J., & Scott, J. (2000, July). Seamless, Accessible Travel: Users' Views of The Public Transport Journey And Interchange. *Transport Policy*, *7*(3), 217–226. DOI: 10.1016/S0967-070X(00)00022-6

Hinestroza-Ramirez, J. E., Lopez-Restrepo, S., Yarce Botero, A., Segers, A., Rendon-Perez, A. M., Isaza-Cadavid, S., Heemink, A., & Quintero, O. L. (2023). Improving Air Pollution Modelling in Complex Terrain with a Coupled WRF–LOTOS–EUROS Approach: A Case Study in Aburrá Valley, Colombia. *Atmosphere (Basel), 14*(4), 738. Advance online publication. DOI: 10.3390/atmos14040738

Hinestroza-Ramirez, J. E., Rengifo-Castro, J. D., Quintero, O. L., Yarce Botero, A., & Rendon-Perez, A. M. (2023). Non-Parametric and Robust Sensitivity Analysis of the Weather Research and Forecast (WRF) Model in the Tropical Andes Region. *Atmosphere (Basel), 14*(4), 686. Advance online publication. DOI: 10.3390/atmos14040686

Hinestroza-Ramirez, J. E., Soto Barbosa, J. E., Yarce Botero, A., Suárez Higuita, D. A., Lopez-Restrepo, S., Cruz Ruiz, L. M., Solorzano Araque, V., Céspedes, A., Lorduy Hernandez, S., Caceres, R., Jiménez-Sánchez, G., & Quintero, O. L. (2023). Evaluation of the 3DVAR Operational Implementation of the Colombian Air Force for Aircraft Operations: A Case Study. *Climate (Basel), 11*(7), 153. Advance online publication. DOI: 10.3390/cli11070153

Hnatyuk, V., Pshenychna, N., Kara, S., Kolodii, V., & Yaroshchuk, L. (2024). Education's role in fostering environmental awareness and advancing sustainable development within a holistic framework. *Multidisciplinary Reviews, 7.*

Holland, J., & Holland, J. (2014). Implications of Shifting Technology in Education. *TechTrends, 58*(3), 16–25. DOI: 10.1007/s11528-014-0748-3

Hong, A., Nam, C., & Kim, S. (2020). Estimating the potential financial risk of smart homes: A case study in South Korea. *Sustainability, 12*(17), 6947. DOI: 10.3390/su12176947

Hongisto, V., Mäkilä, M., & Suokas, M. (2015). Satisfaction with sound insulation in residential dwellings – The effect of wall construction. *Building and Environment, 85*, 309–320. DOI: 10.1016/j.buildenv.2014.12.010

Hoyos-Restrepo, M., & Montilla-Rosero, E. (2021). Development and Validation of a Scanning Depolarization Lidar System for Studying Urban Aerosols in a Tropical Valley. In *European Lidar Conference (ELC).*

Hoyos-Restrepo, M., & Montilla-Rosero, E. (2022). *Measurements of urban aerosol properties by developing a scanning depolarization lidar system*. Universidad EAFIT.

Hubert, M., Blut, M., Brock, C., Zhang, R. W., Koch, V., & Riedl, R. (2018). Acceptance of smart home technologies: An empirical investigation. *Journal of Business Research, 94*, 295–304. DOI: 10.1016/j.jbusres.2018.01.002

Hui, C. X., Dan, G., Alamri, S., & Toghraie, D. (2023). Greening smart cities: An investigation of the integration of urban natural resources and smart city technologies for promoting environmental sustainability. *Sustainable Cities and Society*, *99*, 104985. DOI: 10.1016/j.scs.2023.104985

Hunt, A., & Watkiss, P. (2011). Climate change impacts and adaptation in cities: A review of the literature. *Climatic Change*, *104*(1), 13–49. DOI: 10.1007/s10584-010-9975-6

Ibem, E. O., Ayo-Vaughan, E. A., Oluwunmi, A. O., & Alagbe, O. A. (2018). Residential Satisfaction Among Low-Income Earners in Government Subsidized Housing Estates in Ogun State, Nigeria. *Urban Forum, 30*(1), 75–96.

Ibrahim, A. N. H., Borhan, M. N., & Yusoff, Md. N.I. & Ismail, A. (2020). Rail-Based Public Transport Service Quality and User Satisfaction – A Literature Review. *Promet – Traffic & Transportation*, Vol. 32, 2020, No. 3, 435-447. https://doi.org/ DOI: 10.7307/ptt.v32i3.3270

Ibrahim, A. N. H., Borhan, M. N., Osman, M. H., Khairuddin, F. H., & Zakaria, N. M. (2022). An Empirical Study of Passengers' Perceived Satisfaction with Monorail Service Quality: Case of Kuala Lumpur, Malaysia. *Sustainability (Basel)*, *14*(11), 6496. DOI: 10.3390/su14116496

IdeasXChange. (2017, March 6). *Urban mining in Japan*. https://ideasxchange.org/2017/03/06/urban-mining-in-japan/

IEA. (2021). Global Energy Review 2021. International Energy Agency. Paris https://www.iea.org/reports/global-energy-review-2021, Licence: CC BY 4.0

Ikevuje, A. H., Anaba, D. C., & Iheanyichukwu, U. T.Augusta Heavens IkevujeDavid Chinalu AnabaUche Thankgod Iheanyichukwu. (2024). Exploring sustainable finance mechanisms for green energy transition: A comprehensive review and analysis. *Finance & Accounting Research Journal*, *6*(7), 1224–1247. DOI: 10.51594/farj.v6i7.1314

Infante-Perea, M., Román-Onsalo, M., & Navarro-Astor, E. (2018). Expected career barriers in building engineering: Does gender matter? *Journal of Women and Minorities in Science and Engineering*, *24*(1), 43–59. DOI: 10.1615/JWomenMinorScienEng.2017018301

International Renewable Energy Agency (IRENA). (2020). *Renewables in cities: 2020 global status report*. International Renewable Energy Agency. https://www.irena.org/ /media/Files/IRENA/Agency/Publication/2020/Oct/IRENA_Renewables_in_cities_2020.pdf

International Telecommunication Union. (2016). Smart sustainable cities: An ITU perspective. ITU-T Focus Group on Smart Sustainable Cities. https://www.itu.int/en/ITU-T/focusgroups/ssc/Pages/default.aspx

Inza-Aguirre, A. (2014). Estudio de series temporales y composición química del material particulado atmosférico en distintas áreas del país vasco. *Phd Thesis.* Universidad del País Vasco. https://addi.ehu.es/handle/10810/12248

IPCC. (2021). *Climate Change 2021: The Physical Science Basis.* IPCC Sixth Assessment Report. https://www.ipcc.ch/report/ar6/wg1/

Isa, A., & Yusoff, Z. (2015). State of physical facilities of higher education institutions in Nigeria. *International Journal of Scientific and Research Publications*, *5*(4), 1–5.

Islam, I. N. (2016). Human resource management practices : Architects' perception and job satisfaction. *International Journal of Ethics in Social Sciences*, *4*(1), 89–102.

Ismagilova, E., Hughes, L., Dwivedi, Y. K., & Raman, K. R. (2019). Smart cities: Advances in research—An information systems perspective. *International Journal of Information Management*, *47*, 88–100. DOI: 10.1016/j.ijinfomgt.2019.01.004

Jaakkola, E. (2020). Designing conceptual articles: Four approaches. *AMS Review*, *10*(1–2), 18–26. DOI: 10.1007/s13162-020-00161-0

Jacobson, M. Z. (1997). Development and application of a new air pollution modeling system—II. Aerosol module structure and design. *Atmospheric Environment*, *31*(2), 131–144. DOI: 10.1016/1352-2310(96)00202-6

Jaenicke, R. (2001). Ernö Mészáros: Fundamentals of Atmospheric Aerosol Chemistry. *Journal of Atmospheric Chemistry*, *39*(1), 99–103. DOI: 10.1023/A:1010753724116

Jalal, A. (2023). Smart Cities: Integrating Technology for Sustainable and Efficient Urban Development. *Liberal Journal of Language and Literature Review*, *1*(01), 92–102.

Jamieson, C. (2011). The future for architects? Building Futures. *RIBA Building Futures*. Retrieved from http://www.buildingfutures.org.uk

Janhunen, E., Leskinen, N., & Junnila, S. (2020). The economic viability of a progressive smart building system with power storage. *Sustainability (Basel)*, *12*(15), 5998. DOI: 10.3390/su12155998

Jiménez-Castillo, D., & Sánchez-Fernández, R. (2019). The role of digital influencers in brand recommendation: Examining their impact on engagement, expected value, and purchase intention. *International Journal of Information Management*, *49*, 366–376. DOI: 10.1016/j.ijinfomgt.2019.07.009

Ji, W., & Chan, E. H. W. (2019). Smart home energy management systems: A review of technologies and applications. *Renewable & Sustainable Energy Reviews*, *109*, 112–123. DOI: 10.1016/j.rser.2019.04.016

Joan, R. (2013). Flexible Learning As New Learning Design In Classroom Process To Promote Quality Education. *I-Manager's Journal on School Educational Technology*, *9*(1), 37–42. DOI: 10.26634/jsch.9.1.2401

Johnson, L., Becker, S. A., & Cummins, M.. (2016). *NMC horizon report: 2016 higher education edition*. The New Media Consortium.

Joyce, M., & Dunn, R. (2009). A Proposed Methodology For Measuring Public Transport Accessibility To Employment Sites In The Auckland CBD. Retrieved from https://www.researchgate.net/publication/254609293_A_proposed_methodology_for_measuring_public_transport_accessibility_to_employment_sites_in_the_Auckland_CBD

Karagulian, F., Barbiere, M., Kotsev, A., Spinelle, L., Gerboles, M., Lagler, F., Redon, N., Crunarie, S., & Borowiak, A. (2019). Review of the Performance of Low-Cost Sensors for Air Quality Monitoring. *Atmosphere (Basel)*, *506*(10), 506. DOI: 10.3390/atmos10090506

Karn, R., Bhandari, B., & Jha, N. (2012). Original Article Practices of Personal Hygiene and Sanitation in a village. *Journal of Nobel Medical College*, *1*(2). Advance online publication. DOI: 10.3126/jonmc.v1i2.7298

Karthik, S. A., Naga, S. B. V., Satish, G., Shobha, N., Bhargav, H. K., & Chandrakala, B. M. (2025). AI and IoT-Infused Urban Connectivity for Smart Cities. In *Future of Digital Technology and AI in Social Sectors* (pp. 367–394). IGI Global.

Kasai, S., Li, N., & Fang, D. (2015). A system-of-systems approach to understanding urbanization–state of the art and prospect. *Smart and Sustainable Built Environment*, *4*(2), 154–171. DOI: 10.1108/SASBE-07-2014-0038

Kaziev, K. V., Sherstobitova, A. A., & Kazieva, B. V. (2020). University IT infrastructure in the context of evolutionary transformations of the digital economy. *Personality Society*, *1*(1), 12–19. DOI: 10.46502/issn.2712-8024/2020.1.2

Kennedy, C., Cuddihy, J., & Engel-Yan, J. (2007). The changing metabolism of cities. *Journal of Industrial Ecology*, *11*(2), 43–59. DOI: 10.1162/jie.2007.1107

Kerres, M. (2004). Beyond Learning Platforms: Infrastructures for the Digital Campus. In: *Proceedings of 6th International Conference on New Educational Environments (ICNEE04)*.

Khadka, K., & Maharjan, S. (2017). *Customer Satisfaction And Customer Loyalty*. Thesis. Centria University of Applied Sciences Pietarsaari. Retrieved from https://core.ac.uk/download/pdf/161421179.pdf

Khadka, N. (n.d). Service Quality: What it is + Top 5 Components. Online. Retrieved from https://www.questionpro.com/blog/service-quality/#:~:text=What%20is%20Service%20Quality%3F,quality%20is%20a%20valuable%20art

Khadka, U., Hossain, S., Sarkar, S., & Khan, N. (2024). Cyber-Physical Systems and IoT: Transforming Smart Cities for Sustainable Development. *AIJMR-Advanced International Journal of Multidisciplinary Research, 2*(5).

Khalid, U. A., Bachok, S., Osman, M. M., & Ibrahim, M. (2014). User Perceptions of Rail Public Transport Services in Kuala Lumpur, Malaysia: KTM Komuter. *Procedia: Social and Behavioral Sciences, 153*, 566–573. DOI: 10.1016/j.sbspro.2014.10.089

Khan, J. A., Raman, A. M., Sambamoorthy, N., & Prashanth, K. (2023). *Research Methodology (Methods, Approaches And Techniques)*. San International Scientific Publications., DOI: 10.59646/rmmethods/040

Khatoun, R., & Zeadally, S. (2016). Smart cities: Concepts, architectures, research opportunities. *Communications of the ACM, 59*(8), 46–57. DOI: 10.1145/2858789

Khekare, G., Khetan, U., & Doshi, P. N. (2025). Artificial Intelligence (AI)-Driven Traffic Solutions: Enhancing Green Transportation Through Predictive Analytics and Deep Learning. In *Driving Green Transportation System Through Artificial Intelligence and Automation: Approaches, Technologies and Applications* (pp. 319–334). Springer.

Khider, K. H. (2024). The Impact of Innovation and Sustainable Development in Smart Cities. In *The Emerald Handbook of Smart Cities in the Gulf Region: Innovation, Development, Transformation, and Prosperity for Vision 2040* (pp. 171–180). Emerald Publishing Limited. DOI: 10.1108/978-1-83608-292-720241009

Khodeir, L. M., & Nessim, A. A. (2020). Changing skills for architecture students employability: Analysis of job market versus architecture education in Egypt. *Ain Shams Engineering Journal, 11*(3), 811–821. DOI: 10.1016/j.asej.2019.11.006

Kholiavko, N., Popelo, O., & Tulchynska, S. (2021). Priority directions of increasing the adaptivity of universities to the conditions of the digital economy. *Revista Tempos e Espaços Em Educação, 14*(33), e16383. DOI: 10.20952/revtee.v14i33.16383

Kim, Y., Soyata, T., & Behnagh, R. F. (2018). Towards Emotionally Aware AI Smart Classroom: Current Issues and Directions for Engineering and Education. *IEEE Access : Practical Innovations, Open Solutions*, *6*, 5308–5331. DOI: 10.1109/ACCESS.2018.2791861

Kitchin, R. (2014). The real-time city? Big data and smart urbanism. *GeoJournal*, *79*(1), 1–14. DOI: 10.1007/s10708-013-9516-8

Klett, J. D. (1985). Lidar inversion with variable backscatter/extinction ratios. *Applied Optics*, *24*(11), 1638–1643. https://doi.org/https://doi.org/10.1364/AO.24.001638. DOI: 10.1364/AO.24.001638 PMID: 18223768

Kolotouchkina, O., Ripoll González, L., & Belabas, W. (2024). Smart cities, digital inequalities, and the challenge of Inclusion. *Smart Cities*, *7*(6), 3355–3370. DOI: 10.3390/smartcities7060130

Kostina, S. N. (2021). Is the infrastructure of regional universities ready to meet the challenges of digital transformation? *University Management: Practice and Analysis*, *25*(3), 14–32. DOI: 10.15826/umpa.2021.03.024

Kovaleva, N. N., Eresko, P. V., Izotova, V. F., & Gafarov, Y. R. (2022). *Optimizing The Implementation Of University Digitalization Practices*. European Proceedings of Social and Behavioural Sciences., DOI: 10.15405/epsbs.2022.01.57

Krug, J. D., Dart, A., Witherspoon, C. L., Gilberry, J., Malloy, Q., Kaushik, S., & Vanderpool, R. W. (2017). Revisiting the size selective performance of EPA's high-volume total suspended particulate matter (Hi-Vol TSP) sampler. *Aerosol Science and Technology*, *51*(7), 868–878. DOI: 10.1080/02786826.2017.1316358 PMID: 32025079

Kubisch, A. C., Auspos, P., Taylor, S., & Dewar, T. (2013). Resident-Centered Community Building: What Makes It Different? *National Civic Review*, *102*(3), 61–71. DOI: 10.1002/ncr.21128

Kumar, A., Jimenez, R., Belalcázar, L. C., & Roja, N. Y. (2016). Application of WRF-Chem Model to Simulate PM10 Concentration over Bogotá. *Aerosol and Air Quality Research*, *16*(5), 1206–1221. DOI: 10.4209/aaqr.2015.05.0318

Kummitha, R. K. R. (2020). Smart cities and entrepreneurship: An agenda for future research. *Technological Forecasting and Social Change*, *149*, 119763. DOI: 10.1016/j.techfore.2019.119763

Laufer, M., Leiser, A., Deacon, B., Perrin de Brichambaut, P., Fecher, B., Kobsda, C., & Hesse, F. (2021). Digital higher education: A divider or bridge builder? Leadership perspectives on edtech in a COVID-19 reality. *International Journal of Educational Technology in Higher Education, 18*(1), 51. Advance online publication. DOI: 10.1186/s41239-021-00287-6 PMID: 34778538

Laughlin, C. (2021). Security challenges in the smart home: A systematic literature review. *Journal of Network and Computer Applications, 177*, 102964. DOI: 10.1016/j.jnca.2020.102964

Le, T.-V. ChuDuc, H., & Tran, Q. X. (2024). Optimized Integration of Renewable Energy in Smart Buildings: A Systematic Review from Scopus Data. *2024 9th International Conference on Applying New Technology in Green Buildings (ATiGB)*, 397–402.

Lee, J. H., Hancock, M. G., & Hu, M.-C. (2014). Towards an effective framework for building smart cities: Lessons from Seoul and San Francisco. *Technological Forecasting and Social Change, 89*, 80–99. DOI: 10.1016/j.techfore.2013.08.033

Lee, M. M., Lin, M. F. G., & Bonk, C. J. (2007). OOPS, Turning MIT Opencourseware into Chinese: An analysis of a community of practice of global translators. *International Review of Research in Open and Distance Learning, 8*(3). Advance online publication. DOI: 10.19173/irrodl.v8i3.463

Lees, L., Slater, T., & Wyly, E. (2008). *Gentrification* (1st ed.). Routledge., DOI: 10.4324/9780203940877

Lei, Z., Zhou, H., Hu, W., Deng, Q., Zhou, D., Liu, Z.-W., & Gao, X. (2020). 3-D Interactive Control Laboratory for Classroom Demonstration and Online Experimentation in Engineering Education. *IEEE Transactions on Education, 64*(3), 276–282. DOI: 10.1109/TE.2020.3041070

Leow, B. Y., & Krishnaswamy, J. A. (2021). Smart mobility in smart cities: Emerging challenges and opportunities. *Journal of Urban Technology, 28*(1–2), 167–185. DOI: 10.1080/10630732.2020.1824847

Lewinski, P. (2015). Effects of classroomsâ€™ architecture on academic performance in view of telic versus paratelic motivation: A review. *Frontiers in Psychology, 6*. Advance online publication. DOI: 10.3389/fpsyg.2015.00746 PMID: 26089812

Licina, D., Wargocki, P., Pyke, C., & Altomonte, S. (2021). The future of IEQ in green building certifications. *Buildings & Cities, 2*(1), 907–927. DOI: 10.5334/bc.148

Li, L., Liu, J., Cheng, B., & Li, X. (2016). Cybersecurity challenges in intelligent transportation systems. *IEEE Transactions on Intelligent Transportation Systems*, *17*(9), 2445–2456. DOI: 10.1109/TITS.2016.2524064

Lim, C., Kim, K. J., & Maglio, P. P. (2018). Smart cities with big data: Reference models, challenges, and considerations. *Cities (London, England)*, *82*, 86–99. DOI: 10.1016/j.cities.2018.04.011

Li, T., Yang, S., & Tan, M. (2019). Simulation and optimization of water supply and demand balance in Shenzhen: A system dynamics approach. *Journal of Cleaner Production*, *207*, 882–893. DOI: 10.1016/j.jclepro.2018.10.052

Liu, C., Xiao, Q., & Wang, B. (2008). An Ensemble-Based Four-Dimensional Variational Data Assimilation Scheme. Part I: Technical Formulation and Preliminary Test. *Monthly Weather Review*, *136*(9), 3363–3373. DOI: 10.1175/2008MWR2312.1

Lokhande, P. (2016). Garbage Collection Management System. *International Journal of Engineering and Computer Science*, *5*(11).

Lopez-Restrepo, S., Quintero, O., Segers, A., Rodríguez, M., Pinel, N., Posada-Marín, J., & Rendón, A. M. (2017). Challenges and opportunities for Open LOTOS-EUROS model to reproduce the Dynamics for Tropical Andes Domain. *CMAS Conference Proceedings*.

Lopez-Restrepo, S., Yarce, A., Pinel, N., Quintero, O. L., Segers, A., & Heemink, A. W. (2022). A Knowledge-Aided Robust Ensemble Kalman Filter Algorithm for Non-Linear and Non-Gaussian Large Systems. *Frontiers in Applied Mathematics and Statistics*, *8*, 830116. Advance online publication. DOI: 10.3389/fams.2022.830116

Luchkov, A., Korolev, A., & Kodabashyan, L. (2022). *The Architecture of Digital Enterprise in the University Infrastructure*. In: 2022 15th International Conference Management of large-scale system development (MLSD). IEEE. pp. 1-5. DOI: 10.1109/MLSD55143.2022.9934605

Lv, Y., & Sarker, M. N. I. (2024). Integrative approaches to urban resilience: Evaluating the efficacy of resilience strategies in mitigating climate change vulnerabilities. *Heliyon*, *10*(6), e28191. DOI: 10.1016/j.heliyon.2024.e28191 PMID: 38545232

MacArthur, E. (2019). Cities and circular economy for food. *Ellen MacArthur Found*, 1-66. https://www.ellenmacarthurfoundation.org/cities-and-a-circular-economy-for-food/overview

Machado-León, J. L., de Oña, R., Baouni, T., & de Oña, J. (2017). Railway transit services in Algiers: Priority improvement actions based on users perceptions. *Transport Policy*, *53*, 175–185. DOI: 10.1016/j.tranpol.2016.10.004

MacInnis, D. J. (2011). A Framework for Conceptual Contributions in Marketing. *Journal of Marketing, 75*(4), 136–154. DOI: 10.1509/jmkg.75.4.136

Mahajan, R., Gupta, P., & Singh, T. (2019). Massive Open Online Courses: Concept and Implications. *Indian Pediatrics, 56*(6), 489–495. DOI: 10.1007/s13312-019-1575-6 PMID: 31278230

Maina, J. J. (2018). Reliability of self-assessment questionnaire : Do architecture postgraduates students overestimate their employability skills? Feedback from graduates and employers. *GU Journal of Science, 6*(2), 71–81.

Maina, J. J., & Daful, C. K. (2017). Do they measure up? Architecture graduates' perception of acquired skills, employers' expectations and what is obtained. *Journal of Research in National Development, 15*(1), 165–174.

Mainkandan, P., Golla, S. D., & Gatikoppu, S. P. P. K. ChaithanyaPuttaparthi, S., & AchyuthNarahari, S. (2024). Early Flood Warning System using Machine Learning. *2024 5th International Conference on Smart Electronics and Communication (ICOSEC)*, 1088–1092.

Makvandi, M., Li, W., Li, Y., Wu, H., Khodabakhshi, Z., Xu, X., & Yuan, P. F. (2024). Advancing Urban Resilience Amid Rapid Urbanization: An Integrated Interdisciplinary Approach for Tomorrow's Climate-Adaptive Smart Cities—A Case Study of Wuhan, China. *Smart Cities, 7*(4), 2110–2130. DOI: 10.3390/smartcities7040084

Malik, K., & Thakur, R. R. (2010). Creating value through IT – emerging patterns in brick-and-mortar b-schools. *International Journal of Innovation in Education, 1*(2), 148. DOI: 10.1504/IJIIE.2010.036857

Mandal, J., & Mohammed, I. A. (2024). Implementation of AI Transportation Routing in Reverse Logistics to Reduce CO2 Footprint. *International Journal of Supply Chain Management, 9*(5), 1–12. DOI: 10.47604/ijscm.3079

Manisalidis, I., Stavropoulou, E., Stavropoulos, A., & Bezirtzoglou, E. (2020). Environmental and Health Impacts of Air Pollution: A Review. In *Frontiers in Public Health* (Vol. 8). Frontiers Media S.A. DOI: 10.3389/fpubh.2020.00014

Manley, S., & De Graft-johnson, A. (2008). Women in Architecture Five years on. In Dainty, A. (Ed.), *Proceedings 24th Annual ARCOM Conference* (pp. 891–900). Cardiff, UK: Association of Researchers in Construction Management.

Margulies, A. H. (2004). A New Model for Open Sharing: Massachusetts Institute of Technology's OpenCourseWare Initiative Makes a Difference. *PLoS Biology, 2*(8), e200. DOI: 10.1371/journal.pbio.0020200 PMID: 15314645

Marsal-Llacuna, M.-L. (2020). The people's smart city dashboard (PSCD): Delivering on community-led governance with blockchain. *Technological Forecasting and Social Change, 158*, 120150. DOI: 10.1016/j.techfore.2020.120150

Matas, A. (2007). Demand And Revenue Implications of An Integrated Public Transport Policy: The Case Of Madrid. Transport Reviews. Vol. 24, 2004 - Issue 2 Pages 195-217. DOI: 10.1080/0144164032000107223

Matin, N. H., Eydgahi, A., & Gharipour, A. (2025). Sustainable Design: Minimizing Discomfort Glare Through Data-Driven Methods for Responsive Facades. *Sustainability (Basel), 17*(2), 783. Advance online publication. DOI: 10.3390/su17020783

Mazzetto, S. (2024). A Review of Urban Digital Twins Integration, Challenges, and Future Directions in Smart City Development. *Sustainability (Basel), 16*(19), 8337. DOI: 10.3390/su16198337

McAuliffe, G., Danner, M., Grothaus, T., & Doyle, L. (2008). Social inequality and social justice. *Culturally Alert Counseling: A Comprehensive Introduction*, 45–83.

McCracken, G. (1988). *The long interview*. Sage Publications. DOI: 10.4135/9781412986229

McFarlane, C. (2012). Rethinking informality: Politics, crisis, and the city. *Planning Theory & Practice, 13*(1), 89–108. DOI: 10.1080/14649357.2012.649951

McKinnon, A. (2010). Environmental sustainability. *Green Logistics: Improving the Environmental Sustainability of Logistics. London.*

McPhearson, P. T., Feller, M., Felson, A., Karty, R., Lu, J. W., Palmer, M. I., & Wenskus, T. (2010). Assessing the effects of the urban forest restoration effect of MillionTreesNYC on the STructure and functioning of NEW York City ecosystems. *Cities and the Environment, 3*(1), 1–21. DOI: 10.15365/cate.3172010 PMID: 21874148

Md Amin, N. D., Yip, C. F., Adnan, N. A., Sabil, A., & Noor Hisham, N. (2022). Simulation Study on Natural Lighting Projection Through Façade Optimisation for A Proposed Disaster and Relief Center. *IOP Conference Series. Earth and Environmental Science, 1022*(1), 012006. Advance online publication. DOI: 10.1088/1755-1315/1022/1/012006

Meerow, S., Newell, J. P., & Stults, M. (2016). Defining urban resilience: A review. *Landscape and Urban Planning, 147*, 38–49. DOI: 10.1016/j.landurbplan.2015.11.011

Mehmood, R., Katib, S. S. I., & Chlamtac, I. (2020). *Smart infrastructure and applications*. Springer International Publishing. DOI: 10.1007/978-3-030-13705-2

Meninato, P., & Marinic, G. (2024). Transforming Medellín: Architecture and urban design as agents of social change. *Journal of Architecture and Urbanism, 48*(1), 83–90. DOI: 10.3846/jau.2024.17793

Mishchenko, M. I., Travis, L., & Lacis, A. (2000). *Scattering, Absorption, and Emission of Light by Small Particles*. Cambridge University Press.

MITHUN, R., & Roopadarshini, S. (2024). *Technological Innovations and Renewable Integration in Smart Cities: Enhancing Sustainability, Governance, and Security.*

Mohammad Nasser AL-Arifi, T.AL-Arifi. (2023). Decorative aesthetic aspects and their use in Islamic architecture. *Al-Academy*, (107), 77–92. DOI: 10.35560/jcofarts107/77-92

Mohit, M. A., Ibrahim, M., & Rashid, Y. R. (2010). Assessment of residential satisfaction in newly designed public low-cost housing in Kuala Lumpur, Malaysia. *Habitat International, 34*(1), 18–27. DOI: 10.1016/j.habitatint.2009.04.002

Moh, J. (2012). *Design for Smart Transport: An Integrated Multi-Modal Transport Interchange in Central Christchurch*. Open Access Te Herenga Waka-Victoria University of Wellington.

Moná-Bedoya, W. (2022). *Airyx Skyspec - Instrumento Max-DOAS. Operating Manual*. Universidad EAFIT.

Moná-Bedoya, W., & Montilla-Rosero, E. (2023). *Determinación de la Densidad Óptica Diferencial de Columna de Gases Traza en el Valle de Aburrá Utilizando la Técnica MAX-DOAS. Report*. Universidad EAFIT.

Monin, A. S., & Obukhov, A. (1954). Basic laws of turbulent mixing in the surface layer of the atmosphere. *Contrib. Geophys. Inst. Acad, 6*(2).

Morrison, H., Curry, J. A., & Khvorostyanov, V. I. (2005). A New Double-Moment Microphysics Parameterization for Application in Cloud and Climate Models. Part I: Description. *Journal of the Atmospheric Sciences, 62*(6), 1665–1677. DOI: 10.1175/JAS3446.1

Mosteanu, N. R. (2020). Digital university campus–change the education system approach to meet the 21st century needs. *European Journal of Human Resource Management Studies, 4*(4), 79–93. DOI: 10.46827/ejhrms.v4i4.959

Mouwen, A. (2015). Drivers of customer satisfaction with public transport services. *Transportation Research Part A, Policy and Practice, 78*(August), 1–20. DOI: 10.1016/j.tra.2015.05.005

MRT. (2023). Kajang Line. Online. Retrieved from https://www.mymrt.com.my/projects/kajang-line/

MRT. (2023). Putrajaya Line. Online. Retrieved from https://www.mymrt.com.my/projects/putrajaya-line/#:~:text=The%20Putrajaya%20Line%20is%20the,Putrajaya%2C%20Malaysia's%20federal%20administrative%20centre

Mugion, R. G., Toni, M., Raharjo, H., Di Pietro, L., & Sebathu, S. P. (2018). Does the service quality of urban public transport enhance sustainable mobility? *Journal of Cleaner Production*, *174*, 1566–1587. DOI: 10.1016/j.jclepro.2017.11.052

Muhammad Das, A., Ladin, M. A., Ismail, A., & Rahmat, R. O. K. (2013). Consumers Satisfaction of Public Transport Monorail User In Kuala Lumpur. *Journal of Engineering Science and Technology.*, *8*(3), 272–283. https://www.researchgate.net/publication/286541188_Consumers_satisfaction_of_public_transport_monorail_user_in_Kuala_Lumpur

Mukim, M., & Roberts, M. (2023). *Policies for Promoting Green*. Resilient, and Inclusive Urban Development.

Müller, L. (2024). Driving Forces and Enablers for Universal Design in Urban Planning. *Studies in Health Technology and Informatics*, *320*, 287–294. DOI: 10.3233/SHTI241017 PMID: 39560252

Muller, M. (2018). Cape Town's drought: Don't blame climate change. *Nature*, *559*(7713), 174–176. DOI: 10.1038/d41586-018-05649-1 PMID: 29980735

Munonye, W. C., & Ajonye, G. O. (2024). *The Role of Urban Design in Facilitating a Circular Economy: From Linear to Regenerative Cities*.

Muñoz, J. L. R., Ojeda, F. M., & Jurado, D. L. A.. (2022). Systematic review of adaptive learning technology for learning in higher education. *Eurasian Journal of Educational Research*, *98*(98), 221–233.

Musa, M. F., & Ahmad, Z. (2012). Higher Education Physical Assets and Facilities. *Procedia: Social and Behavioral Sciences*, *50*, 472–478. DOI: 10.1016/j.sbspro.2012.08.051

Musiitwa, V. (2019). Obsolete? Relevance of the architect's role and the changing nature of the architectural profession. *Journal of Design Studio*, *1*(1), 45–53.

Mutambik, I. (2024). The sustainability of smart cities: Improving evaluation by combining mcda and promethee. *Land (Basel)*, *13*(9), 1471. DOI: 10.3390/land13091471

MyRapid. (2024). Ridership Archive. Online. Retrieved By https://myrapid.com.my/bus-train/ridership-archive/

Navarro-Astor, E., & Caven, V. (2012). Architects in Spain: A profession under risk. In Dainty, A. (Ed.), *Proceedings 28th Annual ARCOM Conference* (Vol. 1, pp. 577–587). Edinburgh, UK: Association of Researchers in Construction Management.

Nawaz, M. A., & Kaldeen, M. (2020). Impact of digital marketing on purchase intention. *International Journal of Advanced Research, 8*(4), 1254–1260. DOI: 10.21474/IJAR01/10887

Neirotti, P., De Marco, A., Cagliano, A. C., Mangano, G., & Scorrano, F. (2014). Current trends in Smart City initiatives: Some stylised facts. *Cities (London, England), 38*, 25–36. DOI: 10.1016/j.cities.2013.12.010

Nelson, H. G., & Stolterman, E. (2014). *The design way: Intentional change in an unpredictable world.* MIT press.

Németh, B., Issa, O., Diba, F., & Tuckett, A. (2020). Learning cities and learning communities: Analyzing contextual factors and their impacts on adult and lifelong learning in urban settings. *Andragoske Studije, 2*(2), 17–52. DOI: 10.5937/AndStud2001017N

Nguyen, D. (2018). The University in a World of Digital Technologies: Tensions and Challenges. *Australasian Marketing Journal, 26*(2), 79–82. DOI: 10.1016/j.ausmj.2018.05.012

Nieuwenhuijsen, M., & Khreis, H. (2018). Integrating Human Health into Urban and Transport Planning. In *Springer eBooks*. DOI: 10.1007/978-3-319-74983-9

Nikou, S. (2019). Factors driving the adoption of smart home technology: An empirical assessment. *Telematics and Informatics, 45*, 101283. DOI: 10.1016/j.tele.2019.101283

Ni, P., Kamiya, M., Shen, L., Gong, W., & Xu, H. (2019). Reviews of Global Urban Competitiveness 2017–2018 Driving Force, Agglomeration, Connectivity and the New Global City. *House Prices: Changing the City World: The Global Urban Competitiveness Report*, (2017–2018), 49–131. DOI: 10.1007/978-981-32-9111-9_2

NOAA. (2021). *Hurricane Costs*. National Oceanic and Atmospheric Administration. https://coast.noaa.gov/states/fast-facts/hurricane-costs.html

Noichan, R., & Dewancker, B. (2018). Analysis of Accessibility in an Urban Mass Transit Node: A Case Study in a Bangkok Transit Station. *Sustainability (Basel), 10*(12), 4819. DOI: 10.3390/su10124819

Nowak, D. J., Crane, D. E., & Stevens, J. C. (2006). Air pollution removal by urban trees and shrubs in the United States. *Urban Forestry & Urban Greening, 4*(3-4), 115–123. DOI: 10.1016/j.ufug.2006.01.007

NYC Environmental Protection. (2020). *NYC Green infrastructure 2020 annual report*. New York City Environmental Protection. https://www.nyc.gov

Obaidat, M. S., & Nicopolitidis, P. (2016). *Smart cities and homes*. Elsevier.

Obaidat, M. S., & Nicopolitidis, P. (2016). *Smart cities and homes: Key enabling technologies*. Morgan Kaufmann.

Oftedal, L. A. (2020). *National digital infrastructure for higher education*.

Okeke, N. I., Bakare, O. A., & Achumie, G. O.Njideka Ihuoma OkekeOluwaseun Adeola BakareGodwin Ozoemenam Achumie. (2024). Integrating policy incentives and risk management for effective green finance in emerging markets. *International Journal of Frontiers in Science and Technology Research, 7*(1), 76–88. DOI: 10.53294/ijfstr.2024.7.1.0050

Oke, T. R. (1982). The energetic basis of the urban heat island. *Quarterly Journal of the Royal Meteorological Society, 108*(455), 1–24. DOI: 10.1002/qj.49710845502

Okwandu, A. C., Akande, D. O., & Nwokediegwu, Z. Q. S.Azubuike Chukwudi OkwanduDorcas Oluwajuwonlo AkandeZamathula Queen Sikhakhane Nwokediegwu. (2024). Green architecture: Conceptualizing vertical greenery in urban design. *Engineering Science & Technology Journal, 5*(5), 1657–1677. DOI: 10.51594/estj.v5i5.1114

Olfindo, R. (2021). Transport accessibility, residential satisfaction, and moving intention in a context of limited travel mode choice. *Transportation Research Part A, Policy and Practice, 145*, 153–166. DOI: 10.1016/j.tra.2021.01.012

Oluwatayo, A. A. (2014). Employee architect's perception of human resource practices and their job satisfaction. *Built Environment Project and Asset Management, 5*(1), 89–102. DOI: 10.1108/BEPAM-04-2013-0008

Oña López, J. J. D., Oña López, R. D., Eboli, L., & Mazzulla, G. (2013). Perceived service quality in bus transit service: A structural equation approach.

Organisation for Economic Co-operation and Development. (n.d.). Smart cities and inclusive growth. OECD Publishing. https://www.oecd.org/cfe/cities/OECD_Policy_Paper_Smart_Cities_and_Inclusive_Growth.pdf

Oyedele, L. O. (2010). Sustaining architects' and engineers' motivation in design firms: An investigation of critical success factors. *Engineering, Construction, and Architectural Management, 17*(2), 180–196. DOI: 10.1108/09699981011024687

Oyedele, L. O. (2013). Analysis of architects' demotivating factors in design firms. *International Journal of Project Management, 31*(3), 342–354. DOI: 10.1016/j.ijproman.2012.11.009

Padmanabhan, S. (2024). Digital Transformation in Higher Education. *Advances in Educational Technologies and Instructional Design*, •••, 59–69. DOI: 10.4018/979-8-3693-0433-4.ch005

Papaioannou, D., & Martinez, L. M. (2015). The Role of Accessibility and Connectivity in Mode Choice. A Structural Equation Modeling Approach. *Transportation Research Procedia, 10*, 831–839. DOI: 10.1016/j.trpro.2015.09.036

Papargyropoulou, E., Lozano, R., Steinberger, J. K., & Wright, N., & bin Ujang, Z. (. (2014). The food waste hierarchy as a framework for the management of food surplus and food waste. *Journal of Cleaner Production, 76*, 106–115. DOI: 10.1016/j.jclepro.2014.04.020

Pardo, N., Avellaneda, J. D., Rausch, J., Jaramillo-Vogel, D., Gutiérrez, M., & Foubert, A. (2020). Decrypting silicic magma/plug fragmentation at Azufral crater lake, Northern Andes: Insights from fine to extremely fine ash morpho-chemistry. *Bulletin of Volcanology, 82*(12), 79. DOI: 10.1007/s00445-020-01418-z

Parekh, R., & Smith, C. (2024). Eco-friendly urban design: An analysis of sustainable building practices and their community impact. *World Journal of Advanced Research and Reviews, 23*(3), 2857–2864. DOI: 10.30574/wjarr.2024.23.3.2901

Park, E., Del Pobil, A. P., & Kwon, S. J. (2018). The role of Internet of Things (IoT) in smart cities: Technology roadmap-oriented approaches. *Sustainability (Basel), 10*(5), 1388. DOI: 10.3390/su10051388

Parra-Pulido, R. A., Hernández-Peña, Y. T., & Zafra-Mejía, C. A. (2024). Systematic Review of Dimensions and Indicators in Sustainable and Smart Cities: Trends, Interdependencies, and Continental Variations. *Urban Science (Basel, Switzerland), 8*(4), 202. DOI: 10.3390/urbansci8040202

Pastore, L., & Andersen, M. (2022). The influence of façade and space design on building occupants' indoor experience. *Journal of Building Engineering, 46*, 103663. Advance online publication. DOI: 10.1016/j.jobe.2021.103663

Patel, A., & Shah, P. (2021). Rethinking slums, cities, and urban planning: lessons from the COVID-19 pandemic. *Cities & Health, 5*(sup1), S145-S147.

Pawlasowa, P. (2015). *The Factors Influencing Satisfaction with Public City Transport: A Structural Equation Modelling Approach.* Online. Retrieved from https://pdfs.semanticscholar.org/fcb4/6fcd525ee3da344814edbb58cd2a5e07baa6.pdf

Pawłowski, A., & Rydzewski, P. (2024). Pathways to Carbon Neutrality: Integrating Energy Strategies, Policy, and Public Perception in the Face of Climate Change—A Global Perspective. *Energies*, *17*(23), 5867. DOI: 10.3390/en17235867

Petrichenko, L., Sauhats, A., Diahovchenko, I., & Segeda, I. (2022). Economic Viability of Energy Communities versus Distributed Prosumers. *Sustainability (Basel)*, *14*(8), 4634. DOI: 10.3390/su14084634

Pfeffer, T. (2011). *Virtualisation of universities: Digital media and the organisation of higher education institutions.* Springer Science & Business Media.

Pihlak, S., & Tuksam, S. (2019). Algorithmic craftsmanship for bespoke timber architecture. *Digital Wood Design: Innovative Techniques of Representation in Architectural Design*, 1439-1458.

Piketty, T. (2014). *Capital in the Twenty-First century.* Harvard University Press. DOI: 10.4159/9780674369542

*Planning for Rapid Urbanisation Survey of the Architectural Profession in the Commonwealth.* (2018). Commonwealth Association of Architects.

Pope, C. A.III. (2002). Lung Cancer, Cardiopulmonary Mortality, and Long-term Exposure to Fine Particulate Air Pollution. *Journal of the American Medical Association*, *287*(9), 1132. DOI: 10.1001/jama.287.9.1132 PMID: 11879110

Popova, O. I., Gagarina, N. M., & Karkh, D. A. (2020). *Digitalization of Educational Processes in Universities: Achievements and Problems.* Proceedings of the International Scientific Conference “Digitalization of Education: History, Trends and Prospects” (DETP 2020). DOI: 10.2991/assehr.k.200509.131

Qistina, N. (2023, January 27). Video shows the struggle pedestrians have to endure to get to MRT station in PJ. *Says*. Retrieved from https://says.com/my/news/struggle-pedestrians-have-to-endure-to-get-to-mrt-station

Quintero, O. L., Niño-Ruiz, E. D., & Pinel, N. (2020). On the mathematical modelling and data assimilation for air pollution assessment in the Tropical Andes. In *Environmental Science and Pollution Research* (Vol. 27, Issue 29, pp. 35993–36012). Springer. DOI: 10.1007/s11356-020-08268-4

Rabang-Alonzo, F. N. (2013). Employment status of architecture graduates of the University of Northern Philippines. *UNP Research Journal*, *XXII*, 96–109.

Radhamani, R., Sasidharakurup, H., & Kumar, D.. (2015). Role of Biotechnology simulation and remotely triggered virtual labs in complementing university education. *2015 International Conference on Interactive Mobile Communication Technologies and Learning (IMCL)*. DOI: 10.1109/IMCTL.2015.7359548

Rahman, B. Q. Y. A. (2024). The role of renewable energy in achieving sustainable Development. *Journal of Sustainable Studies, 6*(3 (3).

Raju, S. T. (2022, August 18). *Public transport is not the preferred choice of many*. The Sun. 2022. Retrieved from; https://www.thesundaily.my/local/public-transport-not-preferred-choice-of-many-GB9614181

Rane, N. L., Kaya, O., & Rane, J. (2024). Integrating internet of things, blockchain, and artificial intelligence techniques for intelligent industry solutions. *Artificial Intelligence, Machine Learning, and Deep Learning for Sustainable Industry, 5*.

Ranjazmay Azari, M., Bemanian, M., Mahdavinejad, M., Körner, A., & Knippers, J. (2023). Application-based principles of Islamic geometric patterns; state-of-the-art, and future trends in computer science/technologies: a review. In *Heritage Science* (Vol. 11, Issue 1). Springer Science and Business Media Deutschland GmbH. DOI: 10.1186/s40494-022-00852-w

Rausch, J., Grobéty, B., & Vonlanthen, P. (2015). Eifel maars: Quantitative shape characterization of juvenile ash particles (Eifel Volcanic Field, Germany). *Journal of Volcanology and Geothermal Research, 291*, 86–100. DOI: 10.1016/j.jvolgeores.2014.11.008

Rausch, J., Jaramillo-Vogel, D., Perseguers, S., Schnidrig, N., Grobéty, B., & Yajan, P. (2022). Automated identification and quantification of tire wear particles (TWP) in airborne dust: SEM/EDX single particle analysis coupled to a machine learning classifier. *The Science of the Total Environment, 803*, 149832. DOI: 10.1016/j.scitotenv.2021.149832 PMID: 34525712

Reeves, T. C., & Oh, E. (2008). Generational Differences. In Spector, J. M., Merrill, M. D., van Merrienboer, J., & Driscoll, M. P. (Eds.), *Handbook of Research on Educational Communications and Technology* (3rd ed., pp. 295–303). Taylor & Francis Group.

Remix. (2021). *8 Benefits of Public Transportation*. Retrieved from; https://www.remix.com/blog/8-benefits-of-public-transportation

ReportLinker. (2022). Global smart cities market to reach USD 2.8 trillion by 2027. https://www.reportlinker.com/p06285854

Rezende, D. A., Almeida, G. G. F., & Fumagalli, L. A. W. (2024). Strategic digital city: Multiple projects for sustainable urban management. *Sustainability (Basel), 16*(13), 5450. DOI: 10.3390/su16135450

Riazi, M., & Emami, A. (2018). Residential satisfaction in affordable housing: A mixed method study. *Cities (London, England), 82*, 1–9. DOI: 10.1016/j.cities.2018.04.013

Rios-Lugo & Hernández-Mendoza. H. (2020). Fundamentos teóricos de icp-ms y su importancia en el análisis de elementos tóxicos en agua subterránea. 14. 4-15. https://www.researchgate.net/publication/341310570_Fundamentos_teoricos_de_icp-ms_y_su_importancia_en_el_analisis_de_elementos_toxicos_en_agua_subterranea. *Report.*

Robertson, A., Cleaver, E., & Smart, F. (2019). *Beyond the metrics: Identifying, evidencing and enhancing the less tangible assets of higher education*. QAA Scotland.

Rodríguez-Abitia, G., & Bribiesca-Correa, G. (2021). Assessing Digital Transformation in Universities. *Future Internet, 13*(2), 52. DOI: 10.3390/fi13020052

Rojas González, L., & Montilla-Rosero, E. (2025). Evaluation of In-Situ Low-Cost Sensor Network in a Tropical Valley, Colombia. *Sensors (Basel), 25*(4), 1236. DOI: 10.3390/s25041236 PMID: 40006467

Rubin, V. (1998). The Roles of Universities in Comnunity-Building Initiatives. *Journal of Planning Education and Research, 17*(4), 302–311. DOI: 10.1177/0739456X9801700405

Ruiz-Vanoye, J. A., Díaz-Parra, O., Ruiz-Jaimes, M. A., Ortiz, J. A., Simancas-Acevedo, E., Rodriguez-Flores, J., Mireles, J. R. M., Xicoténcatl-Pérez, J. M., & Jimenez, M. A. V. (2025). The Role of Smart Cities in Creating Sustainable Urban Environments Through Strategies and Innovative Solutions. In *Interdisciplinary Approaches to Transportation and Urban Planning* (pp. 23–46). IGI Global.

Saaty, T. L. (1980). The analytic hierarchy process (AHP). *The Journal of the Operational Research Society, 41*(11), 1073–1076.

Saelens, B. E., & Handy, S. L. (2008, July). Built Environment Correlates of Walking: A Review. *Medicine and Science in Sports and Exercise, 40*(7, Suppl), S550–S566. DOI: 10.1249/MSS.0b013e31817c67a4 PMID: 18562973

Sage, R. (2023). *Tackling Tradition in Education*. Qeios., DOI: 10.32388/CDVBT5

Salleh, R., Md Yusoff, M. A., Harun, H., & Memon, M. A. (2015). Gauging industry's perspectives on soft skills of graduate architects : Importance vs satisfaction. *Global Business and Management Research, 7*(2), 95–102.

Salleh, R., Md Yusof, M. A., & Memon, M. A. (2016). Attributes of graduate architects: An industry perspective. *Social Sciences, 11*(5), 551–556. DOI: 10.3923/sscience.2016.551.556

Sampson, R. J. (2012). *Great American city: Chicago and the enduring neighborhood effect*. University of Chicago Press. DOI: 10.7208/chicago/9780226733883.001.0001

Sang, K. J. C., Dainty, A. R. J., & Ison, S. G. (2007). Gender: A risk factor for occupational stress in the architectural profession? *Construction Management and Economics, 25*(12), 1305–1317. DOI: 10.1080/01446190701546177

Sang, K. J. C., Dainty, A. R. J., & Ison, S. G. (2008). The impact of self-employment on architect's job satisfaction. In Dainty, A. (Ed.), *Proceedings 24th Annual ARCOM Conference* (Vol. 1, pp. 13–22). Cardiff, UK: Association of Researchers in Construction Management.

Sang, K. J. C., Dainty, A. R. J., & Ison, S. G. (2014). Gender in the UK architectural profession: (re)producing and challenging hegemonic masculinity. *Work, Employment and Society, 28*(2), 247–264. DOI: 10.1177/0950017013491306

Sang, K. J. C., Ison, S. G., & Dainty, A. R. J. (2009). The job satisfaction of UK architects and relationships with work-life balance and turnover intentions. *Engineering, Construction, and Architectural Management, 16*(3), 288–300. DOI: 10.1108/09699980910951681

Sargent, M. (2015). Wall to wall. *Nursery World,* 2015(Sup10), 16–18. DOI: 10.12968/nuwa.2015.Sup10.16

Sargsyan, T. (2024). *Sustainable urban development policies and practices in the United States*.

Sasano, Y., & Nakane, H. (1984). Significance of the extinction/backscatter ratio and the boundary value term in the solution for the two-component lidar equation. *Applied Optics, 23*(1), 11–13. DOI: 10.1364/AO.23.0011_1 PMID: 20407534

Satterthwaite, D. (2011). How urban societies can adapt to resource shortage and climate change. *Philosophical Transactions of the Royal Society A: Mathematical, Physical and Engineering Sciences, 369*(1942), 1762-1783.

Savickas, M. L. (2006). Career construction theory. *Encyclopedia of Career Development*, 85–88.

Savitri, C., Hurriyati, R., Wibowo, L. A., & Hendrayati, H. (2022). The role of digital marketing in influencing purchase intention: A study on e-commerce platforms. *The Journal of Business and Retail Management Research, 16*(2), 45–53.

Schachter, E. N., Moshier, E., Habre, R., Rohr, A., Godbold, J., Nath, A., Grunin, A., Coull, B., Koutrakis, P., & Kattan, M. (2016). Outdoor air pollution and health effects in urban children with moderate to severe asthma. *Air Quality, Atmosphere & Health, 9*(3), 251–263. DOI: 10.1007/s11869-015-0335-6

Schill, M., Godefroit-Winkel, D., Diallo, M. F., & Barbarossa, C. (2019). Consumers' intentions to purchase smart home objects: The role of environmental concern and technological innovativeness. *Journal of Business Research, 103*, 541–553. DOI: 10.1016/j.jbusres.2019.02.026

Schmidt, J. T., & Tang, M. (2020). Digitalization in Education: Challenges, Trends and Transformative Potential. *Führen Und Managen in Der Digitalen Transformation,* 287–312. DOI: 10.1007/978-3-658-28670-5_16

Scholl, K. G., & Gulwadi, G. B. (2015). Recognising campus landscapes as learning spaces. *Journal of Learning Spaces, 4*(1), 53–60.

Schwaen, R., Sarpaneva, P., & Alenjery, N.. (2018). Bricks and books: Reinventing the teaching of architectural history and theory. In: *National Conference on the Beginning Design Student.*

Seinfeld, J. H., & Pandis, S. N. (2006). Atmospheric Chemistry and Physics. In *Air Pollution to Climate Change* (2nd ed.). John Wiley & Sons.

Setiawan, T., Samith, M. F., & Mughits, M. H. (2024). Urban Resilience: Navigating Challenges and Opportunities in Indonesia. [SSHJ]. *Social Science and Humanities Journal, 8*(12), 5965–5984. DOI: 10.18535/sshj.v8i12.1491

Seto, K. C., Guneralp, B., & Hutyra, L. R. (2012). Global forecasts of urban expansion to 2030 and direct impacts on biodiversity and carbon pools. *Proceedings of the National Academy of Sciences of the United States of America, 109*(40), 16083–16088. DOI: 10.1073/pnas.1211658109 PMID: 22988086

Sferrazza, A. (2018). The Nature of the Space: Walls to Bridges as Transformative Learning. *Engaged Scholar Journal: Community-Engaged Research, Teaching, and Learning, 4*(1), 241–250. DOI: 10.15402/esj.v4i1.321

Shah, V. M., & Shah, D. (2023). Impact of digitalisation in education-a literature review analysis. *Towards Excellence,* 15(2), 333–343. Internet Archive. DOI: 10.37867/TE150234

Shannon, S. J. (2012). "I wish for more than I ever get": Employers' perspectives on employability attributes of architecture graduates. *Creative Education, 03*(06), 1016–1023. DOI: 10.4236/ce.2012.326153

Shannon, S. J., Webb, N., Zeng, Y., & Holder, J. (2014). Why architecture graduates do not register as architects: A quantitative and qualitative South Australian study 1999-2011. *Creative Education, 05*(16), 1540–1558. DOI: 10.4236/ce.2014.516171

Shanthana, L. S., & Gupta, P. (2021). Adoption of smart home technologies: An empirical study using UTAUT2. *International Journal of Business Information Systems, 38*(3), 321–341. DOI: 10.1504/IJBIS.2021.119123

Sharma, A., Iyer, G. R., Mehrotra, A., & Krishnan, R. (2010). Sustainability and business-to-business marketing: A framework and implications. *Industrial Marketing Management, 39*(2), 330–341. DOI: 10.1016/j.indmarman.2008.11.005

Sharma, R. S. (2015). Role of universities in development of civil society and social transformation. In: *Proceedings of International Academic Conferences*. International Institute of Social and Economic Sciences.

Shekhar. C. (2024). Sustainable Tourism Development: Balancing Economic Growth And Environmental Conservation. *Available at* SSRN *4901174*.

Shiau, W. L., & Luo, M. M. (2012, November). Factors affecting online group buying intention and satisfaction: A social exchange theory perspective. *Computers in Human Behavior, 28*(6), 2431–2444. DOI: 10.1016/j.chb.2012.07.030

Shill, H. B., & Tonner, S. (2003). Creating a Better Place: Physical Improvements in Academic Libraries, 1995–2002. *College & Research Libraries, 64*(6), 431–466. DOI: 10.5860/crl.64.6.431

Shin, J., & Lee, S. (2018). Adoption of smart homes: A technology acceptance model perspective. *International Journal of Human-Computer Interaction, 34*(12), 1131–1142. DOI: 10.1080/10447318.2018.1426899

Shuhaiber, A., & Mashal, I. (2019). Understanding users' acceptance of smart homes. *Technology in Society, 58*, 101110. DOI: 10.1016/j.techsoc.2019.01.003

Silva, B. N., Khan, M., & Han, K. (2018). Towards sustainable smart cities: A review of trends, architectures, components, and open challenges in smart cities. *Sustainable Cities and Society, 38*, 697–713. DOI: 10.1016/j.scs.2018.01.053

Singh, J., Steele, K., & Singh, L. (2021). Combining the Best of Online and Face-to-Face Learning: Hybrid and Blended Learning Approach for COVID-19, Post Vaccine, & Post-Pandemic World. *Journal of Educational Technology Systems, 50*(2), 140–171. DOI: 10.1177/00472395211047865

Singla, A. (2024). The economics of climate change: Assessing the costs and benefits of mitigation and adaptation strategies. *Shodh Sagar Journal of Commerce and Economics, 1*(1), 18–23. DOI: 10.36676/ssjce.v1.i1.04

Sinha, K., Sinha, S., & Shrivastava, V. (2024). A Study of Social Equity in Urban Spaces: Insights from Recent Urban Development Projects and Government Schemes in India. *Library of Progress-Library Science, Information Technology & Computer, 44*(3).

Sivakarthi, G., Gobinath, A., Abikannan, P. R., Balasubramani, T., Baranisri, K., Melba, J. E., & Harinisri, T. R. SanthoshKumar, V., & Devi, C. M. (2024). Intelligent Street Light Management and Monitoring System with IoT Integration. *2024 15th International Conference on Computing Communication and Networking Technologies (ICCCNT)*, 1–6.

Smart, F., Cleaver, E., & Robertson, A. (2020). Beyond the metrics: The importance of intangible assets in the HE context. *Journal of Perspectives in Applied Academic Practice, 8*(2), 3–6. DOI: 10.14297/jpaap.v8i2.432

Smith, N. (2016). Book Interview: Making sense of bricks and mortar. *Engineering & Technology, 11*(5), 84–85. DOI: 10.1049/et.2016.0528

Sokolova, M. V., Fath, B. D., Grande, U., Buonocore, E., & Franzese, P. P. (2024). The Role of Green Infrastructure in Providing Urban Ecosystem Services: Insights from a Bibliometric Perspective. *Land (Basel), 13*(10), 1664. DOI: 10.3390/land13101664

Sommer, F., Dietze, V., Baum, A., Sauer, J., Gilge, S., Maschowski, C., & Gieré, R. (2018). Tire Abrasion as a Major Source of Microplastics in the Environment. *Aerosol and Air Quality Research, 18*(8), 2014–2028. DOI: 10.4209/aaqr.2018.03.0099

Song, M., Berends, H., Van Der Bij, H., & Weggeman, M. (2006). The Effect of IT and Co-location on Knowledge Dissemination. *Journal of Product Innovation Management,* 24(1), 52–68. Portico. DOI: 10.1111/j.1540-5885.2006.00232.x

Spurk, D., & Straub, C. (2020). Flexible employment relationships and careers in times of the COVID-19 pandemic. *Journal of Vocational Behavior, 119*(May), 1–4. DOI: 10.1016/j.jvb.2020.103435 PMID: 32382161

Srirangam, S., Chun, L. W., Mari, T. S., & Gunasagaran, S. (2022). *CHILDREN'S SAFETY: THE COMMON SPACES IN PPR HOUSING IN KUALA LUMPUR.*

Statista. (2019). Smart cities ranking worldwide in 2019. https://www.statista.com/statistics/1053441/smart-cities-ranking-worldwide/

Statista. (2021). Smart home market revenue worldwide 2017–2025. https://www.statista.com/statistics/1100922/smart-home-market-revenue-worldwide/

Strengers, Y., Kennedy, J., Abu Bakar, A., & Nicholls, L. (2022). Digital literacy and smart home technology: Challenges for older adults. *Journal of Consumer Culture*, *22*(3), 672–690. DOI: 10.1177/14695405211016031

Sturges, J. (2013). A matter of time: Young professionals' experiences of long work hours. *Work, Employment and Society*, *27*(2), 343–359. DOI: 10.1177/0950017012460318

Su, K., Li, J., & Fu, H. (2011). Smart city and the applications. *2011 International Conference on Electronics, Communications and Control (ICECC)*, 1028–1031. DOI: 10.1109/ICECC.2011.6066743

Sullivan, S. E., & Al Ariss, A. (2021). Making sense of different perspectives on career transitions: A review and agenda for future research. *Human Resource Management Review*, *31*(1), 100727. Advance online publication. DOI: 10.1016/j.hrmr.2019.100727

Summerfield, R. (2022). Hybrid working can help recruit and retain talent, upskill leaders and boost team working, suggests a case study from an international professional services firm. *Strategic HR Review*, *21*(1), 34–40. https://doi.org/https://doi.org/10.1108/SHR-11-2021-0060. DOI: 10.1108/SHR-11-2021-0060

Sun, Y. (2024). Sustainable Smart Cities Planning in Conjunction with Environment Governance. *Advances in Economics. Management and Political Sciences*, *112*, 62–69.

Susskind, R., & Susskind, D. (2015). *The Future of The Profession: How Technology will Transform the Work of Human Experts* (1st ed.). Oxford University Press. DOI: 10.1093/oso/9780198713395.001.0001

Suzuki, H., Cervero, R., & Iuchi, K. (2013). *Transforming cities with transit: Transit and land-use integration for sustainable urban development.* World Bank Publications.

Tabassum, M., Kusiak, A., & Wang, J. (2019). Privacy and security in smart homes: A review. *IEEE Access : Practical Innovations, Open Solutions*, *7*, 153665–153678. DOI: 10.1109/ACCESS.2019.2948897

Tan, V. (2022, July 9). Commuters In Malaysia's Klang Valley Are Addicted To Their Cars. What Can Be Done To Encourage Use Of Public Transport? *Channel News Asia*. Retrieved from https://www.channelnewsasia.com/asia/malaysia-klang-valley-cars-traffic-congestion-encourage-public-transport-use-rail-lrt-mrt-ktm-2794391

TechTarget. (2024). *SPSS (Statistical Package for the Social Sciences)*. Online. Retrieved from https://www.techtarget.com/whatis/definition/SPSS-Statistical-Package-for-the-Social-Sciences

Teixeira, J., Zuazua-Ros, A., Jesus, M., Rangel, B., & Sofia Guimarães, A. (2023). *How 3DPC Will Transform Architectural Design. In 3D Printing for Construction with Alternative Materials*. Springer International Publishing.

Terziradeva, I. (2018). Sensor technologies for smart city applications. *2018 International Conference on Smart City and Emerging Technology (ICSCET)*, 1–5. https://doi.org/DOI: 10.1109/ICSCET.2018.8537372

Thomas, M. A. (2017). On The Benefits of Affordable Housing. *Table de Quartier Sud de L'Ouest-De-L'Île.*

Tiwary, A., & Kumar, P. (2014). Impact evaluation of green–grey infrastructure interaction on built-space integrity: An emerging perspective to urban ecosystem service. *The Science of the Total Environment*, *487*, 350–360. DOI: 10.1016/j.scitotenv.2014.03.032 PMID: 24793331

Topchiy, I., & Fatkullina, A. (2019). Career Guidance of Architects in the System of Continuous Education. *The Annual International Conference on Cognitive-Social, and Behavioural Sciences*, 285–293. https://doi.org/https://doi.org/10.15405/epsbs.2019.12.02.34

Transparency International. (2021). *Corruption Perceptions Index 2021*. Transparency International. https://www.transparency.org/en/cpi/2021

Tyrinopoulos, Y., & Antoniou, C. (2008). Public transit user satisfaction: Variability and policy implications. *Transport Policy*, *15*(4), 260–272. DOI: 10.1016/j.tranpol.2008.06.002

Tzoulas, K., Korpela, K., Venn, S., Yli-Pelkonen, V., Kaźmierczak, A., Niemela, J., & James, P. (2007). Promoting ecosystem and human health in urban areas using Green Infrastructure: A literature review. *Landscape and Urban Planning*, *81*(3), 167–178. DOI: 10.1016/j.landurbplan.2007.02.001

Ullah, A., Quddusi, S. A., & Haider, I. (2024). *Incorporation of Artificial Intelligence in Enhancing Quality of Life in Smart Cities.*

Ullah, F., Qayyum, S., Thaheem, M. J., Al-Turjman, F., & Sepasgozar, S. M. E. (2021). Risk management in smart cities: A systematic literature review. *Sustainable Cities and Society*, *74*, 103225. DOI: 10.1016/j.scs.2021.103225

UNE Normalización Española. (2006). UNE-EN 14907:2006. Calidad del aire ambiente. método gravimétrico de medida para la determinación de la fracción másica pm2.5 de la materia particulada en suspensión.*Report.*

UNEP. (2023). *Annual Report: Climate Action.* https://www.unep.org/resources/annual-report-2023

UN-Habitat. (2020). *World Cities Report 2020: The Value of Sustainable Urbanization.* UN. https://unhabitat.org/world-cities-report-2020-the-value-of-sustainable-urbanization

United Nations Environment Programme. (2018). Global status report 2018: Towards a zero-emission, efficient and resilient buildings and construction sector. https://www.unenvironment.org/resources/report/global-status-report-2018

United Nations Habitat. (2020). World cities report 2020: The value of sustainable urbanization. https://unhabitat.org/sites/default/files/2020/10/wcr_2020_report.pdf

United Nations. (2015). *Transforming our world: The 2030 Agenda for Sustainable Development.* United Nations. https://sdgs.un.org/2030agenda

United Nations. (2018). *Revision of World Urbanization Prospects.* Department of Economic and Social Affairs. https://www.un.org/en/desa/2018-revision-world-urbanization-prospects

Urban Green Council. (2017). *2016 annual report.* Urban Green Council. https://www.urbangreencouncil.org/wp-content/uploads/2022/11/2017.08.09-2016-Annual-Report.pdf

Valtonen, T., Leppänen, U., Hyypiä, M., Kokko, A., Manninen, J., Vartiainen, H., Sointu, E., & Hirsto, L. (2020). Learning environments preferred by university students: A shift toward informal and flexible learning environments. *Learning Environments Research, 24*(3), 371–388. DOI: 10.1007/s10984-020-09339-6

van der Walt, I. D. (2023). *Navigating the digital groove: Crafting a user-centric odyssey for libraries.*

Van Dut, V. (2017). Accessibility And Connectivity Challenges of Mass Rapid Transit In Kuala Lumpur, Malaysia. *Malaysia Sustainable Cities Program, Working Paper Series* Pg. 1-33.Retrieved from https://malaysiacities.mit.edu/sites/default/files/documents/dut.pdf

Van Zoonen, L. (2016). Privacy concerns in smart cities. *Government Information Quarterly, 33*(3), 472–480. DOI: 10.1016/j.giq.2016.06.004

Vargo, S. L., & Lusch, R. F. (2004). Evolving to a New Dominant Logic for Marketing. *Journal of Marketing*, *68*(1), 1–17. DOI: 10.1509/jmkg.68.1.1.24036

Veiga Ávila, L., Beuron, T. A., Brandli, L. L., Damke, L. I., Pereira, R. S., & Klein, L. L. (2019). Barriers to innovation and sustainability in universities: An international comparison. *International Journal of Sustainability in Higher Education*, *20*(5), 805–821. DOI: 10.1108/IJSHE-02-2019-0067

Viana-Rodríguez, M. del M. (2003). *Niveles, composición y origen del material particulado atmosférico en los sectores Norte y Este de la Península Ibérica y Canarias. Tesis doctoral.* Universidad de Barcelona.

Videka, L., Blackburn, J. A., & Moran, J. R. (2008). Building Research Infrastructure in Schools of Social Work: A University Perspective. *Social Work Research*, *32*(4), 294–301. DOI: 10.1093/swr/32.4.294

Vidhya, V. (2021). Digital marketing and its impact on consumer purchase intention. *Journal of Critical Reviews*, *8*(2), 123–130.

Vitunskaite, M., He, Y., Brandstetter, T., & Janicke, H. (2019). Smart cities and cyber security: Are we prepared? *Computers & Security*, *87*, 101568. DOI: 10.1016/j.cose.2019.101568

von Hauff, M., & Nguyen, T. (2014). Universities as Potential Actors for Sustainable Development. *Sustainability (Basel)*, *6*(5), 3043–3063. DOI: 10.3390/su6053043

Wahid, A. R., Yatmo, Y. A., & Paramita, K. D. (2020). More than Just a Material Perfection: Preserved Human-Environment Relationship in Traditional Brick-Making Scenarios. *Journal of Physics: Conference Series*, *1655*(1), 012125. DOI: 10.1088/1742-6596/1655/1/012125

Waldrep, L. W. (2010). *Becoming an Architect* (2nd ed.). John Wiley & Sons.

Waldrep, L. W. (2017). The Career Paths of an Architect. In *The Architecture Student's Handbook of Professional Practice* (15th ed., pp. 46–56). American Institute of Architects.

Wampler, B. (2010). *Participatory budgeting in Brazil: Contestation, cooperation, and accountability*. Penn State Press.

Wang, C., Zhang, F., Wang, J., Doyle, J. K., Hancock, P. A., Mak, C. M., & Liu, S. (2021). How indoor environmental quality affects occupants' cognitive functions: A systematic review. In *Building and Environment* (Vol. 193). Elsevier Ltd., DOI: 10.1016/j.buildenv.2021.107647

Wang, D., Xu, P.-Y., An, B.-W., & Guo, Q.-P. (2024). Urban green infrastructure: Bridging biodiversity conservation and sustainable urban development through adaptive management approach. *Frontiers in Ecology and Evolution*, *12*, 1440477. DOI: 10.3389/fevo.2024.1440477

Washburn, D., Sindhu, U., Balaouras, S., Dines, R. A., Hayes, N., & Nelson, L. E. (2009). Helping CIOs understand "smart city" initiatives. Forrester Research. https://www.forrester.com/report/Helping+CIOs+Understand+Smart+City+Initiatives/-/E-RES55959

Watif, M., JT, A. R., Tahir, L. S. A., & Hikmah, N. (2024). Ketimpangan Sosial dan Kemiskinan Pada Masyarakat Perkotaan. *PESHUM: Jurnal Pendidikan. Sosial Dan Humaniora*, *3*(4), 536–547.

Weinstein, A. (2000). Customer Satisfaction Among Transit Riders: How Customers Rank the Relative Importance of Various Service Attributes. *Transportation Research Record: Journal of the Transportation Research Board*, *1735*(1), 123–132. DOI: 10.3141/1735-15

Westraadt, L., & Calitz, A. (2020). A framework for the development of smart cities in South Africa. *South African Journal of Information Management*, *22*(1), a1173. DOI: 10.4102/sajim.v22i1.1173

WHO. (2016, May 13). *Ambient air pollution: A global assessment of exposure and burden of disease*. World Health Organization. https://www.who.int/publications/i/item/9789241511353

WHO. (2024). *Sustainable Development Goal indicator 3.9.1 mortality attributed to air pollution*. https://www.who.int/publications/i/item/9789240099142

Wibisurya, A. (2018). The impact of digital marketing on consumer purchase intention. *Journal of Business and Management*, *7*(2), 45–52.

Wijekoon, A., & Sabri, M. F. (2021). Environmental concerns and purchase intention of smart home objects: The moderating role of happiness. *Journal of Cleaner Production*, *312*, 127767. DOI: 10.1016/j.jclepro.2021.127767

Wilkins, S., Hazzam, J., & Ireland, J. J. (2022). Servicescape in transnational higher education: The effects of campus design, physical environment and facilities on student experience and satisfaction. *Journal of Marketing for Higher Education*, •••, 1–20. DOI: 10.1080/08841241.2022.2139792

Wimalasena, N. N., Chang-Richards, A., Wang, K. I. K., & Dirks, K. (2022). Housing quality indicators. *Systematic Reviews*.

Winter, A., Wiseman, J., & Muirhead, B. (2006). university-community engagement in Australia. *Education, Citizenship and Social Justice*, *1*(3), 211–230. DOI: 10.1177/1746197906064675

Woldeamanuel, M. G., & Cyganski, R. (2011). Factors Affecting Travellers' Satisfaction With Accessibility To Public Transportation. Association For European Transport and Contributors. Retrieved from https://aetransport.org/public/downloads/Kdg5v/4913-514ec5fd92570.pdf

Won, A. S. (2015). The virtual human interaction labStanford, California. XRDS: Crossroads. *The ACM Magazine for Students*, *22*(1), 64–65. DOI: 10.1145/2830324

Wood, A. J., Graham, M., Lehdonvirta, V., & Hjorth, I. (2019). Good Gig, Bad Gig: Autonomy and Algorithmic Control in the Global Gig Economy. *Work, Employment and Society*, *33*(1), 56–75. DOI: 10.1177/0950017018785616 PMID: 30886460

World Bank. (2010). *Cities and climate change: An urgent agenda*. World Bank. https://hdl.handle.net/10986/17381

World Bank. (2018). *What a Waste 2.0: A Global Snapshot of Solid Waste Management to 2050*. World Bank. https://openknowledge.worldbank.org/entities/publication/d3f9d45e-115f-559b-b14f-28552410e90a

World Bank. (2023, April 3). *Urban Development*. World Bank. https://www.worldbank.org/en/topic/urbandevelopment/overview

Wu, Q., Huang, Y., Irga, P., Kumar, P., Li, W., Wei, W., Shon, H. K., Lei, C., & Zhou, J. L. (2024). Synergistic control of urban heat island and urban pollution island effects using green infrastructure. *Journal of Environmental Management*, *370*, 122985. DOI: 10.1016/j.jenvman.2024.122985 PMID: 39461153

Yadav, Y., Colucci, E., Boccardo, P., & Zlatanova, S. (2024). A Geodatabase Design for the Development of a Digital Twin for Urban Environments: A Case Study from Turin, Italy. *The International Archives of the Photogrammetry, Remote Sensing and Spatial Information Sciences*, *48*, 525–532. DOI: 10.5194/isprs-archives-XLVIII-4-2024-525-2024

Yahia, A. K. M., Rahman, D. M. M., Shahjalal, M., & Morshed, A. S. M. (2024). Sustainable materials selection in building design and construction. *International Journal of Science and Engineering*, *1*(04), 106–119. DOI: 10.62304/ijse.v1i04.199

Yap, J. B. H., & Ng, X. H. (2018). Yap, J. B. H., & Ng, X. H. (2018). Housing affordability in Malaysia: Perception, price range, influencing factors and policies. *International Journal of Housing Markets and Analysis*, *11*(3), 476–497. DOI: 10.1108/IJHMA-08-2017-0069

Yarce Botero, A., Lopez Restrepo, S., Sebastian Rodriguez, J., Valle, D., Galvez-Serna, J., Montilla, E., Botero, F., Henzing, B., Segers, A., Heemink, A., Quintero, O. L., & Pinel, N. (2023a). Design and Implementation of a Low-Cost Air Quality Network for the Aburrá Valley Surrounding Mountains. *Pollutants*, *3*(1), 150–165. DOI: 10.3390/pollutants3010012

Yarce Botero, A., Lopez-Restrepo, S., Pinel Peláez, N., Quintero, O. L., Segers, A., & Heemink, A. W. (2021). Estimating nox lotos-euros ctm emission parameters over the northwest of south america through 4denvar tropomi no2 assimilation. *Atmosphere (Basel)*, *12*(12), 1633. Advance online publication. DOI: 10.3390/atmos12121633

Yarce-Botero, A., Heemink, A. W., & Quintero Montoya, O. L. (2024). Data assimilation in a LOTOS-EUROS chemical transport model for Colombia using satellite measurements. *PhD Thesis*. Delft University of Technology. https://doi.org/https://doi.org/10.4233/uuid:e202a1f3-9c73-42d1-b7f6-d45f9631df74

Yarce-Botero, A., Lopez-Restrepo, S., Pinel, N., Quintero, O., Segers, A., Schaap, M., & Heemink, A. W. (2019). *Implementation of the Chemical-Transport Model LOTOS-EUROS in Northwest South America for the identification of ecosystems affected by contaminant deposition*. EGU General Assembly.

Yilmaz, K. (2013). Comparison Of Quantitative and Qualitative Research Traditions: Epistemological, Theoretical, And Methodological Differences. *European Journal of Education*, *48*(2), 311–325. DOI: 10.1111/ejed.12014

Zadeh, L. A. (1965). Fuzzy sets. *Information and Control*, *8*(3), 338–353. DOI: 10.1016/S0019-9958(65)90241-X

Zain, Z. M., Taib, M. N., & Baki, S. M. S. (2007). Hot and humid climate: Prospect for thermal comfort in residential building. *Desalination*, *209*(1–3), 261–268. DOI: 10.1016/j.desal.2007.04.036

Zender, R., & Tavangarian, D. (2009). Service-Oriented University: Infrastructure for the University of Tomorrow. *Communications in Computer and Information Science*, *53*, 73–84. DOI: 10.1007/978-3-642-10263-9_7

Zhang, Y., Liu, S., & Mathews, E. (2015). Convergence of digital humanities and digital libraries. *Library Management*, *36*(4/5), 362–377. DOI: 10.1108/LM-09-2014-0116

Zhang, Y., & Liu, X. (2022). Eco-friendly smart home services: Design and implementation challenges. *Sustainable Cities and Society*, *78*, 103616. DOI: 10.1016/j.scs.2021.103616

Zhao, S., De Angelis, E., & Ma, D. (2018). Reflecting on the architecture curriculum through a survey on career switching. *Journal of Design and Technology Education, 23*(1), 76–87.

Zhou, L., & Lu, Y. (2022). Evaluation Model for Spatial Allocation Efficiency of Modern Educational Campus Building Using Big Data. *Mobile Information Systems, 2022*, 1–10. DOI: 10.1155/2022/9705618

Zhuang, M., Zhu, W., Huang, L., & Pan, W.-T. (2021). Impact of corporate social responsibility for smart cities on consumers' purchase intention. *Frontiers in Psychology, 12*, 674726. DOI: 10.3389/fpsyg.2021.674726

# About the Contributors

**Kenn Jhun Kam** stands as a Senior Lecturers within the esteemed School of Architecture, Building, and Design at Taylor's University. He has a Degree in Building Technology, a Master's Degree in Building Technology, and a Ph.D. in Building Quality and Assessment. He is a Chartered Surveyor from the Royal Institution of Chartered Surveyors (RICS), a registered Professional Technologist with the Malaysian Board of Technologists (MBOT) and a registered Engineering Technologist with the Board of Engineers Malaysia (BEM). He has experience in construction for 5 years and has completed 2 high-rise projects from IJM before joining the education industry. He has almost 10 years of experience in academia. He also held a management position such as Associate Dean at his current institution. Most of the subjects that he has been teaching are construction-related subjects such as Construction Technology, Building Services, Research Methodology and Dissertations.

**Sujatavani Gunasagaran** stands as a distinguished Program Director and Senior Lecturer within the esteemed School of Architecture, Building, and Design at Taylor's University. Her academic journey is marked by excellence, having earned a BSc in Architecture from the University of Malaya, an MSc in Building Technology from the University Science of Malaysia, and a Doctorate of Education from the University of Selangor. Dr. Suja is recognized as a Professional Technologist and holds membership in prestigious organizations such as the Malaysia Board of Technologist (MBOT), Malaysian Institute of Architects (PAM) Education, Malaysia Green Building Council (malaysiaGBC), Society of Building Science Educators (SBSE), and is a Green Building Index (GBI) Facilitator. Her commitment to advancing the realms of architectural education has not gone unnoticed, with several awards honouring her innovative approaches to teaching and learning. At the heart of her teaching philosophy and research lies a fervent dedication to sustainability, creativity and cutting-edge technology use such as Building Information Modeling

(BIM) and digital simulation. Dr. Suja extends her expertise to guide and mentor students pursuing advanced degrees, overseeing both master's and PhD programs. Beyond her role in academia, she plays a pivotal role in shaping the academic landscape, contributing significantly as a member of the Committee for Curriculum, Design, Assessment, and Delivery. Her administrative responsibilities involve designing novel programs and ensuring the ongoing quality of existing ones. In addition to her teaching and administrative roles, Dr. Suja is a distinguished Editor for two journal publications, further establishing herself as an active and influential figure in the realm of research and publication in built environement. Her multifaceted contributions underscore her commitment to advancing the field of architecture, construction management and education, making her a respected and integral part of the academic community.

***

**Khairool Aizat Ahmad Jamal** is a well-rounded professional who is both knowledgeable and passionate about the field of Building Information Modelling (BIM). With a strong background in architecture and construction, he holds a Bachelor of Architecture (Hons.) from Universiti Teknologi Malaysia (UTM), an M.Sc degree in Integrated Construction Project Management from Universiti Teknologi MARA (UITM), and a Post-Graduate Certificate of Teaching and Learning from Taylor's University. He is also registered as a Graduate Architect with the Malaysia Board of Architects (LAM) and a Professional Technologist with the Malaysia Board of Technologists (MBOT). Khairool's prior expertise in the construction industry was honed through his work with both local and international firms, where he gained valuable experience in the process. His role as an academician has allowed him to expand his knowledge and perspectives, working with students from a variety of disciplines within the built environment. His passion for BIM and Integrated Project Delivery (IPD) has inspired him to further pursue a PhD studies in the topic of Historic-BIM Retrofit. He is currently active in research and supervision activities and has made significant contributions to the field through presentations at various workshops and conferences, and by publishing research books, articles, and proceedings in indexed journals and magazines

**Shirley Chin Ai Ling** is an experienced Senior Lecturer and Stream Coordinator with a strong background in the field of cost management and professional practice. With a postgraduate degree in Teaching & Learning, as well as a Master's degree in Project Management, she possesses a comprehensive understanding of the subject matter. Sr Shirley has excelled in her teaching and administrative responsibilities at the School of Architecture, Building & Design, where she leads the Bachelor of

Quantity Surveying (Honours) program. Most of her subjects taught are related to measurement and management, including subjects such as measurement, construction economics, and quantity surveyor's studio.

**Manish Bisht** is Professor and Director at Graphic Era Hill University, Haldwani. He is having more than 25 years of experience of teaching. He is MBA, Ph.D. and fellow from IIM Kashipur. He is an expert of Strategic Marketing and Strategic Management, Advertisement, and Consumer Behaviour.

**Francisco Botero** graduated with honors in 2002 as a Mechanical Engineer from Universidad EAFIT in Colombia and completed his Ph.D. in 2012 with a thesis focused on non-intrusive diagnostic techniques for hydraulic turbomachinery. His research covers energy generation, technical diagnostics, mechanical vibrations, signal processing, monitoring, and air quality. He participates in international research projects and has a strong academic output, with presentations at scientific forums and publications in well-known journals. He also provides consulting services to regional industry leaders. Currently, he is an active member of high-ranking research groups in Colombia's Ministry of Science and Technology. As a faculty member at Universidad EAFIT, he teaches undergraduate courses in Solid Mechanics and Fluid Mechanics, and graduate courses in Mechanical Design, Industrial Maintenance, and Turbomachinery.

**Jose Duque** is interested in regional tectonic processes, using the relationships between magmatism, deformation, and geodynamic processes to understand the evolution of continental margins over time. His work is supported by tools such as fieldwork, structural geology, geochronology (U-Pb and 40Ar-39Ar), geochemistry, and paleomagnetism. Since his arrival at Eafit University, professor Duque has gained interest in the field of environmental magnetism, especially in the use of magnetic techniques used to evaluate environmental pollution.

**Jen LingGan** is a senior lecturer at Taylor's Business School, Taylor's University, Malaysia. She holds a Ph.D. in Management and has several years of teaching experience, primarily in the areas of management and marketing. Her research interests include employee well-being, organisational behaviour, and the integration of emerging technologies in business education. Dr. Gan has published in peer-reviewed journals and contributed book chapters on topics related to the future of work, mental health, and smart systems in education. She is actively involved in curriculum development and cross-border academic collaborations.

**Oindrilla Ghosh** is a Research Scholar hailing from the School of Law at Christ (Deemed to be University) Bangalore, India, who focuses her research on the health of tribal communities. Her work includes Neuroscience on Organizational Behavior publications at IGI Global and Environmental Disasters, of which 12 publications are indexed in SCOPUS and Web of Sciences conference proceedings. She completed her early education at Loreto Day School, Bowbazar, and achieved distinction in her undergraduate (B.A/LL.B) and postgraduate (LL.M) studies at Calcutta University. Having served as an Assistant Professor of Law at Kingston Law College, Barasat, Kolkata, Ghosh has actively participated in numerous National Conferences, International Conferences, UN Global Summits, webinars, and seminars organized by prestigious academic institutions. Her expertise lies in health perspectives, environmental studies, human behavior, and related areas. Additionally, she has conducted various workshops and lectures in educational institutions, and is engaged with NGO's to help the needy

**Nor Azlin Hamidon** is currently an associate professor of Fine Art Department at the College of Creative Art, Universiti Teknologi Mara, Malaysia. Upon the completion of her first degree from the Faculty of Usuluddin, University of Malaya with first class degree, she was granted with the Royal Educational Award (Anugerah Pelajaran DiRaja) by the Kings Council in 1995 for not only for the academic achievement, but also for her active involvement with various clubs and student associations in the university, and her relentless contribution for the society as well. Her area of expertise is Islamic and Malay visual art, specializing in Islamic calligraphy. She also covers some issues pertaining to Malay Performance Arts. Her inclination towards Islamic calligraphy was caused by her own skill and ability to write Islamic calligraphy. She was the first prize winner for Islamic Calligraphy Contest at national level in 1988 and the second prize winner in the Islamic Calligraphy on Ceramic Contest in 1994. For Nor Azlin Hamidon, her works of art is defined in her lines and movements, in diptych paintings and also motifs and collage style. Since 1988, her involvement in calligraphy is of great force. By winning the first place in the national Islamic Calligraphy contest, she embarks her journey in this field by producing art works and completing her PhD in Contemporary Islamic Calligraphy Paintings of Malaysia. Her participation in University of Malaya's art exhibitions shows another strength in terms of contemplating the contemporary artwork within this style. Her feminism style appears, in choice of colours and the soft strokes. Having most of her works in purple, green and blue, the gradation of colours is so soft and balanced. Most of her paintings are proposing the pairing-binary concept, the interdependent elements in life and balance, either in ecosystem or basic human needs.

**Gabriel Ho Sin Yin** is a graduate in Quantity Surveying from Taylor's University. I currently work as a BIM Modeller, where I specialize in utilizing Building Information Modeling (BIM) technologies to optimize project delivery, enhance collaboration, and improve efficiency in the construction industry.

**Manuela Hoyos-Restrepo** is a Physics Engineer and MSc. in Applied Physics from EAFIT University, Colombia; currently a PhD student-researcher at ONERA - The French Aerospace Lab. Since 2016 she has participated in research projects as student research assistant for developing in situ and remote sensing instruments to study the optical properties of atmospheric aerosols. She is interested in developing and implementing new techniques and technologies applicable to studying the atmosphere based on knowledge from the physical and computer sciences.

**Habizah Ilmi** is an experienced lecturer and stream coordinator at the School of Architecture, Building and Design. She is a member of the Royal Institution of Surveyors Malaysia (RISM) and the Royal Institution of Chartered Surveyors (RICS), and is also a registered Consultant Quantity Surveyor with the Board of Quantity Surveyors Malaysia (BQSM). Prior to entering academia, she accumulated over 13 years of professional experience in the construction industry. Since then, she has been actively involved in teaching in the quantity surveying and construction management program for more than 15 years. Her teaching and research interests include the professional practice, contract administration and construction management.

**Binod Kumar** is a graduate student known for his academic excellence, with 8 scholarly publications indexed in Scopus database. Hailing from Ranchi, Jharkhand in India, Binod is currently pursuing a Master of Laws (LL.M) at the prestigious Radha Govind University. His passion for technology and innovation along with climate changes is evident through his high academic performance and numerous projects. Binod has a keen interest in artificial intelligence, machine learning, neuropsychology, climate changes and disaster management, fields in which he has undertaken several research projects. He is particularly fascinated by the potential of AI to solve real-world problems and is dedicated to learning and applying new techniques in these areas. He volunteers at local NGOs, teaching underprivileged children basic computer skills. With a strong foundation in law and a commitment to making a positive impact, Binod Kumar is poised to become a future leader in the legal industry.

**Sze-ee Lee** embarked on her academic career in 2018 as a senior lecturer at the School of Architecture, Building, and Design (SABD), Taylor's University in Malaysia. She completed her Postgraduate Certificate in Teaching and Learning in 2020, and PhD in 2024, focusing on interdisciplinary research into the evolving career paths of 21st-century architects. Her research interests encompass social, heritage, and sustainable architecture. In addition to her academic role, Sze-ee is also a practicing architect with over 15 years of diverse experience in residential, commercial, and institutional projects, both locally and overseas. She has worked with international architectural firms in Sydney and London before returning to Malaysia in 2011. Sze-ee believes that thoughtful design and careful planning in architecture bring a better quality of life to people.

**Lim Tze Shwan** has a degree in Quantity Surveying and a master degree in Construction Contract Management. She is a member of Royal Institution of Surveyors Malaysia (RISM) and registered Professional Quantity Surveyor with Board of Quantity Surveyors Malaysia (BQSM). She has experiences in the construction industry specializing quantity surveying for years before joining an education industry. Most of the subjects that she had been teaching are quantity surveying subjects such as Measurement, Software Application for Quantity Surveying, Price Analysis, Construction Economic, Industrial Training and Integrated Project

**Elena Montilla-Rosero** is an Associate Professor and Researcher at EAFIT University. Physicist Engineer by University of Cauca (Colombia). MSc. Physics Instrumentation and Ph.D. Physical Sciences by University of Valladolid, Spain. She had two postdoctoral research positions in atmospheric optics in the CEFOP-UdeC (Chile) and the IPEN-UFRN (Brazil). In addition, she had participated in collaborative projects at the Alomar Atmospheric Observatory (Norway), the University of Beira Interior (Portugal), and the Latin American LIdar NETwork (LALINET). Her research career has been dedicated to atmospheric aerosols study through in-situ instrumentation and especially by Lidar techniques.

**Nurul Aini Osman** has a decade of expertise spanning academia and construction, Nurul Aini Osman specialize in waste management, sustainability projects, electronic waste, and community engagement within construction. Her robust background includes securing research grants from universities and the government, reflecting her dedication to innovation. She adept communication and negotiation skills enhance my ability to drive collaborative and impactful initiatives.

**Jorge E. Pachon** works for the Universidad de La Salle in Bogota. He is responsible for the research area in "Energy and Environmental Management" that supports both graduated and undergraduate programs. Jorge´s main area of expertise is Air Quality and Public Health, where he has led several research and consulting projects for the Environmental Authority and the private sector. In this research project Jorge was responsible for leading the component 2 of multi-technical characterization of particle matter.

**John H. Reina** is a Professor of Physics at the Universidad del Valle, Colombia. He is also the founding director of the Centre for Bioinformatics and Photonics, CIBioFi, created in the Faculty of Natural and Exact Sciences in 2015. John Henry leads a team of researchers studying theoretical aspects that exploit the physical properties of quantum objects to design devices that outperform conventional systems. Of particular importance are the issues of quantum coherence and decoherence in the design of software and hardware tolerant to the imperfections of quantum technologies under development. He is also interested in computational methods and laser spectroscopy for remote sensing (e.g. Lidar and DOAS) of particulate material and trace gases.

**Néstor Rojas** is a Chemical Engineer from Universidad Nacional de Colombia, Bogotá (1996). He received his Ph.D. from the University of Leeds, UK in 2002. He is a Full Professor at Universidad Nacional de Colombia. His research focuses on air quality and includes the chemical characterization of particulate matter in ambient air and in emissions from various sources; the determination of the contribution of pollution sources; the estimation of pollutant emissions inventories; exposure to particulate matter in microenvironments; and the estimate of impacts of air pollution on public health. He was a Fulbright visiting researcher at the University of Wisconsin - Madison in 2015 and a visiting reestructurar at the CNRS Laboratoire d'Aérologie in Toulouse, France. He is a member of the scientific committee of the IGAC - International Global Atmospheric Chemistry project.

**Ungku Norani Sonet** is an architecture and urbanism senior lecturer. After several years of architectural practise, she opted to pursue postgraduate studies and finished her PhD research. Her primary area of interest in architecture education is the responsive architectural design approach to local context and identity. In addition to the responsive design approach, she is particularly interested in doing research on public participation exercises in development frameworks. Her current research delves deeper to increase public involvement toward a holistic approach of sustainable built environment.

**Soon Lam Tatt** received his Doctor of Philosophy, MSc in Quantity Surveying, and BSc (Hons) in Housing, Building and Planning (Quantity Surveying) from Universiti Sains Malaysia. He has more than 15 years of industrial and academic experience in the field of quantity surveying. He is currently a senior lecturer at Taylor's University, Malaysia. Prior to this, he held several management positions, such as Programme Director, Associate Dean, and Stream Coordinator, at his current institution. He specializes in Building Information Modelling (BIM) and Real Estate Development. Mr. Soon is currently a chartered member of the Royal Institution of Chartered Surveyors and a registered Quantity Surveyor under the Board of Quantity Surveyors Malaysia.

**Keith Kay Hin Tan** is a UK-registered architect and the author of two previous books about the heritage of Malaysia's colonial-era Catholic mission schools. He obtained a doctorate in Tourism studies from Taylor's University Malaysia in 2017, where he is also an Associate Professor at the School of Architecture, Building and Design. In addition to his teaching role, he is also a member of the university's Liveable Urban Communities (LUC) Impact Lab. This has also allowed him to lead and/or participate in research and scholarly activities together with Think City Sdn Bhd and ICOMOS Malaysia. He has a strong interest in the architectural heritage of Southeast Asia, and was the editor of several books dealing with these topics. In addition, Keith has a strong publication record in SCOPUS - indexed journals dealing with architectural heritage and tourism, and is a regular architectural contributor on Malaysian radio and other media outlets.

**Aqilah Yaacob** is a senior lecturer, programme director and certified trainer at Taylor's University. Recognized with the 2023 President Award for Transformational Teaching and Learning, she pioneers innovative educational approaches, fostering transdisciplinary projects with students to address Sustainable Development Goals. Her initiatives have garnered numerous accolades, including innovative teaching and learning awards, and successfully guiding students to win national and international business competitions. Dr Aqilah engages with communities and industries, judging social entrepreneurship programs and securing research grants for sustainability initiatives. With a Ph.D. from Cardiff University, her work appears in prestigious journals, book chapters and conferences worldwide. Passionate about ethical business practices, she shares her insights through media appearances and advisory roles, empowering underprivileged communities globally.

**Andrés Yarce Botero** received a Ph.D. in Applied Mathematics/Mathematical Engineering from Delft University of Technology (TU Delft), the Netherlands, and Universidad EAFIT, Medellín, Colombia. His doctoral thesis was titled Data assimilation in a LOTOS-EUROS chemical transport model for Colombia using satellite measurements. During his Ph.D., he also worked as a postdoctoral researcher in the TuDelft–KNMI–VU PIPP project "High Resolution to Exploit Nitrogen Chemical Compound Observations from Space in the Netherlands" (2021–2024). His academic journey began with studies in Physics at Universidad de Antioquia (2006–2009, not completed), followed by a degree in Physical Engineering at

Universidad EAFIT (2010–2014), and later a Master's in Applied Physics at the same university (2015–2016). Born on December 24, 1987, in Medellín, Colombia, he spent part of his childhood and adolescence in Bogotá due to his father's work. There, he attended Colegio Italiano Leonardo Da Vinci (1994–2000). After returning to Medellín in 2001, he completed his secondary education at Colegio Padre Manyanet (2001–2005). Since 2024, Andrés Yarce Botero has been a recognized researcher at the Barcelona Supercomputing Center (BSC), working in the Earth Sciences Department, within the Data Assimilation and Forecasting Group.

**Ahmad Fahmi Zainazlan** got recognized as a Graduate Architect (Board of Architect) and Professional Technologist (Board of Technologist) specialized in Building Construction and BIM and Parametric Design. Experienced for more than 10 years in construction industries, Building Information Modelling in Schematics, Submissions and Site Implementation as well as teaching BIM as an academician. Aside from architecture, Fahmi also trained in the art of Islamic Calligraphy and Islamic Ornamentation since childhood, bridging his architecture world to Islamic Artistic Design. Ts. Fahmi passions on digital architecture and Islamic architecture uncovers BIM spectrum in Heritage and Archaeology through a systematic review paper, which evolves from the narrative of Heritage BIM. He continues developing portfolio through Heritage digital BIM reconstruction of a conservation archaeological building. He also teaches digital modules such as Parametric Modelling, IT Application for sustainable and Advance Architectural Construction other than Leading Design Studio. He is at present active in prototyping new adaptation in architectural design as well as consulting architecture firms for the betterment of the industry.

# Index

## L



## M



## P



## Q



## R



## S



## T

## U



## W